Depth *of* Field

Patrick McGilligan | Series Editor

Depth *of* Field

———◆———

STANLEY KUBRICK,
Film, and the Uses of History

edited by

Geoffrey Cocks, James Diedrick,
and Glenn Perusek

THE UNIVERSITY OF WISCONSIN PRESS

The University of Wisconsin Press
1930 Monroe Street
Madison, Wisconsin 53711

www.wisc.edu/wisconsinpress/

3 Henrietta Street
London WC2E 8LU, England

5   4   3   2   1

Printed in the United States of America

Library of Congress Cataloging-in-Publication Data
Depth of field :
Stanley Kubrick, film, and the uses of history / edited by
Geoffrey Cocks, James Diedrick, and Glenn Perusek.
p. cm.—(Wisconsin film studies)
Includes bibliographical references and index.
ISBN-13: 978-0-299-21610-8 (hardcover : alk. paper)
ISBN-10: 0-299-21610-1 (hardcover : alk. paper)
ISBN-13: 978-0-299-21614-6 (pbk. : alk. paper)
ISBN-10: 0-299-21614-4 (pbk. : alk. paper)
1. Kubrick, Stanley—Criticism and interpretation. I. Cocks, Geoffrey.
II. Diedrick, James. III. Perusek, Glenn. IV. Series.
PN1998.3.K83D47   2006
791.4302'33'092—dc22   2005022821

On s'engage et puis on voit.

The strong do what they can and the weak suffer what they must.

In the most general sense of progressive thought, the Enlightenment has always aimed at liberating men from fear and establishing their sovereignty. Yet the fully enlightened earth radiates disaster triumphant.

Contents

Acknowledgments   ix

Introduction: Deep Focus   3
GEOFFREY COCKS, JAMES DIEDRICK, AND GLENN PERUSEK

First Take: Words and Pictures

The Written Word and the Very Visual Stanley Kubrick   31
VINCENT LOBRUTTO

Writing *The Shining*   55
DIANE JOHNSON

The Pumpkinification of Stanley K.   62
FREDERIC RAPHAEL

Mazes and Meanings

Kubrick's Armies: Strategy, Hierarchy, and Motive in the
War Films of Stanley Kubrick   77
GLENN PERUSEK

Subjected Wills: The Antihumanism of Kubrick's Later Films   101
PAT J. GEHRKE AND G. L. ERCOLINI

2001: A Cold Descent   122
MARK CRISPIN MILLER

Deviant Subjects in Foucault and *A Clockwork Orange:*
Criminological Constructions of Subjectivity 146
PAT J. GEHRKE

Pictures, Plurality, and Puns: A Visual Approach to *Barry Lyndon* 165
BILLE WICKRE

Death by Typewriter: Stanley Kubrick, the Holocaust, and
The Shining 185
GEOFFREY COCKS

Full-Metal-Jacketing, or Masculinity in the Making 218
PAULA WILLOQUET-MARICONDI

Final Take: *Eyes Wide Shut*

In Dreams Begin Responsibilities 245
JONATHAN ROSENBAUM

Freud, Schnitzler, and *Eyes Wide Shut* 255
PETER LOEWENBERG

Introducing Sociology 280
TIM KREIDER

Filmography 301

Bibliography 305

Contributors 309

Index 313

Acknowledgments

Depth of Field: Stanley Kubrick, Film, and the Uses of History grew directly out of a symposium held in spring 2000 at Albion College in Michigan: "The Eyes Have It: Stanley Kubrick, Film, and the Uses of History." The symposium was sponsored by the college's Center for Interdisciplinary Study in History and Culture. Our first debt, then, is to Albion College for its generous support of the symposium and for interdisciplinary inquiry more generally. The symposium itself attracted some of the most important Kubrick critics and scholars from around the country, several of whom have contributed essays to this volume—Vincent LoBrutto, Pat J. Gehrke, Mark Crispin Miller, Jonathan Rosenbaum. In addition to their prepared remarks, they visited classes and met with students, giving graciously of their time and expertise. The preparation of the manuscript itself was expedited by Marilyn Kniburys, secretary in the Philosophy and Religious Studies Department at Albion College; Kay Pierce, secretary in the English Department at Albion College; and Alice Moore of the Albion College Library. The editors also wish to thank Sarah Cocks and LeeAnne Richardson for their patience during the gestation of this challenging, demanding, and rewarding project.

Depth *of* Field

Introduction

Deep Focus

============>•◆•<============

GEOFFREY COCKS, JAMES DIEDRICK,

AND GLENN PERUSEK

"Film giant Stanley Kubrick dies at 70" reads the headline in a March 1999 issue of the *British Journal of Photography*. The obituary notes proudly that Kubrick was a faithful reader of the *BJP* and that while he was of course best known as one of the great film directors, "[h]is interest in still pictures never diminished."[1] Indeed, Kubrick's passion for photography remained an essential part of his filmmaking not just in terms of camera work or lighting but in his conviction of the sheer power of the visual image to capture truths about the world. Like many film directors, from Jean Renoir to William Wyler, Kubrick displayed a predilection in his camera shots for deep focus, "an effect of lens and lighting that makes everything in the composition, from the closest object in the frame to the farthest, appear to be equally clear."[2] In photography this technique is called "depth of field" and is a way of expanding the visual choices open to both photographer and viewer. In film, it is most closely associated with the mise-en-scène school of film theorist André Bazin, who stressed the importance of the camera's shot—as oppposed to the editor's cut—in portraying the world of human feeling and action realistically. For Kubrick, depth of field was a vital means of opening up the space created by the visual image for the inclusion of the many details of setting, lighting, color, property, and action that would allow him to communicate a—his—world of ideas.

Depth of field is an appropriate description both of Kubrick's work and the contents of this volume of essays. Kubrick focused deeply on a broad array of subjects and film genres. Likewise, *Depth of Field: Stanley Kubrick, Film, and the Uses of History* probes deeply and broadly into Kubrick's oeuvre. Kubrick's thirteen feature films from 1953 to 1999 cover a range of genres

3

from film noir, crime thriller, war film, historical epic, and black comedy to love story, science fiction, social satire, horror movie, and murder mystery. But each of the carefully, even painstakingly, crafted films Kubrick directed betrays the consistent themes and concerns of an acute and pessimistic observer of the modern world and the twentieth century in particular. The essays in this volume come from a variety of disciplines appropriate—indeed, necessary—for understanding the wide range of issues and events Kubrick addressed from the depth and breadth of his own reading, research, and observation.

Kubrick's Worldview

Kubrick's worldview is captured, we think, in the epigraphs to this volume. Napoleon fascinated Kubrick and was to be the subject of a film he exhaustively planned but never made. Napoleon's words, "One begins a battle and then one sees," capture the contingent whirl of events in battle and in the world to which Kubrick in his own time was a witness. The words also characterize Kubrick's method of filmmaking. While he was famous for exercising rigorous control over all aspects of his films, he also encouraged his collaborators to experiment and create as they went along. Kubrick believed in being surprised by how things developed. This habit of "waitful watching" was a response to the volatile world of human experience rich in possibilities. It was also in line with Kubrick's experience as a chess player, where strategy is a matter not only of preparation but of adapting different approaches and tactics as the game develops. His identification with Napoleon was also a result of the "will to power" within himself, all those antisocial and aggressive drives he, like Sigmund Freud, saw acted out in everyday life and in history, and which in his case were sublimated into imperial control over his films. His realistic, resigned and—because he was a skeptic and a moralist rather than a cynic—outraged view of a world dominated by systems of power and oppression reflects Thucydides' famous observation from *The Peloponnesian War:* "The strong do what they can and the weak suffer what they must." These words apply to the world into which Kubrick was born, in which modern states had at their disposal unprecedented technical and bureaucratic powers and resources. Like the photojournalist he was before turning to film, Kubrick used the camera to capture truths about this world, believing that film could transcend the ability of words and traditional narrative to do so. His only affirmation in the face of twentieth-century disasters was a limited pragmatic faith in democracy and the limited potential for art to effect change.[3]

Kubrick's work can be seen as bringing the terrible news of twentieth-century history—and the humbling message of twentieth-century social and psychological theory—to a mass audience in the form of the characteristically twentieth-century medium of film. In this sense he is part of a tradition of cultural criticism that includes writers like Freud, Friedrich Nietzsche, Max Weber, Theodor Adorno, and Michel Foucault. For Weber, modern capitalist societies are in the grips of a rational calculus of self-interest and gain generalized into a force that disciplines all members of these societies. The Protestant ethic's ascetic self-denial and devotion to calling dovetailed with the imperatives of a rising capitalist *system,* Weber observed. In the modern world, the desire for gain, which Weber sees as irrational, was harnessed to rational calculation. Weber identifies capitalism with the "taming of this irrational motivation, or at least with its rational tempering."[4] With the ascetic work ethic dominating "inner-worldly morality," we witness the rise of a powerful ideology that "determines, with overwhelming coercion, the style of life *not only* of those directly involved in business but of every individual who is born into this mechanism." While seventeenth-century puritanism characterized concern for outward possessions as a thin coat, it had, for Weber, been transformed into a *stahlhartes Gehäuse,* a steel-hardened housing, or, as some would translate it, an iron cage.[5] This rationalist macrocosm could be confronted by "new prophets" or possibly "powerful old ideas and ideals will be reborn at the end of this monstrous development." But Weber was not optimistic. It was also possible that "'Chinese' ossification, dressed up with a kind of desperate self-importance," could result, in which would arise *letzte Menschen,* "specialists without spirit, hedonists without heart . . . nonentities imagin-[ing] they have attained a stage of humankind never before reached."[6] For those familiar with Kubrick's films, these words eerily evoke the image of General Buck Turgidson in *Dr. Strangelove* (1964).

This Weberian vision of capitalism as a fearful new power haunted social theorists and commentators throughout the twentieth century. And while social theory has emphasized how the deep wellspring of human desires is channeled and appropriated by hierarchical social systems so that we become complicit in the inescapable circulations of power, Freudian and post-Freudian psychoanalysis has challenged cherished notions of individual consciousness and autonomy, reconceptualizing the human subject as decentered and thus hostage to anarchic unconscious desires.

Kubrick's austere intellectual temper, his use and interrogation of popular film genres, and his mordant view of the human prospect made him a powerful voice of postmodern skepticism about the whole Enlightenment project, which enshrined scientific rationalism and spawned a myriad of systems-builders bent on reforming the world. Indeed, a film like *Dr. Strangelove* might be said to enact the deeply ironic view of the Enlightenment famously expressed in our third epigraph, from Theodor Adorno's and Max Horkheimer's *Dialectic of Enlightenment:* "In the most general sense of progressive thought, the Enlightenment has always aimed at liberating men from fear and establishing their sovereignty. Yet the fully enlightened earth radiates disaster triumphant."[7]

Linking Kubrick and Adorno may seem counterintuitive given Adorno's skepticism about the dialectical possibilities of film. He viewed most movies as mere extensions of what he called the "culture industry,"[8] where "art and ideology are becoming one and the same thing,"[9] and he feared that film would replace the more "difficult" critical art forms capable of cultivating critical awareness: "The film has succeeded in transforming subjects so indistinguishably into social functions, that those wholly encompassed, no longer aware of any conflict, enjoy their own dehumanization as something human, as the joy of warmth. The total interconnectedness of the culture industry, omitting nothing, is one with total social delusion."[10] Yet Adorno was not totally dismissive of film—he was a great admirer of Charlie Chaplin—and his belief that the formally innovative nature of certain twentieth-century art makes it critical of and relatively autonomous from the prevailing political and socioeconomical system suggests that he might have admired the technical adventurousness and dialectical openness of Kubrick's work.[11] Indeed, Kubrick's entire film career, including his insistence on artistic autonomy, his perfectionism, his antisentimentality, and his intellectual rigor, is at one with Adorno's presentation of his theory of aesthetics in *Aesthetic Theory:* both participate in an effort to circumvent the reduction of art and thought to the culture industry.

Like Adorno, who famously declared that poetry became impossible after Auschwitz, Kubrick believed that the calamities of the twentieth century rendered certain kinds of art difficult if not impossible (he considered but never completed a film about the Holocaust). Kubrick was born in 1928, fourteen years after the outbreak of World War I in 1914 and fourteen years before the full implementation of the Nazi Final Solution in 1942, at the midpoint, as it were, of "the horror, the horror" that Joseph Conrad prophesied in *Heart of Darkness* (1902). Kubrick's films offer no easy satisfactions or solutions—only invitations to critical dialectic. As a postmodernist, Kubrick interrogated the genres he utilized and erased the transparency of the film form through an "open narrative" that invites critical engagement and reflection on the part of the audience. This erasure of transparency represented a conscious use of what German dramatist Bertolt Brecht called an "alienation effect," whereby the viewers are reminded that they are watching a performance whose conventions are designed to divert attention from actual social conditions and problems. These problems, according to Brecht, were the real subjects of art. They are also Stanley Kubrick's subjects.

Kubrick and Film Theory

The sea of literature on Kubrick is vast and, like any sea, has its depths and its shallows. The great bulk of this literature comes out of the discipline of Film Studies, although since the "linguistic turn" in the 1970s, scholars in literature and language have also contributed significant critiques. These critiques are particularly appropriate since Kubrick habitually adapted works of literature for the screen. But with two exceptions, Vladimir Nabokov's *Lolita* (1955) and Stephen King's *The Shining* (1977), Kubrick chose literary sources that were not generally well known. He did this so that neither he nor the audience was burdened with established interpretations of what the sources "meant." This strategy allowed him to create something thematically and artistically distinctive at all stages of the film's production. It also allowed him to present his own point of view and to exercise artistic control over the subject matter. Even his *Lolita* (1962) and *The Shining* (1980) differ significantly from the originals, allowing him to engage various philosophical, social, and historical concerns free from the constraints not only of expectation but literary and film genre.[12] Such license reinforces the importance of a formal Film Studies component to the literature on Kubrick, since in both form and content Kubrick's films departed from the traditional canons of theatrical and filmic performance and presentation. But this very comprehensiveness of approach to both subject matter and form in Kubrick's films also demands the type of unprecedented multidisciplinary and interdisciplinary research presented in *Depth of Field*. Our collection by turns challenges and complements other major works on Kubrick such as Michel Ciment's *Kubrick* (1983, 2000), Alexander Walker's *Stanley Kubrick, Director* (1971, 1999), and Thomas Allen Nelson's *Kubrick* (1972, 2000). It is also the case that Kubrick's death in 1999, and the flood of material on his life and work that has resulted, makes possible for the first time a comprehensive assessment of his oeuvre.[13]

Such an approach actually strengthens a trend within Film Studies itself toward a more comprehensive scholarly examination of the phenomenon of film in general from a variety of perspectives. Film, the distinctive art form of the twentieth century, combines in provocative and even contradictory ways the mechanical process of reproduction born of the industrial age with a product that often evokes and mimics the world of dreams. Film was and is also undeniably an entertainment medium and thus a commercial venture, but even early in the century it was clear that film had a claim to serious attention. Filmmakers like Kubrick, Orson Welles, Akira Kurosawa, and many others not only reflected their time and place but also actively addressed their eras on various levels of artistic and didactic discourse. The realist school, as we noted above, argued for such things as long takes and available light in order to exploit photography's capacity to record actual physical events. The "montage" school, championed above all by Sergei Eisenstein, argued for the use of editing and other artificial effects to create a unique and artistic film reality. Both approaches make the viewer aware of the formal apparatus, in André Bazin's case for aesthetic purposes, in Eisenstein's for political ones. The Hollywood "continuity style," in the successful search for a marketable product, appropriated Bazin's mise-en-scène but made the form invisible, allowing the audience to become lost in the story and characters for purposes of entertainment rather than reflection. Auteur theory originally sought to distinguish films made by individual directors for artistic purposes from the collectively mass produced studio "movies" churned out for purposes of profit. By the 1960s, however, scholars interested in film were arguing that even mass-produced Hollywood films had a "voice," at least in terms of wider discourses within the surrounding culture. They also questioned, particularly along the lines of structuralist, Marxist, psychoanalytic, and gender theory, the "reactionary" implications of auteur theory in its preference for aesthetics at the expense of a critical social and political consciousness.

This volume emphasizes the historical contexts, and historiographical implications, of Kubrick's career and oeuvre. Kubrick himself was vitally interested in history, particularly in the history of the twentieth century. Of his thirteen films, ten were about the century in which he lived. These films confront in particular the unprecedented organization of power and violence among people and states that dominated much of the first half of the century. Kubrick was also alert, as we have seen, to the issues of analysis and interpretation that modern social theorists were bringing to these twentieth-century crises. He was convinced that art addressing these crises and issues has value even in a world that often seemed disastrously beyond the control of its inhabitants. Kubrick followed the realist tradition of emphasizing human actions within shots and scenes, but he was not merely a realistic and certainly not a naturalistic filmmaker. Even though he started out as a documentary filmmaker in order to earn money and learn the craft, it was not the purpose of his feature films simply to record the reality of society or nature. For Kubrick, photography and film existed to interrogate and analyze in an active and dynamic way the contingencies of the modern world. Kubrick absorbed the legacy and the lessons of German Expressionist filmmaking, a tradition that emphasized the depiction of subjective states through setting and acting. But Kubrick's films also evoke the gritty postwar realism of American film noir.[14] Even within Expressionism, emotional affect is not an end in itself, but is rather a means of confronting social structures and conflicts. Kubrick's favorite author was Franz Kafka (another affinity with Adorno), whom he admired for his ability to survey the eruption of the fantastic and the grotesque out of the quotidian in order to represent and interrogate the disruptions and displacements of modern history.

Kubrick often spoke of his films as dreams.[15] But even this conception does not imply disengagement from the world, since psychoanalysis in the twentieth century has demonstrated the powerful presence of fantasy in human motives and actions. Films resemble dreams insofar as they emerge from and operate on multiple levels of consciousness. Kubrick believed that film is most effective as a means of communication, artistic expression, and argument about social realities when its audience is actively engaged in constructing its meanings rather than being passively manipulated and entertained. His films, therefore, are all "open narratives"; they generate ambiguity and invite engagement by frustrating conventional expectations. For this reason, Kubrick was always loath to discuss the "meaning" of his films. He articulated this reticence in response to a question about *2001: A Space Odyssey* (1968):

> I tried to create a *visual* experience, one that bypasses verbalized pigeonholing and directly penetrates the subconscious with an emotional and philosophical content. . . . I intended the film to be an intensely subjective experience that reaches the viewer at an inner level of consciousness, just as music does. . . . You're free to speculate as you wish about the philosophical and allegorical

meaning of the film—and such speculation is one indication that it has succeeded in gripping the audience at a deep level.[16]

This statement echoes the argument of *Aesthetic Theory,* where Adorno
seeks to preserve the sanctity of subjectivity embodied in the work of art
against the onslaught of the market, where value is equated with price. For
both Adorno and Kubrick, therefore, art is not only possible after Auschwitz, it is more necessary than ever, whatever doubts one might have about
its moral or political efficacy.

Kubrick was a hybrid, an auteur of high aesthetic and intellectual ambition who self-consciously hijacked Hollywood genres in order to interrogate their assumptions and thereby tease his viewers into thought. Well
versed in popular culture and especially popular film conventions, he was
more acutely aware of cultural assumptions and their effects on popular
consciousness than more formally "artistic" filmmakers. He was also free
to explore formal and substantive intellectual concerns beyond the reach
of filmmakers dependent on studios and the marketplace—a dependence
that Kubrick, almost alone among major filmmakers, did not have to endure. This is not to say that Kubrick's films somehow exist outside the ide-
ological forces that surrounded their creation or attend their reception. As
semiotic theory reminds us, films are "texts," which do not (merely) convey the ideas intended by their makers, but "construct, not necessarily
coherently or without contradiction, a perception of social reality."[17] The
meanings of these aesthetic constructions will in turn be constructed by
each viewer, constructions that are themselves shaped by prevailing economic, political, and social conditions. Rather, Kubrick's self-consciousness
about these conditions, his relative independence from studio systems that
respond reflexively to cultural predispositions (*pace* Frederic Raphael below), and his postmodern predilection for critiquing cultural conventions
arguably permitted him greater agency in creating a cinema shaped by his
own point of view.

Reception theory is also relevant to the mass medium of film. Audiences
are disposed—and have been trained—to accept the cinema as a "natural"
three-dimensional experience, independent of external constructions,
whose artificial qualities have been rendered transparent. But such transparency is of course impossible, since the audience always imposes its own
cognitive and cultural constructions upon films. Moreover, the artificiality
of the experience is always registered by such things as the movement of
figures and objects back and forth over the boundary of the screen and the
dark space around it. Writers and directors inevitably direct the viewer's

attention in specific ways. Many viewers in Weimar Germany, for instance, responded to *The Cabinet of Dr. Caligari* (1919) in the way the screenwriters planned in spite of the producers' attempt by means of a framing story to undercut the screenplay's antiwar, iconoclastic point of view.[18] At the same time, audiences, like filmmakers and film theorists, exist in specific historical, political, social, and cultural contexts that influence and thus limit the interpretative possibilities they bring to film. Certainly the wide range of responses to Kubrick's oeuvre is a powerful instance of the dialectical nature of serious films in the way they can excite dialogue between artist and audience by means both of the intention of their maker and the ineffability of their effects. Kubrick was far from what critics like Pauline Kael and Stanley Kauffmann reduced him to—a cynic, a misogynist, a misanthrope, or a pseudointellectual tyrant.[19] While he did, as Diane Johnson has written, possess a "comic and pessimistic view of things in general," she adds the important qualification that "tragedy after all has an optimistic side, paradoxically affirming as it does the dignity of the human being."[20]

Kubrick's Filmmaking

Kubrick has often been characterized as a director obsessed with controlling all aspects of filmmaking. But as we learn more about how he worked from those with whom he worked, we discover that there was a great deal of experimentation and improvisation in the collective realization of the ideas he wished to address. Certainly Kubrick was firm and consistent in making his films vehicles for his ideas. But he was a far different filmmaker than Alfred Hitchcock, who famously claimed that once the storyboards for a film were worked out, he considered the film finished. When it came to crew, cast, and audience, Kubrick's refusal to explain exactly what he was after helped him retain control over the ideas his films addressed, but this refusal also encouraged active engagement in the process of the production and exploration of meaning, sabotaging film and genre conventions and inviting audience involvement. The many takes Kubrick demanded of his actors (and himself) were not (only) evidence of a desire for control but a method by which he and the actors could be surprised by something interesting that also rang true beyond the tricks of traditional acting. For the same reason Kubrick would write and rewrite scenes on the set and encourage actors in rehearsals and during filming to participate in finding what worked. Until the posthumously produced *A.I.* Kubrick never used the usual director storyboards to chart out action beforehand. Rather, he reshaped the narrative as it was being filmed. This allowed for maximum

flexibility for himself and the actors, who took scenes in directions that resonated emotionally with the intellectual and artistic concerns of the film
as a whole.

In the words of Nicole Kidmann, Kubrick sought performances that
were "slightly odd, slightly off," emphasizing again his debt to German
Expressionist film of the 1920s and its obsession with internal conflict and
disorder.[21] Thus, scenes in Kubrick's films (like the films themselves) tend
to run long, as the characters act and react to each other in ways that
may be hyperbolic but hew closer to the rhythm and flow of life than to
the kinetic pace of conventional film dialogue and editing. Predictably,
Kubrick criticized Eisenstein's passion for elaborate editing, claiming it led
to the diminution of content for the sake of form.[22] He wanted something
to *happen* in front of the camera. He observed in a hyperrealistic way that
compels the audience to connect the film's concerns with those of the
world. As Kidman described her eleven-minute confession scene in *Eyes
Wide Shut* (1999),

> We worked on it for three weeks. It's rare as an actor that you're asked to
> speak for more than two or three minutes, and that speech is a major mono-
> logue. Stanley rewrote and we worked on it again. It was incredible how he
> decided to shoot it—he constructed the shot watching us. We got to play the
> whole scene without having to cut—so it was more like theater. Stanley liked
> extremes.[23]

From the start, Kubrick was a careful strategic thinker. His love of chess
was an expression of this love of strategy, and it carried over into his filmmaking. As Michael Herr has said, "as he grew older and moved beyond
still photography, chess became movies, and movies became chess by other
means."[24] The strong chess player must be both a thoroughgoing planner
and capable of assessing new dangers and opportunities in ever-changing
conditions. In planning for contingencies, for new openings and possibilities, Kubrick approached the filmmaking process with care and gravity,
committed to the view that his vision demanded no less.

Organization of the Volume

THE FIRST TAKE: WORDS AND PICTURES

Kubrick was a voracious reader and he was drawn to serious and challenging literature. Perhaps this is one of the reasons that his films are so

effective at representing the relationship, or the discrepancy, between what is seen and what is said. As Michel Foucault has written,

> it is not that words are imperfect, or that, when confronted by the visible they prove insuperably inadequate. Neither can be reduced to the other's terms: it is in vain that we say what we see: what we see never resides in what we say. And it is in vain that we attempt to show, by the use of their images, metaphors, or similes, what we are saying; the space where they achieve their splendor is not that deployed by our eyes.[25]

With the exception of his first two films (*Fear and Desire* [1953] and *Killer's Kiss* [1955]), Kubrick always wrote or co-wrote screenplays on the basis of works of literature. Thus, our volume begins with three essays dealing with the intersection of the written word and film in Kubrick's cinema. The first provides an historical overview of Kubrick's individual and collaborative writing for the screen, while the other two represent first-person accounts by two of the screenwriters with whom Kubrick worked. Adaptations of literature for film have a long and controversial history, and controversy has raged around most of Kubrick's adaptations. This is due in part to his choice of culturally explosive texts, from *Lolita* to *A Clockwork Orange*—designed both to generate maximum audience interest and to allow the filmmaker to contribute to the cultural dialectic generated by the texts themselves.

The Killing (1956) was based on Lionel White's *Clean Break* (1956) and co-written with Jim Thompson, author of hardboiled detective novels. Thompson and Kubrick needed each other. Thompson was near the end of his career; Kubrick was at the beginning of his but needed a story to make a breakthrough film.[26] He and producer James Harris took a chance on the unique narrative structure of the novel, and the collaboration was a success. Diane Johnson has observed that "[a] good film has to have a talented writer who is involved, because the writing is the most important part of the film, and when the artistic fun is taken away from the screenwriter, he becomes an automaton, the proverbial Mr. Nobody with his Underwood."[27] Kubrick understood this and consistently sought the participation of talented writers, even though his relations with them were often contentious. Contentiousness certainly characterized Kubrick's next project, *Paths of Glory* (1957), which involved screenwriting contributions from Kubrick, Thompson, and Calder Willingham. Both of Kubrick's co-screenwriters were unhappy with Kubrick's insistence on control of the final screenplay, and the screen credits for the film were ultimately submitted to the Writers Guild for arbitration. Thompson was so incensed by his perception that his contributions were being effaced that he characterized Kubrick as "a curious study of the artist as psychopath in our time."[28]

As a replacement for director Anthony Mann, Kubrick had little control over the production of *Spartacus* (1960), but he did cut a great deal of screenwriter Dalton Trumbo's dialogue.[29] On *Lolita,* as Vincent LoBrutto tells us, Kubrick left the screenwriting to author Vladimir Nabokov, but he and his co-producer James Harris had to pare down a long screenplay. Nabokov went on record with both praise and criticism for the film, as would Anthony Burgess when Kubrick's adaptation of his novel *A Clockwork Orange* appeared.[30] When Nabokov published his own version of his original screenplay as a book, however, he graciously noted in his foreword that he did so "not in pettish refutation of a munificent film but purely as a vivacious variant of an old novel."[31]

The black comedy *Dr. Strangelove* represented a severe departure from its source, *Two Hours To Doom* (1958, aka *Red Alert*), a nuclear thriller by an ex-RAF pilot named Peter George. Kubrick, George, and satirist Terry Southern shared writing credit, although Southern later commented on the control over the project Kubrick exercised by noting that he "scarcely let as much as a trouser pleat go unsupervised."[32] Kubrick's collaboration with science-fiction writer Arthur C. Clarke on *2001* was unusual in that the film was based on a short story, and Clarke wrote the novel while Kubrick made the film of the screenplay on which they collaborated.[33] The screenplay for *A Clockwork Orange* (1972) was written by Kubrick alone and was based on the American edition of Anthony Burgess's 1962 novel that omitted the last chapter. Burgess has expressed regret that the fame of the film has overshadowed other works of his he regards as better than *A Clockwork Orange* and concludes that the "Kubrickian *Orange* is a fable, the British or world one is a novel."[34] Author reaction was no problem for Kubrick on his next project, *Barry Lyndon* (1975), from the 1844 picaresque novel by William Makepeace Thackeray. Kubrick typically reworked the book not only in terms of narrative economy but in problematic ways that transform the protagonist from a roguish into an ironic figure.[35] Kubrick's 1980 adaptation of Stephen King's *The Shining* (1977) left the author as cold as he believed Kubrick to be.[36] Michael Herr, who wrote with Kubrick on *Full Metal Jacket* (1987), found him extremely sensitive to language but often focused to the point of oppressiveness, while Gustav Hasford, the author of *The Short-Timers* (1979) upon which the screenplay was based, had to fight for credit.[37] As we shall see with Frederic Raphael's essay, there was significant conflict between Kubrick and his co-writer on *Eyes Wide Shut* (1999). Contention also marked the long preparations for what would become Kubrick's posthumous production of Steven Spielberg's *A.I.* (2001).

The three essays in this section focus on Kubrick's career history at both the macro and micro level. Vincent LoBrutto, author of *Stanley Kubrick: A Biography* (1997), offers an overview of Kubrick's idiosyncratic method of writing for the screen. LoBrutto argues that screenwriting is the only major gap in Kubrick's list of artistic achievements. Kubrick, as in all other aspects of the preparation of a film, knew how to get good people to do good work for him in the realm of writing; but he was also was a master visualist who had an eye (and ear) for good literature that would make a good film.[38] LoBrutto first documents Kubrick's early and ongoing interest in literature of all types, his regular recourse to writing screenplays alone or in collaboration with others, as well as the early origins of his need for artistic control of a film's subject matter and treatment. Kubrick's distinctive way of constructing a screenplay reflected his lifelong investment in reading as well as his lack of formal training. He also wrote constantly on the screenplay during the production of the film, consistent with his artistic modus operandi of "waitful watching."

The novelist Diane Johnson, who co-wrote the screenplay for *The Shining,* has written briefly elsewhere about her work with Kubrick, but in her essay for this volume she elaborates on that experience and on her response to the completed film. From the beginning of her work with Kubrick, Johnson was impressed by his literary sensibility, noting in a 1985 essay that he "talked like a novelist" and that "considerations of motivation, suspense, plausibility, characterization and meaning" were always paramount in his discussions.[39] Writing in detail about her collaboration for the first time since Kubrick's death, Johnson sheds light on everything from Kubrick's working methods to the themes and symbolic patterns that circulate through his films.

Kubrick worked on a script while also attending to all aspects of the production process in an "evolving and organic way," an approach Johnson believes is superior to that of most other directors, who have the script finished before doing the production planning. The result was a "consistency and deeply mediated effect" of the finished product. This process also corresponds with Kubrick's ongoing openness to sources of inspiration and experimentation in building a film over a long period of time. At the same time, it is clear from Johnson's account that *The Shining* was

Kubrick's film. Just as he and Johnson changed King's novel in accord with Kubrick's purposes, Johnson found upon viewing the film that the character of Wendy, for whom Johnson wrote the dialogue, was a less "rounded" character than the one she had constructed on paper. Johnson objects to Kubrick's cutting of a scene that makes clear "Jack's transition from depressed and blocked writer to one suddenly filled with demonic energy," because it leaves the viewer in the dark about Jack's motivation. But it is also clear from Johnson's account that she had a profound effect on the transformation of *The Shining* from a novel of supernatural terror to a film of psychological horror. Johnson's account demonstrates that Kubrick, in pursuing his particular artistic view of the world, was discriminating—and also extremely demanding—in his choice of collaborators.

Despite her disagreements with Kubrick about some of the choices he made in producing a final cut of *The Shining,* Johnson has described her work with the director as a "marvelous experience."[40] This was not true of Kubrick's final collaboration—his work with Frederic Raphael turning Arthur Schnitzler's *Dream Story* into *Eyes Wide Shut.* The reasons have something to do with the intense (and psychologically complex) relationship between writers and directors. Johnson has written that this relationship can be compared to the relationship between analyst and patient,

> and perhaps partly explains why screenwriters always seem to be in a state of infatuation or rage with the person they are working for. They are going through negative or positive transference with the difference that it is the doctor whose dreams are under discussion, or, at any rate, whose interpretations are going to prevail. Unhappy screenwriter! His words are the enemy of images; he himself is perhaps therefore the enemy, not the collaborator, of the controlling artist, the director who "sees"—perhaps, paradoxically, in the pages of a book—his film. Obviously it is much the best thing for the filmmaker to write his film himself.[41]

Johnson's analogy illuminates both her work with Kubrick, which occupied a middle ground between infatuation and rage, and novelist Frederic Raphael's battle of wills with the director.

In his essay Raphael transforms his dissatisfaction into a fascinating analysis of the culture of the auteur. Raphael has given a detailed account of his work on *Eyes Wide Shut* in *Eyes Wide Open: A Memoir of Stanley Kubrick* (1999), but here he provides the first account of his collaboration with Kubrick since having seen *Eyes Wide Shut* and endured brickbats from

Kubrick family and friends for writing critically about his collaboration. While in his book and in an interview with Michel Ciment in 1999 Raphael has positive things to say about Kubrick and his collaboration with him, in this account he is highly critical of what he sees as the myth of Kubrick the genius, a myth constructed and preserved assiduously by the film industry, the media studies establishment, and the Kubrick family.[42] Raphael sees this mythmaking as part of a larger project of media conglomerates to cover their commercial pandering to popular tastes in film with the fig leaf of art. Raphael sees the studio production of films as bearing little artistic resemblance to the creativity of the individual novelist, even for the relatively independent Kubrick who is still dependent, in Raphael's view, not only on the collaborative necessities of film production but on his own myth. Raphael's screenwriting collaboration with a man he viewed as arrogant, overrated, and inscrutable only confirmed his view, in contrast to that of Johnson, that screenwriting is the poor relation to writing.[43]

MAZES AND MEANINGS

Kubrick's films often employ the image of mazes to explore the dangerous labyrinthine corridors of human consciousness and human systems. Political theorist Glenn Perusek brings modern social theory to bear on Kubrick's early war films—*Fear and Desire, Paths of Glory,* and *Dr. Strangelove*—as well as his unproduced *Napoleon*. Kubrick was always fascinated by war and, like many film directors, likened his profession to that of a battlefield commander. But Perusek demonstrates that Kubrick's view of warfare goes far beyond an interest in the visual appeal of guns and trumpets to questions of human motivation and human nature. He argues that Kubrick's war films are concerned both with strategic calculations of power and domination, and the ways in which these calculations are often thwarted by emotion and circumstance. He also focuses on the frustrated role of intermediaries in maintaining the circulation of power within social systems. Even in a nonwar film like *Eyes Wide Shut*, physician Bill Harford is clearly a servant to the powerful, an economic and social beneficiary of that power and yet in contact and sympathy with those below him. Colonel Dax in *Paths of Glory* clearly fits this mold and, like the soldiers below him and those in *Fear and Desire,* he is unable to change the power hierarchy and able to mitigate the situation with which he is confronted only to a very small degree. *Dr. Strangelove*, even more than the other films, focuses on the eruption of the irrational within a governmental and military hierarchy that ultimately defeats intercession by the intermediary figure of

Group Captain Lionel Mandrake. This failure of intermediaries also high-lights Kubrick's evolution from a Rousseauian point of view in *Paths of Glory* to a less hopeful view of human nature in his later films. Kubrick came of age at a time when Enlightenment faith in the ability of great sys-tems to change the world radically and finally for the better was coming to an end, and he had little faith in political movements to substantially better the human condition. It was the new and more disheartening world slouching, as it turned out, toward Auschwitz that Kubrick would con-template with an increasingly disillusioned gaze.

The essay by Pat Gehrke and Gina Ercolini elaborates on some of the ideas sketched out in the first part of this introduction, arguing that Kubrick's later films constitute a critique, whether intentional or not, of "humanist subjectivity and, more specifically, rational autonomous will." Gehrke and Ercolini focus on *2001*, *A Clockwork Orange*, *The Shining*, *Full Metal Jacket*, and *Eyes Wide Shut*. The "repeating topographies" of "resolu-tion and reason, subjectedness and will, and identification and otherness" they map in these films are in accord with other studies of Kubrick's films that highlight the characters' inability to act independently of the condi-tions that surround and shape them. And yet Gehrke and Ercolini con-clude that Kubrick's "anti-humanism . . . is not anti-human," since his films detail the capacity of human beings to make choices within the conditions of their subjection. Their conclusion that Kubrick's films engage in "a cel-ebration of otherness" is a provocative one and also in line with much recent research into what Diane Johnson has termed his "outraged yearn-ing for a better order."[44]

Cultural critic Mark Crispin Miller offers a probing examination of how *2001* exemplifies Kubrick's worldview in myriad subtle ways. In contrast to all other analyses of *2001*, Miller focuses not on the astronauts, the computer HAL, and the voyage "To Jupiter and Beyond" but on the early sections of the film featuring Dr. Heywood Floyd. He thereby foregrounds Kubrick's traditional theme of male dominance over females and the cold isolation from each other in which people often reside. He also discerns in *2001* the "detumescence" of the type of violent—though also self-destructive—patriarchal power that dominates world affairs in *Dr. Strangelove*. This decline is a function of the growth of scientific and technological instru-mentality as embodied in the computer HAL. Modern man is just as pow-erless and isolated as the apes in the hostile environment of "The Dawn of Man" sequence. Moreover, according to Kubrick, modern man is fur-ther dehumanized by what in the late nineteenth century Max Weber labeled the "disenchantment of the world" and Friedrich Nietzsche termed the "death of God" spawned by the triumph of science and materialism. The way out for Nietzsche was the "overman," a morally superior and autonomous being that Kubrick allegorizes in *2001*.[45] The profit and enjoyment that one can take from Kubrick's bleak view of humankind resides, Miller seems to say, in the combination of concern, artistry, and critique that informs his films. Comprehending the contours of the dark within and around is an achievement in itself and might promise the mitigation that comes from critical self-awareness and concern.

A Clockwork Orange reflects not only Kubrick's usual pessimistic outlook but also the social criticism of the 1960s that was the counterpart of that decade's utopianism and hedonism. In his essay, Pat Gehrke offers a Foucauldian analysis of how Kubrick's adaptation of the novel by Anthony Burgess (1962) also reflects deeper contemporaneous "discursive formations [contesting] social scientific and criminological constructions of subjectivity." According to Gehrke, *A Clockwork Orange* is an admonition against acceptance of scientific or state authority "as unimpeachable guardians of our civilization." Gehrke identifies four roles assumed by the protagonist Alex: criminal, convict, patient, and citizen, categories whose unstable and shifting boundaries demonstrate the arbitrary nature of ethical distinctions made by dominant hierarchies. Of particular importance to Kubrick, Burgess, Foucault, and Gehrke is the trend in the social sciences of the time toward behaviorism, especially aversion therapy of the type hyperbolized in *A Clockwork Orange*. Such techniques, especially when employed by the state, represent a fundamental threat to what Foucault the atheist—and Burgess the Christian—regarded as essential to ethics: choice. Gehrke's emphasis on the issue of resistance to power and authority represented by this line of thought is another indication of the creative tension in Kubrick's oeuvre between hope and resignation.

Barry Lyndon and *2001* are the only Kubrick films not set in the twentieth century, but *Barry Lyndon* is a record of a civilization before our own that died with the eruption of the modern world in 1789, the year in which Kubrick's film ends. While *Barry Lyndon* was a commercial failure and its critical reception was, as usual, mixed, no one questions the beauty of its settings and cinematography. Kubrick even sacrificed deep focus in scenes filmed in candlelight through a supersensitive lens. The result was the simulation of the flat surface of paintings that were the original visual record of the age and which also reflect the static ethos of the hierarchical society of the *ancien regime*. Paintings, portraits, and sculptures composed in the style of famous eighteenth-century works appear in the film, both as artifacts within scenes and as shots composed in the style of eighteenth-century land-scapes and scenes of daily life. Kubrick is not simply trying to create the look, feel, and pace of the surface decorum of eighteenth-century aristo-cratic society through story, settings, costumes, and music;[46] he also aims to reveal the stultifying effects of the artifice of eighteenth-century decorum.

As art historian Bille Wickre demonstrates, the subject matter and com-position of these paintings "create a subtext for the narration of the film, to focus the viewer on the act of looking and being the object of the gaze, and to provide a series of ironic visual puns." In particular, *Barry Lyndon* alludes to paintings by Watteau and Chardin—paintings that criticize the false decorum, cruelty, and hypocrisy of the ruling estates of the *ancien regime*. The static order of the ruling classes, reproduced by Kubrick in the stately pace, architecture, and the still-life shots of the film, snuff the life out of the protagonist and everyone else.[47] This point of view mirrors that of the satirist Thackeray, whose novel Kubrick chose as his point of artis-tic departure. Among other things, such visual subtexts also underscore the continuity of theme that runs through all of Kubrick's films and thus joins the only film of his not set in the modern age with his work on the discontents of the world after 1789. Indeed, *Barry Lyndon* and *2001* may be viewed as elegies for bygone ages, an eighteenth century segueing to the more dangerous age of "bourgeois technological society"[48] and a twenti-eth century evolving via alien intervention into a new and perhaps better human race.[49]

The history of the modern age, and especially the twentieth century, that so affected Kubrick informs historian Geoffrey Cocks' study of *The Shining*. Adapted from Stephen King's 1977 novel, *The Shining* is a dark musing upon the maze that is the human mind. The Minotaur at the cen-ter of this Kubrickian labyrinth, Cocks argues, is the Holocaust. This may be detected through careful attention to the many visual and aural details with which Kubrick habitually fills the screen. Kubrick grew up as a secu-lar New York City Jew at a time when the Nazis were embarking on their campaign to exterminate the Jews of Europe. Kubrick, whose family came to the United States from Poland in 1900, became a keen photographic observer of what was an increasingly dangerous world. In the 1950s he married into a German family. Consequently his films betray an approach-avoidance syndrome with regard to the history of Germany, Jews, and the Holocaust. The 1970s, which witnessed a series of horror films reflecting social contradictions and a wave of popular interest in Nazi Germany and the Holocaust, gave Kubrick a chance to address a subject that, in spite of long-standing plans to make a film about the Holocaust, he never addressed directly. That he could not address the subject explicitly was due to a number of personal, philosophical, and aesthetic considerations that Cocks analyzes. *The Shining,* like other Kubrick films, parodies a genre, here horror, to interrogate the immanent horrors of the modern world. Cocks claims that the film functions on one level as a retelling of Thomas Mann's *The Magic Mountain* (1924). As such, *The Shining* offers an artistic response to the horrors of World War II just as Mann's novel represents a response to the decline of European civilization to and through World War I.

Psychoanalytic and gender theory provide important tools for analyzing Kubrick's films, as demonstrated in Paula Willoquet-Maricondi's essay on *Full Metal Jacket.* Surrealism during the 1920s and 1930s originally exploited the psychoanalytic fixation on dreams and the unconscious. By the 1970s, film theorists had begun to examine the psychodynamic interrelationships among viewer, structure, and ideology. According to Jean-Louis Baudry, film creates the illusion for the viewer that he or she is a privileged spectator of reality, that the camera eye is the eye of the viewer over which he or she has control. Baudry draws from the post-Freudian psychoanalytic theory of Jacques Lacan, according to which a child sees his or her self only in an idealized way through the eyes of others. For Baudry, the film viewer is like a child. The screen is a mirror and not a window. Christian Metz's *Psychoanalysis and the Cinema* (1975, 1982), however, argues that the cinema not only reflects the spectator's image like a mirror but also acts as a window in simulating and encouraging voyeurism. Metz points to Lacan's emphasis on the sexual difference between the male child and the mother, as a result of which male identity becomes associated with desire, loss, and absence. In film, Metz maintains, this process produces a male audience's fetishization of "the phallic woman." This "apparatus" theory of film has been criticized for devoting insufficient attention to a number of factors inherent in the viewing of film, in particular gender. In 1975 Laura Mulvey, in an article in *Screen* titled "Visual Pleasure and Narrative Cinema," conceptualized film as a function of "the male gaze" in which women are objects to be observed—and thus controlled—by men. This view was in turn criticized for reducing women on screen and in the audience to passive victims, not accounting for the agency of women or the objectification of men, ignoring the range of sexual identity and response to film beyond the heterosexual, and discounting the role of conscious, cognitive, processes in the viewing of films.

Full Metal Jacket is almost completely devoid of women, and has been assailed for participating in a 1980s trend that reasserted solidaristic masculine American values challenged by the Vietnam War.[50] Willoquet-Maricondi argues, however, that *Full Metal Jacket* is not a reaffirmation of masculinity as an oppressive social construction but a devastating critique of it and the war films made about—or around—it. Willoquet-Maricondi sees the psychodynamics of the film's portrayal of the Marine molding of the masculine in terms of male separation from the infantile source of primary identity, which in our society is almost always a female. The culture demands this separation in terms of what it means to be "masculine," and organizations like the Marine Corps exploit the resultant sense of loss of a part of original identity by being "Mother Green and her lean, mean killing machine." This process of "remasculinization" is, Willoquet-Maricondi argues, represented and criticized in *Full Metal Jacket*. Kubrick's film world has always been dominated by males—in *Full Metal Jacket* there are only two women, a prostitute and an enemy sniper. To contrast two films about the Cold War, for instance—*Dr. Strangelove* and Tony Richardson's *Blue Sky* (1994)—is to notice the degree to which Kubrick's film focuses almost exclusively on the destructive tendencies and perversions of phallocentric power, whereas Richardson is concerned with the lives of women married to Cold Warriors.[51] But it is also worth emphasizing that there are strong women in Kubrick's films who resist subordination to men, although usually in vain—from Sherry Peatty in *The Killing* to Alice Harford in *Eyes Wide Shut*. Kubrick was of course a male member of a patriarchal society, and more than half of his films were made before the emergence of the women's movement. It is also worth noting that Kubrick's reflexive form of filmmaking interrogates female stereotypes in popular literature and film, revealing the ways in which women are often shaped by male desires and designs. So even in *Dr. Strangelove*, in which only one woman appears, it is her (bikinied) body, according to a Lacanian reading, that, as Peter Baxter has written, "fills in the mysterious object, lack of which is signified in the first shot, and becomes the place of the joyous annihilation of the final sequence" over Vera Lynn's World War II rendition of "We'll Meet Again."[52] As Willoquet-Maricondi's essay shows, post-Freudian psychoanalytic thought focusing on the dynamics of gender formation from infancy on is a useful tool in unpacking Kubrick's representations of women.

FINAL TAKE: *Eyes Wide Shut*

The last section of our volume draws together three very different critical appreciations of Kubrick's last film. Film critic Jonathan Rosenbaum, author of *Movies as Politics* (1997), puts Kubrick's last film in three larger contexts: that of his film career as a whole; the comparable work of directors like John Huston, Orson Welles, and Martin Scorsese; and the literary tradition from which Arthur Schnitzler's original story comes. Rosenbaum notes that *Eyes Wide Shut* presents dreamlike settings that invoke the past in general and filmmaking styles of various twentieth-century decades in particular. Anticipating the emphasis of Tim Kreider's essay, he also detects a theme of social exclusion reflecting Kubrick's Jewish origins and connected, among other things, to his major addition to the novella. The figure of Ziegler represents those powerful alpha males who manipulate and dominate the men and, especially, the women in the social orders below them. It is interesting to note that the great house in *Eyes Wide Shut* recalls in its contradictory associations the Overlook Hotel in *The Shining*. Somerton, like the Overlook, is a symbol of social and sexual power, and social and sexual anxiety. Its name in Anglo-Saxon means "summer dwelling" in a story that takes place at Christmas, while the Overlook is a hotel that is open only in the summer in a story that takes place during the winter.

Historian and psychoanalyst Peter Loewenberg provides essential historical and theoretical background for an understanding of the psychological form and content of *Eyes Wide Shut*. Viennese physician and writer Arthur Schnitzler and Viennese physician and psychoanalyst Sigmund Freud admired each other's work on the human psyche. They were major representatives of the intellectual and artistic hothouse that was Vienna in the last decades of the nineteenth century and the first decades of the twentieth. Freud's analysis of the uncanny in mental life is a foundational element in Schnitzler's *Dream Story* just as it is in Kubrick's *The Shining*. It is thus no surprise, at least in retrospect, that Kubrick had long been obsessed with making a film of *Dream Story*. Loewenberg also notes that some of the dreams in Schnitzler's story are more "intensely sexual and sadistic" than those in the film, an observation supporting Rosenbaum's judgment that Kubrick is more of a moralist than was Schnitzler. It is perhaps also relevant in terms of the sexual infidelity of Schnitzler himself that Loewenberg documents, contrasting as it does with Kubrick's own apparently lifelong marital fidelity. Another factor, as Loewenberg observes, is that Kubrick was compelled for commercial reasons by American censorship to moderate scenes of explicit sexual activities and necrophilia. This continues to be a greater problem for filmmakers than for novelists, who can produce books on their own, unlike directors even as powerful as Kubrick, who must (or choose to) bow to external masters for commercial reasons. This is the Western liberal analogue to the political censorship inherent in Soviet Communism: Jerzy Kozinski once observed that Andrzej Wajda's film *Ashes and Diamonds* (1958) could not be as probing as a novel because filmmakers in Communist Poland had to censor themselves for political reasons in a way writers, not dependent on the expensive production organization of film, did not.[53] Loewenberg also illuminates the psychodynamics behind the homosexual fantasies in *Eyes Wide Shut,* a subject Kubrick has addressed in several of his films.

While Loewenberg concentrates on the psychological dynamics created by the nexus of Freud, Schnitzler, and Kubrick, cartoonist and film critic Tim Kreider foregrounds the sociological concerns and implications of *Eyes Wide Shut.* Kreider begins by noting Kubrick's eye for telling detail, as with the book in a prostitute's bedroom that gives his essay its title. Two major characteristics of Kubrick's filmmaking are reflected in his observation that the Steadicam tracking shots, like a narrator, function as "an omniscient presence . . . afloat as the disembodied point of view in a dream." Kubrick's work is reminiscent of Max Ophuls, whose camera in *La Ronde* (1950), his film of Schnitzler's play *The Roundelay* (1897), likewise floats in and out of rooms recording the sumptuous and decadent manners of old Europe. What strikes Kreider most of all, however, is the commodification of people during the most commercialized time of the year, Christmas. And it is not only products that can be consumed but also people themselves: "everyone can be bought." Thus the central theme in *Eyes Wide Shut,* according to Kreider, is the exploitation of the powerless many by the powerful few, a consistent theme, as we have seen, in Kubrick's oeuvre. Women in particular are commodities. Doctor Bill Harford is associated with money (his first words are "Honey, have you seen my wallet?") while his wife (whose first words are "Ah . . . isn't it on the bedside table?" and "How do I look?") and all other women in the film are necessarily preoccupied with their physical appearance, in or out of clothes. Kreider argues that Kubrick's last three films, *The Shining, Full Metal Jacket,* and *Eyes Wide Shut,* "form a sort of thematic trilogy about our culture's hatred of the female." In the end, Kubrick's style of "open narrative" contributes powerfully to the film's content. We, like Bill, whose role recalls Perusek's discussion of intermediaries, cannot be sure of the true nature of anything that has happened. This is not only consistent with the interchangeability of dreams and reality in the film but reflects the machinations of powerful men like Ziegler to promote ambiguity as well as intimidation among those over whom they rule. For Kubrick, power, like sex, remains constant—from Vienna in 1900 under a declining Austrian Empire to New York in 1999 under a decadent American one. Fear and desire are the human lot from first to last.

NOTES

1. Geoffrey Crawley, "Film Giant Stanley Kubrick Dies at 70," *British Journal of Photography* 145.7215 (March 10, 1999): 3.
2. Robert P. Kolker, "The Film Text and Film Form," in *Film Studies: Critical Approaches,* ed. John Hill and Pamela Church Gibson (Oxford: Oxford University Press, 2000), 14.
3. Michael Herr, *Kubrick* (New York: Grove, 2000), 12; *Stanley Kubrick Interviews,* ed. Gene Phillips (Jackson: University Press of Mississippi, 2001), 70–71.
4. Max Weber, "'Prefatory Remarks' to Collected Essays in the Sociology of Religion" (1920), in *The Protestant Ethic & the Spirit of Capitalism,* trans. Stephen Kalberg (Los Angeles: Roxbury, 2002), 152.
5. Max Weber, *The Protestant Ethic and the "Spirit" of Capitalism,* trans. and ed. Peter Baehr and Gordon C. Wells (New York: Penguin, 2002), 120–21; Arthur Mitzman, *The Iron Cage: An Historical Interpretation of Max Weber* (New York: Knopf, 1970).
6. Weber, *Protestant Ethic,* 121. Alternatively, Kalberg, 24, writes: A "mechanized ossification, embellished with a sort of rigidly compelled sense of self-importance" might result, bringing with it "narrow specialists without mind, pleasure-seekers without heart; in its conceit, this nothingness imagines it has climbed to a level of humanity never before attained."
7. Theodor Adorno and Max Horkheimer, *Dialectic of Enlightenment,* trans. John Cumming (New York: Herder and Herder, 1972), 179.
8. See Max Horkheimer and Theodor W. Adorno, "The Culture Industry: Enlightenment As Mass Deception," in *Dialectic of Enlightenment.*
9. Theodor Adorno, *Aesthetic Theory,* ed. Gretel Adorno and Rolf Tiedemann, trans. Robert Hullot-Kentor (Minneapolis: University of Minnesota Press, 1997), 464.
10. Theodor Adorno, *Minima Moralia: Reflections from Damaged Life,* trans. E. F. N. Jephcott (London: Verso, 1974), 206.
11. See Theodor W. Adorno, "Chaplin Times Two" (trans. John MacKay), *Yale Journal of Criticism* 9.1 (1996): 57–61. What Adorno says here of Chaplin's approach to film could apply with equal force to Kubrick: "It is well known that he does not confine his mimetic arts strictly to the films which, since his youth, he produces only over great intervals of time and in an intensely and openly self-critical spirit. He acts incessantly, just like Kafka's trapeze artist, who sleeps in the baggage rack so as not to ease off training even for a moment."

12. See Tony Pipolo, "The Modernist and the Misanthrope: The Cinema of Stanley Kubrick," *Cineaste* 27.2 (Spring 2002): 4–15, 49; Ron Magid, "Quest for Perfection," *American Cinematographer* 80.10 (October 10, 1999): 40–51; Rainer Rother, "Das Kunstwerk als Konstruktionsaufgabe," *Merkur: Deutsche Zeitschrift für europäisches Denken* 43.5 (May 1989): 384–96.

13. For extensive bibliographies of works on Kubrick, see Michel Ciment, *Kubrick: The Definitive Edition*, trans. Gilbert Adair (New York: Faber and Faber, 2001); and Wallace Coyle, *Stanley Kubrick: A Guide to References and Resources* (Boston: G. K. Hall, 1980).

14. Alexander Walker, *Stanley Kubrick, Director* (New York: W. W. Norton, 1999), 208.

15. Herr, *Kubrick*, 84; *Kubrick Interviews*, 110.

16. *Kubrick Interviews*, 47–48.

17. Richard Dyer, "Introduction to Film Studies," in *Film Studies*, 6.

18. Neil. H. Donahue, "Unjustly Framed: Politics and Art in *Das Cabinet des Dr. Caligari*," *German Politics and Society* 32 (1994): 76–88. See also Michael Dunne, "*Barton Fink,* Intertextuality, and the (Almost) Unbearable Richness of Viewing," *Literature/Film Quarterly* 28 (2000): 303–11.

19. See, for example, Stanley Kauffmann, "Blank Cartridge," *New Republic,* July 27, 1987, 28–29; Pauline Kael, "Devolution," *New Yorker,* June 9, 1980, 130.

20. Diane Johnson, "Stanley Kubrick (1928–1999)," *New York Review of Books,* April 22, 1999, 28.

21. Rick Lyman, "A Perfectionist's Pupil with a Major in Creepy," *New York Times,* Feb. 22, 2002, B7.

22. Joseph Gelmis, *The Film Director as Superstar* (Garden City, NY: Doubleday, 1970), 315–16.

23. *Facets Features,* Spring 2000, 24.

24. Herr, *Kubrick*, 24.

25. Michel Foucault, *The Order of Things: An Archaeology of the Human Sciences,* ed. R. Readman and S. Miller (London: Routledge, 1992), 9.

26. Robert Polito, *Savage Art: A Biography of Jim Thompson* (New York: Knopf, 1995), 393.

27. Diane Johnson, "Writing for the Movies Is Harder Than It Looks," *New York Times Book Review,* April 14, 1985, 11.

28. Polito, *Savage Art,* 406.

29. Peter Hanson, *Dalton Trumbo, Hollywood Rebel* (Jefferson, NC: McFarland & Company, 2001), 136.

30. Nabokov, *Strong Opinions* (New York: McGraw-Hill, 1973), 21, 210. For more on the *Lolita* adaptation see Richard Corliss, *Lolita* (London: British Film Institute, 1994); and Christopher MacGowan, "Kubrick's Lolita: One of 'Those Foreign Films'?," in *Proceedings of the Conference on Film and American Culture,* ed. Joel Schwartz (Roy R. Charles Center, College of William and Mary, 1994), 74–79. See also Elizabeth Power, "The Cinematic Art of Nympholepsy: Movie Star Culture as Loser Culture in Nabokov's Lolita," *Criticism* 41 (Winter 1999): 101–18, which includes comparisons of Kubrick's adaptation with the 1999 Adrian Lyne version.

31. Vladimir Nabokov, *Lolita: A Screenplay* (New York: McGraw-Hill, 1974), xii.

32. Terry Southern, "Strangelove Outtake: Notes from the War Room," *Grand Street* 13.1 (Summer 1994): 69.

33. Arthur C. Clarke, *2001: A Space Odyssey* (New York, 1999), xiii.

34. Anthony Burgess, "A Clockwork Orange Resucked," in Burgess, *A Clockwork Orange* (New York: W. W. Norton, 1986), viii.

35. Walter Coppedge, *"Barry Lyndon:* Kubrick's Elegy for an Age," *Literature/Film Quarterly* 29.3 (2001): 172–78.

36. Greg Jenkins, *Stanley Kubrick and the Art of Adaptation: Three Novels, Three Films* (Jefferson, NC: McFarland, 1997), 72–73.

37. Vincent LoBrutto, "The Written Word and the Very Visual Stanley Kubrick," in this volume; Herr, *Kubrick,* 45–46, 53–54; Gerri Reaves, "The Fracturing of Identification," *Literature/Film Quarterly* 16.4 (1988): 232–37.

38. See also Vincent LoBrutto, "The Old Ultra-Violence," *American Cinematographer* 80.10 (October 1999): 52–60.

39. Johnson, "Writing for the Movies," 35. In a 1981 interview, Johnson praised Kubrick's literary sensibility and his contributions to the screenplay for *The Shining:* "He's quite a good writer, as well as a great director, and he really improved my version a lot" (*Chicago Review* 33 [1981]: 75–79, 77). See also "Diane Johnson, Screenwriter," in Ciment, *Kubrick,* 293–95.

40. Diane Johnson, interview with Barbara Lane, Commonwealth Club of California. http://www.commonwealthclub.org/01-05johnson-speech.html (July 1, 2002).

41. Johnson, "Writing for the Movies," 35.

42. "Frederic Raphael, Screenwriter," in Ciment, *Kubrick,* 269–71.

43. See also Michael Harrington, "Painful Weight of Pretension," *The Spectator,* July 24, 1999, 36–37.

44. Johnson, "Stanley Kubrick (1928–1999)," 28.

45. Leonard F. Wheat, *Kubrick's 2001: A Triple Allegory* (Lanham, MD: Scarecrow, 2000).

46. Elise F. Knapp and James Pegolotti, "Music in Kubrick's *Barry Lyndon:* 'A Catalyst to Manipulate,'" *Eighteenth-Century Life* 19 (May 1995): 92–97.

47. John Engell, *"Barry Lyndon,* a Picture of Irony," *Eighteenth-Century Life* 19 (May 1995): 83–88.

48. Frank Cossa, "Images of Perfection: Life Imitates Art," *Eighteenth-Century Life* 19 (May 1995): 82.

49. Benjamin Ross, "Eternal Yearning," *Sight and Sound* 5.10 (October 1995): 42.

50. Susan Jeffords, *The Remasculinization of America* (Bloomington: Indiana University Press, 1989), 116, 173, 176.

51. We are grateful to Molly Mullin, associate professor of anthropology at Albion College, for pointing out the instructive contrast between these two films.

52. Peter Baxter, "The One Woman," *Wide Angle* 6.1 (1984): 41.

53. Jerzy Kosinski, "Postwar Poland," Albion College, April 21, 1988.

First Take

WORDS AND PICTURES

The Written Word and the Very Visual Stanley Kubrick

⟫◈⟪

VINCENT LOBRUTTO

Film director Stanley Kubrick (1928–99) was a consummate visualist. Although he will be remembered for the astonishing cinematic images he created, his pictorial obsessions did not begin with the camera—they emerged from the word. Kubrick was a man who lived only for family and the movies, but his passion for filmmaking was nurtured and fueled by literature. Kubrick influenced generations of filmmakers raised on moving image narratives, yet Stanley Kubrick's personal cinematic journey began with his head buried in books in the Bronx, New York.

Kubrick's father Jacques, a physician, maintained a large library where Stanley spent hours reading and dreaming. In addition to reading, Stanley's father also introduced Stanley to his two other lifelong passions: chess and photography. Kubrick was a poor student, distracted from his studies by the wonders of still photography. A photo sale to *Look* magazine began his career as a wunderkind still photographer. The picture captured a forlorn New York newsstand operator and featured bold tabloid headlines announcing the death of the beloved American president Franklin Delano Roosevelt. After graduating from William Howard Taft High School, Kubrick and his friend Alexander Singer walked the streets of New York City's film district in Times Square in search of inspiration and contacts. Singer had a detailed notebook filled with ideas for a film adaptation of Homer's *Iliad* under his arm and tucked under Kubrick's was a volume of abbreviated novels of classic literature. Animated film creator Faith Hubley remembers seeing the young men on their quest. "Stanley would stop people at 1600 Broadway and say, 'Dostoyevsky, what do you think?' He couldn't pronounce the names."[1] Another member of the New York film community from the fifties remembers Kubrick with a treasured tome that contained every possible variation of dramatic narrative.

As a *Look* photojournalist, Kubrick rendered stories with his camera. With a series of images, the young photographer created a visual narrative—he was in fact searching for the movies. Kubrick's first encounter with a professional writer was a pairing with *Look* staff writer G. Warren Scholat Jr. They did not collaborate on the process of connecting words with images, but when Kubrick learned that Scholat had worked for the Walt Disney Studio, the quiet photographer talked to him about his plan to become a filmmaker.

Kubrick and Singer decided to make a short film together. Alex had written a short story to adapt and direct, Stanley was to be the director of photography. Singer described the story this way: "It's about some teenagers at the beach and a wistful love, a chance encounter that doesn't materialize. Very much a teenage experience." The two young men met on the top of a Fifth Avenue double-decker bus to discuss the project. Singer handed Kubrick the script and continuity sketches, and specified every camera setup for the short. "This is beautiful, Alex, you should make it yourself," Kubrick responded. "You've just taken away all of the choices from me and what's left is to sort of fill the frame—and while that takes some photographic knowledge and some doing, the real creativity and the real choices have already been made."[2] Kubrick made it clear early on that as a cinematic storyteller he had to have complete control of the story, script, and visualization.

Stanley Kubrick proceeded to create his own short, *Day of the Fight* (1951), his first film. The documentary was based on a photostory he shot for *Look*. "Prizefighter" was a study of twenty-four-year-old middle-weight boxer Walter Cartier. The title of the short came from a *Look* headline, "THE DAY OF A FIGHT." The concept of following a fighter's day hour by hour evolved from Kubrick's photos documenting the process of Cartier preparing for battle in the ring. The film has no synchronous dialogue. Kubrick developed the narrative working closely with Cartier, constantly asking him questions about the details of his life.[3] *Day of the Fight* was sold to RKO-Pathe for their *This Is America* Series and released in 1951. The script is credited to Robert Rein, but the narration spoken by Douglas Edwards, the veteran CBS newsman, reveals the voice of a young film director who was already grappling with serious themes. Heavily influenced by the tabloid language of newspapers and magazines and the philosophy of existentialism, the film ends with these words: "One man has skillfully, violently overcome another—that's for the fan. But K. O., name of opponent, time, date, and place—that's for the record book. But it's more than that in the life of a man who literally has to fight for his very existence. For him, it's the end of a working day."

Kubrick's second short film *Flying Padre* (1953) developed its documentary narrative from a human-interest story, a genre popular among photojournalists in the 1950s. The story follows the Reverend Fred Stadtmueller, a priest who flies his own single-engine plane to serve his New Mexico congregation. Half of the eight-minute-thirty-second film presents slice-of-life moments of the kindhearted priest. For the remainder of the story, Kubrick attempts a linear dramatic structure as the padre flies to rescue a sick baby at an isolated ranch. The film's story line is again presented through narration. There are no writing credits on *Flying Padre,* but the text skillfully imitates the comforting tone of the form. The young auteur again worked on every aspect of the project.

After *Flying Padre,* Kubrick resigned from *Look* and declared himself a professional film director. In 1953, he was commissioned to create an industrial film for the Seafarers International Union. *The Seafarers* (1953) is a goodwill promotional film for the offices at the Atlantic and Gulf Coast District of the American Federation of Labor. The screenplay was written by Will Chasan with research from the staff of the *Seafarers Log,* the union's house organ. The narrator, Don Hollenbeck, appears on camera reading from a script set before him. As an industrial film of the era *The Seafarers* is typical, but the filmmaker was not. During a montage of machines, the narration makes the point that machines serve man, a theme that would surface fully realized in *2001: A Space Odyssey* (1968). The thirty-minute film is Kubrick's first color work; a fifty-eight-second dolly shot across a cafeteria is an element of cinematic grammar he would employ to illustrate his stories. A photograph of a young naked woman with a string of pearls draped above her breasts is revealed in a cut to be a calendar in the barbershop. This nudity is the first sign of Kubrick's adolescent sexuality, sensibility, and the devilish sense of humor inherent in *Lolita* (1962), and *A Clockwork Orange* (1971). *The Seafarers* concludes with a dramatic speech delivered during an impassioned union meeting. Kubrick develops his sense of visual storytelling, accelerating a montage of the members reacting to the fiery oration as it comes to a climax. The skeleton of this dramatic interplay may have been buried in Kubrick's subconscious when he came up at the last minute with the ending for *Paths of Glory* (1957).[4]

Out of a life's work of thirteen feature films, only two of Kubrick's films are based on original stories—the first two. Throughout his career Kubrick emphasized the importance of a good story. To a man who had mastered the cinematic crafts of cinematography, production design, sound, and editing, the most difficult task of all was to invent and write an original story. Kubrick was never able to achieve solo creation of an original narrative. His first feature, eventually titled *Fear and Desire* (1953), began a forty-nine-year relationship with novelists, writers and screenwriters that embraced collaboration, confrontation, and above all control over the sanctity of content, thematic purity, and narrative style.

Kubrick had met Howard O. Sackler, who later wrote the Pulitzer Prize–winning play *The Great White Hope,* when Sackler was a member of the *Taft Review* and the William Howard Taft High School's literary club. Kubrick brought the script to producer Richard de Rochemont and told him it was co-written by Howard O. Sackler, a contemporary poet. In 1951 Kubrick formed Stanley Kubrick Productions. He raised almost $10,000 from friends, his father, and his uncle Martin Perveler, who owned a string of drugstores in Los Angeles and was credited as associate producer on the project, then known as *The Trap.* After independently producing the film, de Rochemont's Vavin Inc. financed completion costs. Kubrick changed the title when de Rochemont told him there were already three films titled *The Trap.* The project was renamed *Shape of Fear* and upon release *Fear and Desire.*[5] The subject is war—one Kubrick would return to repeatedly. Kubrick expresses his view of the horror and futility of war through a surreal visual and figurative style. *Fear and Desire* portrays a nameless war with a faceless enemy in an undisclosed locale. Four soldiers are shot down behind enemy lines. They acquire a shack, food, and guns from the enemy. The men hold a young woman hostage and tie her to a tree. The woman has an emotional breakdown; one of the men goes mad and performs spurts of Shakespeare's *The Tempest.* Two of the soldiers try to assassinate a general and his aide, portrayed by the same actors. One of the men sees his own face in the dead general. *Fear and Desire* closes with the four men reunited. One is dead, another insane, the others have lost their desire for life. Kubrick relies on the literary device of narration to set the motif of the film. The influence of Sartre, Camus, and American existentialists such as Norman Mailer can be heard in the opening voice-over: "There is a war in this forest. Not a war that has been fought, nor one that will be, but any war. And the enemies that struggle here do not exist unless we call them into being. For all of them, and all that happens now is outside history. Only the unchanging shapes of fear and doubt are from our world. These soldiers that you see keep our language and our time, but we have no other country but the mind."[6] In a letter to the eventual distributor, Joseph Burstyn, Kubrick revealed his aspiration for a poetic, mythological cinema, where meaning should be left to the perceptions of the beholder. "Its structure: allegorical. Its conception: poetic. A drama of 'man' lost in a hostile world—deprived of material and spiritual foundations—seeking his way to an understanding of himself, and of life around him. He is further imperiled on his *Odyssey* by an unseen but deadly enemy that surrounds him; but an enemy who, upon scrutiny, seems to be almost shaped from the same mold. . . . It will, probably, mean many things to different people, and it ought to be."[7] In *Fear and Desire*, the twenty-five-year-old Stanley Kubrick metabolized a thesis surrounding the cruel nature of man— one that would inspire and inform one of the most important cinematic oeuvres in film history.

Kubrick returned to boxing for his second feature. The original story was first called *Kiss Me, Kill Me* but released as *Killer's Kiss*. The screenplay was again co-written with Howard O. Sackler, but this time Kubrick did not give his collaborator screen credit. The opening credits state "Story by Stanley Kubrick." *Killer's Kiss* is Kubrick's interpretation of film noir. The story follows a down-on-his-luck boxer and his relationship with a dance-hall girl controlled by a gangster club owner. The script is structured in flashbacks, and the story is told in a first person narration from the boxer's point of view. Kubrick's doomed lovers conform to the conventions of the genre, but in the final moment the filmmaker violates the strict noir narrative code by bringing the boxer and the girl together for a happy ending. The dialogue and plot are a pastiche of B-movie elements. Kubrick's New York story reveals the underbelly of Times Square nightlife, and his images are a noir tone poem of old New York. In a memorable sequence, Kubrick creates a surrealistic effect by staging a fight scene in a mannequin factory.

Kubrick and James B. Harris met and formed Harris-Kubrick Pictures in 1957, opening an office on Fifty-seventh Street.[8] They both began to look for material for their first film. Harris searched through titles in Scribner's Bookstore on Fifth Avenue until he came upon *Clean Break* (1955), a novel by Lionel White. The story of a racetrack robbery intrigued Harris, who purchased the book and read it immediately. He saw cinematic potential in the story, which is told in a series of flashbacks that unfold the prismatic story from multiple viewpoints. Kubrick devoured *Clean Break* in one sitting. They both were attracted to the time-shifting elements and the way White told the story from many different character and timeline perspectives. Harris-Kubrick purchased the rights to *Clean Break* for $10,000. They tried to make a deal with United Artists, who were interested but needed to see a script. Kubrick suggested they hire legendary hard-boiled crime novelist Jim Thompson to write his first film script.[9]

Kubrick worked closely with Thompson, who was not familiar with the screenplay format. The structure for the adaptation called *The Killing* (1956) was largely transposed from the novel. Kubrick organized the scenes, and Harris made several contributions to the script. Kubrick concentrated on the dialogue with Thompson, who wrote on legal-size paper instead of the standard 8½ by 11. The screenplay was bound on the top rather than on the left. The screen credits state, "Screenplay by Stanley Kubrick and Dialogue by Jim Thompson."[10] The ownership of a screen story was imperative to Kubrick. He needed writers to create a screenplay but was not quite willing to bestow equal acknowledgment. Kubrick's major impact on *The Killing* narrative was his inventive use of a stark camera style that not only emphasized movement within space but also the complex editing structure that flashed back and forth in time. The story is heavily dependent on a narration that keeps constant track of the shifting time frame and thus defines each character's point of view and state of mind.

The Killing represents daring cinematic storytelling, featuring nonlinear construction decades before Quentin Tarantino's *Pulp Fiction* (1994). When the film was completed, Harris and Kubrick screened *The Killing* in Hollywood. The reaction was mixed; many felt the story was confusing and that the flashbacks prevented audience involvement.[11] Disheartened, Harris and Kubrick flew back to their home base in New York and actually began re-editing the film as a straight-line narrative before handing in the final cut to United Artists. In the end they trusted their cinematic instincts and returned to their original vision of hard cutting the time shifts in the narrative. *The Killing* is often recognized as the first mature Stanley Kubrick film. The audacious narrative style and fatalist point of view established Kubrick's hallmark filmic virtuosity and jaundiced moral vision.

After *The Killing*, Harris-Kubrick made a deal with Dore Schary to produce films for MGM. Harris and Kubrick agreed they wanted the subject of their next film to be war. Kubrick suggested Humphrey Cobb's novel *Paths of Glory*, which he had read as a teenager in his doctor father's office while waiting for him to finish with a patient. The 1935 novel is the story of three World War I soldiers executed for cowardice in France in order to cover up the actions of a power-mad general who was willing to fire upon his own troops to further his military ambitions. Schary found *Paths of*

Glory too downbeat and was concerned by the box-office failure of another antiwar film, John Huston's adaptation of Stephen Crane's *The Red Badge of Courage* (1951). He sent Harris and Kubrick to MGM's literary library to find a suitable property to adapt. After searching hundreds of titles in the archive, Kubrick selected Stefan Zweig's *The Burning Secret* (1914), a novel concerning a child who protects his mother when his father finds out she has had an affair. Schary greenlighted the project. Although the deal was for Harris-Kubrick to write, produce, and direct a film in forty weeks, the duo felt they needed to work with a writer to adapt the novel. The well-read Kubrick suggested Calder Willingham,[12] the southern novelist who was script-doctoring *The Bridge on the River Kwai* (1957) at the time. Schary was reluctant, but Harris and Kubrick were able to convince him to bring on Willingham. Kubrick continued to seek out literary writers to create a story he could visualize cinematically. He was drawn to Willingham's sense of irony, savagery, and dark knowledge of the military mind. While Kubrick and Willingham worked on *The Burning Secret*, Harris-Kubrick secretly put Jim Thompson on assignment adapting *Paths of Glory*—even though MGM had flatly turned it down.

Schary was fired during an MGM boardroom shake-up, Harris-Kubrick ran out of time in producing *The Burning Secret*, and the deal was terminated. Kubrick's moonlighting with Jim Thompson had produced a draft of *Paths of Glory*, and Harris-Kubrick moved forward with the project. United Artists rejected the Kubrick/Thompson script, and it was rewritten by Calder Willingham. Kirk Douglas bought the script for his Bryna Productions and signed Harris-Kubrick to a five-picture deal. When Douglas arrived on location in Germany, he was presented with a new script reworked by Kubrick. After reading lines like, "You've got a big head, You're so sure the sun rises and sets up there in your noggin' you don't even bother to carry matches," and "You've got the only brain in the world. They made yours and threw the pattern away. The rest of us have a skull-ful of cornflakes," Douglas threw the script across the room. Douglas told Kubrick he was committed to the Willingham script and wanted it reinstated immediately, so they returned to that draft. The final screenplay is credited to Stanley Kubrick, Calder Willingham, and Jim Thompson.[13]

In August 1958, Richard de Rochemont wrote to Kubrick to compliment *Paths of Glory* and suggested the director consider Vladimir Nabokov's novel *Lolita* for his next production.[14] Marlon Brando was so impressed with Kubrick he hired him to direct what eventually became *One-Eyed Jacks*. The screenplay was adapted from Charles Neider's *The Authentic Death of*

Hendry Jones (1956), a Western novel that reconceived the Billy the Kid legend. Sam Peckinpah wrote the screenplay, and Brando's production company Pennebaker approved it. Kubrick was given a six-month contract to rewrite the Peckinpah script and to prepare the film with Brando. Peckinpah was fired, and Brando, Kubrick, and Calder Willingham worked on the project together. In the end, Calder Willingham was fired too, and it became all too clear that Kubrick wasn't a "yes" man. Guy Trosper was hired to rewrite the project, and Brando fired Kubrick. The project became the only film directed by Marlon Brando.

As Harris continued to work the Harris-Kubrick desk, he learned about *Lolita*'s publication and got a copy of the controversial novel. Calder Willingham had also been telling Kubrick about Nabokov's nymphet tale. The team was so excited about reading the book that when it arrived Harris cracked the spine and, as he finished reading each page, passed the loose ones to Kubrick so they could read it simultaneously. Nabokov resisted selling his work to the movies: "My supreme, and in fact only, interest in these motion picture contracts is money. I don't give a damn for what they call 'art.' Moreover I would veto the use of a real child. Let them find a dwarf-ess."[15] Eventually Harris struck a two-year deal with superagent Swifty Lazar for $150,000 plus 15 percent of the profits.

Harris and Kubrick proceeded to develop their production of *Lolita* when Kirk Douglas called to tell Kubrick that he would replace Anthony Mann as the director of *Spartacus*. The screenplay for the film had been written by blacklisted screenwriter Dalton Trumbo. The relationship between Douglas, producer Edward Lewis, Trumbo, and Howard Fast, the author of the novel, was contentious. Kubrick had little control over the production and meager input into the script, but he managed to bring the material to the screen with majesty and intelligence. Douglas had, in fact, grappled with an ethical struggle over the writing credit. The shooting script was credited "by Eddie Lewis and Sam Jackson." Lewis and Douglas vehemently detested the blacklist, so the producer's name had been used as a front—Jackson was Dalton Trumbo's pseudonym. Lewis would not take credit for Trumbo's work, and Douglas felt that using Jackson was morally wrong. Now Kubrick suggested a solution: "Screenplay by Stanley Kubrick." At this point Douglas was so enraged that Kubrick would consider taking credit for someone else's work that the suggestion propelled him to give Dalton Trumbo his rightful credit. At the same time Otto Preminger credited Trumbo with the screenplay for his production of *Exodus* (1960). The dreaded era of the blacklist was finally over.

Spartacus (1960) was the first feature film directed by Stanley Kubrick on which he didn't receive a writing credit. *Lolita* became the second—and last—but for very different reasons. Kubrick and Harris wisely decided to give Nabokov solo credit to preserve the literary quotient of the project and to avoid personalizing responsibility for the explosive content. On March 1, 1960, Nabokov and Kubrick met in Hollywood to exchange ideas about the screen adaptation of *Lolita*. The next day Nabokov sat on a public park bench in Beverly Hills mentally constructing the screenplay. Over the next several months Kubrick and Nabokov met infrequently. Outlines, criticism, and advice from the director eventually stopped coming. Nabokov spent from eight in the morning until noon each day pursuing his beloved butterfly-hunting pastime and structuring the cinematic narrative in his head. After lunch the Russian literary giant sat in a lawn chair for four hours writing the morning's ideas for scenes on individual index cards. By the end of April, Nabokov delivered the completed second act of the script. Swifty Lazar struggled with Kubrick's lawyer over the rights for Nabokov to publish his version of the screenplay. Kubrick was secretive about re-rewriting Nabokov's draft and was looking to avoid comparison between his film and Nabokov's screenplay for as long as possible. As June came to a close, Nabokov amassed more than one thousand index cards and presented a four-hundred-page typed screenplay to Kubrick, a version that would have made a three-hour-and-forty-minute film. Kubrick visited Nabokov's home in person and told him it had too many scenes and would make a seven-hour film. Kubrick gave Nabokov a list of deletions and changes; the author made some and created still more new sequences. "You couldn't lift it," remarked James B. Harris, referring to Nabokov's mammoth draft.[16]

After working on the script for six months, Nabokov delivered a shorter version of his work and Kubrick accepted it. Fearful of an X-rating that would have spelled box-office disaster, the producers negotiated with the League of Decency and the Motion Picture Association of America, and in August 1961 *Lolita* officially received Code Seal approval. Nabokov may have received the sole screenwriting credit, but Harris and Kubrick proclaimed their control over the sensitive material in the opening credits: "MGM Presents in Association with Seven Arts Productions James B. Harris and Stanley Kubrick's *Lolita.*" Kubrick rewrote the script before and during shooting, especially by embracing the wild improvisations of Peter Sellers as Quilty. In 1974 Nabokov finally published his revised script, adding a few scenes from his four-hundred-page opus. No voices were raised during the creation of the adaptation, but Kubrick retained complete artistic control over what he put on the screen. The resulting film captures the spirit of Nabokov,[17] while at the same time possessing the sardonic comic tone that would fully emerge in Kubrick's next film. Kubrick had preserved something essential in Nabokov's vision while continuing to develop as a filmmaker with an individual point of view.

Dr. Strangelove, or How I Learned to Stop Worrying and Love the Bomb (1964) began a new phase in Kubrick's career. Harris-Kubrick extricated themselves from their commitment to Kirk Douglas's Bryna Productions, and with *Lolita* Kubrick had begun working in London, England . . . far from Hollywood. For his next project Kubrick started with a subject, thermonuclear war, which had preoccupied him since 1958. Kubrick asked Alastair Buchan, the head of the Institute for Strategic Studies in London, to recommend a syllabus so he could study all aspects of nuclear weapons. The list included *Red Alert,* a dramatic novel about nuclear global conflict by Peter George, a former Royal Air Force navigator and a British intelligence agent. Kubrick purchased the motion picture rights and began working on the screenplay with Peter George. During one work session, Harris and Kubrick departed from *Red Alert*'s solemn premise. "What would happen in the War Room if everybody's hungry and they want the guy from the deli to come in and a waiter with an apron around him takes the sandwich order?" they joked. "Do you think this could be a comedy or a satire? Do you think this is funny?"[18] When they came out of their silly jag, Harris took the dramatic script to Seven Arts and presented it as their second picture commitment. It was then, however, that Harris-Kubrick Pictures came to an end. James B. Harris wanted to set out on his own directing career; Stanley Kubrick was looking for greater control as his own producer so that he could pursue a series of obsessions, themes, and subjects.

As Harris was leaving, Kubrick told him he had brought writer Terry Southern onto the project since he was now convinced the film should be a satiric comedy. Kubrick proceeded to do serious research on nuclear weapons, reading forty-six books on the topic. These included *The Effects of Nuclear Weapons, Soviet Military Strategy, Man's Means to His Ends, The Causes of World War III,* and *Nuclear Tactics.* He also studied the work of Herman Kahn, Thomas Schelling, Edward Teller, Erich Fromm, Bruno Bettelheim, Albert Einstein, and Leopold Infeld. Kubrick and Terry Southern worked closely to transform *Red Alert* into an outrageous black comedy.[19] Before production began, Kubrick sent the script to Geoffrey Shurlock of the MPAA to make sure he wouldn't have any problems getting a Code

Seal for the irreverent film. Shurlock was concerned about the use of "hell" and "damn" throughout the script, the phrase "rotten sons of bitches," the references to prophylactics, and a pie-throwing sequence that involved the president of the United States. Kubrick assured Shurlock the MPAA would find the completed film acceptable. Privately Kubrick felt that if he brought the scandalous *Lolita* to the screen he could certainly get approval for his new comedy.

During production Southern and Kubrick continued to work on the screenplay. At five o'clock each morning they would work on two table-tops in their moving office in the back seat of Kubrick's old Bentley while they headed to Shepperton Studios. Kubrick posed questions and situations to the madly ingenious Terry Southern, who developed outrageous dialogue and came back with even more bizarre situations. *Dr. Strangelove* went through another rewrite during postproduction. Kubrick and film editor Anthony Harvey took the whole story structure apart, rearranging index cards on a large corkboard until they found a more interesting way to present the narrative.

The first critics' screening for *Dr. Strangelove* was scheduled for November 22, 1963; it was canceled when the afternoon news announced President John F. Kennedy's assassination in Dallas. Kubrick then changed Major Kong's line, "A fella could have a pretty good weekend in Dallas," to "A fella could have a pretty good weekend in Vegas." Later, after a disastrous screening for Columbia Pictures executives, Kubrick cut the pie-throwing sequence, which also contained a line that would reflect the horror in Dallas when Buck Turgidson said, "Gentlemen, our beloved president has been struck down in his prime." Kubrick stated he removed the scene because "[i]t was too farcical and not consistent with the satiric tone of the rest of the film."[20]

The screenplay was credited to Stanley Kubrick, Peter George, and Terry Southern; it received an Academy Award nomination and won the Writer's Guild Award for 1964. Kubrick became incensed when an ad for *The Loved One* (1964) read, "What happens when the director of *Tom Jones* meets the writer of *Dr. Strangelove?*" Kubrick had his lawyers force the ad out of print and in a formal statement downplayed Southern's participation on the film.[21] Kubrick fiercely protected his auteur status and was punitive about the contributions of other writers. Southern's contribution, however, was instrumental in transforming *Dr. Strangelove* into the first contemporary black comedy, a model that continues to influence the genre today.[22]

Kubrick's landmark film *2001: A Space Odyssey* (1968) began with the director's notion to make "a really good sci-fi movie." Kubrick's collaboration with well-known science fiction author Arthur C. Clarke was his most satisfying and substantive work with a writer; it broke new ground in screenplay methodology and in cinematic storytelling. The four-year process of bringing *2001* to the screen began with Kubrick optioning Clarke's "The Sentinel" (1948),[23] a nine-page short story that suggested highly intelligent extraterrestrials had explored the earth before the arrival of man and left a physical marker (later visually interpreted by Kubrick and his design team as a monolith). Kubrick wanted to use "The Sentinel" as a jumping-off point, and he also purchased a group of six other Clarke stories.[24] The original writing schedule included twelve weeks to complete the screenplay, two weeks of consultation, and four weeks of revisions. Clarke's actual participation on the film spanned the four years of production. Kubrick began their professional relationship as collaborators by judging the conventional screenplay "[t]he most uncommunicative form of writing ever devised."[25] Although much of the film would be crafted during the filmmaking process, Kubrick needed a words-on-paper draft to enlist MGM's participation in distributing the highly secretive cinematic project. Kubrick proposed that he and Clarke collaborate first on writing a full-length novel with attention to film adaptation, and then evolve a shooting script from that novel.

Clarke began writing the novel in Kubrick's Central Park West office on an electric typewriter; he later chose to avoid the director's intense scrutiny by working quietly in the literary atmosphere of the famed Chelsea Hotel in the company of Arthur Miller, Allen Ginsberg, and William Burroughs. During daily meetings, Clarke and Kubrick screened countless science fiction films but found them lacking from a narrative and technical point of view.[26] The two men consulted Carl Sagan and other leading thinkers, scientists, engineers, and designers from IBM, Honeywell, Boeing, Bell Telephone, RCA, Chrysler, and General Electric. After an estimated 2,400 hours of writing, the manuscript of the novel was complete, and MGM and Cinerama greenlighted the project at $6 million. Kubrick and Clarke changed the project's original title *Journey Beyond the Stars* to embrace the coming millennium. At this stage Clarke began revising and expanding the first draft of the novel. Kubrick discarded entire sections he had once approved. Ideas continued to shift and turn. In 1965, Clarke returned to his home in Ceylon to rewrite the story, and Kubrick moved the production to MGM at Boreham Wood outside of London. On Christmas Day, Clarke handed in a completed draft of the script; Kubrick complained that it was too wordy. He wanted the film to rely on visuals and sound to communicate ideas and narrative. (The completed 139-minute film has only 46 minutes of dialogue.) At one point narration was considered but then dropped. A documentary opening, featuring interviews with leading space authorities, was researched but also discarded. Clarke, on set during the shooting in England, continued to write, consult, and answer Kubrick's innumerable questions. Clarke even functioned as an emissary to the director, flying to MGM in Hollywood to calm the jittery nerves of anxious executives who had been kept in the dark about the project.

Kubrick and Clarke had an agreement allowing Clarke to publish the novel under his own name. During production Clarke finished what he considered the final draft of the novel, but Kubrick had never intended for Clarke to publish the novel before his film was finished and released. He made sure of a delay by presenting the writer with a nine-page memo questioning the smallest literary and factual detail, stating minutiae like, "Can you use the word *veldt* in a drought-stricken area?," "I don't think the verb *twittering* seems right," and "Do leopards *growl?*"[27] Confident that he had the final corrections in hand, Clarke instructed his agent Scott Meredith to proceed with a publishing deal. Dell agreed to publish the book as a Delacorte hardcover and a Dell paperback. The $160,000 deal was predicated on releasing the book *before* the movie opened. Kubrick balked at this and refused to sign the contract; Clarke desperately tried to keep up with Kubrick's criticisms and modifications. Unfortunately, these were still the days of hard type, and Delacorte had moved ahead in setting the book. The type and plates were ordered to be broken up and destroyed as the project continued to change.

In 1968, the movie was released and the novel published. The film credits read "Screenplay by Stanley Kubrick and Arthur C. Clarke," and the novel states that it was written by Arthur C. Clarke, based on a screenplay by Stanley Kubrick and Arthur C. Clarke. The script was nominated for an Oscar but lost to Mel Brooks for *The Producers*. *2001* may be best known for its ground-breaking special effects, and indeed it had a seismic impact on future cinematic narratives.[28] *2001* is driven by ideas, potent visual images, and a philosophic, spiritual search for the mysteries of the universe, not by conventional plot, character development, and dialogue devices.

Now, with *2001* over, Kubrick began reading hundreds of books about Napoleon. He developed a consulting relationship with Professor Felix Markham of Oxford University, who had studied the subject for more than thirty-five years and was considered to be one of the world's foremost

Napoleon scholars. Kubrick researched everything from the French emperor's taste in food to the weather on the day of a specific battle. All the
data was cross-indexed in a research file, including information on every
person who was in any way connected with Napoleon's life. Kubrick would
be able to use specific time- and place-related material whenever he wanted
by way of this encyclopedic research. Kubrick began preproduction on the
project and showed some interest in Jack Nicholson for the title role.
Kubrick learned that Anthony Burgess was planning to write a novel con-
figured like a symphony, and he convinced Burgess to apply the concept
to the life of Napoleon. The plan was for Burgess to write the novel, then
adapt it into a screenplay in collaboration with Kubrick, reiterating the *2001*
approach. Financing for this epic project fell through, but Burgess did
write *Napoleon Symphony: A Novel in Four Movements,* published in 1974.

With *Napoleon* on the shelf, Kubrick considered an adaptation of Arthur
Schnitzler's *Traumnovelle*—beginning a thirty-year obsession that eventually
became *Eyes Wide Shut* (1999). Kubrick had also read through the Anthony
Burgess canon and optioned the author's *A Clockwork Orange* (1962). Film
director Ken Russell and the Rolling Stones had been interested in this
property, which Burgess no longer owned—he had sold the rights to a
New York lawyer and a clothing-chain executive from Philadelphia for a
few hundred dollars. Kubrick's initial reaction to *A Clockwork Orange*
revealed his attraction to a story and the potential for cinematic adaptation. "It has everything: great ideas, a great plot, external action, interesting side characters and one of the most unique leading characters I've ever
encountered in fiction—Alex. The only character comparable to Alex is
Richard III and I think they both work on your imagination in much in
the same way. They both take the audience into their confidence, they are
both completely honest, witty, intelligent and unhypocritical."[29] Kubrick
recognized in *A Clockwork Orange* a moral investigation of free will.
Heretofore, computers had taken command of nuclear weapons that could
destroy the world in *Dr. Strangelove;* they had been responsible for the
murder of an astronaut in *2001.* In *A Clockwork Orange,* science found a way
to control aberrant behavior and attempted to obliterate the human spirit.
The mechanization of man was becoming a central Kubrickian metaphor.

For the first time, Stanley Kubrick wrote a feature screenplay without
collaboration. He based this screenplay on the American edition of the
novel, which omitted the twenty-first and final chapter of the original
British edition—the chapter that demonstrates Alex's mature rejection of
his teenage rebellion and violence. The first draft screenplay, completed on

May 15, 1970, was created by Kubrick in an experimental format that expanded the formal aspects of the craft. In a traditional screenplay, the descriptive prose runs from the left to the right margins and the dialogue is centered in a smaller block. Kubrick did the opposite for the screenplay for *A Clockwork Orange*. The dialogue runs from the left to the right margins and the descriptive prose is centered in a smaller block. This shifts the emphasis, allowing the description of the environments and action to take on a poetic quality so that the reader clearly understands the world in which the characters are living. The writing style evokes color, mood, and atmosphere for the imagery and a sparse directness for the dialogue written in the spirit of the Nadsat language Burgess invented for Alex and his droogs.[30] The story as Kubrick wrote it retained Burgess's first-person narration but leaves out Alex's maturation into adulthood and his embrace of responsibility. At the end of the screenplay, Alex is much like he is at the beginning of the novel—driven and delighted by his violent desires.

Kubrick received solo credit for the adaptation, linking him, once again, directly to another literary figure. The solo credit showed up on his next project when Kubrick set out to explore the genre of the historic period film. After extensive study he selected William Makepeace Thackeray's *The Memoirs of Barry Lyndon Esq., of the Kingdom of Ireland* (1844). Kubrick was especially secretive about this project. He did not want anyone to know he was making a film based on material held in the public domain, lest anyone might do a knockoff of the story and get it to theaters before he himself completed his project. There was speculation that Kubrick had returned to adapting Schnitzler's *Traumnovelle,* but Stanley swore his stars Ryan O'Neal and Marisa Berenson to secrecy and proceeded to film the project without revealing the plot or the source.

Literary academics and critics reproached Kubrick for choosing a minor novel and one of Thackeray's lesser works. *Barry Lyndon* (1975) received attention for its lush period production values and the landmark use of photographing by candlelight, but the film also extends Kubrick's preoccupation with individual and social corruption. Barry, Kubrick's antihero, is a scoundrel and cheat who, as a soldier, deserter, gambler, and lover, rises to the heights of fortune only to return to his beginnings as petty gentry. The film is also Kubrick's most literary, structured in novelistic sections with narrative cards and narration that spans the 185-minute film. Thackeray presented the broken-spirited Barry as a first-person narrator; Kubrick employed an anonymous narrator whose dryly ironic tone functions as a critical commentary on his protagonist and aristocratic society.

Kubrick next settled on the notion of revivifying the horror film. He began by reading his way through the genre, and eventually chose Stephen King's best seller *The Shining* (1977). King was already a phenomenon: his books had sold twenty-two million copies; Brian DePalma had adapted *Carrie* (1976) to the screen; Tobe Hooper made *Salem's Lot* (1979) into a television movie; and George Romero was scheduled to direct an adaptation of *The Stand*.[31]

Kubrick was attracted to King's ghost story because of the "cascade of inventions" it offered.[32] He was determined to make *The Shining* a commentary on human malevolence, personified by writer, father, and husband Jack Torrance. Kubrick intensified King's themes of family dysfunction, child abuse, and violence, and he united the forces of ghosts, alcoholism, and mental illness that haunted Jack. Kubrick was not actually telling King's story, but he was using *The Shining* to restate a favorite theme: "There's something inherently wrong with the human personality. There's an evil side to it."[33]

Kubrick had read and admired Diane Johnson's novel *The Shadow Knows* (1974), which deals with themes of anxiety, paranoia, and violence, and he enlisted her help on the screenplay.[34] The two of them worked together in England for three months, first creating separate outlines for the film, then comparing the two and discussing each scene. This process was completed three times as the plot line for the film developed. Kubrick cultivated a good working relationship with Johnson, as he had with Arthur C. Clarke, and he spent hours discussing a wide range of subjects with her. They talked about H. P. Lovecraft, Bruno Bettelheim's psychoanalysis of fairy tales, and Freud's insights into how individuals express parapsychological experiences. Kubrick and Johnson had several copies of *The Shining* that they cut up and filed into envelopes marked for the individual characters in the book. "He [Kubrick] has a strong literary sense," Johnson remarked. "In all respects he thinks like a novelist."[35]

Kubrick didn't ask Stephen King to participate in the adaptation, but he fired a volley of questions (during transatlantic phone calls) at the writer about the novel's philosophic, conceptual, and narrative elements. Initially, King was honored that such a prestigious filmmaker was interested in adapting his work but was later disappointed that his novel was used as a jumping-off point for Kubrick's personal, psychological, and philosophical examination of the central character. Eventually King decided to mount a television miniseries to faithfully adapt his novel. When King asked permission to go ahead with his production Kubrick agreed, with one stipulation: that King stop criticizing his film.[36]

After reinventing the horror genre, Kubrick returned to his obsession with war, this time focusing on Vietnam. Kubrick began the process that culminated in *Full Metal Jacket* (1987) by talking with Michael Herr, a Vietnam war correspondent who had written the acclaimed *Dispatches* (1977) and had worked with Francis Ford Coppola on *Apocalypse Now* (1979). Kubrick and Herr both were impressed with *The Short-Timers* (1979), a first novel by Gustav Hasford, a former marine and war correspondent who had served in Vietnam.[37] The novel was not as celebrated as *The Shining, A Clockwork Orange,* or *Lolita,* so Kubrick changed the title. He was inspired by the phrase "full metal jacket" he had seen in a gun catalog referring to a lead bullet encased in a copper jacket. The film did retain the overall structure of Hasford's novel and the darkly comic nature of the dialogue.

In 1985, Kubrick and Herr formally began work on the screenplay. Kubrick had written a detailed treatment, and Herr met with him every day to break it down into scenes on index cards. Herr then proceeded to write the first draft of the screenplay; he and Kubrick discussed the day's work each evening by phone. Kubrick and Hasford had marathon telephone conversations about the screenplay but met only once. Kubrick rewrote Herr's first draft, and Herr reworked Kubrick's. Hasford also came to London to work on the script, which was in a constant state of rewrite throughout production.

The screenplay contained a section that followed Private Joker to Phu Bai to see Captain January and tracked his disillusionment with the Marine Corps propaganda machine, linking the Parris Island segment with the in-country fighting finale. The scenes were shot but deleted during the editing process. At one point during postproduction the film began at Joker's funeral, and the story was told as a flashback, but Kubrick wanted to stress Joker's affirmation of life and abandoned the structure. Again Kubrick employed narration as Joker led the viewer through the war via his cynical and morbidly funny viewpoint. When the film came out, the screen credits read "screenplay by Stanley Kubrick, Michael Herr, Gustav Hasford," even though Kubrick and Herr had wanted Hasford to be solely credited with additional dialogue. Hasford fought—without an agent or a lawyer—for a screenplay credit throughout the production of the film, and he finally won his place alongside Kubrick and Herr.

In the twelve years between *Full Metal Jacket* and the release of *Eyes Wide Shut,* Kubrick pursued the adaptation of several literary works. Rumors persisted that he was interested in Patrick Süskind's novel *Perfume* (1986), but he denied he was considering it for adaptation. Subsequent reports revealed Kubrick had adapted Louis Begley's novel *Wartime Lies* (1991). The story takes place during the Holocaust and would have been the only Kubrick project to touch directly on themes connected with his Jewish heritage. Begley did not work with Kubrick on the screenplay; in fact he and Kubrick never met or spoke. The project was scheduled to be photographed on location in Denmark, but it was suddenly canceled. Speculation asserted that Kubrick was dissuaded from making the film because of Steven Spielberg's upcoming *Schindler's List* (1993).

In November of 1993, Warner Brothers announced Kubrick's next film was to be *A.I.* (2001), the abbreviation for "artificial intelligence." The project inception began in the mid-1970s when Kubrick optioned science-fiction writer Brian Aldiss's short story "Super Toys Last All Summer Long" (1969). Aldiss was under contract to co-write the screenplay and spent long sessions talking and spinning ideas with Kubrick. After six months with little to show, Kubrick took a break from the project, and Aldiss took off for a vacation in Florida. Upon his return, Kubrick told the writer he had broken the contract that stipulated he could not leave the country. *A.I.* went through other writers, including Bob Shaw, Ian Watson, and Sara Maitland.

On December 15, 1995, Warner announced Kubrick's next film would be *Eyes Wide Shut* (1999), a tale of jealousy and sexual obsession, starring Tom Cruise and Nicole Kidman, to be followed by *A.I.* And now, thirty years later, Kubrick began work with novelist and screenwriter Frederic Raphael on the transformation of Arthur Schnitzler's *Traumnovelle* or *Dream Story* (1926) into a film script.[38] The dreamlike state of the novel presented cinematic potential for Kubrick, who believed that the act of watching a film put the viewer in a dream mode. Schnitzler's investigation of marriage and the realm of sexual experience was one of the last frontiers for Kubrick, who had examined the dark side of sexuality in *Lolita* but was shackled by the morality of the times. Embracing the thriller genre and inspired by the epic *Metamorphoses* by the ancient poet Ovid, Kubrick examined the psychology, diversity, and physicality of sexual experience with Hollywood's power couple of the day.

In the months before Kubrick's death, Frederic Raphael was in dispute over whether his name would appear on the film's credits. Kubrick's relationship with Raphael was possibly the most contentious of all his collaborations; even John le Carré [David John Moore Cornwell] once considered working on the project, but he and Kubrick could not agree on the story. In his memoir *Eyes Wide Open* (1999), published just after Kubrick's death, Raphael levels many accusations against the director, including the claim that Kubrick was a self-hating Jew and that he was not interested in character or dialogue. These and other allegations outraged the Kubrick family and admirers of the filmmaker, and the film described in *Eyes Wide Open* bears little resemblance to the actual film—no surprise given the fact that Raphael did not watch it before completing his book.

Eyes Wide Shut may not be the film to sum up the career of Stanley Kubrick, but he had little choice in the matter. At the time of his death he was moving into the final phase of postproduction, touching up the sound mix, approving prints, and overseeing the release. After his death, the Kubrick estate asked Steven Spielberg to move ahead with *A.I.* During the 1990s Kubrick and Spielberg had long discussed collaborating on this film project: Kubrick was to produce, Spielberg to direct. Spielberg took on the project and based his film on Kubrick's plans, but he wrote his own screenplay. Kubrick does not in fact receive a writing credit although he had been developing the narrative with several writers and had detailed story discussions with Spielberg.

Stanley Kubrick once noted that "[o]ne man writes a novel. One man writes a symphony. It is essential for one man to make a film."[39] Throughout his career Kubrick "collaborated" with writers on his own terms. In *Citizen Kane* (1940), Charles Foster Kane, speaking through the actor, co-writer, and director Orson Welles remarked, "Those are the only terms anybody knows—his own." Stanley Kubrick lived this philosophy—*his* terms were the *only* terms to consider.

Throughout his life Stanley Kubrick was an avid reader. His home was filled with books; he studied Kirkus for the latest titles. Although Kubrick may have worked with writers on his own terms, he honored their literary knowledge by asking them countless questions about narrative and engaging in stimulating conversations about the art of the story. Stanley Kubrick has taken his place in the international pantheon of great twentieth-century film directors. He created unforgettable images: the Star Child of *2001*, the trenches of World War I doom in *Paths of Glory*, and the maze in *The Shining*. But Kubrick should also be remembered as a man of ideas, of thematic integrity, a man who embraced world literature, a man with a love of words who transformed sentences into visions.

NOTES

1. Author's interview with Faith Hubley. Vincent LoBrutto, *Stanley Kubrick: A Biography* (New York: Donald I. Fine Books, 1997), 55.

2. Author's interview with Alexander Singer.

3. Although *Day of the Fight* appears to be a documentary, Kubrick did add at least one human-interest touch of his own. In the film, Walter is shown playing with his puppy. According to his surviving brother Vincent, Walter never owned a dog.

4. In the ending of *Paths of Glory,* a beautiful young German girl (played by Kubrick's widow, Christiane) is forced to sing for the battle-weary French soldiers. As the song strikes an emotional chord, the men's expressive faces are intercut with hers as she stands center-stage mesmerizing the soldiers with a folk ballad that reminds them of their youth. The dramatic staging and editing strategy in *The Seafarers* (made four years earlier) are remarkably similar. As an impassioned speaker addresses his union brethren, Kubrick intercuts the faces as they react with emotion to the words from the podium.

5. Fear and desire are very close emotions, longtime Kubrick associate Robert Gaffney explained to the author. To illustrate his point, Gaffney described World War II reportage documenting soldiers in foxholes masturbating to deal with their fear while on watch for the enemy.

6. Norman Kagan, *The Cinema of Stanley Kubrick* (New York: Continuum, 1972), 9–10.

7. Ibid., 9.

8. Stanley Kubrick met James B. Harris through Alexander Singer. Harris and Singer made training films together from 1950 to 1952 in the U.S. Army Signal Corps during the Korean War. In 1949 Harris was a founder of Flamingo Films with David L. Wolper and Sy Weintraub. The company was financed by Harris's father. Harris and Singer planned to make an independent fifteen-minute detective film. Singer told Harris about his friend Stanley Kubrick who came to visit the weekend set as Singer photographed and Harris directed. After his army discharge, Harris ran into Kubrick. They met at Flamingo Films to discuss getting *Fear and Desire* into television distribution. After talking, both men decided to form Harris-Kubrick Pictures, an independent company where Kubrick would direct and Harris would produce.

9. Jim Thompson was a master of modern crime fiction. Prior to working with Stanley Kubrick on the screenplay of *The Killing,* he was the author of *Now and Earth* (1942), *Heed the Thunder* (1946), *Nothing More Than Murder* (1949), *The Killer Inside Me* (1952) (a particular favorite of Kubrick's), *Cropper's Cabin* (1952), *Recoil* (1953), *The Alcoholics* (1953), *Bad Boy* (1953), *The Golden Gizmo* (1954), *Roughneck* (1954), *A Swell-looking Babe* (1954), *A Hell of a Woman* (1954), *The Nothing Man* (1954), and *After Dark, My Sweet* (1955).

10. According to Thompson's biographer, Robert Polito, in *Savage Art* (New York: Knopf, 1995), Thompson felt cheated out of a screenplay credit when he first saw the film. James B. Harris found the "dialogue by" credit to be fair, explaining that Kubrick laid out the narrative and that Thompson did not work alone. Alexander Singer, who was the associate producer, attributes the writing of *The Killing* screenplay to Thompson. After study and investigation, Polito determined that Thompson should have received a co-writing credit.

11. Friends, agents, and other film industry insiders told Harris and Kubrick

that the nonnarrative story structure was confusing and just didn't work. Bill Shiffen, Sterling Hayden's agent, told Harris and Kubrick that *The Killing* hurt his client, who starred in the film. After a screening Shiffen told the filmmakers, "This movie is all mixed up. What is all this business of back and forth, back and forth? Just when you're getting to the crux of the robbery you cut. You're going to irritate the audience. I'm very disappointed in you guys." Quoted in LoBrutto, *Kubrick,* 122.

12. Calder Willingham is the author of the novels *End as a Man* (1948), *Geraldine Bradshaw* (1950), *Reach to the Stars* (1951), *Natural Child* (1952), *To Eat a Peach* (1955), *Eternal Fire* (1963), *Providence Island* (1969), *Rambling Rose* (1972), and *The Big Nickel* (1975). Willingham was also a successful screenwriter. He began writing for the small screen in 1948 on *The Philco Television Playhouse* series. Willingham's feature film credits as a screenwriter include *The Strange One* (1957), based on his novel and play, *End as a Man, The Vikings* (1958), *One-Eyed Jacks* (originally to be directed by Kubrick, who was replaced by the star Marlon Brando), *The Graduate* (1967), *Little Big Man* (1970), and *Thieves Like Us* (1974). In addition to working on the *Paths of Glory* screenplay, Willingham also wrote a draft of *Lolita* for Kubrick, but it was rejected by the director.

13. Polito, *Savage Art,* 406. Calder Willingham claimed that Jim Thompson had little to do with the final script of *Paths of Glory.* Willingham was on the set in Munich, Germany, and reports that he wrote 99 percent of the screenplay (with Kubrick contributing only two lines) and that none of the dialogue was written by Thompson. Polito compares Thompson's draft screenplay with the completed film and concludes that Thompson crafted seven scenes: the opening meeting between the French generals; Roget's reconnaissance patrol—the murder and cover-up of the killing of one of his own men; Dax's confrontation with Mireau over taking the Ant Hill; Arnaud and Duval's discussion about dying; Mireau's order to fire on his own troops; the conversations between Mireau and Dax after the Ant Hill debacle; and the court-martialed soldiers on the eve of their execution. On September 24, 1957, the screen credits for *Paths of Glory* were submitted to the Writers Guild for arbitration. The result put Willingham's name into second position.

14. Vladimir Nabokov's novel *Lolita* had caused an international scandal when it was published in the United States in 1958. *Lolita,* the story of an older man's obsession with a prepubescent girl, shocked the literary and societal establishments. Civic, conservative, and religious groups called for a ban on the Russian master's first book written in English. Controversy was good for sales: 236,700 copies sold in bookstores, 50,000 through book clubs, a year on the bestseller list, and an astounding 14 million copies sold by the mid-1980s. Despite the instant success, the major film studios wouldn't touch the explosive subject until Harris-Kubrick Pictures took the risk.

15. LoBrutto, *Kubrick,* 162.

16. Richard Corliss interview with James B. Harris in Corliss, *Lolita* (London: BFI Publishing, 1994).

17. In 1997, Adrian Lyne directed an adaptation of *Lolita* with a screenplay by Tom Stoppard. Narratively the film is considerably closer to Nabokov's novel, but compared to the Kubrick film it plays like a conventional period film. Lyne did not have the censorship constraints that confronted Kubrick, but he fails to capture the

black humor and delicious perversity of Nabokov's prose. By implication rather than presentation, and by utilizing innuendo and double-meanings, Kubrick captures the spirit of Nabokov's intent. Ironically, Lyne experienced a form of industry self-censorship when the film was unable to find a distributor. The times had changed, but Nabokov's novel still caused enough controversy to instill fear in an entertainment community unwilling to take risks. Eventually the cable television network Showtime was courageous enough to premiere the film. Once Showtime committed to air Lyne's *Lolita,* it was then picked up for theatrical distribution and had a modest run in a limited release.

18. LoBrutto, *Kubrick,* 228.

19. *Dr. Strangelove* is often cited by film critics, theorists, and historians as the first contemporary black comedy. Every genre has a prehistory, and the sensibilities of Eric von Stroheim, Preston Sturges, Billy Wilder, and *Kind Hearts and Cornets,* directed by Robert Hamer (1949), certainly contributed to the development of the genre.

20. Gene D. Phillips, *Stanley Kubrick: A Film Odyssey* (New York: Popular Library, 1975.)

21. Lee Mishkin, "Kubrick Threatens Suit on 'Strangelove Writer,'" *New York Morning Telegraph,* Aug. 12, 1964. In Kubrick's formal statement concerning the MGM and Filmways advertisement for *The Loved One* he stated, "I have been strongly advised by my attorney to publicly place Mr. Southern's contribution in its proper perspective and to take legal action to restrain MGM and Filmways from repeating the advertisement." Kubrick stated that the script for *Dr. Strangelove* was primarily written by Peter George and himself. To put Southern in his place, Kubrick contends Southern was brought on eight months into the process and contributed from November 16 to December 28, 1962. Kubrick categorized his decision to bring Southern on "To see if more decoration might be added to the icing on the cake." The final blow came with the notion that Southern took no part in changing the script during the shooting process. After demolishing a writer who made an indelible contribution to the anarchic tone of *Dr. Strangelove,* Kubrick ended with "I'm glad he worked on the script and that his screenplay credit in third place is completely fitting and proportionate to his contribution."

22. Films as diverse as *Catch-22* (1970), *The End* (1978), *Heathers* (1989), *There's Something About Mary* (1998), and *I Love You to Death* (1990) have been inspired by and are in the tradition of *Dr. Strangelove.*

23. "The Sentinel" was written for a BBC contest during the Christmas holiday of 1948. The story lost the prize but was sold to *Ten Story Fantasy* magazine under "Sentinel of Eternity," Clarke's original title.

24. On May 20, 1964, Clarke signed a contract to work on Kubrick's project. The agreement was for the sale of "The Sentinel" and the Clarke stories "Breaking Strain," "Out of the Cradle," "Endless Orbiting . . . ," "Who's There?," "Into the Comet," and "Before Eden." Kubrick wanted the ability to draw from all of these works for the creation of his sci-fi film. Clarke was given ten thousand dollars for the stories and a thirty-thousand-dollar step-deal to compose a treatment based on "The Sentinel." The contract also included a percentage of all sequel novels and film rights relating to *2001* to go to Stanley Kubrick. As of now this deal includes

the film *2010* (1984), directed by Peter Hyams, and the novels *2010: Odyssey Two,* *2061: Odyssey Three,* and *3001: The Final Odyssey.*

25. LoBrutto, *Kubrick,* 263.

26. Some of the films screened by Clarke and Kubrick were *Destination Moon* (1950), *The Day the Earth Stood Still* (1951), *The Thing from Another World* (1951), *Forbidden Planet,* (1956), and *Things to Come* (1936).

27. Arthur C. Clarke, *The Lost World of 2001* (New York: New American Library, 1970), and *Report on Planet Three* (London: Victor Gollancz, 1973).

28. The narrative of *2001* was a clean break with the traditional three-act structure of the classical Hollywood film. The tableau structure, the lack of dialogue, and the idea of a pure film experience where the characters and action are presented through cinematic expression was Kubrick's attempt to film a new narrative structure. This revelation in screen storytelling had a far-reaching impact on the films of the American New Wave of the 1970s and into the 1980s in the work of Ridley Scott and Nicholas Roeg. *Blade Runner* (1982), the films of David Lynch, and countless others were inspired and liberated by the nonnarrative approach of *2001*.

29. Andrew Bailey, "A Clockwork Utopia: Semi-Scrutable Stanley Kubrick Discusses His New Film," *Rolling Stone,* Jan. 20, 1973.

30. The May 15, 1970, draft of *A Clockwork Orange* is in the collection of the Margaret Herrick Library in Los Angeles, California.

31. The George Romero film of *The Stand* never made it into production but a miniseries was directed by Mick Garris and aired on the ABC Television Network in 1994.

32. John Hofsess, *New York Times,* June 1, 1980.

33. Jack Kroll, *Newsweek,* May 26, 1980. Kubrick wrote an earlier treatment of the novel, before he began his collaboration with Diane Johnson, which is now at the Warner Brothers film archives at the University of Southern California. In this treatment Wendy stabs Jack in the stomach. He dies, and Danny has a vision of Halloran arriving in a lunatic state and trying to kill the boy and his mother. Danny stops Halloran with his power and Wendy stabs him to death.

34. Johnson's other novels include *Lying Low* (1991), *Terrorists and Novelists* (1982), *Le Divorce* (1998), *Health and Happiness* (1998), and *Le Marriage* (2001).

35. From an interview with Diane Johnson by Denis Barbier translated from the French and reprinted in LoBrutto, *Kubrick,* 413.

36. During an address to librarians aired on C-Span, King explained that when he wanted to make *The Shining* into a television miniseries, he had to get Kubrick's permission because the director still held the rights to the King novel. Kubrick agreed, providing King would never again speak negatively about *The Shining* directed by Stanley Kubrick.

37. Gustav Hasford was born and raised in rural Alabama. At fourteen, he was a reporter for the *Franklin County Times* and the *Northwest Alabamian,* covering sporting events and car accidents. At the same time an article he wrote about coin collecting was published in *Boy's Life.* Hasford didn't graduate from high school; instead he started a quarterly magazine for writers. In 1967 at age eighteen, Hasford joined the Marines and was assigned as a 4312 Basic Military Journalist. Transferred to North Carolina, he assisted in putting out the base newspaper. Articles

about Vietnam inspired him to a tour of duty with ten months left on his hitch. As a combat correspondent with the First Marine Division he was stationed at Red Deal in Da Nang Bay in 1968. Hasford was at the Tet Offensive and was discharged in August 1968. Stateside he settled in Kelso, Washington, got married, and worked as a hotel clerk at night where he spent time reading and thinking about writing. He had a poem published in a war veteran anthology, his marriage broke up, and he moved to Los Angeles where he lived with science fiction writer Art Cover and speculative fiction author Harlan Ellison. In Los Angeles, Hasford worked as a staff editor for adult magazines. He had been developing a draft of *The Short-Timers* since his Vietnam tour of duty. After seven years of writing and three years of making the rounds, the book was finally published by Harper and Row and Bantam Books in 1979.

38. Frederick Raphael is the author of many novels including *California Time, After the War, The Trouble with England,* and *The Glittering Prizes.* An accomplished and respected screenwriter, Raphael's screen credits include *Darling* (1965), *Two for the Road, Far from the Madding Crowd* (both 1967), and *Daisy Miller* (1974).

39. The authorized Kubrick web site, www.kubrickfilms.com.

Writing *The Shining*

⇒•◇•⇐

Over the years, other screenwriters have told about their work with Stanley Kubrick; since his death their accounts seem of particular interest, both
as a way of explicating his earlier work, which has remained the subject of
critical discussion, and particularly, perhaps, as a way of illuminating his
last work, *Eyes Wide Shut* (1999). There is still no unified critical opinion
about this last film except perhaps an impression, among American critics
at least, that it doesn't quite work, and among French ones that it does.
No one quite agrees about its "meaning," and in several ways it seems to
contradict some of his stated filmmaking ideas.

My own work with Kubrick in 1979 came about as a result of his reading my novel *The Shadow Knows* (1974), a psychological novel with certain
connections to the detective story, in my mind dealing with racial issues
and urban violence, or, in the minds of some readers, about the deterio-
rating state of mind of a young woman under stress who is perhaps, or
perhaps not, being stalked. Kubrick had been browsing in the "horror"
genre because he wanted, he said, to make the scariest move he could.
Kubrick rose to genre challenges and had already made a great science
fiction movie, a historical film, and so on; during the making of *The Shining* (1980) he was thinking ahead about a war movie, partly challenged
perhaps by Francis Ford Coppola's *Apocalypse Now* then underway (1979),
and about the Schnitzler novella (*Dream Novel* [1926]) that would become
Eyes Wide Shut.

When it came to the horror film, he did not want to make a movie that
depended unduly on ghosts and gimmicks for horrific effect. Though he
did not rule out the supernatural, he wanted to create a film in which the

horror generated from human psychology. This was the case with my novel and also to some extent with Steven King's novel *The Shining* (1977); there are some apparitions in the latter that can be taken for projections of the disturbed mind of the hero, Jack Torrance, and are also supernatural. For whatever reason, in part certainly because my novel was a first-person narrative and therefore more difficult to film, Kubrick chose to use *The Shining;* he did, however, choose me to write the script. For one thing, in connection with my university teaching, I had some acquaintance with the classic texts of Gothic literature—*The Mysteries of Udolfo* (1794), or *The Monk* (1796) for example. In fact, these texts would hardly affect *The Shining*, but at least I could recommend some books for him to read.

Literary himself, Kubrick believed in having an academic foundation, if only in his collaborators. He wanted to know what the King novel was about, in the deepest psychological sense; he wanted to talk about that and to read theoretical works that might shed light on it, particularly works of psychology and especially those of Freud. Perhaps he also thought I would be freer, less respectful, and more flexible than the author himself in tampering with the text of *The Shining*—almost certainly the case, since one is always more willing to tamper with somebody else's text than one's own. He sweetly soothed any disappointment I might have felt that he didn't choose my novel for his film by saying it was easier to make a film of a lesser literary work, just as it was easier to make a film of an author's minor work, for example Thackeray's *Barry Lyndon* (1844) instead of *Vanity Fair* (1848).

Kubrick believed in adapting already existing books rather than working from original scripts. There were several reasons for this, most importantly that one could gauge the effect, examine the structure, and think about the subject of a book more easily than a script. Novelists, he thought, were apt to be better writers than screenwriters are—an idea that many would debate, no doubt. For whatever reasons in his personal experience, he didn't have much respect for screenwriters.

I would come to London for as long as it took, and work with him. In his view, it did not matter that I had had no screenwriting experience—he seemed to view it as a craft that anyone could learn—and from my point of view it was an excellent chance to learn something about this elusive craft from a great teacher. My arrangement with him was similar to that of other writers he had worked with. Terry Southern (author of the *Dr. Strangelove* [1964] script for Kubrick) advised: "Be sure you don't live out there [near the Kubricks]; stay in London or your life won't be your own."

I followed this advice, rented a place in London, and was conveyed to

Kubrick's house every day in an orange Mercedes driven by the chauffeur named Emilio, a trip of an hour or so. (Kubrick's view of Terry Southern's participation was: "He would come out once or twice a week and shout a few words from the window of the taxi.")

Kubrick and I would work in the morning, face to face across a table in a big workroom. In the afternoon he turned to the other ongoing matters of the set, casting (which was mostly done), costume, the music, and so forth, and I was invited to comment and participate as part of the process, as were members of his family, who wandered in and out, with views of their own: "Oh, Daddy, no one dresses like that." I remember objecting to some detail of the set—the way the tile in a bathroom went all the way up to the ceiling "like a gas-chamber. Bathroom tiles mostly stop at the height of the shower door." Kubrick had the tiles torn out. He would try out different tapes and records on the family, and everyone commented on the music. I believe this evolving and organic way of attending to all the aspects of a film at the same time is an improvement on the more common practice, by many directors, of seeing how the script will come out before beginning to plan the production; the commitment built into the process in the former situation explains the consistency and deeply meditated effect of Kubrick's films. But perhaps an ongoing group effort works only when the family is in harmony, like the Kubricks, all interested in the ongoing process. Still, it was certainly Kubrick himself who presented the options and initiated discussion of the various elements of music, casting, décor, and the like.

I would hang around until evening; then we'd have dinner and watch movies. We watched other horror movies, old Jack Nicholson films (was he better in his depressed or in his manic mode?), classics, and shows that were playing in the West End at the moment. Eventually, however late, Emilio would take me back to London. Meanwhile, the script was written in eleven weeks altogether.

Much of this time was spent in talking about it and planning the sequence of scenes; the words themselves, when we arrived at them, were relatively simple. It is not a very "talky" script, and the final version even less so than my script, which initially had much more for Wendy Torrance to say than she ultimately says. I was interested in the Wendy character and gave her some sympathetic lines. Although I did not watch the filming, Shelley Duval told me later that she and Kubrick were a little at odds, and he had cut a lot of her lines. He said, as I remember, that she couldn't say them. Whichever it was, the result was not the "round" Wendy as I had hoped to characterize her (and so did King), but a moist character reduced to tears and whimpers.

There were a couple of other cuts from the script—one I found unfortunate when I finally saw the film at a screening Kubrick arranged in London a few weeks after it had actually come out. For me, the important scene, taken from Steven King's book, is where Jack discovers a scrapbook of clippings in the boiler room of the hotel, and finds in it plots and details he needs for his writing. In King's book, this scrapbook is the poison gift of fairy tales, which, when he accepts it, entangles the hero in consequences he will regret. In accepting material to help him earn literary glory, Jack barters his soul, becomes the creature of the hotel. This motivation scene existed in the script and I understand was filmed; it was simply taken out at the last minute for reasons of time. It would be interesting to see it restored, to know what it would add. Without the scene, which explains Jack's transition from depressed and blocked writer to one suddenly filled with (demonic) energy, writing at great speed and piling high the pages of manuscript, his change seems abrupt and unmotivated.

For Stephen King, I gather from his remake of *The Shining* (1997), the character flaws of the father were of less interest than the supernatural powers of foresight of Danny, the little boy; and the hotel was the true villain, evil locked in combat with the good child. It was the character of the father that interested Kubrick; the powers of the boy were mainly metaphorical, a child's heightened sensitivity to the demons rising in the adults who have power over him. To what extent supernatural forces existed and to what extent these were psychological projections was something we discussed at length, finally deciding that the ghosts and magical apparitions at the Overlook Hotel were both, that the supernatural was somehow generated by human psychology, but, once generated, really existed and had power. Could Lloyd, the ghostly caretaker/bartender open a door, for instance to let Jack out of the freezer? Pour him a drink? Hand him a baseball bat? The answer had to be yes.

He was concerned that the movie be scary. We sought in the works of Freud, especially his essay on the uncanny and in other psychological theories, some explanation for why things are frightening, and what things are frightening, for instance the sudden animation of an inanimate figure. Dark is scary. Eyes can be scary. Kubrick would avail himself of these and other traditional ingredients of horror, for instance the moldering corpse of the woman in the bathtub, which was also in King's text. But it was typical of Kubrick to want an explanation for the nature of horror, wanting to understand the underlying psychological mechanism but also willing to accept the convention of the supernatural. Thus he wanted a "rational" explanation for the haunting of the hotel; he was drawn to the idea that the place rested on the site of Indian massacres or that building it had desecrated some Native American tombs, with all the ghosts and hauntings summoned thereby. Clearly, he had no objection to the idea of something being haunted, that is, of the supernatural per se, it was just that there had to be a *reason* for it. He was quite capable of living with the paradox of something being both true and untrue at the same time.

Geoffrey Cocks, in his essay on some of the symbols in *The Shining* (see page 185), has suggested Kubrick's preoccupation with the Holocaust is demonstrated in such details as the 237 room number, or the recurrence of sevens. Certainly this focus was never mentioned to me or discussed as part of his conscious intention, but his interest in the extermination of Indian peoples might argue for Cocks's idea. The whole notion that certain unconscious motifs creep into Kubrick's films the way they would into any novelist's works, without the conscious collusion of the artist, is certainly valid. In the finished film, the idea of tainted ground and Indian ghosts malevolently hovering over the hotel does not really achieve visual or other expression, but it served to generate some of the creativity of the filmmaker, and indeed some of the décor.

Kubrick's alleged intellectualism—one could almost say he has been accused of it—by which is usually meant overintellectualism, is one of the strangest objections to art, and one that is accepted too easily and without examining the ways in which intellectualism is in fact the correct approach to art. To me it seemed that Kubrick's rational and analytic approach to the complex matters of filmmaking was part of the essence of his genius. Film is not a medium where one is advised to plunge in with high hopes and a vague idea. The novelist can, to a certain extent, wing it in a new work, though even with the novel, a certain amount of preplanning is indispensable, and the more that can be known in advance of the writing, the greater the room for inspiration.

We each began by deconstructing King's novel separately, reducing it to essential scenes, comparing our lists of scenes, and winnowing them down to a hundred or so. I tore bits of exposition and dialogue out of a paperback copy of the novel and put them in little envelopes on which were written "# 1 The Arrival," and so on. I still use the scissors I used to cut the pages! Kubrick was considerate of his writers and insisted they have the equipment most comfortable for them: Which typewriter would you like? (An Adler, just as Kubrick used and Jack uses in the film.) Scissors? Size and color of paper? He had his own habits when it came to colors of paper; for some reason the pages I still have are pink or blue. These colors represented the drafts at various stages. Left to myself I would never use pink or blue paper to write on (only yellow), but it seems I was docile in the case of this system of color-coding.

Next came the process of deciding on a structure, that is, which scenes, which additional scenes, and in which order. We used an eight-act structure divided roughly into timed sequences, sketched out by Kubrick: First Day, Day of the Psychiatrist; Arrival; Before the Snow things are going well; Snow (lull); Big Day (argument, radio dead, finds scrapbook, key to room 217, Lloyd, Jack to room 217 [see 216n77]); Night scene, with Sno-Cat distributor cap; last, Elevator, calls to Halloran, last twenty-four hours of terror. He saw the first four sections as lasting forty-six minutes and the rest seventy-six—which of course the film greatly exceeded.

The Overlook Hotel was a world in which supernatural things happened. The ghosts of the hotel had appropriated the soul of Jack; they showed him shades and past events. But . . . certain rules applied. No artist would be an artist if he did not review and modify his principles, and one of Kubrick's firmest was that there should be no violations in the basic verisimilitude. I believe he never modified this principle. He would permit no unbelievable things of the kind that are seen in too many films, for example the common one where the character who decides to jump into a car and escape, finds the keys already in it. The world of the film can be a fantasy world, but within its terms it must conform to what we know of the real world. We had long and animated discussions about whether ghosts, immaterial beings, could open material things like doors, as when Lloyd lets Jack out of the freezer, and who "was" the hotel? This was a point-of-view question, since the point of view was often the hotel itself in its material, personified, seeing, incarnation.

People have complained about the "unbelievable" things in *Eyes Wide Shut*—how does the Tom Cruise character have so much money in his wallet? Why are the street names incorrect? It could be argued that if they were constructing a dream New York, Kubrick would have told the screenwriter Frederick Raphael; but then, he did not ever mention to me the Holocaust allusions that Geoffrey Cocks argues for in his article on *The Shining*. How many of such details are conscious, and at what point they enter the filmmaking process remains unclear. In a sense the dream nature of *Eyes Wide Shut* is self-evident, and certainly the Schnitzler title *Dream*

Novel specifies the dream nature of the hero's experience. As in a dream, a texture of fears and wishes unfold—a lover waltzes away with one's wife, a patient's pretty daughter confesses her passion, a prostitute both beckons and threatens death, the erotic fantasies of men about little girls are made frighteningly specific. The wallet always has enough money in it. . . .

The film is a kind of ground plan of the male psyche, mapping the fear, desire, omnipresence of sex, preoccupation with death, the connection of death and Eros, the anxiety generated in men by female sexuality—Freudian subjects, Schnitzler's subjects—and it seems to me that Kubrick took some pains to situate the action not in the real but in some dream version of the world, just as in Schnitzler's story. It could be argued that this would have been clearer and more effective set in the period of Schnitzler's writing, when certain ideas, for instance, that women had sexual desires, were less commonplace than they are today. In fact, the modern setting fades to a timelessness of décor and dress—Tom Cruise's evening dress, the clichéd costumes of the orgiasts—and all the archetypes of the unconscious wear the costumes they might have worn for Schnitzler and Freud.

The Pumpkinification
of Stanley K.

———◆———

FREDERIC RAPHAEL

When Roman emperors died, it was common for the senate to decree their
deification. In cases of conspicuous iniquity, vilification could be substi-
tuted for apotheosis. If (as was not unusual) the previous incumbent had
been done away with by his successor, or by his sponsors, it was convenient to blacken the dead man's memory. In the case of the emperor Claudius, something more unusual, and two-faced, occurred. In public, he was
granted divine status; in private, he became the target of ribaldry and
ridicule, which fell little short of diabolization.

Claudius had been an improbable emperor. As a shambling and reclusive
pedant, he was, during the previous reign, an avuncular figure of fun to
his nephew and predecessor, the appalling but glamorous Caligula. When the
latter was assassinated, after bingeing once too often on the blood of family
and friends, Claudius was dragged into the open by the rampaging Prae-
torian guard. Expecting to share Caligula's fate, he was elevated to the purple by those who he assumed had come to dispatch him. As emperor *malgré
lui*, he became a protractedly judicious supreme justice and a commander
in chief who, seconded by efficient professional backup, managed to enjoy
a Triumph (the Oscar, you might say, of Roman military achievement).

As for the downside, readers of Robert Graves's novels *I, Claudius* and
Claudius the God (1934) will remember, Claudius was also notoriously
cuckolded by his wife, Messalina (whose exploits might have furnished an
early draft of Catherine Millet's *The Sexual Life of Catherine M.* [2002]).
He made no friends among the aristocracy by preferring to trust in a sec-
retariat of "freedmen" (liberated slaves). However, Claudius's posthumous
reputation suffered most enduringly at the hands of the intellectual and

dramatist Annaeus Seneca in the satire which bears the traditional title of the *Apocolocyntosis,* an unsubtle play on the word "apotheosis." Seneca's (now mutilated) squib was a lampoon deriding the late emperor's affectations of divinity. As with most powerful men, there was something to be said for Claudius, and not a little against. Seneca contrived to say both, in different contexts.

The *Apocolocyntosis* was not written without spontaneity nor without calculation. Seneca had bided his time and had had time to do it. Having been charged with committing adultery with Caligula's sister, the Spanish-born arriviste had been banished to the island of Corsica by Claudius. For eight years, he petitioned dolefully for recall. Like some prosaic Ovid, he alternated philosophical resignation (he was a prominent Stoic) with groveling flattery, not least of Polybius, Claudius's most influential freedman. So shameless was Seneca's *Consolatio ad Polybium* that, after Claudius' death, he sought to suppress it. He had by then been returned to favor and appointed tutor to the new, immature young emperor, Nero.

Written very early in Nero's reign, the *Apocolocyntosis* was at once appetizingly irreverent and implicitly didactic. Its farcical comedy had a moral for Nero: do not repeat Claudius's murderous mistakes. The young emperor laughed, but he did not learn his lesson. Seneca himself was ordered to commit suicide in the later, gory years of the emperor's reign. Favorites who entertain, or instruct, tyrants often imagine that they cam be exceptions to the general rule of tyrannical ingratitude and vindictiveness.

Apocolocyntosis is routinely translated as "The Pumpkinification (of Claudius)." However, my late friend Professor John Sullivan, in the preface to his exemplary Penguin translation, remarks that it might as well be rendered "The Transfiguration of a Pumpkin-head into a Pumpkin." The satire would, in that case, be against a pulp-brained emperor fatuously aspiring to be a god. Once arrived on Olympus, Seneca's buffoon is judged by those he takes to be his peers, the presiding deities, and relegated, ignominiously, to The Other Place.

There is supplementary irony in the fact that as well as secretly ridiculing Claudius, for Nero's imperial entertainment, Seneca had also composed the fulsome encomium which Nero pronounced at the late emperor's funeral (in 54 AD). Seneca's ambitions warred with his Stoicism; his aptitude for both solemnity and skittishness reflected the split in his character and his talents. Having it both ways, alternating aloof disdain with the urgent fulfillment of commissioned assignments, is a recurring feature of Seneca's life. Writers, some will say, are like that.

What has all this to do with Stanley Kubrick? It reminds us, at least, that when famous men die it is hardly unusual for their reputations to be re-assessed upward, or downward, or both. Dominique Janicaud's recent two-volume *Heidegger en France* (2001) charts the ups and downs of that egregious operator's postwar reputation. Heidegger is regarded by some as the greatest philosopher of his era, by others as a time-serving obscu-rantist, indelibly tainted by his infatuation with Nazism. The fluctuations of the intellectual bourse reflect the influence of critical bulls and bears.[1] Kubrick's stock is similarly volatile. This is no argument for not attempt-ing an evaluation or for regarding all opinions as equally valid (nor are all accountants equally trustworthy). As Nietzsche remarked, "You say there can be no argument about matters of taste? All life is an argument about matters of taste!"

When a patron has been quasi omnipotent, his erstwhile clients find it difficult to accept that there are no longer favors to be culled by continued obsequiousness. Nor can they quite believe that no one need any longer be intimidated by the menace of the great man's disapproval or litigation. As for the promptness with which Seneca punctured Claudius's posthu-mous pretensions, Sullivan remarks, justly, that "satire against those long-dead . . . tends to fall flat." The same is true of memoirs as tactful as mine of Stanley Kubrick.

Michael Herr's little pamphlet about Kubrick, and about me, deserves attention only as an instance of the self-serving appropriation of a dead man's laurels and the preening assumption of, as the philosophers say, privileged access. Antony pulled the same trick in Shakespeare's *Julius Caesar*.

The reception of *Eyes Wide Open* (my short, truthful memoir of 1999) highlights the conflicting emotions and hopes of surviving courtiers, huck-sters, and apparatchiks. The last category takes me easily to a story told about the period immediately after Stalin's death. Since the cinema was a key aspect of his propaganda machine, the top Soviet screenwriters had always made sure that their scripts were as devout toward Stalin as if that atheist's divinity had already, and forever, been established. They were so thoroughly institutionalized that they continued to write in the same vein after the tyrant's death.

At a meeting of the Politbureau, during which nervous moves toward de-Stalinization were already being mooted (the first business on the agenda had been the execution of Lavrenti Beria by his fellow-mafiosi),[2] the chief screenwriter burst into the room waving a sheaf of pages. "I've done it," he is said to have said, "the first draft of the immortal Josef Vissarionovich's biopic! It's going to be great."

Khruschev and his chums looked balefully at this obsolete enthusiast for the monster who had terrorized them, and Russia, for so many decades and whom they had been fortunate to survive. The scrip was not green-lighted (or should one say—recalling the red light that released the traffic in Bertolucci's *The Last Emperor* [1987]—redlighted?). Changes of moral and aesthetic climate often follow the deaths of tyrants, great or petty, much more abruptly than their entourages can quite digest. What might once have seemed wanton, or treasonous, or self-destructively brave (like the anti-Stalin squib, which sealed Osip Mandelstam's fate) becomes—in almost no time—hardly more than a mild footnote to the revision of an inflated reputation. There is no scandal in looking again at important figures; and little wisdom in merely repeating the kind of gush which ideology or careerism once demanded. What is more vacuous than certain critics' notion that they were Stanley Kubrick's confidants because he fed them, in private, with scraps which, in their articles, would fatten his fame?

If I began with a digression about Seneca, Claudius, and Nero, it was not by chance. The intellectual, as instanced by Seneca, but never only by him, is both drawn to, and repelled by, the powerful; he craves advancement but another side of him cannot wholly endorse his own worldly ambitions. It is typical of such a man, if he is creative, to project his apprehensions of unworthiness onto the crass milieu of politics, money, high society, business: Fellini's *La Dolce Vita* (1960) and many of Oliver Stone's "socially conscious" movies manifest a no less furious duplicity. *Saeva indignatio* is often fueled by desire for big bucks, and (in Federico's case at least) big tits.

To direct films is a career unsuited to the squeamish or those with a suspicion that there may be better things to do than scheme, work, and bluff your way to the top. Such halfway men, of whom Seneca was archetypal (he wrote lurid melodramas, one of which Shakespeare cannibalized for *Titus Andronicus*), have been known to imagine themselves somewhat too fine for their own mundane good. That excellent scholar, Erich Segal, had the unusual strength of character to return to his cloister after a season of unscholastic fame and fortune as the author of *Love Story* (1970). He never looked back, happy that he could now afford his own set of Pauly-Wissowa's arcane, and very expensive, *Classical Dictionary* (1894–1963).

When Seneca saw that Nero was turning into something much more poisonous than a pumpkin, he excused himself from the court and went into rustic retirement. Having become a millionaire as Nero's intimate, the retiring philosopher thought it prudent to hand over his personal fortune to the emperor. In this way, he meant to advertise both his devotion to the man whom he now despised and his small appeal as a target for confiscatory greed (which, as Louis XIV's finance minister, Fouquet, was to discover, often provokes the impeachment of ostentatiously well-heeled courtiers).

Seneca might as well have saved himself the trouble of jettisoning his profits. Proving more paranoid than avaricious, Nero harbored a long grudge against the man who preferred his own company to his emperor's. Detached intelligence is a virtue as little admired in courtiers as in screenwriters. When delivered from below, condescension can be a life- or livelihood-threatening luxury. Yet the better screenwriters are (and the more desirable to good directors), the less likely are they to be driven only by a servile appetite for promotion. As Bill Goldman's caustic rogueries regularly prove, even the best screenwriters swear no reliable allegiance to "the Industry."

After some time in retirement, Seneca was required to commit suicide for taking part in a putative plot against the fun-loving, spendthrift, sanguinary Nero. It says something about the latter's alleged fostering of the arts that both Petronius (Nero's *arbiter elegantiae* and author of the emperor-pleasing *Satyrica*) and the precocious young genius Lucan (author of the unfinished epic *Pharsalia*) were called upon to kill themselves at the same time. Admiration and jealousy alternate in the tyrant's mind; what he respects at once diminishes him and must be cut down. Love entails hate, since it implies need or deficiency.

In the preface to my new translation of *Satyrica* (published by The Folio Society in 2003), I argue that Petronius's wilfully Epicurean suicide—which took the form of an all-night party—was intensely literary. Even as he died, Petronius was parodying Seneca's self-consciously Stoic response to Nero's last order to him. In such circumstances, writers can still be more interested in striking stylish attitudes than any reader (or publicity machine) can well imagine. It will be remembered that, as he received his deathblow, like a bad review, from a slave, Nero cried out *"Qualis artifex pereo,"* usually rendered as "What an artist dies with me!" He had made sure that the best of his rivals already had. The desire to be unique knows no equals.

My Hollywood ex-agent told me, not long ago, that I treated screenwriting as a "hobby." I had not checked every detail of a contract which I was paying him 10 percent to vet and which he had counseled me to sign. No such accusation of dilettantism could ever be made against Stanley

Kubrick. Carlyle's notion of genius as "an infinite capacity for taking pains" fitted Stanley's obsessive personality to perfection. No less obsessively bus- inesslike especially when it came to inserting contractual conditions that put collaborators at a furtive disadvantage (ask Brian Aldiss), he added a capacity for inflicting pains to Carlyle's definition. By some clerical over- sight, I was the only person Kubrick ever employed who was not embar- goed from writing about his experiences with him. Achilles always has his heel. There is petty, mythic comedy in this omission, although panicky executives and apprehensive acolytes did not see the joke. I had to be anathematized by the producers (I was not invited to the première) and consigned to oblivion by ranting apparatchiks, one of whom, in London, simultaneously plagiarized my encomium on Kubrick in the BAFTA mag- azine [British Academy of Film and Television Arts]. Cavafy's barbarians are not now at the gate; they are its salaried keepers.

The most frequent change which artists wish to bring about in any soci- ety is their own promotion in it. Such ambitions are often presaged by apparently high-minded critical manifestos such as François Truffaut's notorious *Une Certaine Tendance dans le Cinema Francais* (1954). This seemingly selfless denunciation of dated aesthetics, and their practitioners in the *ancien régime* of French directors, was followed, in very short order, by the revelation that its author and his friends meant to replace the Old Guard with themselves and their (eventually perishable) aesthetics. The drive to direct is no more principled than Roman ambition for the princi- pate. While in opposition, François Mitterand wrote a polemic, denounc- ing General de Gaulle's Fifth republic, entitled *Le coup d'etat permanent.* However, when elected president of the same republic, Mitterand behaved with, to put it mildly, no more scruple, and in no less an autocratic man- ner, than its founder.

We live in an age where immortals are wise to stay alive for as long as possible (even obituaries in the London *Times* have ceased always to speak well of the dead, though Stanley's never mentioned that he was—signifi- cantly?—a Jew). When people are conscripted to eulogy, or excoriated for honesty, in assessing a so-called artist, it is likely to be a consequence more of corporate policies than of private emotion.

Philip Bobbitt's brilliant book, *The Shield of Achilles* (2002), warns of a shift in international politics as a result of, as he puts it, the replacement of the "nation-state" by the "market-state." The United States is the supreme instance of this phenomenon. The market-state is heralded by a revised notion of the essential aims of government. Social welfare is no longer a prime concern. Instead, the well-being of the citizens has to follow from the maximization of commercial opportunity, and profits, even at the risk of individual citizens' security (in the street and with regard to pensions, Medicare, and the like). Corporate success alone is the determining evidence that the right targets are being addressed.

This new (ish) national ethos may not have a direct causal effect on morals, and on aesthetics, but—as Bobbitt remarks—we do better to think of society as a "field of forces" rather than as a pool table on which one ball has a measurable impact on whatever it hits. Our arts and our nexus of moralities are, and are not, transformed, if not pumpkinified, by revised economic conditions (Marx was right about most things, wrong only about the remedy).

Even gods are altered by new attitudes; the unchangeable changes too. Bobbitt quotes a professorial colleague who, inspired by the emergent Zeitgeist, recently, and straight-facedly, described Jesus as a "*moral entrepreneur.*" The Sermon on the Mount has become a "pitch" (Sinclair Lewis's Babbit can find a renovated home, in a better neighborhood, in Bobbitt's mercenary new world.) In an altered socioeconomic climate, we can expect a modified morality and revised aesthetics. The best work of art in our brave newer world has to be the one that will raise the most revenue. Any attempt to attribute value to anything alien to the cash nexus is counterrevolutionary treason to the mercantile state, in whose interest the great corporations stand guard, inflexibly uniformed in righteous greed.

Political Correctness is one thing and Commercial Correctness is very nearly the same thing. We now find ourselves in thrall to a soft Stalinism, which demands that we follow the party line, even when the party is over. The Stalinist state demanded one-hundred-percent endorsement by the electors; the market-state's ideal product solicits one hundred percent of consumers. Hence a film that is not intended, in theory, to appeal to everyone is—as the Stalinists would say if they were Free Enterprisers (and many now are)—counterrevolutionary, unpatriotic, and (what else?), oh, elitist. So far as the movies are concerned, Political Correctness demands that no one be discriminated against, even in speech (of which, in our society, advertising is a key part), less because the previously excluded or undervalued should be admitted as critics than because they are potential customers. Any work of "art" which has specific appeal (for instance, to the literate, the intelligent or—as they used to say—the discriminating) must be suspected of commercial treason: it is (Newspeak) undemocratic not to seek to appeal to everyone. A dated notion of modernity claimed distinction for those who sought, by their show of genius, to "amputate the audience" (leaving only the initiates). Postmodern art is interested primarily in the amplification of the audience, and the receipts (only the art can bear amputation). Kubrick's duplicity, in being at once of Hollywood and not in Hollywood, was at the heart of his attempt to retain the kudos of lonely genius without losing his reputation as a man with the universally golden touch. His films had, for that reason, to be both mainstream and, since he was such a maverick, against the current.

Eyes Wide Shut (1999) was his culminating effort to have things both ways. It was calculated to be a shocker that would shock everyone into seeing it. The esoteric and the erotic had always had affinities; they were now to become identical. In the course of that assimilation, all the specifics of Schnitzler's *donnée* were slowly whittled away. The Jewishness of "Arthur's" hero was an early erasure in this process. What was said (never by me) to be the result of Stanley's "self-hatred" as a Jew was, I am certain, the result of an utterly unselfish, commercial decision by the producer, who just happened to be Stanley Kubrick. If the film were to be about a Jewish doctor, it would "discriminate" against those who might otherwise identify with its hero. The elimination of "art" was pursued in the systematic removal of any signs of wit (a function of class) in the dialogue. Believe it or not, I say this without rancor: for a variety of reasons, Stanley could not allow the sign of any mind, or art, but his own to remain on the piece, and even this had to yield to the demands for success on which his standing with the studio was postulated.

Kubrick had a curious creative intelligence, even for a director. His work was at once idiosyncratic and impersonal. How much about the "author" himself could a stranger deduce from his oeuvre except, maybe, that he was obsessed with violence and killing? Could anyone but a lover of paradox have concluded from the text of his films that Stanley was morbidly afraid of the dangers of flying, driving, seeing a doctor, and even leaving the precincts of his own house?

The work was an advertisement for an almost invisible man who hid, like the Minotaur, at the center of a maze which was, in Stanley's case, of his own devising. This almost superstitious self-effacement—which the old Flaubertian aesthetics deemed wholly proper in an artist—was accompanied by determination to advertise his name as often as possible, in as big letters as possible, on the work on which he left his hallmark, though it bore no palpable impression of the man himself. His name was that of a bigger character than he was. His style was Stanley Kubrick . . . but was Stanley Kubrick?

Let me establish something very clearly. Working with Stanley on *Eyes Wide Shut* was the culmination of a youthful dream. It remains a marginal event in my life as a writer. To put it with convincing immodesty, my opinion of myself was not enhanced by becoming Kubrick's scribe. If I imagined very briefly that we were going to make a film "together," I was experienced enough in the habits of sacred monsters to know that they have a tendency to consume all their collaborators. The greatest tribute Stalin could pay to the genius of his early comrades was to write them out of history and erase the smallest trace of their contributions to his achievements. The first evidence I had that Stanley was actually going to make the movie on which I had worked for so many months was an announcement in the Trades in which he claimed sole credit for the screenplay. Only when threats of legal action were made did his lawyer concede the justice of my complaint.

Kubrick's image as an artist was sustained by bullyboys, bluff, and reticent braggadocio. It does not follow that it was unmerited. His greatest misfortune was that his last work, *Eyes Wide Shut*, was so nearly finished, and was at least presentable as such, at the moment of his death. The marketing machinery of Warner Brothers was thus able to maintain that the public, and the critics, were about to see a masterpiece on which the master had already put his imprimatur. Does any serious, or knowledgeable, person still maintain this?

Like most artists of painstaking quality, Kubrick was an obsessive tweaker. He died in March; his film came out in July. Had he lived, he would have cut, rearranged, perhaps reshot, with maddening meticulousness (never forget the element of fear, Latin *metus*, at the root of that word). Those who were financially (very heavily) invested in *Eyes Wide Shut* were caught in a difficult fix. Had Kubrick not been marketed as a genius, some ruthless hand might well have put the scissors into his work. The score would have been radically revised, and there would have been a lotta lotta editorial rejigging. Since Kubrick was Kubrick, no such ruthlessness could be sanctioned. His (alas) culminating work had to be declared what it was not: both finished and beyond criticism.

I sympathize with those who were forced to market the film as though it were everything they, and we, had hoped for. But now, when the commercial pressure is off, we (and probably they) can see its faults as well as its tantalizing merits. Its main weaknesses were not, I suspect, ever going to be susceptible of remedy, because they were present, very often, in the work that Stanley did complete to his own satisfaction, in so far as he was ever satisfied. If we look at the whole oeuvre, we can salute (or condemn) it as remarkably eclectic as well as consistently wanting in humanity: there are no love scenes, not even any recognition of love, as opposed to desire, which is more photogenic.

The eclecticism is marked by a persistent recourse to, on the whole, classy source material; S. K. had no appetite for "originals." Plato once said that the degenerate form of an architect is a pastry-cook. Kubrick was more of a *charcutier:* he could make something delicious and seemingly exotic out of a pig of a subject. My friend, the painter and sculptor Michael Ayrton, had similarly protean gifts. If you went around an art gallery with him and stopped in front of something you seemed to admire, Michael would say, "I can do you one of those."

Like a cinematic decathlete, Stanley worked his way through most of the standard genres; since he never lived to work on *A.I.* (2001) he never attempted any of them twice. He was probably wise to eschew the musical, but *Eyes Wide Shut* was to be his proof that he could do the erotic love story. It was also, as is widely know, the fulfillment of a bet with himself that the "blue movie" could, under the right management, aspire to "art" (a category of achievement to which Kubrick, a cynic in many regards, had naïve—dare one say good-Jewish-boyish?—aspirations).

He was hampered when it came to a love story, partly because (and this is not a criticism, and might even be praise) he abstained from sentiment ("as a director" is a qualification which is universally implicit, from now on, in what I am saying). The avoidance of kitsch is a "noble" motive for such abstention, but the treatment of the couple in *Eyes Wide Shut* demanded a mastery of the nuances of what even the Viennese called "love," in which, of course, there was more eros than agape. Schnitzler too would have thought it callow to speak of affection, but his novella becomes entirely lurid if there is not "play" between the love which Fridolin feels for his wife and the vindictive lust by which he is simultaneously, or sequentially, possessed.

Kubrick's systematic refusal to invest his experience, as opposed to his expertise, in his work alarmed him when it came to dealing with marriage. He turned to me for an ability to dramatize the play between husband and wife, but my work was (maybe) too imprinted with a style that was not his, although he consented, at first, to admire it.

He then became fixed on the idea that a "real" married couple would bring some automatic certificate of authenticity to his portrayal of the doctor and his wife. He might have thought that a medical husband would make the Tom Cruise part even more authentic, but he did not. Not only did he choose a couple who, soon afterwards, turned out to have a marriage at least in part of convenience, but he gave them no reliable text to play, imagining—and here intelligence collapsed into unsuspected naiveté— that if they improvised chunks of their scenes something more valid would emerge. The result was the sorry sight and sound of the pink, nakedish Tom Cruise uttering shrill and improbable, unerringly platitudinous, reproaches to the overactress who was supposed to be (but never was) the mother of his child. Nothing is less certain to produce authenticity than an actor bereft of an informative text (one that also gives form to the scene), and forced to rely on his own unactorly life to supply words and actions. What made Stanley yield to so misguided a method? The genre of Love Story was the one (apart from the musical) in which he was least practiced, and—more important perhaps—with which he seems to have had little sense of touch.

It is neither my pleasure nor my purpose to go through the many symptoms of manifest inauthenticity which resulted from the casting of so coldly calculating a couple of careerists as Cruise and Kidman. The evidence of imaginative frigidity, as far as specific human beings are concerned, is of a piece with the general formality of the work. Kubrick made fables, not dramas; he toyed with generalities and their illustration by using grotesque and exaggerated puppets to people his pictures. This does not disqualify him from high regard nor make him unworthy of serious attention, but there it certainly is: he was afraid of human beings, their feelings, their violence, their savagery, their mortality; and he would not, perhaps could not, invest himself in them. In a metaphorical sense, he was impotent: he had to be externally empowered by his clout, his skill, his ingenuity, his wilfulness, his acumen, but he took no personal joy as an artist (if you want to call him that) in humanity. It was not foolish of him, nor was it shameful, but it was sad. The genre he chose to prove how polyvalent he was, to convince himself that there was nothing he could not do, was one he tried when his physical energy was waning and which his imagination was incapable of inhabiting. There are clever and "typical" sequences in *Eyes Wide Shut;* neither passion nor even the erotic scandal are realized. D. H. Lawrence's "sex in the head" was as near as Kubrick came to the heart of the matter. It would be nice to think that, given time to tinker and eliminate and rejig, something superb could have been contrived, but I am not so sure. He did not necessarily get the recipe wrong but, on this occasion, the *charcutier* misjudged the ingredients.

The corporate determination to insist on Stanley's apotheosis was always likely, with time, to look excessive. His qualities were rare, but they were not unbounded. He, too, tried, like Seneca and Petronius, both to be a force in the world and to be above mundane considerations. This does make a pumpkin of him, but it must cast doubt on his claims to divinity.

NOTES

A slightly different version of this essay appeared in Frederic Raphael, *The Benefits of Doubt: Essays* (Manchester: Carcanet Press, 2003). Copyright © 2002 by Volatic Ltd.

1. Who will now insist that Lucchino Visconti was a significant director? What was said, at the time, to be his sellout film, *The Leopard* (1962), is the only one I should care to see again, thanks to Burt Lancaster. Visconti's aristocratic air and social clout were the enforcers of his claim to artistic distinction.

2. In his memoirs, Beria's son, Serge, maintains that his father was much misunderstood (the same has been said, seriously, of Nero). Beria was a murderous secret policeman and a regular rapist, but his family saw a "different man." What is less astounding than the alleged "paradox" that concentration camp guards were loving parents who hummed along with Mozart? Kubrick's family made much of not having "authorized" my little book. What did they know of my working relationship with a man whom they, in a sense, had never met? Kubrick's domestic virtues, whatever they were, had nothing to do with his professional conduct. I never heard him say a single word about his beloved wife and children. He gave the impressions of being an insomniac solitary, most at home with his computer. He slept, and died, alone.

Mazes and Meanings

Kubrick's Armies

Strategy, Hierarchy, and Motive in the War Films of Stanley Kubrick

GLENN PERUSEK

Stanley Kubrick strove not to repeat himself and worked in many different genres, but he returned again and again in his career to the theme of war. Here I will examine three aspects of Kubrick's worldview as expressed in his war films *Fear and Desire* (1953), *Paths of Glory* (1957), *Dr. Strangelove* (1964), the screenplay for the unmade *Napoleon* (1969), and *Full Metal Jacket* (1987)—and, in passing, in two other early films of strategic interaction, *Killer's Kiss* (1955) and *The Killing* (1956): Kubrick's carefully nuanced treatment of strategic thinking; his appreciation for the implications of hierarchical organization; and his changing views on meaning and the motivation of human social/political actors. Kubrick's war films emphasize the importance of careful assessments of situations and enemy strength in carrying out strategic plans. They treat overextension of forces as a tragic flaw of leadership, whether stemming from misassessments based on overconfidence or personal ambition. Kubrick's concern with the iterated quality of decision making and the interrelationship between strategy and the mood of collectivities underline the sophistication of his treatment of strategic thinking. The implications of hierarchical organization, present in all of the war films, are perhaps most compellingly treated in *Paths of Glory*. A Rousseauian perspective on the transformation of human selves under civil society is offered as one useful way to understand this work. Kubrick's war films consistently looked away from political explanations. Instead of providing explanations for world-historic events, Kubrick's films on Napoleon, the Great War, the Cold War, and Vietnam each put the trauma of war into a story. The Rousseauian fatalism of *Paths of Glory*

77

gives way in the other war films to a portrait of man as fundamentally corrupted in his very nature. A Weberian perspective on bureaucratic rationality is offered as a way to view the war films after *Paths of Glory*.[1]

Strategic Assessments in Kubrick's War Films

Kubrick, the chess player, was fascinated with strategic interaction. *Dr.
Strangelove* descends into a fantasy extension of nuclear strategic interaction in the early cold war, as an American general, Jack D. Ripper, goes
mad from conspiracy thinking and orders a bomber wing to strike Russian targets with nuclear weapons. We discover that the Russians, meanwhile, had built a "doomsday device" that cannot be knocked out by a first
strike. Irrationally, they fail to inform the other side of the existence of this
ultimate deterrent weapon, whereas the whole point of such a weapon is
to publicize its existence so the enemy will not be tempted to strike first.
What interested Kubrick in the Strangelove project was the paradox at the
heart of all thinking about nuclear deterrence. As he told Jeremy Bernstein, "When you start reading the analyses of nuclear strategy, they seem
so thoughtful that you're lulled into a temporary sense of reassurance. But
as you go deeper into it, and become more involved, you begin to realize
that every one of these lines of thought leads to a paradox." The idea at
the core of Strangelove was "the intellectual notion" of "the inevitable
paradox posed by following any of the nuclear strategies to their extreme
limits."[2]

In the *Napoleon* screenplay, Kubrick traces the rise and decline of the
supremely capable military strategist.[3] An indispensable scene portrays the
negotiations at Tilset in 1807 between Napoleon and the Russian tsar
Alexander. Napoleon convinces Alexander to abandon his alliance with England. While Alexander thought he would be treated "as a fallen enemy,"
instead he finds that "to be defeated by Napoleon seemed equivalent to
winning a great victory." Gracious and friendly, Napoleon makes no demands for territory or reparations, "only an intoxicating proposal to divide
the world between them." And so, Napoleon and Alexander spend two
weeks together, becoming friends, talking "of everything together, as two
brothers—philosophy, women, politics, war, science." Each man is taken
with the other. In the most telling scene in the whole screenplay, the two
emperors sit together in a sauna. Napoleon displays his talent for estima-
tions on the battlefield.

NAPOLEON: You can always tell at a glance whether retreating infantry are being pursued by cavalry, because they hurry along and keep turning around and looking back. When they are retreating before infantry, they merely trudge along, head down.

ALEXANDER: Fascinating! Tell me, leaving aside the question of grand strategy, for the moment, what would you say is the single most difficult tactical skill to master?

NAPOLEON: Without a doubt, to estimate the enemy's strength on the battlefield. This is something that is only acquired by experience and instinct. At Jena, there were as many opinions about strength of the enemy as there were generals present. Murat said there were 50,000, preparing to attack. Berthier said there were no more than 25,000, about to withdraw. "Berthier sees only what is in the open," Murat said. "But don't forget there is a second force hidden in the forest." And so it would always go, each of them would judge things according to his own ability, character and state of mind, at the moment.

ALEXANDER: Ah, my dear Napoleon, sometimes I feel that I am not really an Emperor as you are.

NAPOLEON: What do you mean?

ALEXANDER: I know absolutely nothing of war—and I am still totally dependent upon my generals.

[Napoleon laughs, reassuringly.]

NAPOLEON: That is a problem, and I can appreciate your feelings. But I'm sure you have great talent for war, and I could teach you a lot. If we are ever at war again together, you should lead, say, 30,000 men, under my orders—you would soon get the feel of it.[4]

The foundational task in strategic thought is the art of careful assessment of situations and personnel. Napoleon's great victories were based in part on his superior capacity at assessments. Yet, in the end, Napoleon misassessed both Alexander and the situation in Russia and was forced finally into a catastrophic retreat from Moscow. The screenplay also emphasizes Napoleon's systematic inability to assess Josephine. His love for her seems so great that his feelings blind him to her duplicity.

Strategic Miscalculations

In the twentieth century, chess strategists recognized the importance of careful assessment of positions and the building up of small advantages before embarking on a dramatic combination. A combination, a bold series of moves that will bring a decisive edge to one side, should not be attempted unless it is founded upon significant advantages (in material or maneuverability) that had been built up previously. As *Lasker's Manual of Chess* puts it, "In the beginning of the game ignore the search for combinations, abstain from violent moves, aim for small advantages, accumulate them, and only after having attained these ends search for the combination. . . ."[5] One kind of tragedy on the chess board is the insufficiently prepared combination. Hubris in chess leads to overly aggressive moves that expose pieces to insufficiently protected positions. The result is regularly a fatal counterattack after the foray fails.

Launching premature, unprepared forays—combinations in chess, aggressive offensive actions in military situations—can result in the failure of strategic plans. It is a theme that recurs in Kubrick's films of strategic interaction. In *The Killing* (1956), a deep account of the failure of Johnny Clay's plan must take account of overly ambitious nature. Johnny's bold plot is matched by Val Cannon's immediate grasping for the opportunity to seize, not just George's share of the take, which would have been relatively riskless, but the whole operation's take. Both Johnny Clay and Val Cannon come to ruin because they have allowed their aspirations to overreach what is realistically achievable. In *Paths of Glory,* Generals Broulard and Mireau both acknowledge the impossibility of the goal of taking the Ant Hill. Troop morale is already low; too many casualties must be endured just to get to the position, let alone to take it; little artillery support is available. But Mireau's judgment is clouded by narrow considerations of personal advancement.

Napoleon's demise comes from overextension in Russia: He is drawn deeper and deeper into the country, all the way into Moscow. But the Grand Army's supply lines are tenuously stretched; Napoleon cannot hold the ground he has taken. He is forced into a dismal and disastrous winter retreat.[6] These are all instances of strategic failure resulting from some measure of arrogance or overconfidence. Overly ambitious plans are the Achilles heel of great leaders, whether we are led otherwise to sympathize with the characters (Napoleon) or not (General Mireau). Not only did Broulard and Mireau, like Clay and Cannon, and like Napoleon in Moscow, misassess their situations, they overextended their forces, leading to defeat. Historians of military strategy recognize overreaching as a fundamental strategic error, committed time and again through history.[7]

Decision Making Under Changing Circumstances

Kubrick highlights how changing circumstances alter the nature of the choices of these strategic actors. Key moments in each film highlight the changes. The key moment in *Fear and Desire* is the opportunity of stumbling upon the foreign general. Prior to this point, these soldiers have no purpose but to escape back to safe territory. Only when they stumble upon the opportunity to kill an enemy general does their situation change. Mac sees killing the enemy general as a way to do something meaningful with his life; he is willing to sacrifice his own life in a gambit to expose the enemy general so that his unit can accomplish the task. Conflict among the characters arises. It is as if Kubrick were examining a chess combination from the point of view of the pieces. At a vital moment in *Killer's Kiss*, when Rapallo gains the upper hand against Davey in the warehouse, the alliance between Gloria and Davey breaks down: both calculate that they must act in individual self-interest in order to save their own lives. Both Davey and Gloria are forced to maneuver when Rapallo gains the upper hand against them in the warehouse. Gloria throws herself at Rapallo to save herself. Formerly, she said she found Rapallo repulsive. Now she recants:

GLORIA: I didn't mean it, you know I didn't mean it.
  [They kiss.]
RAPALLO: We could go away . . . sure, I got lots of money, we could have loads of fun someplace, sure, London, Paris, Sicily.
GLORIA: I'll do anything you want.
RAPALLO: Maybe we could get married, settle down, have a couple of kids.
GLORIA: Sure.
RAPALLO: Sure. What do you take me for, a 14-carat sucker? You and lover boy aren't going to put me in the hot seat.
GLORIA: Vinnie, you liked me once, remember? Remember how nice it was? It could be like that again, Vinnie.
RAPALLO: You forgetting about him?
GLORIA: I don't care about him.
RAPALLO: Look baby, you could have had anything once but, no, you were too good for me . . .

As Rapallo goes on to explain the prior action, Davey makes his own run for it. All three characters have trimmed their interests back: each is looking

out solely for himself. Later, at Grand Central, as he's waiting for his train
to Seattle:

DAVEY (voice over): On the ride to the police station, Gloria didn't say
    much. I guess she was trying to work out in her own mind why I ran
    and left her alone like that. I don't suppose she might have thought about
    how I might have felt listening her talk to Rapallo that way. At the sta-
    tion house they separated us for questioning. Five hours later they had
    chalked off Rapallo as self-defense . . .

Thus, the characters are not just self-interested in their dealings with one
another. At significant moments, we hear Davey thinking through strategy,
move, and countermove. Reflecting on an earlier conversation over break-
fast with Gloria, Davey thinks to himself: "I started talking about myself,
about what a washup I was, and how I was going back to Seattle to work
on my uncle's horse ranch. But when I think back about it now, I realized
that all the while I was talking, the thing that was really in my mind was
to remember not to ask what it was her boss Rapallo was so sorry for."
    For the chess player, decision making is necessarily done in iterated
stages through the game. This continual process of making plans and then
having to adjust them to new situations is expressed powerfully in *Dr.
Strangelove*. After General Jack D. Ripper sends his bomber wing into Russia, General Turgidson seeks to transform the dangerous situation into a
tactical knockout.

TURGIDSON: Mr. President, there are one or two points I'd like to make,
    if I may.
MUFFLEY: Go ahead, General.
TURGIDSON: One, our hopes for recalling the 843rd bomb wing are
    quickly being reduced to a very low order of probability. Two, in less
    than fifteen minutes from now the Russkies will be making radar con-
    tact with the planes. Three, when they do, they are going to go abso-
    lutely ape, and they're gonna strike back with everything they've got.
    Four, if prior to this time, we have done nothing further to suppress
    their retaliatory capabilities, we will suffer virtual annihilation. Now,
    five, if on the other hand, we were to immediately launch an all out and
    coordinated attack on all their airfields and missile bases we'd stand
    a damn good chance of catching 'em with their pants down. Hell, we
    got a five to one missile superiority as it is. We could easily assign three

missiles to every target, and still have a very effective reserve force for any other contingency. Now, six, an unofficial study which we undertook of this eventuality, indicated that we would destroy ninety percent of their nuclear capabilities. We would therefore prevail, and suffer only modest and acceptable civilian casualties from their remaining force which would be badly damaged and uncoordinated.[8]

Strategic thinkers have a strong sense of timing: Necessarily concerned not to waste time with needless moves, they see orchestrating an enterprise as a matter of maintaining careful timing and coordination of resources. In *Killer's Kiss,* a failure to hold to a set schedule signals a significant shift in the action. Davey plans to meet his boss, Albert, outside Rapallo's Pleasureland dance hall — Gloria will go in for her final paycheck, and Albert is to deliver Davey's pay. But men in fezzes, who are a complete diversion and not part of Rapallo's plan, steal Davey's scarf; he runs down the street after them. Meanwhile, Albert pulls up in a cab, and takes a place in front of the Pleasureland door. Rapallo sends his lieutenants down to work over Davey; they do not know that Albert now stands outside. They divert Gloria—"The boss said he was sorry and if you go upstairs, you can collect your money"—and back Albert into an alley.

In *The Killing,* the whole heist plot is centered upon split-second coordination of the actions of a half-dozen men. Here again a diversion— Johnny Clay gets stuck in traffic after the successful robbery—signals a failure to maintain the timing of the operation. Clay is late for the distribution of the money. Here, again, the opponent, Val Cannon, makes a move in the space where timing has been thrown off by unforeseen circumstances, leading to the shootout in the apartment. The dramatic tension of *Dr. Strangelove* is maintained through the problem of working against the clock: without securing the proper recall code, the "clock will expire" on American efforts to halt the bombers.

Strategy and Mood

Rationalist paradigms have trouble coming to terms with the relationship between strategy and mood. Strategy is about calculation, reasoned estimation of advantage. Mood seems emotional, removed from reason. This dichotomy, first of all, "forgets" that a mood of cool calculation may be necessary to make good choices. And that hysteria could be a mood ("out of control"), but it could also be a strategy to throw off one's opponent.

Strategy and mood are interrelated. Strategies are adopted within a prevailing mood. Strategic actors respond to new choice situations with some degree of enthusiasm, relish, optimism, and the prevailing mood will affect the decisions that are taken.

In *The Killing,* every character is motivated by material gain. For the most part, the solidarity of thieves is maintained. Individual interests seem to cement the collectivity. At the outset we are shown three couples — Johnny and Fay, Mike O'Reilley and Ruthie, and George and Sherry. The material self-interest of all of these characters is consonant with their human connections. Each of these characters holds to his obligations, and indeed, we gain a sense of sympathy with at least one of these couples, as the bartender appears to be interested in the robbery because he wants to get better doctors for his bedridden spouse. But Sherry's self-interest is the corrosive for the whole scheme: She plans to leave Georgie, is already involved with Val. She plays Georgie to get him to reveal enough information so that Val can investigate.

Napoleon is a portrait of innocence with women, even as his instrumental/strategic nature expresses itself. The shy young officer is breathtakingly decisive in his dealings with revolutionaries of 1789. When he goes with a small group of soldiers to arrest Varlac, before a crowd of three hundred supporters, Varlac refuses to come peacefully.

NAPOLEON: Monsieur Varlac, do not pretend to speak for these good people whom you have misled and inflamed with violent speech. Now, I order you to come down from the cart.

[Another whispered conference.]

VARLAC: I do not recognize the authority of the King or any of his lackeys.

[Laughter from the crowd.]

VARLAC: I suggest that you leave with your men while you can.

NAPOLEON (drawing his pistol): Monsieur Varlac, I will count slowly to five, and if you have not begun to get down from the cart by then, I will carry out your execution, on the spot.

[Without giving Varlac time for further discussion, he begins to the count.]

NAPOLEON: One . . . Two . . . Three . . .

[Several of the committee move away from Varlac.]

NAPOLEON: Four . . . This is your last chance, Monsieur Varlac.

[Varlac is frightened, but makes an obscene gesture. The crowd laughs nervously.]

NAPOLEON: Five . . .
[Napoleon rides up to the cart, carefully aims his revolver and shoots Varlac in the head. His entourage leaps to safety. A gasp of astonishment from the stunned crowd, who stand hypnotized.]

This Napoleon is an intuitive master of the relation between strategic and tactical maneuver and the mood of crowds. His seizure of the initiative is so decisive that the crowd's superior numbers are irrelevant. In the midst of the revolution, Louis XVI's Tuileries Palace is overrun by a rowdy mob. Napoleon comments, "Incredible . . . Incredible . . . How could he let that rabble into the Palace? If he had ridden out among them on a white horse, they would all have gone home. If he lacked the courage to do that, a whiff of grapeshot—and they would still be running." Later, Napoleon comes to the rescue of Barras and the Convention. The Convention placed Barras in charge of defense of the revolution against a monarchist revolt, but he is not up to the task.

NAPOLEON: What do you have in mind?
BARRAS: To be perfectly honest, I haven't the vaguest idea.
NAPOLEON: Are you serious?
BARRAS: I don't even know whether a defense is possible.

Napoleon immediately steps in to the mode of conducting assessments of the sides. He asks about the troops, cavalry, and cannon at Barras's disposal.

BARRAS: Is this enough to oppose 40,000 men?
NAPOLEON: Properly arranged, yes.
BARRAS: These are odds of 8 to 1.
NAPOLEON: The numbers are not particularly relevant. You are not up against soldiers—this is a mob, and they will run as soon as things become sufficiently unpleasant.

Napoleon agrees to Barras's proposal that he assume de facto command of the defense.

BARRAS: You realize what is at stake?
NAPOLEON (smiling): Our lives, the revolution, my career?

Barras levels with Napoleon, suggesting that he (Barras) could flee and live comfortably outside the country. But Napoleon is sure he can orchestrate a successful defense. Commenting in voice-over on the cannon fire the next day, Kubrick's Napoleon says:

> I ordered the artillery to fire ball immediately, instead of blanks, because, to a mob, who are ignorant of fire arms, it is the worst possible policy to start out firing blanks. When they first hear the terrific noise of the guns, they are frightened, but, looking around them and seeing no effect from the cannon, they pick up their spirits, become twice as insolent and rush on fearlessly. It becomes necessary then to kill ten times their number to make an impression.

Napoleon was the ever cognizant calculator of the impact of military force upon collective moods.

Is it hard to see the mind of a chess player behind Kubrick's films of strategic interaction? The supreme problems of the chess player revolve around the proper deployment of resources in an iterated interaction with the opponent. The absolute necessity is to maximize the impact of each move, that is, the need to economize on time, so as to hold the resources with which to achieve tactical objectives. The strategist recognizes that action is a constant dance, an interplay, with the opponent: the plans we make are always contingent on the moves and plans of our opponent. Every plan must really be a decision tree with a thousand different branches.

Hierarchy

Killer's Kiss has a class element: Davey is a modestly successful professional boxer, living in a tenement-style apartment building. When his manager suggests he take a cab to his fight, he opts for the subway instead. His opponent in the struggle for Gloria's affections, Rapallo, drives a big convertible. Rapallo makes a lifestyle appeal to Gloria—the boxer is washed up, he says, suggesting she would be poor with him. Later, when they are reduced to hand-to-hand combat, Davey clearly has the physical edge, even though Rapallo holds an ax.

All of the confederates in the heist in *The Killing* are of modest means. We see no wealthy horsemen; indeed, the track is portrayed as a working-class entertainment. Johnny's friend, Marvin Unger, has a small amount of cash, but his wealth is far from ostentatious—his investments appear to be in a small number of apartment buildings, perhaps only one. The poverty of Johnny and the rest of the conspiracy is emphasized by the fact that Unger must get a full cut from the take, just for putting up a few thousand dollars. But of course the values of consumerist society are pervasive: the goal of the heist is to hit the jackpot in order to have enough money to live opulent, leisured lives.

The power of *Paths of Glory* is that it slides up and down the military hierarchy, portraying motives and methods from the top generals down to corporals and sergeants. When General Broulard first presents the mission to capture the Ant Hill, Mireau emphatically insists that it is impossible. But the offer of a promotion leads General Mireau to reverse himself.

MIREAU: It's out of the question, George. Absolutely out of the question. My division was cut to pieces. What's left of it is in no position to hold the Ant Hill, let alone take it. I'm sorry, but that's the truth.

BROULARD: Well, Paul, there was something else I wanted to tell you, although I'm sure you'll misunderstand my motives in mentioning it.

MIREAU: What was it?

BROULARD: Oh, you'd be bound to misunderstand. However, as your friend, maybe I should tell you.

MIREAU: What are you trying to say, George?

BROULARD: The talk around headquarters is that you are being considered for the Twelfth Corps. . . . and with that, another star. Now, I've pushed it all I can. The Twelfth Corps needs a fighting general and you are overdue on that star. Now, we both know that your record is good enough to refuse this assignment on the grounds you've stated. No one would question your opinion. They'd simply get someone else to do the job. So you shouldn't let this influence your opinion, Paul. . . .

MIREAU: George, I'm responsible for the lives of 8,000 men. What is my ambition against that? What is my reputation in comparison to that? My men come first of all, George. And those men know it, too.

BROULARD: I know that they do.

MIREAU: You see, George, those men know that I would never let them down.

BROULARD: That goes without saying.

MIREAU: The life of one of those soldiers means more to me than all the stars and decorations and honors in France.

BROULARD: So, you think this attack is absolutely beyond the ability of your men at this time.

MIREAU: I didn't say *that,* George. Nothing is beyond those men, once their fighting spirit is aroused.

BROULARD: Paul, I don't want to push you into it if you think it is ill-advised.

MIREAU: Don't worry, George. You couldn't do that if you tried. Of course, artillery would make an enormous difference. What artillery support can you give me?

BROULARD: Well, I'll see.

MIREAU: What about replacements?

BROULARD: We'll see what we can do. I feel sure that you can get along with what you have . . . Now, as far as that star is concerned . . .

MIREAU: That had nothing to do with my decision. If anything, it would sway me the other way.

BROULARD: I realize that perfectly, Paul.

Both the impossibility of the mission and Mireau's self-seeking hypocrisy are simultaneously established. Meanwhile, the trenches are populated by a mixture of honest and brave men, miserable shell-shocked soldiers, and self-serving cowards. Lieutenant Roget, who must fortify himself with drink before a mission, panics while on reconnaissance, kills Corporal Lejeune, and then covers up his mistakes in the written report. Paris, who appeared principled in challenging Roget, in the end acquiesces in the presence of a superior officer. Between these extremes are Colonel Dax, in the trenches a brave, principled, and respected leader of the men; and at home, perhaps the most capable defense lawyer in all of France, and the suggestively named Captain Rousseau, the Battery Commander, who refuses Mireau's order to train his guns on the French trenches, in the midst of the failed attack on the Ant Hill.

In his closing statement to the court martial, which clearly intends to railroad the three defendants, Colonel Dax implores, "Gentlemen of the court, there are times when I am ashamed to be a member of the human race . . . I can't believe that the noblest impulse of man, his compassion for another, can be completely dead here." In the aftermath of the execution ("The men died wonderfully . . ."), Broulard confronts Mireau with the evidence that Mireau had ordered artillery to fire on his own men. While it would be consistent with officer solidarity for Broulard to look the other way, he decides that an inquiry must be conducted. He turns to Dax:

BROULARD: Colonel Dax, how would you like General Mireau's job?

DAX: His what sir?

BROULARD: His job.

DAX: Let me get this straight, sir. You're offering me General Mireau's command?

BROULARD: Come, come, Colonel Dax, don't overdo the surprise. You've been after the job from the start. We all know that, my boy . . .

BROULARD: It would be a pity to lose your promotion before you get it. A promotion you have so very carefully planned for.

DAX: Sir, would you like me to suggest what you can do with that promotion?

BROULARD [*yelling*]: Colonel Dax, you shall apologize at once or shall be placed under arrest.

DAX [*his voice rising to a fever pitch*]: I apologize for not being entirely honest with you. I apologize for not revealing my true feelings. I apologize sir for not telling you earlier that you are a degenerate, sadistic old man. And you can go to hell before I apologize to you now or ever again.

BROULARD: Colonel Dax, you are a disappointment to me. You have spoiled the keenness of your mind by wallowing in sentimentality. You really did want to save those men. And you were not angling for Mireau's command. You are an idealist, and I *pity* you, as I would the village idiot. We're fighting a war, Dax, a war that we've got to win. Those men didn't fight, so they were shot. You bring charges against General Mireau, so I insisted that he answer them. Wherein have I done wrong?

DAX: Because you don't know the answer to that question, I pity you.

And it is pity, sympathy for others, which is expressed in the closing scene, the scene with the German singing girl, that has so perplexed critics. This innocent woman can still arouse pity in the aggressive, catcalling crowd of ordinary French soldiers. Their impulse to sympathy for others has not been entirely eviscerated, even by years of trench warfare and self-serving duplicity by their own generals. Let me suggest that Jean-Jacques Rousseau's perspective on the transformation of human selves under civil society is one useful way to understand *Paths of Glory*.

In Rousseau's state of nature, men are motivated not only by an impulse to self-preservation, but also by pity, by sympathy—compassion for others. The capacity of identification with others, which is necessary for sympathy, is greater in natural man than in man living under civilization. Civilization developed the faculty of reason. "It is reason that engenders amour propre, and reflection that reinforces it; reason that turns man back upon himself; reason that separates him from everything that troubles and afflicts him: It is Philosophy that isolates him; by means of Philosophy he secretly says, at the sight of a suffering man, perish if you wish, I am safe."[9] The impulse of sympathy is not entirely extinguished in modern society, but it is the simplest folks who will exhibit this decency. "In Riots, in Street-Brawls, the Populace gathers, the prudent man withdraws; it is the rabble, it is the Marketwomen who separate the combatants" (153–54).

Civilization developed reason but destroyed sympathy. Complex human interdependencies grew up and with them private property. Self-interested men, with ever-more acutely developed reasoning capacity, created hierarchical society. Promoting self-advantage became their prime cause, and honesty of self-presentation was sacrificed. "To be and to appear became two entirely different things, and from this distinction arose ostentatious display, deceitful cunning, and all the vices that follow in their wake." Men who were formerly free and independent were now "subjugated by a multitude of new needs" (170). Society became an inescapable web of interdependency, subjugating all. Even the wealthy and the powerful depended on others to achieve their designs in the world. A man was dependent "especially to those of his kind, whose slave he in a sense becomes even by becoming their master; rich, he needs their services; poor, he needs their help."

> He must therefore constantly try to interest them in his fate and to make them really or apparently find their own profit in working for his: which makes him knavish and artful with some, imperious and harsh with the rest, and places him under the necessity of deceiving all those he needs if he cannot get them to fear him, and does not find it in his interest to make himself useful to them. Finally, consuming ambition, the ardent desire to raise one's relative fortune less out of genuine need than in order to place oneself above others, instills in all men a black inclination to harm one another, a secret jealousy that is all the more dangerous as it often assumes the mask of benevolence in order to strike its blow in greater safety: in a word, competition and rivalry on the one hand, conflict of interests on the other, and always a hidden desire to profit at another's expense. (170–71)

The wealthy and powerful become especially depraved in modern society, for they develop a taste for domination of others. "The rich, for their part, had scarcely become acquainted with the pleasure of dominating than they disdained all other pleasures, and using their old Slaves to subject new ones, they thought only of subjugating and enslaving their neighbors; like those ravenous wolves which once they have tasted human flesh scorn all other food, and from then on want to devour only men" (171).

The growth of unequal society led to an unleashing of all passions, with the exception that "natural pity" was stifled (171)—the great irony of the development of reason within the structure of a privately-interested society. "Humankind, debased and devastated, no longer able to turn back or to renounce its wretched acquisitions, and working only to its shame by the abuse of the faculties that do it honor, brought itself to the brink of ruin" (172). For Rousseau, the seeds of a universal struggle for recognition are sown in the transition from the natural state to civil society. Whereas natural man lives within himself, in society man lives "always outside himself," on reputation, deriving "the sentiment of his own existence solely from their judgment" (187). In civil society there is a "universal desire for reputation, honors, and preferment which consumes us all, exercises and compares talents and strengths, how much it excites and multiplies the passions and, in making all men competitors, rivals, or rather enemies, how many reverses, how many successes, how many catastrophes of every kind it daily causes by leading so many Contenders to enter the same lists" (184).

While *Paths of Glory* is bitter in its criticism of the hypocrisy of the military command, it is sympathetic in its portrayal of Dax, who is carrying out orders to the end, and the men. The Rousseauian theme is clearly though subtly stated: Modern men, stuck in trench warfare and a struggle for recognition and advancement behind the lines, will step on one another to defend their reputation or gain promotion. Broulard is perplexed when Dax deviates from this logic, expecting him to have been struggling against Mireau for personal gain. When Dax demonstrates that he was genuinely interested in principle, Broulard recoils, as he would at *natural man*. While I would agree with Kolker and others that Dax is constrained throughout in his tactical options, he does manage to effect Mireau's dismissal. Nor is the cabaret scene that follows a mere "bit of sentimentality" if we view the film in Rousseauian terms.[10] The war will go on; the 701st regiment must return to the front lines. The miserable conundrums of civilized man will continue. But there is a spark of hope in the fact that sympathy for others still exists among ordinary soldiers.

Although it is tempting to cast *Paths of Glory* in Marxian terms, this would be imprecise. Self-serving hypocrisy pervades characters above and below Dax on the social hierarchy. The extent of "class solidarity" portrayed in the film is the hesitancy of troops to leave the trenches to face nearly certain death. More broadly, the 1916–23 period witnessed a highwater mark of a social revolutionary process—the formation of workers' and soldiers' councils in Russia and Germany, the brief experiment of a participatory democratic workers' state in Russia in 1917–18, the possibility of spreading proletarian revolution to the advanced industrial countries. All of this is not only untreated in Kubrick's film but unmentioned. The spirit of the film is not Marxian but rather a looser Rousseauian critique of society as having nearly extinguished human sympathy.

Motive and Meaning

Like anyone with eyes open in the twentieth century, Kubrick was affected by world war, depression, holocaust, and nuclear stalemate, the unfolding traumas of modern imperialist conflict after 1914. His chosen way to respond was *not* to give a political explanation. *Fear and Desire* sets us down with a unit of soldiers caught behind enemy lines in an abstract war. As they make their way back to safe territory, they are faced with an existential crisis: Should they risk their lives to take out a single enemy general whom they happen upon, or should they simply take the least risky path to saving their own lives. The choice is between purpose and security. The relative justice of the cause is unrepresented; it has no bearing on their considerations. *Paths of Glory* begins *in media res,* in the trenches and in the opulent mansion that serves as General Mireau's headquarters. World War I provides a rich opportunity to analyze modern, great power imperialism and the rise of military competition, but *Paths of Glory* does not even make side comments on the geopolitical situation. Its representation of human evil operates below a political analysis of the root causes of this war. *Dr. Strangelove* gives no explanation for the rise of the Cold War or the nuclear stalemate. Instead, it portrays the breakdown of this rational system in the actions of a mad, maverick general and then explores subsequent iterated decision-making. *Full Metal Jacket* provides no rationale for American involvement in Vietnam. Instead, it shows the establishment of the rational system, in the actions of the drill sergeant on the Marine recruits, and then its breakdown—at an individual level (Pyle's latrine meltdown) and at a collective level, for the whole platoon, in Vietnam itself. All we do get is an uncomprehending "conversation" between a fatalistic soldier pointing to evil within the souls of men, and an officer seeking to hold the side together amid criticism of the whole war effort.[11]

Later, after a fire fight, the platoon stands over the body of Lieutenant Touchdown, offering fragmentary words of account. "You're going home now . . . *Semper fi* . . . We're mean Marines, sir . . . Go easy, bros . . . Better you than me . . ." "We'll at least they've died for a good cause," suggests Rafterman.

ANIMAL MOTHER: What cause was that?
RAFTERMAN: Freedom?
ANIMAL MOTHER: Flush out your head gear, new guy. You think we waste Gooks for freedom? This is a slaughter. If I'm gonna get my balls blown off for a word, my word is poontang.

Later still, this fragmentary viewpoints structure is repeated, as the platoon is interviewed in Hué City by a television crew. None of the soldiers can articulate a reasonable justification for American involvement in the war; they speak words of competitive bravado, or express dismay that the Vietnamese themselves are uncommitted to the cause.[12] Others are impressed with the bravery of the enemy. Animal Mother, one of the bravest marines, goes so far as to say, "Well, if you ask me, we're shooting the wrong Gooks." But the next words out of his mouth are: "What do I think of America's involvement in the war? Well, I think we should win." How would that be done? "Well, if they'd send us more guys, and bomb the hell out of the north, they might, they might give up." But he clearly has no courage of this conviction. Joker sums up the absurdity of the whole situation: "I wanted to see exotic Vietnam, the jewel of Southeast Asia. I wanted to meet interesting and stimulating people of an ancient culture and kill them." The war is absurd, and the troops have no decent explanation for their own involvement. The troops themselves are divided in their understanding of the war; it seems pointless, it would make sense to apply greater firepower if the United States is to win; but perhaps we have not even selected the appropriate enemy. Yet they have no choice but to continue to strive for their military objectives, even though it entails suffering and death without meaning.

Similarly, the meaning of the French revolution, and Napoleon's complicated relationship to its principles, is beyond Kubrick's purpose in the *Napoleon* screenplay. The French revolution extended the principle of democratic revolution and popular self-government against royal absolutism. From the point of view of the liberal, democratic, and republican elements that had fomented revolution, the rise of Napoleon was at the time a great defeat. Yet, Napoleon's coup of 1799 did not fully turn its back on the principles of the revolution. Although Napoleon contrived a series of constitutions, each giving him more absolute power than the former, he consistently claimed that his power was founded on popular authority and staged plebiscites to ratify each of the new constitutions. Napoleon's reorganization of French law, in the *Code Napoléon,* was the practical embodiment of the principles of the revolutionary orators of the 1790s. The freedom of contract, civil marriage and divorce, and the principle of equality before the law (the abolition of class differences) had far-reaching implications. The *Code Napoléon* was the basis for legal and social reform throughout Europe as Napoleon's armies advanced. Although Napoleon himself was eventually defeated, it proved more difficult for these principled reforms to be dislodged, as the European heads of state only made headway against Napoleon once they started to copy the French appeals to the mood and interests of their own peoples.[13] Yet, Kubrick's Napoleon does offer a political philosophy, centered upon the inherent evil within humans.

NAPOLEON: The revolution failed because the foundation of its political philosophy was in error. Its central dogma was the transference of original sin from man to society. It had the rosy vision that by nature man is good, and that he is only corrupted by an incorrectly organized society. Destroy the offending social institutions, tinker with the machine a bit, and you have Utopia—presto!—natural man back in all his goodness. [Laughter at the table.]
NAPOLEON: It's a very attractive idea but it simply isn't true. They had the whole thing backwards. Society is corrupt because man is corrupt—because he is weak, selfish, hypocritical and greedy. And he is not made this way by society, he is born this way—you can see it even in the youngest children. It's no good trying to build a better society on false assumptions—authority's main job is to keep man from being at his worst and, thus, make life tolerable for the greater number of people.[14]

We might say that the *Napoleon* screenplay carries on Kubrick's discussion of Rousseau, but that Kubrick has become more pessimistic in the meantime. But the lines quoted above are essentially an aside within the screenplay. The main focus in this projected film was to be the personal successes and failings of the great strategist. In general, instead of providing explanations for world-historic events, Kubrick's films on Napoleon, the Great War, the Cold War, and Vietnam each put the trauma of war into a story. The message of *Paths of Glory* is Rousseauian fatalism, in which society has corrupted man, even though a spark of natural sympathy can still dwell in the hearts of ordinary soldiers. But the other Kubrick war films present a vision of man as fundamentally corrupted—"the Jungian thing, sir"—not by society, as Rousseau would have it, but in their very nature. This corruption is consistently presented in *Full Metal Jacket,* where it is not only generals and drill sergeants who are brutal and vicious to others; the troops themselves are driven by murderous desires. The sympathy of the troops listening to the German girl singing, at the close of *Paths of Glory,* is a redeeming moment that stands out from the other films. But even here, the crowd seems dangerous and changeable, for a moment earlier they were catcalling boisterously, threateningly.

Kubrick himself has indicated that his films after *Paths of Glory* reflect precisely a shift away from Rousseauian idealism. *A Clockwork Orange's* "view of man is less flattering than the one Rousseau entertained," he acknowledges, emphasizing inherent human weakness. "Man isn't a noble savage, he's an ignoble savage. He is irrational, brutal, weak, silly, unable to be objective about anything where his own interests are involved . . . and any attempt to create social institutions based on a false view of the nature of man is probably doomed to failure." Kubrick wanted his post-Rousseauian position to be seen *not* as pessimism but its opposite. "Rousseau's romantic fallacy that it is society which corrupts man, not man who corrupts society, places a flattering gauze between ourselves and reality . . . but, in the end, such a self-inflating illusion leads to despair." Perhaps it was Rousseau, Kubrick argues, who was truly the pessimist. "[T]he question must be considered whether Rousseau's view of man as a fallen angel is not really the most pessimistic and hopeless of philosophies. It leaves man a monster who has gone steadily away from his original nobility."[15] That Kubrick's interpretation of Rousseau is insufficiently nuanced is secondary to his grim emphasis on the inherence of human failing.[16]

Let me suggest that another perspective, which may be useful in coming to terms with some of Kubrick's war films, is provided by Max Weber. *Dr. Strangelove* and *Full Metal Jacket* in particular are preoccupied with the establishment and breakdown of rational systems. The opening sequences of the latter film powerfully portray the creation of disciplined unity of Marines under the tutelage of a brutally efficient drill sergeant. The subsequent action of *Full Metal Jacket* and the whole action of *Dr. Strangelove* are centered, respectively, upon the disintegration of the rational systems of the disciplined unity of the marines at the infantry level in Vietnam, and on the high international system of nuclear deterrence. In both cases, the signal for the disintegration of the rational system is an individual going mad—General Jack D. Ripper, with his delusions of a poisoned water supply, sending his bomber wing against its targets in Russia, and Pyle's "major malfunction" in the latrine at the end of basic training. (Ironically, Pyle had *successfully* negotiated the difficult training; he was on his way to Vietnam. Was his breakdown a fulfillment of the training?) The breakdown of rationality, however, is far more extensive than these two individuals' madness. The ordered symmetry of the rational system of deterrence and the close discipline of the marine unit are obliterated as these two films proceed.

In the work of Max Weber, rationality as an all-encompassing system is identified not with military organization but with the rise of capitalism. Capitalism required that people internalize a self-denying discipline and embrace a professional calling. Ironically, the Protestant variant of Christianity was the initial vehicle for this new ethic in the secular realm. Weber insisted that the passion for profits alone, the greedy drive for gain, could not be identified with modern, systematic, hierarchical capitalism. This sentiment could be found "in all epochs and in all countries of the globe. It can be seen both in the past and in the present wherever the objective possibility for it somehow exists."[17] Capitalism required that this "irrational motivation" be tamed or at least tempered. Capitalism is a system of the pursuit of profit "in a rational, continuous manner." "There are no choices. If the entire economy is organized according to the rules of the open market, any company that fails to orient its activities toward the chance of attaining profit is condemned to bankruptcy" (152). Capitalism as a system, as opposed to particular capitalist enterprises, is distinguished by its systematic organization, based upon calculation of gain, of the skills or capacities of individuals. "Calculation lies (as long as each case is rational) at the foundation of every single activity . . ." (153). Systematic capitalism organizes workers into companies oriented to market opportunities, separates the household from productive enterprise, and employs rational accounting (155–56).

Importantly, Weber viewed the modern economic order as framing an inescapable cosmos that enveloped and determined "the style of life of all individuals born into it, *not* only those directly engaged in earning a living" (123). For Weber, once capitalist rationality became dominant in the economic realm, essentially all organized activity adhered to its patterns. By the twentieth century, asceticism and devotion to calling created a calculating mind-set that constituted a steel-hard casing or "iron cage" [*stahlhartes Gehäuse*]. The rational, calculating mind-set was inescapable. Weber was far from sanguine about these developments. The pursuit of gain, channeled through asceticism and devotion to a calling, lost its connection to religious meaning. It came to be "associated with purely competitive passions. Not infrequently, these passions directly imprint this pursuit with the character of a sporting contest" (124). Without a dramatic transformation, the revival of new prophesy or "a mighty rebirth of ancient ideas and ideals," this society would likely descend into a "mechanized ossification." Humans in such a society would become as automatons, "narrow specialists without mind, pleasure-seekers without heart," occupants of a nothingness (124). The greatest irony of all is that this society predicated on rationality could become enmeshed in profoundly irrational pursuits and outcomes. Rational calculations could not decide upon ends, only means. Narrow specialists without mind: the assembled generals in the War Room. The ordinary soldiers fighting street to street in Hué, in an unwinnable, unfathomable war, reduced to hollowly carrying out their orders. When off duty, they negotiate with prostitutes: pleasure-seekers without heart. Both *Dr. Strangelove* and *Full Metal Jacket* show worlds populated by organizational men seeking only to carry out their orders. They have lost the capacity to reason about ends; they are obedient occupants of a bureaucratic order, following narrow rules established for them, even if they make no sense in their present context. Consider Group Captain Lionel Mandrake's attempt to phone the president with the recall code. He struggles to convince Colonel "Bat" Guano to allow him to make the call at all—Guano was merely following orders. But the operator will not allow him to place the call without the proper change; and the White House operator will not accept a collect call.[18] In *Dr. Strangelove*, Captain Mandrake is a lonely figure struggling against the bureaucratic logic of the deterrence machine in its headlong rush to world disaster. Everyone around him is simply carrying out orders. Joker plays a similar role in *Full Metal Jacket*, although I would argue that he has been reduced to ironic commentary as he carries out his orders.

NOTES

1. I appreciate the help I've received from discussions with Angela Benander, Andrew Grossman, and Adam Lutzker. Especially valuable was Michael Bastian's sharply critical reaction to an earlier draft of this essay.

2. Jeremy Bernstein, "Profile: Stanley Kubrick," in *Stanley Kubrick: Interviews,* ed. Gene D. Phillips (Jackson: University of Mississippi Press, 2001), 28, 29.

3. Kubrick was forced to abandon the film because he was unable to secure sufficient funding.

4. Stanley Kubrick, *Napoleon: A Screenplay,* September 29, 1969, accessed from www.filmforce.net on August 1, 2000, 78–79.

5. Emanuel Lasker, *Lasker's Manual of Chess* (New York: Dover, 1947), 199.

6. The Russian strategy of withdrawal echoes one already known in the ancient world. When the Persian king Darius invaded Scythia, the nomadic Europeans recognized they were no match for his forces. The Scythians "determined that they could not wage an open stand-up fight . . . [so] they would withdraw and, withdrawing, fill in the wells and springs as they passed and destroy the grass from the land." Their policy of continuous retreat led Darius on a futile pursuit; in the end the Persians barely managed to remove themselves back to their own land. See Herodotus, *The History,* trans. David Grene (Chicago: University of Chicago Press, 1987), 4.118–42.

7. Basil H. Liddell Hart, *History of the Second World War* (New York: G. P. Putnam's Sons, 1970); Basil H. Liddell Hart, *Strategy* (New York: Praeger, 1955); Sun Tzu, *The Art of War,* trans. Samuel B. Griffith (London: Oxford University Press, 1963).

8. *Dr. Strangelove:* A Continuity Transcript, accessed from http://161.210.220.100/doc/0055.html on May 5, 1999, 18–19. This dialogue continues:

MUFFLEY: General, it is the avowed policy of our country never to strike first with nuclear weapons.
TURGIDSON: Well, Mr. President, I would say that General Ripper has already invalidated that policy.
[Laughs.]
MUFFLEY: That was not an act of national policy and there are still alternatives left open to us.
TURGIDSON: Mr. President, we are rapidly approaching a moment of truth both for ourselves as human beings and for the life of our nation. Now, the truth is not always a pleasant thing, but it is necessary now to make a choice, to choose between two admittedly regrettable, but nevertheless, distinguishable post-war environments: one where you got twenty million people killed, and the other where you got a hundred and fifty million people killed.
MUFFLEY: You're talking about mass murder, General, not war.
TURGIDSON: Mr. President, I'm not saying we wouldn't get our hair mussed. But I do say . . . no more than ten to twenty million killed, tops. Uh . . . depending on the breaks.

9. Jean Jacques Rousseau, "Discourse on the Origin and Foundation of Inequality among Men," *The Discourses and Other Early Political Writings,* ed. and trans. Victor Gourevitch (Cambridge: Cambridge University Press, 1997), 153; hereafter cited in text.

10. Robert Kolker, *A Cinema of Loneliness,* 3rd ed. (Oxford: Oxford University Press, 2000), 113.

11. The dialogue:
COLONEL: Marine, what is that button on your body armor?
JOKER: A peace symbol, sir . . .
COLONEL: What is that you've got written on your helmet?
JOKER: "Born to kill," sir.

COLONEL: You write "born to kill" on your helmet *and* you wear a peace button. What's that supposed to be, some kind of sick joke? . . . What is it supposed to mean?

JOKER: I don't know, sir.

COLONEL: You don't know very much, do you?

JOKER: No, sir.

COLONEL: You better get your head and your ass wired together, or I *will* take a giant shit on you.

JOKER: Yes, sir.

COLONEL: Now answer my question or you'll be standing tall before the man.

JOKER: I think I was trying to suggest something about the duality of man, sir.

COLONEL: The what?

JOKER: The duality of man. The Jungian thing, sir. [The screenplay is a bit more expansive: "The dual nature of man? . . . You know, sir, the Jungian thing about aggression and xenophobia on one hand, and altruism and cooperation on the other?" Stanley Kubrick and Michael Herr, *Full Metal Jacket: A Screenplay* accessed from www.alta.demon.co.uk/amk/doc/0065.html on Aug. 14, 2000, 68.]

COLONEL: Whose side are you on, son?

JOKER: Our side, sir.

COLONEL: Don't you love your country?

JOKER: Yes, sir.

COLONEL: Then how about getting with the program? Why don't you jump on the team and come on in for the big win?

JOKER: Yes, sir.

COLONEL: Son, all I've ever asked of my Marines is that they obey my orders as they would the word of God. We are here to help the Vietnamese because inside every Gook, there is an American, trying to get out. It's a hard ball world, son. We've got to try to keep our heads until this peace craze blows over.

12. As Eightball says, "I personally think they don't want to be involved in this war. . . . [I]t's sort of like they took away our freedom and gave it to the Gookers, you know. But they don't want it. They'd rather be alive than free, I guess, poor dumb bastards."

13. William H. McNeill, *A World History,* 3rd ed. (New York: Oxford University Press, 1979), 431.

14. Kubrick, *Napoleon: A Screenplay,* 64–65.

15. Stanley Kubrick, "Now Kubrick Fights Back," *New York Times,* Feb. 27, 1972, 4:1, 11. The parallel between Kubrick's own pessimism and that of his Napoleon, at note 14, should be self-evident. I am grateful to Geoff Cocks for this reference.

16. Offering more than impressionistic remarks on the question of the *inherence* of human evil would require a historical and comparative scope on human societies and prehistory that multitudes of social theorists and theologians, let alone filmmakers, hardly possess. When Rousseau pointed out the truncated historical perspectives of prior social theorists, scientific ethnography had not yet entered its infancy. While Friedrich Engels, *Origin of the Family, Private Property and the State*

(New York: International Publishers, 1972), could be criticized for being founded upon inchoate ethnography, the solid recent work of Eleanor Burke-Leacock, *Myths of Male Dominance* (New York: Monthly Review Press, 1981), and Karen Sacks, *Sisters and Wives* (Urbana: University of Illinois Press, 1982), among others, is surely worthy of careful study before even venturing tentative hypotheses upon this matter. Still, orienting perspectives have seemed necessary to those constructing political institutions and justifying religions, as well as those founding schools of psychotherapy. All I am suggesting is that debates that find Thucydides, Augustine, and Hobbes to provide enduring touchpoints would be enriched by consideration of the ethnographic work that does not prejudge nonhierarchical hunter-gatherer social organization according to standards of later societies.

17. Max Weber, "Prefatory Remarks to Collected Essays in the Sociology of Religion [1920]," in *The Protestant Ethic and the Spirit of Capitalism,* trans. Stephen Kahlberg (Los Angeles: Roxbury, 2002), 152; hereafter cited in text.

18. The dialogue:

MANDRAKE: They won't accept the call. Have you got 55 cents?

GUANO: Well, you don't think I'd go into combat with loose change in my pocket, do you? . . .

MANDRAKE: Colonel, that Coca Cola machine. I want you to shoot the lock off it. There may be some change in there.

GUANO: That's private property.

MANDRAKE: Colonel! Can you possibly imagine what is going to happen to you, your frame, outlook, way of life and everything, when they learn that you have obstructed a telephone call to the President of the United States? Can you imagine?

Subjected Wills

The Antihumanism of
Kubrick's Later Films

———❯◆❮———

PAT J. GEHRKE AND G. L. ERCOLINI

In the summer of 2001, Steven Spielberg released what was supposed to be his homage to the work of the late Stanley Kubrick. Instead, viewers almost unanimously found *A.I.* disappointing. Not only did critics and audiences receive it harshly, but Kubrick fans and Spielberg fans alike largely rejected the film. It was described as "muddled," "a soggy mess," and "a disaster."[1] John Patterson aptly ascribed the failure of *A.I.* to "the incongruity of its two creators."[2] It was, we believe, due to the incongruity between Spielberg's humanism and the antihumanism of Stanley Kubrick.

It is easy to argue that Spielberg is a "dedicated humanist" or that his films express an "innate idealistic humanism."[3] Kate Soper defines humanism as the positive appeal "to the notion of a core humanity or common essential features in terms of which human beings can be defined and understood."[4] Humanism values features such as reason, love, family, or truth and believes these values to be innate qualities of the human being. Similarly, humanism negatively refers to concepts such as alienation or inauthenticity, "designating, and intending to explain, the perversion or 'loss' of this common being."[5] Films such as *Schindler's List, Amistad, Saving Private Ryan,* and even *A.I.* rely upon such a belief system for their explanations of heroes, victims, and villains.

On the other hand, antihumanism, as Reiner Schurman aptly describes it, refuses to place faith in such "metaphysics of man" and rejects "the program derived from such a metaphysics, a program that aims at restoring integral man."[6] It is the dominance of antihumanism in Kubrick's later films that we believe leads some critics to describe him as distrustful of humankind or misanthropic.[7] From at least *2001* forward, Kubrick's films consistently

101

work to critique and undermine notions of humanist subjectivity and, more specifically, rational autonomous will. Robert Kolker argues that Kubrick is an antihumanist in part because his characters undo their own subjectivity.[8] This essay expands his thesis by detailing how Kubrick's later works critique humanism through the deconstructing of three common humanist themes—reason, will, and identification.

In analyzing these films we have tried to avoid turning to the texts upon which the films were based or turning to indications of Kubrick's intent. While many of Kubrick's films are based on books or short stories, we believe that reading material from these prior stories into the films risks distorting how the films themselves function. Kubrick's screenplays, as Lee Siegel noted of *Eyes Wide Shut,* often followed "only the skeleton of the novel" and in some cases radically altered the storyline and tenor of the material, such as the transformation of Peter George's dramatic nuclear thriller, *Red Alert,* into the parodic *Dr. Strangelove.*[9]

Likewise, it is not our desire to ask what Kubrick wanted his movies to do or what he was trying to accomplish with particular choices. How a film or any communication event functions often exceeds or even contradicts the desires of its author, regardless of her or his skill. Whether Kubrick himself was a humanist, an antihumanist, posthumanist, or located elsewhere in the debate is not the concern of this investigation. Rather, we desire to study how the films themselves operate. We have chosen to follow an approach to film criticism similar to the one expressed by Marco Abel, by trying to avoid moral or aesthetic judgment about a film in favor of working "*with* the visceral aspects of the film, *with* the film's forces, according to *their* devices, *their* speeds."[10] We view Kubrick's later films as operative critiques, setting out not representations of the world as it is, will be, or should be, but interrogating both the traditional methods of filmmaking and the common notions of what it means to be an individual acting and operating in a world of others. In this way, we analyze how these films, regardless of origin or intent, operate as critiques of humanist subjectivity by interrogating notions of reason, will, and identification.

Unreasonable Truths

Kubrick's films are notorious for frustrating critics and audiences alike by defying their expectations and the standards of genre. For example, *2001* did not follow the form of a science-fiction film, and critics and audiences criticized *The Shining* for failing to meet the standards of a good horror film. Not only did Kubrick's later films break from generic traditions, they also broke with our basic expectations of storytelling and filmmaking. Through denying our desires for a rationally ordered and resolved narrative, refusing to endorse transcendental or eternal truths, and blurring the separation between reason and unreason, the films of Kubrick's later period consistently withdraw from common humanist belief in an innate human capacity to reason that could provide some access to at least approximate truths.

Eyes Wide Shut, Kubrick's last film, is perhaps the best example of the productivity of unreasonableness and deception. The film not only denies us knowledge of the truth of events and statements in the story, it also fundamentally eschews the value of searching for such truths and devalues reason's capacity to provide truth. The characters themselves are rife with deception, and the film affords us no objective point of view or narrative through which we might organize these deceptions into a reasonable truth. Certainly when Victor Ziegler, Bill's wealthy client, tells him that the entire scene at the mansion was a charade put on for the benefit of scaring Bill off, we are left doubtful of the truth of this statement. Yet, Eyes Wide Shut refuses to resolve the question of what really happened. Alice's story about the naval officer at the hotel likewise has no objective verification in the film—not even Bill remembers seeing him there. Nicole Kidman's overplaying of Alice's drunkenness at the party might also be perceived as Alice's overplaying of her own intoxication to enhance her flirtation. The characters in Eyes are so deceptive that by the end, when Alice and Bill agree that they are "awake now and hopefully for a long time to come," we are wondering what this "awake" can mean, for they have no greater grasp on the truth of the events or even a system of reason through which they might understand the previous few days. They are awake now perhaps only to an awareness that the truth is not what is most important in these events.

What Eyes makes plain is a thematic in much of Kubrick's work. His films consistently refuse to resolve themselves, reveal their truths, or allow audiences to contain the narrative in a set of principles. The very narrative structure of filmmaking is undercut by 2001. The film has no enduring story to provide a prepackaged system of interpretation for the events. Indeed, the first thirty minutes are without a single spoken word. Yet, the lack of a main character and the lack of a narrative that drives 2001 become an excess of potential meanings that will always overflow every attempt to "make sense" out a movie that is fundamentally an experience rather than a story. 2001 is slow, plodding, and takes long pauses—all things that most popular films take great effort to avoid.

Similarly, *Full Metal Jacket* refuses to set the tone for how one should experience or interpret the boot camp sequences. The film precisely does not ask that we be shocked, disgusted, excited, inspired, or amused by Drill Instructor Hartman's abuse of Pyle, Joker, and the other recruits. As Gerri Reaves wrote, the film provides "no prepackaged access" and "demands that we flounder and eventually supply our own narrative moorings."[11] Likewise, the deaths of the soldiers in the film are universally left unmourned and uncelebrated, but likewise are not denigrated. From Hartman's slaying to Joker's killing blow to the sniper, not one of these deaths is justified by or packaged into an outcome or end that might provide a system of reason. Indeed, no one bothers to explain why Joker shoots the sniper or why Pyle shoots Hartman. We are left on our own to provide those reasons and, to further frustrate us, the story pulls away from every attempt we might make to reason its events.

This is why *Eyes Wide Shut* was perhaps an exemplar of how Kubrick's movies disassembled the audience's expectation for a reasoned narrative. Consider this simple question: Who is the mysterious woman in the plumed headdress that intervenes on Bill's behalf at the party? Is it really Mandy, the woman that would later be reported as dead from an overdose? Bill leaps to such a conclusion based on the coincidence of events, and Ziegler only confirms Bill's own suspicion. Bill asks Ziegler if it was her at the party, and after a pause, with his back still turned to Bill and to the camera, revealing nothing of himself, Ziegler replies that it was. Yet, this is in the same conversation that he would make the dubious claim that Bill's unmasking and her intervention were just an act to scare off Bill. Making this story even more dubious, Ziegler told Bill only moments before that if Bill knew who the people at that party were he would not sleep well at night. Perhaps it was not Mandy that intervened on Bill's behalf, but Domino, the prostitute that Bill encounters on the street, or even the love-struck Marion, the daughter of his recently deceased patient. As savvy filmgoers, we might notice that the actor playing the mysterious woman in the credits is a different actor than any of those that played Mandy, Domino, or Marion. Yet, from a director who used Peter Sellers to play three of the main characters in *Dr. Strangelove,* we cannot take this as evidence of a particular meaning. It would be just like a Kubrick movie to use more than one actor to play the same role. This central fact of the events that occurred at the mansion is left irresolvable. Even the credits only muddle the issue.

Eyes is also peppered with odd events that simply have no apparent connection to the narrative of the film on face. Bill's nights are filled with a series of potentially plot-revealing events that are never connected back to any central theme or story. For example, while Milich, the costume shop owner, berates his daughter for her lascivious behavior, she whispers in Bill's ear, almost indiscernibly, "You should have a cloak lined with ermine." Marion's declaration of fanatical love comes and goes, and the group of youths that knock Bill down in the street and call him "fag" drift off screen and out of story like so much flotsam.

Even when these films end, they refuse to make sense of all the events or provide reason for the characters' actions. No film could defy the convention of resolving and uncovering the complete narrative in a grand finale more than did *2001*. There is no reasoning or language that will assemble, from what is provided in the film, a unitary explanation for the last sequence, "Jupiter and Beyond the Infinite." There are no moorings left for Dave or for the audience once he traverses the space of the monolith. Even the flow of time is unhinged, both by the odd juxtaposition of ornate Louis XIV decoration and stark ultramodern architecture, and by Dave's disturbing experience of observing himself at different points in time.

Full Metal Jacket similarly refuses to resolve itself at its conclusion. Contrary to traditional war films such as *Saving Private Ryan,* there is no completion of a quest or act of sacrifice for the nation that resolves or justifies the struggles of the soldiers. Indeed, the war rages on and makes no more or less sense at the end of the movie. The traditional ending of judgment—be that praise or condemnation—is replaced with a simple farce as the soldiers march off to the river, surrounded by combat, singing the *Mickey Mouse Club* theme and thinking only about the "great homecoming fuck." As Janet Moore noted, *Jacket* avoids the traditional narrative conclusion precisely to leave open a space for thought: "If Kubrick were to articulate closure, to provide the weenie of a viable alternative perspective, he would be authorizing a fantasy realm where thought shuts down."[12]

This is not to say that audiences and critics have not worked very hard to give reasons to Kubrick's films. The search for the true meaning of *Eyes Wide Shut* or *2001* or any of his later movies will likely fill volumes of future scholarship. However, the equal validity of multiple contradictory positions on what the films "really mean" combined with the radical polysemy of the films only makes the search for the truth—the reasons and reasoning that will make sense of it all—ultimately fruitless. In this way, Bill's search for the truth of the bizarre events that he encounters in *Eyes* mirrors the experience of audiences and critics seeking to reason their way through Kubrick's films. As Bill learns, this search is not only fruitless but also dangerous. We construct fantasies of meaning that organize events into a logical or reasonable narrative, but in refusing to give up the quest for the truth and meaning of the events, Bill places himself in grave danger. Bill's eyes and those of the critics that would construct systems of reason and meaning from Kubrick's' films are wide shut—that is to say, in being on the lookout for meaning and recognition, in trying to reason their way through the films, both Bill and those critics obsessed with narrative completion shut their eyes to the experience of the film as it operates. In this way, *Eyes Wide Shut* is not only, as Stefan Mattesich argued, an allegory of its own reception, but it is a lesson in how to experience a Kubrick film.[13]

The last refuge of the heroes of meaning is in the transcendental principles of reason and morality. Yet, each of Kubrick's films withdraws from anything transcendent and refuses to either submit to reason or purport a morality. In *Full Metal Jacket* the ultimate reason-machine of military command and control comes apart, revealed to be just a "big shit sandwich" of which every soldier has to take a bite. When Joker, Cowboy, and Animal Mother are in combat, there is no order to their efforts. When one commander of the squad is killed, the next is appointed for no apparent reason other than, perhaps, that he picked up the radio first. The smooth operation of the military machine, in practice, is the lost fumbling of a misread map and an uncoordinated set of assaults and fatalities.

Perhaps *2001* is more to blame for promoting transcendental interpretations of Kubrick's movies than any of his other films. Yet, it is here better than anyplace else that we can see the narrowness of the gap between the sentient mind of the space-faring human and the animalistic behavior of the apish progenitors of humankind. The most startling movement of the film may not be the alignment of the planets as Strauss's *Zarathustra* swells, but the silent, sudden, and timeless moment when that single airborne bone becomes the spacecraft. In that instant *2001* removes all the separation between the ape and human, stripping the fantasticality of space travel down to just a more complicated extension of that simplistic simian tool.

Even more adept at eroding any faith in the transcendence of reason is HAL's irrefutable logic. The 9000 series is an infallible computer. Two 9000 series computers have produced contradictory answers. From these two facts there are only two ways out: first, the abandonment of the principle of noncontradiction, a core concept for reason; or, second, the assignation of the error to a third party that corrupted or interfered with the operation of the 9000 series computers. This latter path, assigning the problem to human error, is of course the only reasonable path. HAL's absolute reason is not corrupted by insanity but is at the very root of his execution of the crew. Given the incredible importance of the mission and the unreliability of the human crew, when faced with the possibility of losing his control over the mission, the only reasonable response, from a purely logical perspective, is HAL's.

The consequences of HAL's reason have brought some critics to believe that *2001* seeks to articulate how HAL's failure to embrace human compassion or transcendent moral truths is the real danger of technology. However, HAL displays compassion and empathy for Dave and Frank at many points during the film. Though his exchanges are programmed and often quite purposeful, he expresses at least as much care for and interest in the well-being of the crew as the astronauts themselves. If Frank or Dave had to decide whether to significantly jeopardize this vital mission or sacrifice a fellow crew member, would their decision have been any less coldly logical? Kubrick films are never long on the idea of human compassion and usually eschew moralizing. Even *Dr. Strangelove*, while making a mockery of the logic of nuclear brinksmanship, lacks any overt moral judgment.

In *Clockwork Orange,* after his release from the Ludovico Institute, Alex is turned away by his parents, he is beaten by homeless people, he is tortured by his former gang members, and he is tormented by the author. This is not, however, moral retribution. These are acts that defy a notion of compassion and are without either moral justification or the cool rationality of institutional punishments. Instead, they are passionate acts of violence that refuse reasoning or moralizing. There is no karmic justice or righteous vindication but only the emergence of new sites of violence, expressions of anger, spite, and a perfectly, totally defenseless new victim.

In *Full Metal Jacket,* Joker, Animal Mother, and the other squad members mock the justification of war by principles such as democracy and freedom. As Reaves notes, acts done "under the guise of idealism and democracy are finally done only for the reward of 'the great homecoming fuck' and the honor of being 'the first kid on the block to get a confirmed kill.'"[14] As Animal Mother says, "You think we waste gooks for freedom? This is a slaughter. If I'm gonna get killed for a word, my word is poontang." *Jacket*'s refusal to provide narrative resolution, absence of organizing reason, and avoidance of moralistic interpretations of war brought Karen Rasmussen and Sharon Downey to conclude that "like *The Deer Hunter, Full Metal Jacket* offers no rationale for American involvement in Vietnam. Unlike *The Deer Hunter,* it highlights the confusion felt by soldiers who were fighting that war. Its ending creates ambiguity rather than resolution or conflict."[15]

Indeed, *Full Metal Jacket* undermines the very distinction between order and confusion, between moral and immoral, and between the real and the fantastic. The ending is indeed a "happy" one, in the sense that Joker is alive and able to narrate that he is happy to be so, but the fantasia of that happiness is emphasized both in Joker's recognition that he is "in a world of shit" and in the dual fantasies that accompany the ending: the fantasy of the "great homecoming fuck" and the ultimate synecdoche for fantasia, Mickey Mouse. *Eyes Wide Shut* repeats this blurring of the real and the fantasy in the recognition, at the close, that Bill and Alice should be grateful to have survived all of their adventures, "whether they were real or only a dream." The question of truth and the tool of reason—two common grounds for humanist values—are at best ineffectual in Kubrick's worlds and at their worst are dangerous, even potentially lethal.

Will as Subjection

One could argue that the removal of reason and truth as the grounding points for events can serve to open a space for absolute human will and agency. One might find in the rejection of reason and truth a sort of absolute humanism, in which the will of the human, unencumbered by any form of logic or prior truths, becomes the creator and measure of all things. In Kubrick's films, however, the characters are driven by something quite the opposite of an absolute will. Instead, from Dave Bowman to Dr. Bill, Kubrick's characters find themselves in a state of subjectedness that is contrary to a vision of will-as-force. Kubrick's characters rarely manifest autonomous will and are far more likely to find themselves subjected to technologies and practices than to be agents expressing their will through technology. Christopher Hoile noted this tendency in Kubrick's films when he wrote that "Kubrick's films have all concerned the illusion that man's will contributes to his progress. Man's progress in *Dr. Strangelove* only leads to destruction; progress in *2001* is not directed by man at all but by a black monolith; and in *A Clockwork Orange* progress equals programmatic sameness."[16] Perhaps most immediately connecting Hoile's three examples is the central role of technology.

In *A Clockwork Orange*, it is the technology of behavior modification rather than an electronic or physical device that places Alex in the most obvious state of subjection. After the doctors at the Ludovico Institute have tested their new treatment upon him, he is incapable of witnessing—much less performing—acts of violence or sex without being gripped by a crippling feeling of illness. He likewise is incapable of ever listening to Beethoven again, as a side effect of the treatment. Nonetheless, this "cure" and Alex's newfound status as the perfect citizen do not arise from a more pure or moral form of will. Quite to the contrary, will is precisely what the treatment seeks to circumvent. Alex now reacts to violence and sex in a strict and programmatic response to stimuli. A certain element of his will has been converted to a single-celled organism. The treatment at the institute is most profound for what it reveals about what came before. The technology of behavior modification is only a more amplified version of the disciplining force of the prisons, which in turn also makes plain the socializing discipline of life as a citizen. As Pat Gehrke has argued elsewhere, regardless of which of these subject-positions Alex occupies, he is more subjected to the technologies of discipline than he is an agent acting autonomously.[17]

In *Full Metal Jacket,* the technology of discipline is again made plain in the boot camp sequences. Here, Drill Instructor Hartman explicitly positions the recruits not as agents who will act upon the world but as agencies through which the Marine Corps and God himself will take actions. Indeed, the will of the recruits is broken quickly and efficiently as they are turned from men into cyborg warriors. Hartman tells them that each of them will become "a weapon." The mechanical symbiont of the rifle becomes inseparable from its organic soldier. Together they become one entity. Hartman says, "The deadliest weapon in the world is a Marine and his rifle." Each recruit chants his recognition of this symbiotic relationship: "Without me, my rifle is useless. Without my rifle, I am worthless." Will and agency give way to obedience and subjection. In the transition from recruit to soldier each person finds a position of subjection, a new name, a new identity, and a new purpose: to do as the U.S. Marines and God himself expect of soldiers and to provide Heaven with a fresh supply of souls.

In *2001,* the technology becomes more physically manifest, but the disciplining effect of the technology is equally apparent. In each human movement we find it acts in reaction to and as limited by its technological symbionts. From the magnetic shoes in the zero-gravity spacecraft to the anxiety-inducing long list of detailed instructions on how to use the zero-gravity toilet, even the most basic of human actions become responses to the human relationship with technology. In each of these circumstances, the clumsiness and physical difficulty of action operates as a metaphor for the difficulty found at the center of human agency. The sound only of heavy labored breathing to accompany the space walk scenes emphasizes this difficulty. At every turn, strained human labor struggles to grab onto or push off of technology just to manage to cross a room or even excrete. In contrast, the movement of the spacecraft as it docks with the space station is smooth, effortless, and artistic—all set to Johann Strauss's *Blue Danube Waltz*.

This is not to say that the humans in Kubrick's films become robots or are without the capacity for any kind of choice. Certainly Alex makes choices even when under the complete sway of his conditioning. Joker, Cowboy, and Animal Mother take actions not preprogrammed. As Hartman says, "the Marine Corps does not want robots—they want killers." Rather, it is to say that they find their capacity for action not in the autonomous will of the hero figure but precisely in rote behaviors and in reactions to their positions of subjection. Rather than being protagonists of the film and pushing the plot forward, they maintain common and mundane behaviors and react to events around them, being pulled—sometimes kicking and screaming—through the film by events and forces well outside of any autonomous rational human agent.

Certainly the mechanization of behavior in the prison scenes of *A Clockwork Orange* displays the sense of rote performance of duties, as Alex is told to strip, get dressed, stand with his toes on the white lines, put things down properly, and the like. Alex obeys all these orders and is fashioned into the model prisoner—a character that maintains the clockwork schedule and behavior of the prison system.

Not far from Alex's experience of the rote are the scenes in *Full Metal Jacket* that transform Fatbody Pyle from the doughnut-eating failure into the "born-again hard" killing machine. In scene after scene of Pyle's subjection we see him incapable of finding a space in which to react until finally he takes on the mechanization in a way no other soldier could match. He becomes the perfect marine and even displays the "thousand-yard stare" that is usually reserved only for veterans of heavy combat. It might be noted here that some scholars have interpreted the violence and sexual objectification of women in *Full Metal Jacket* as a sign of misogyny or patriarchy. Given that, as Moore wrote, "Leonard destroys the DI and himself in a graphic display of the *telos* of 'masculine' aggression and male bonding—hardly an affirmation of confident masculinity," we believe that *Full Metal Jacket*'s misogyny, like that of *A Clockwork Orange* and *Eyes Wide Shut*, functions more compellingly as an interrogative critique of patriarchy.[18]

The programmatic and rote behavior of both the prison and the barracks is likewise mirrored by the shallow and rote behavior of all the humans in *2001*. Consider how the flight attendants and the passengers interact on the spacecraft or how Dave and Frank interact onboard the *Discovery*. Their interactions are ruled by simple and mechanical principles of courtesy and protocol, with no self-revelation, discovery, or serious inquiry. Indeed, it is HAL more than any of the human characters that attempts a conversation of emotional and psychological complexity. Of course, he does so only to facilitate his psychological examinations of the crew.

Shallow dialogue was perhaps the most common criticism of Kubrick's last film, *Eyes Wide Shut*. The conversations between Bill and Alice are dominated by exchanges like this one: "Where is my wallet?"—"On the nightstand." Alice asks Bill how her hair looks, and he responds without even turning around to look at her—the response is already set before the question has even been asked. This is the simple mundane day-to-day life that is usually left out of films, all the way down to Alice using the toilet while Bill puts on his tie. Even when Alice engages Bill about her fantasy lover, the naval officer, his responses are predictable and simple. She says that she is trying to get a straight answer out of him, to which he responds that he thought that is what he had been providing. When Marion announces her engagement to Carl, Bill heartily congratulates her, smiling and speaking of what great news it is, completely setting aside the context of her father's death that very evening. As the corpse lies only a few feet away Bill gives superficial consolation to Marion's grief, speaking with a hollow assuredness characteristic of his profession.

In *The Shining*, rote repetition of form and content is given a new artistry. Not only does Jack set about at repeating the acts of the former caretaker, Grady, but he repeats exact lines spoken by the ghosts of the house. The twins, when they confront Danny in the hallway, invite him to come play with them "forever and ever and ever." Later, when Jack is inquiring about whether Danny likes the hotel, he says that he hopes Danny likes it, because he would like to stay there "forever and ever and ever." Jack's manuscript likewise repeats the rote production of dialogue, as the same line, "All work and no play makes Jack a dull boy" fills every sheet, formatted in paragraphs, stanzas, block quotes, and other styles for hundreds of pages. Jack and Danny both operate not as autonomous willing agents but as subject to the house and its shining. It is Grady and Lloyd, the bartender, who push Jack forward into action. Meanwhile Danny reacts to the visions of the twins and the woman in room 237. Wendy, meanwhile, routinely fulfills her role of mother, only finding agency as a response to the unusual behavior of her husband and her son.

This rote repetition in subjection is expressive of the reactive quality of will in Kubrick's films. Rather than having autonomous wills that would animate them from within themselves, the characters find choice and action come from outside themselves, as with Jack and Danny. It is in being subjected to others that the illusion of will comes to the fore. In *2001* it is precisely not the autonomous will of the protohumans that produces the first tool use but the subjection of the apes to the monolith. Invention and perhaps the very beginning of human thought are here removed from any self-substantiation or any origin within the human. Instead, it is in the mere response to the monolith that invention and will are possible. The limitations of will in *2001* are likewise significant. Dr. Floyd and his colleagues at most are capable of simple deceit as they develop a cover story for the discovery of the strange monolith. All of their other actions are only reactions to the experience of the monolith—an object with no apparent will, purpose, location, or even time. If there is a protagonist in *2001,* the monolith is certainly more qualified to fill that role than any human.

Alex in *A Clockwork Orange* is the most reactive of all senses of will. His attempts to assert agency and autonomy are consistently thwarted by an ever-tightening net of social control. Ultimately his conditioning baffles his capacity to adapt so greatly that he can do nothing but give up and surrender completely to his subjection. This is the act of suicide that sends him out the high window of the author's home. However, that reactive and almost programmatic surrender to his condition—his subjection—is precisely where agency is again made possible for Alex. There is, thus, a notion of will in Kubrick's films; not a will as autonomous, independent, or self-substantiating, but a will that is an effect of constraint and subjection where the very possibility of saying "I" and attempting to act in the world is already due to one's subjection. This is a will that is decidedly antihumanist in its refusal of any metaphysics that might imbue it with intrinsic qualities. Will is found not in the innate being of the human, but rather in the event of subjection that calls forth a response.

In *Eyes Wide Shut* we find a particularly interesting sense in which will is represented as reactive rather than proactive. Bill, in every assertion of agency that he attempts in the film, is interrupted by someone or something that derails his plans. In fact, it is interruptions that drive the story and Bill's own choices. These interruptions perform the gaps in will—the sense in which any agent's will is a fantasy constructed by writing over the interruptions and subjections that burst in and overflow the best laid plans of every person. Consider the series of interruptions that drive the story in

Eyes. First, during their conversation at the party, Nick and Bill are interrupted by a man who asks Nick to assist him. Shortly after this, while speaking to the two models, Bill is interrupted and called to help Ziegler, who is concerned because Mandy has overdosed in his bathroom. Later, when Alice relates her fantasy of the naval officer, their conversation is interrupted by a phone call informing Bill of his patient's death. In the midst of a shallow conversation about how her father passed peacefully, Marion interrupts by declaring her unbridled love for Bill. Their subsequent conversation is then interrupted by the arrival of Marion's fiancé, Carl. While walking on the street, Bill is twice interrupted, first by the group of youths that knock him down and call him "fag" and then later by Domino, the prostitute who invites him into her house. Bill's time with Domino is interrupted by a phone call from Alice.

Amid all of these interruptions there is also the play of chance. This is announced in the film both by the location of Domino's apartment immediately next door to a small shop called "The Lotto Store" and again by the headline of the newspaper that Bill reads the day after his visit to the mansion, which reads, "Lucky to be alive." Bill happens across the Sonata café after leaving Domino, and he wanders in to meet Nick. Their conversation is again interrupted by a phone call. At the costume shop, Bill's selection of a costume is interrupted by Milich's discovery of his daughter with two men in the office. Once at the party, Bill and the mysterious plumed woman are interrupted by a masked man who takes the woman away. Later, while Bill is talking with another woman, sent over to him by the man in the tricorn mask, the mysterious plumed woman interrupts and takes Bill aside to warn him again. Their conversation ends abruptly when a man comes to request that Bill speak with his taxi driver. Finally, during Bill's unmasking at the party, the mysterious plumed woman interrupts to say that she will take his place.

It is at this point that Bill begins his quest to discover the "really real" of the previous night's events. However, in his assertion of agency—when he becomes proactive and seeks to become the protagonist of the story— he is thwarted at every turn. His efforts are, as the letter from the mansion tells him, completely fruitless. What is worse, these fruitless acts only place him and his family in ever-greater peril. Bill, even in his greatest moments of attempted will, is tossed about by the events surrounding him and ruled by subjection and chance. In *Eyes Wide Shut,* will is a myth—an illusion that only frustrates and endangers those that would act upon it as if it were a reality. In place of the autonomous agent that can know and overcome the surrounding world, *Eyes,* like the other films in Kubrick's later period, portrays the dependent subject that is a result of a particular status as subjected to and always already in relation to something alien, foreign, or other.

Otherness and the Return of Agency

Otherness—the denial of identification—is a central part of how Kubrick's later films function. The films, and the characters they contain, often refuse an audience's attempt to identify with them and withdraw from systems of interpretation that would allow an audience to categorize them into a known schema. Indeed, the characters in the films experience and depict this nonrelation in their own interactions. Yet, in this refusal of identification we do not find anything lacking or missing. Instead, we find that the otherness of Kubrick's films and their characters produces an experience of agency that at once closes off those systems of relation that primarily desire knowledge and control, and opens up the possibility of an agency or subjectivity that grounds itself in this relation with otherness, discarding the humanist grounds and purposes of will for an antihumanist subjectivity of response.

A number of elements in Kubrick's later films deny audience identification with the characters. In *2001, The Shining,* and *Full Metal Jacket,* as Reaves noted, we are denied "identification with a consistent point-of-view."[19] Instead, in each of these films we are given a smattering of perspectives and vantage points. In *2001* we are never with any one set of characters long enough to establish enduring identification. The apes, Dr. Floyd, and Dave never overlap in the film and never endure long enough for significant identification with the audience. Further, the strange and alien monolith that does appear in each of the three segments of the film is so absolutely other that it exceeds any reasonable identification. The silence and solidity of the monolith likewise make it an ideal figure for interruption of identification. Indeed, the strange and hauntingly dissonant music of Gyorgi Ligeti that accompanies each appearance of a monolith emphasizes our disorientation and its absolute otherness. Some critics, such as Dale Williams, see this as an affirmation of our capacity to "find communion with God."[20] However, to read a mythic or deific empowerment of humanity into *2001* writes over the film's own operation as well as the fundamental statement it makes about the divine: ultimately, what is divine is what is beyond the possibility of any communion or any understanding. In the infinity of divinity, the divine will always exceed and overflow every attempt to contain it in a system of thought or representation. No human, not even Dave Bowman, comes to know these monoliths or even communicate with them. *2001* uses images of the mythic and images of the divine precisely as articulations of this point. As Paul Miers wrote, to read into the film a "mid-cult mytho-poesis" requires that one look the other way during those scenes that contain the film's best jokes.[21]

In *The Shining* the camera repeatedly swaps between first-person perspectives of Jack, Danny, and Wendy, denying us the convenience of identifying with any one character. From Danny's moments of shining and his witnessing of multiple ghosts in the house to Jack's encounters with Lloyd and with the woman in the bathtub, to Wendy's batting at Jack and visions of the ghosts, we are asked by the camera to identify with each of the three characters. Yet, they are impossible to identify with. The strangeness of Jack's actions, the absolute absurdity of his manuscript, and his giddy homicidal ranting push away the possibility of convenient audience identification. Likewise, Danny's psychic sentience, sheepish behavior, and constant accompaniment by Tony, the little boy that lives in his mouth, make Danny an equally unlikely candidate for identification. Wendy fails to even find persona or voice in most of the film, relegating herself to a whining and groveling creature of fear and loneliness—hardly the kind of character that encourages our identification, regardless of how much she herself might desire it.

In *Full Metal Jacket,* we are again subjected to the roaming point of view that is common to *The Shining*. Alternately, we experience the film through Joker's narration, the vantage point of Pyle in the head, the perspective of the dead soldier as his comrades each narrate their own meaning for his death, and the view of the Vietnamese sniper as she takes aim at the American squad. While we are treated to repeated narrations from Joker, and the storyline seems to follow his experience, it is neither his narration nor his perspective that govern the film. Perhaps Joker's voice-over might best be characterized not as narration, which would organize the story into a coherent and logical narrative, but an internal dialogue or running commentary on the action. It is a shortcut to conveying information but not a revelation of the meaning, purpose, or logic of the story.

While not as plainly represented by elements of narration or point of view, both *A Clockwork Orange* and *Eyes Wide Shut* similarly operate to reduce the chance of significant audience identification. In *Orange,* the only consistent character and point of view we receive is that of Alex, a youth intent on robbery, violence, and rape. He has very little about him that is likable and even less that we might wish to emulate in our own behaviors. His glib and sarcastic comments and his attempts at control and resistance are rarely fruitful and never ultimately very satisfying. He is wounded and abandoned by his own gang, beaten by the police, degraded both by his wardens and fellow inmates, and becomes the subject of a most unkind experiment. His choices are poor, to say the least, and he is not especially bright. Indeed, nothing about him seems exceptional or even desirable. Of course, a certain juvenile masculinity might lead one to worship his voracious attitude and appetite for excitement, violence, and sex without the constraints of social conventions or moral guilt. However, one would have to ignore everything past the first twenty minutes to miss how *Orange* takes apart this juvenile fantasy and emasculates Alex in the most intimate and profound ways. Indeed, Alex is not a character to be identified with but to be loathed and pitied.

The shallow and rote conversations in many of Kubrick's films have already been mentioned briefly, but it bears revisiting when discussing audience identification in *Eyes Wide Shut*. The film works fabulously for exactly the same reason that so many critics disliked it—Bill and Alice are superficial and lead a relatively hollow existence. They have no real substance or meaning in their lives. Indeed, they are caricatures of the rote behavior of day-to-day life that audiences avoid identifying with by engaging the fantastic in a film. Bill and Alice are no less a caricature of their roles as husband and wife than Alex is a caricature of the unruly youth or Hartman is a caricature of the sadistic drill sergeant. The difference is that Bill and Alice are much like the characters the audience does want to identify with—they are the beautiful, professional class, young couple with high incomes who rub shoulders with the rich and powerful. There is no substance to their characters with which the audience might connect. Their shallowness and hollowness, in reflecting the shallowness and hollowness of most human interaction, interrupts the possibility of identification. As Stefan Mattessich notes, the fact that we find Bill and Alice to be inappropriate material for such a caricature "implies a substance to the life they exemplify" that Kubrick's films consistently deny their main characters.[22]

Our inability to identify with Bill and Alice is also reflected in their inability to identify with each other. Even after years of marriage, they cannot understand each other or make a deep intimate connection. Their own interactions are as shallow as their interactions with their babysitter or even their daughter. The most passionate they become is in the verbal and emotional kickboxing that occurs in their bedroom. Yet, even here, in Alice's fantasies and Bill's response, there is no communion or fusion or meeting of minds but only an engagement between two individuals, each other to

the other. Siegel noted that almost every critic found fault in the performances of Tom Cruise and Nicole Kidman—"They seem to be acting like
actors, everyone complained."[23] Yet, as Mattessich wrote, this is precisely
why the film works so well at undermining the easy identification an audience might seek with Bill and Alice.

The capacity for sexual relations to overcome this isolation and otherness is denied in the film both by the passionless sex in the mansion that
fails to efface the otherness of the masked figures and in the soft bars of
"Strangers in the Night" that plays in the background as Bill and Nick are
escorted by the house staff to be interrogated by the man in the crimson cloak.
Even the sex between Bill and Alice is incapable of bridging the absolute
otherness between them. Mattessich wrote that "the trope of non-relation"
governs the film and is announced clearly in the shot of Alice looking into
the mirror while Bill caresses her.[24] In the end, sex is the replacement for
the fusion and understanding that Bill and Alice seek. Her desire to know
what he really thinks and his desire to know the truth of the events must
give way to the one thing Alice says that they must do: "Fuck." Sexual
activities in *Eyes* are not acts of making love. Sex has no fusing or bonding
effect. To fuck is precisely not an act that creates love—it is an act in which
one maintains the experience of otherness.

The characters in other Kubrick films have no more significant relationships than that of Bill and Alice. Alex relates to his mother and father in a
formal behavior governed by cliché. HAL, Dave, and Frank all engage in
purely professional and hollow conversation. Even while *Full Metal Jacket*
establishes the cohesion of the squad and the corps mentality, it undermines
the connectedness of the characters by separating them off against one
another, such as Pyle's victimization by his bunkmates. Joker and Cowboy are ecstatic to see each other in Vietnam but have no relationship
established in the film other than their simple proximity in the boot camp
sequence. Cowboy could have been any other person from that boot camp
sequence, and the reaction would have been identical. It is only in having
shared the experience of being subjected to Drill Instructor Hartman's sadism
that they find any connection.

This, then, is what is left for identification and for agency in Kubrick's
later films: the experience of subjection, being subjected to forces and
events beyond one's control and often beyond one's understanding. Will
re-emerges in these movies not as the triumph of the individual autonomous human agent but as a reaction to subjection, as an effect of being
subject to the absolute otherness of others and the concrete practices and

expectations of social structures. Will is grounded in dependence, rather than independence. This is why every conquering of the other in a Kubrick film strikes back at the self. In conquering that upon which one is dependent, one removes the groundings from underneath one's very will. This is not to say, as Paula Wiloquet-Maricondi argues, that the self and the enemy are the same, but that it is precisely the *otherness* of the other—enemy or most intimate partner—that grounds the possibility for any agency in Kubrick's later films.[25] In the defeat of the other, one erases that otherness, assimilating her or him, and erasing her or his very identity. In this act the very possibility for will is gone, and one becomes exactly what Hartman tells the squad that they will become: agencies to be used by forces not of their making. The assimilation of the Vietnamese into the American ideal is the perfect justification for what Animal Mother calls "a slaughter." It is the view that "inside every gook there is an American trying to get out" and that the Vietnamese are "dumb bastards" who "would rather die than be free" that makes most of the soldiers in *Full Metal Jacket* into perfect weapons.

Yet, each character can find an agency, even in the strictest moments of subjection, by being attentive to how others call her or him into response. In *Full Metal Jacket* that call is felt by Joker both in his inability to remain indifferent to Pyle's whimpering even after having delivered the last blow of the beating and in his need to respond to the request of the Vietnamese sniper who begs him to shoot her. Alex finds agency and will through surrendering to his subjection and leaping from the author's window. Proto-humans find will in responding to the absolute otherness of the monolith. Bill finds will in submitting to the impossibility of containing or controlling the events around him. Wendy finds will in her response to Jack's assault, and Danny finds will ultimately in the incomprehensible maze and snow through which his father chases him. In each case, the film has disassembled the operation of a rational autonomous human will and given in its place the possibility of a reactive will that operates only in the experience of subjection.

Conclusion

If one takes these films at face value we can see that as a body of work, Kubrick's later films repeatedly critique and undermine notions of humanist subjectivity, and more specifically, autonomous and rational will. Yet, Kubrick's films demonstrate the possibility of a will based on dependency and reaction that would abandon dreams of fusion or communion in favor of a celebration of otherness. In this analysis we have examined how Kubrick's later films unhinge reason and truth, diminishing the utility of both. In so doing, rather than establishing a world in which the human will is the sole creator and measure of all things, Kubrick's characters develop agency only as response to subjection and otherness. In radical contrast to Spielberg's characters, who can act independently upon a world largely subject to their will, for Kubrick, it is we who are subjected. Yet, in being so subjected we are given the very possibility for choice and action. In all his later films, Kubrick grapples with the problem of how one can exist after the death of the humanist subject. As Norman Kagan put it, Kubrick's work is about "finding a third alternative to impotent weakness or the corruption of power."[26] In this context it is a third alternative to the choice of either a world of determinism or one of unfettered human will. As a body of philosophical work, Kubrick's films become a sort of phenomenology of antihumanist subjectivity.

In reacquiring a sense of agency in the reactive space of subjection, Kubrick's characters give us an antihumanism that is decidedly not antihuman. In fact, it moves the limits and possibilities for freedoms from transcendental or metaphysical principles of reason, truth, and right, relocating these limitations and openings for action in the lived world. As Kagan notes, the humanist pursuit of "some uncorrupt personal purpose or meaning in life" in Kubrick's world is destructive, damaging to the individual and the lived world.[27] The antihumanism of Kubrick's movies revives the possibility of politics and social existence without returning to the kind of humanist values and faiths that motivate Spielberg and so many other contemporary filmmakers. In response to our lived experiences of subjection, we can ask what choices and freedoms are facilitated by the constraints and structures within which we live. In what ways are new freedoms, new ways of being, and new choices enabled by a particular event or type of subjection?

It is in this space of the reactive will, the will-as-subjected, that Kubrick's later work empowers us to live creatively in the (post)modern world of discipline and subjection rather than merely bemoaning our alienation or the loss of some previous grand faith in the goodness of human nature. Kubrick's work expresses a possibility for thinking, willing, and being after we have found that the fantastic promises of humanism have produced dystopias more like the worlds of *Dr. Strangelove, A Clockwork Orange,* and *Full Metal Jacket* than Spielberg's wonderlands of *E.T., Indiana Jones, Jurassic Park,* and even *A.I.*

NOTES

1. For just a few such reviews, see Peter Bradshaw, "Drowning by Numbers," *Guardian* (Manchester), Sept. 21, 2001, sect. Friday, 12; Mick LaSalle, "*A.I.* Is Spielberg, Kubrick at Worst," *San Francisco Chronicle,* March 8, 2002, D10; John Patterson, "Bad Bedfellows: Spielberg Directing Kubrick Spells Disaster," *Guardian* (Manchester), July 2, 2001, sect. 2, 14.

2. Patterson, "Bad Bedfellows," 14.

3. For examples, see Ann Hornday, "Revising Movie History," *Sun (Baltimore),* Nov. 30, 1997, sect. Art, 1E; and Paul Whitelaw, "Love at First Bite," *Scotsman,* June 15, 2000, 12.

4. Kate Soper, *Humanism and Anti-Humanism* (La Salle, IN: Open Court, 1986), 11.

5. Ibid., 11–12.

6. Reiner Schurman, *Heidegger on Being and Acting: From Principles to Anarchy* (Bloomington: Indiana University Press, 1987), 45.

7. For example, see Tony Pipolo, "The Modernist and the Misanthrope: The Cinema of Stanley Kubrick," *Cineaste* 27 (2002): 4–15, 49.

8. Robert Kolker, *A Cinema of Loneliness: Penn, Stone, Kubrick, Scorsese, Spielberg, Altman,* 3rd ed. (Oxford: Oxford University Press, 2000), 106.

9. Lee Siegel, "*Eyes Wide Shut:* What the Critics Failed to See in Kubrick's Last Film," *Harper's Magazine,* October 1999, 78.

10. Marco Abel, "*Fargo:* The Violent Production of the Masochistic Contract as Cinematic Concept," *Critical Studies in Mass Communication* 16 (1999): 310.

11. Gerri Reaves, "From Hasford's *The Short Timers* to Kubrick's *Full Metal Jacket:* The Fracturing of Identification," *Film/Literature Quarterly* 16 (1988): 233.

12. Janet C. Moore, "For Fighting and for Fun: Kubrick's Complicitous Critique in *Full Metal Jacket,*" *Velvet Light Trap* 31 (1993): 44.

13. Stefan Mattessich, "Grotesque Caricature: Stanley Kubrick's *Eyes Wide Shut* as the Allegory of Its Own Reception," *Postmodern Culture* 10.2 (2001), np.

14. Reaves, "From Hasford's," 236.

15. Karen Rasmussen and Sharon D. Downey, "Dialectical Disorientation in Vietnam War Films: Subversion of the Mythology of War," *Quarterly Journal of Speech* 77 (1991): 188.

16. Christopher Hoile, "The Uncanny and the Fairy Tale in Kubrick's *The Shining,*" *Film/Literature Quarterly* 12 (1984): 11.

17. Pat J. Gehrke, "Deviant Subjects in Foucault and *A Clockwork Orange:* Congruent Critiques of Criminological Constructions of Subjectivity," *Critical Studies in Media Communication* 18 (2001): 270–84, and in this volume, 146–64.

18. Moore, "For Fighting," 41.

19. Reaves, "From Hasford's," 232.

20. Dale E. Williams, "*2001: A Space Odyssey:* A Warning Before Its Time," *Critical Studies in Mass Communication* 1 (1984): 321

21. Paul Miers, "The Black Maria Rides Again: Being a Reflection on the Present State of American Film with Special Respect to Stanley Kubrick's *The Shining,*" *MLN* 95 (1980): 1364.

22. Mattessich "Grotesque Caricature," 8.

23. Siegel, "Eyes Wide Shut," 80.

24. Mattessich, "Grotesque Caricature," 10.

25. Paula Willoquet-Maricondi, "Full-Metal-Jacketing, or Masculinity in the Making," *Cinema Journal* 33 (1994): 19, and in this volume, 218–41.

26. Norman Kagan, *The Cinema of Stanley Kubrick,* 3rd ed. (New York: Continuum Publishing, 1989), 233.

27. Ibid.

2001

A Cold Descent

MARK CRISPIN MILLER

MR. KUBRICK: My pupils are still dilated, and my breathing sounds
like your soundtrack. I don't know if this poor brain will survive another
work of the magnitude of 2001, but it will die (perhaps more accurately
"go nova") happily if given the opportunity: Whenever anybody asks me
for a description of the movie, I tell them that it is, in sequential order:
anthropological, camp, McLuhan, cybernetic, psychedelic, religious.
That shakes them up a lot. Jesus, man, where did you get that incredibly
good technical advice? Whenever I see the sun behind a round sign, I
start whistling *Thus Spake Zarathustra*. My kettledrum impression draws
the strangest looks.

DEAR MR. KUBRICK: Although I have my doubts that your eyes will
ever see this writing, I still have hopes that some secretary will neglect to
dispose of my letter. I have just seen your motion picture and I believe—
please, words, don't fail me now—that I have never been so moved by a
film—so impressed—awed—etc. The music was absolutely on a zenith.
The Blue Danube really belonged in some strange way, and the main
theme with its building crescendos was more beautiful than John
Lennon's "I Am the Walrus" and from me that's a compliment. The
story in *Life* magazine, of course, showed the most routine scenes, as
Life has a tendency to eliminate any overwhelming virtue in a motion
picture, and the three best scenes were lumped together and were almost
unrecognizable. But lest I run off at the mouth, let me conclude by
saying that if the ill-voted Oscars doesn't give you a multitude of awards
in 1969, I will resign from humanity and become a soldier.

It is, at least to me, the first movie to be a true art form. It is one of the few truths I have experienced in my lifetime that has left such a strong impression. I mean more than an impression—it is constantly on my mind and has loosened some of my prejudices.

For the life of me, I cannot understand why the critics (all of which I read when they reviewed the film) haven't stood up and shouted with enthusiasm in their reviews. Sadly, I have come to the conclusion that for so many years films were made for the 12-year-old mind that at last, alas, our critics have emerged with 12-year-old minds. Pity.

I am 14 and loved every minute of 2001. Anybody who says it was dull is an idiot. How can a movie so different, like 2001, be dull. Oh, well, some people are dumb.

Some thirty years after the release of Stanley Kubrick's masterpiece, such fan mail has an unintended poignancy—in part (but only in part) because the letters are so obviously dated. Those fierce accolades are pure sixties. To reread such letters now—and Jerome Agel's 1970 *The Making of Kubrick's 2001*, the ecstatic, crazed homage that includes them—is to look back on a cultural moment that now seems as remote from our own as, say, those hairy screamers of prehistory, erect with murderous purpose at the water hole, might seem from the low-key Dr. Heywood R. Floyd, unconscious on his umpteenth voyage to the moon.

The film's first devotees were knocked out, understandably, by its "incredible and irrevocable splendor" (as another letter-writer phrased it). Others—also understandably—were troubled, or infuriated, by the film's disturbing intimation that, since "the dawn of man" so many, many centuries ago, the human race has gotten nowhere fast. That subversive notion is legible not only in the famous match cut from the sunlit bone to the nocturnal spacecraft (two tools, same deadly white, both descending) but throughout the first two sections of the narrative. Indeed, the negation of the myth of progress may be the film's basic structural principle. Between the starved and bickering apes and their smooth, affable descendants we can discern all sorts of broad distinctions, but there is finally not much difference—an oblique, uncanny similarity that recurs in every human action represented.

In *2001*, for example, the men feed unenthusiastically on ersatz sandwiches and steaming pads of brightly colored mush—edibles completely processed, heated imperceptibly, cooled down, and very slowly masticated, as opposed to the raw flesh bolted furtively by the now carnivorous apes; and yet both flesh and mush appear unappetizing, and both are eaten purely out of need. Similarly, in *2001* the men are just as wary and belligerent, and just as quick to square off against tribal enemies, as their tense, shrieking forebears—although, as well-trained professionals and efficient servants of the state, they confront the others not with piercing screams and menacing gestures but by abruptly turning very still and speaking very quietly and slowly: "I'm . . . sorry, Dr. Smyslov, but, uh . . . I'm really not at liberty to discuss this . . ." Thus Dr. Floyd, although seated in an attitude of friendly languor (legs limply crossed, hands hidden in his lap), fights off his too-inquisitive Soviet counterpart just as staunchly as, eons earlier, the armed apes had crushed their rivals at the water hole (which recurs here as a small round plastic table bearing drinks, and again the locus of contention). Now, as then, the victor obviously wields a handy instrument of his authority (although this time it's a briefcase, not a femur); and now, as then, the females merely look on as the males fight it out. (There is no matriarchal element in Kubrick's myth.)

More generally, the scientists and bureaucrats, and the comely corporate personnel who serve them (polite young ladies dressed in pink or white), are all sealed off—necessarily—from the surrounding vastness: and here too the cool world of *2001* seems wholly unlike, yet is profoundly reminiscent of, the arid world where all began. Back then, the earthlings would seek refuge from the predatory dangers of the night by wedging themselves tightly into certain natural hiding places, and even in daylight would never wander far from that found "home" or from one another, even though the world—such as it was—lay all around them. Likewise, their remote descendants are all holed up against the infinite and its dangers—not in terror any more (they seem, until recently, to have forgotten terror), and surely not in rocky niches (their habitats are state creations, quietly co-run by Hilton, Bell, and Howard Johnson), but in a like state of isolation in the very midst of seeming boundlessness.

Herein the world of *2001* recalls the prehistoric world before the monolith gives "man" his first idea. Once that revelation comes, the species is no longer stuck in place. Made strong by their new carnivorous diet, and with their hands now mainly used to smash and grab, the ape-men have already visibly outgrown their former quadrupedal posture (they are standing, for the first time, when they come back to the water hole), and so are ready to move on. "A new animal was abroad on the planet, spreading slowly out from the African Heartland," writes Arthur C. Clarke in his novelization of the film—which, of course, elides that historic episode, along with all the rest of human history, thereby taking us from one great dusk directly to another. When "Moon-Watcher" (as Clarke calls him) exultantly flings his natural cudgel high into the air, that reckless gesture is the film's only image of abandon and its last "human" moment of potentiality—for, as the match cut tells us, it's all downhill from there.

And yet, although the film takes us straight from one twilight moment to another, the first is very different from the next. Indeed, the two are almost perfect opposites. At first, humankind nearly dies out because there is no science, no technology: no one knows how to make anything, and so those feeble simians cannot fight off the big cats, bring down the nutritious pigs, take over fertile territory, set up proper shelters and otherwise proceed to clear away the obstacles, and wipe out the extremes of mere nature through that gradual subjection turning into men. And yet that long, enlightened course of ours (the film suggests) has only brought us back to something too much like the terminus we once escaped—only this time it is not the forces of mere nature (instincts and elements) that threaten to unmake us but the very instrumentality that originally saved us. In *2001*, in other words, there is too much science, too much made, the all-pervasive product now degrading us almost as nature used to do. The match cut tells us not just that we're on the downswing once again but that, this time, what has reduced us is our absolute containment by, and for the sake of, our own efficient apparatus. Hence Dr. Floyd is strapped inside one such sinking ship and is quite unconscious of it, whereas Moon-Watcher simply used his weapon and did so with his eyes wide open. That first image of the dozing scientist is a transcendent bit of satire, brilliantly implying just how thoroughly man has been unmade—stupefied, deprived, bereft—by the smart things of his own making: a falling-off, and/ or quasi-reversion, imperceptible except through critical contrast with the states that had preceded it.

Emboldened by hard protein, the apes at once start making war—mankind's first form of organized amusement, Kubrick suggests, and (as all his films suggest) one whose attraction can never be overcome by the grandiose advance of "civilization." On the contrary: In Kubrick's universe, the modern state is itself a vast war machine, an enormous engine of displaced (male) aggression whose purpose is to keep itself erect by absorbing the instinctual energies of all and diverting them into some gross spectacular assault against the other. These lethal—and also suicidal—strikes are carried out by the lowliest members of the state's forces (the infantry, the droogs, the grunts; "King" Kong, Jack Torrance) against an unseen enemy, and/or —ultimately—some isolated woman, while those at the rear, and at the top, sit back and take vicarious pleasure in the rout. There is, in other words, a stark division of labor in that cold, brilliant, repetitious world of jails and palaces, hospitals and battlefields. It is the function of the lowly to express— within strict limits, and only at appointed times and places—the bestial animus that has long since been repressed and stigmatized, and that (there- fore) so preoccupies the rest of us. Thus Alex's droogs, the grunts under Cowboy's brief command, and the doomed Jack Torrance all revert, as they move in on their respective prey, to the hunched and crouching gait of their first ancestors sneaking toward the water hole.

Meanwhile, it is the privilege of those at the top—"the best people," as certain characters in *Barry Lyndon* and *The Shining* term them—to sit and (sometimes literally) look down on all that gruesome monkey business, sometimes pretending loudly to deplore it, yet always quietly enjoying it (whether or not they have themselves arranged it in the first place.). Such animal exertion is, for them, a crucial spectatorial delight, as long as it happens well outside their own splendid confines—at the front, or in the ring, or in some remote suburban house, or in the servant's quarters at the Overlook, or in the ruins of Vietnam. (In the desublimated plutocratic underworld of *Eyes Wide Shut,* actors and spectators grimly and oblivi- ously merge, and the sport can take place either in majestic hideaways, well-guarded and remote, or in one's own luxurious bathroom.)

When, on the other hand, someone goes completely ape right there among the members of the audience, that feral show is not at all a plea- sure but an indecorum gross and shattering—whether played as farce, like General Turgidson's clumsy tussle with the Soviet ambassador in *Dr. Strange- love* ("Gentlemen, you can't fight in here! This is the War Room!"), or as a grotesque lapse, like Barry Lyndon's wild and ruinous attack on his con- temptuous stepson. Such internal outbursts threaten "the best people" very deeply: not only by intimating a rebellious violence that might one day destroy them, and their creatures, from without (as nearly happens to Marcus Crassus in *Spartacus*, or as happens to Sgt. Hartman in *Full Metal Jacket*) but by reminding those pale, cordial masters that, although they like to see themselves as hovering high above the brutal impulse, they them- selves still have it in them. That rude reminder the pale masters cannot tol- erate, for their very self-conception and their power, is based directly on the myth of total difference between themselves and those beneath them.

It is the various troops and thugs, those down and out there on the ground, who do the lethal simian dance, because they are primitives. We who do our work in chairs, observing those beneath us, setting them up for this or that ordeal and then watching as they agonize, are therefore beings of a higher order, through this sedentary act confirming our "humanity."

Dr. Heywood Floyd is just such a "human" being. If he never appears gazing coolly down on others as they suffer, as do the generals in *Paths of Glory* or the Ludovico experts in *A Clockwork Orange,* that omission does not connote any relative kindness but is merely one reflection of his total separation from reality: Dr. Floyd never callously looks down on suffering because, within his bright, closed universe-within-a-universe, there *is* no suffering—not any physical intensity or emotional display of any kind—for him to look down on. For that matter, the doctor never really looks at anything, or anyone, until the climax of his top-secret visit to the moon, when he looks intently at the monolith, and even touches it (or tries to). Prior to that uncanny action, the scientist's gaze is, unless opaque (as it becomes in his brief "fight" with Smyslov), consistently casual, affable, and bored, the same pleasant managerial mask whether it confronts some actual stranger's face, the video image of his daughter's face, or the all-too-familiar prospect of a synthetic sandwich.

Although he floats, throughout, at an absolute remove from any site of others' gratifying pain, Dr. Floyd is nonetheless inclined, like all his peers in Kubrick's films, to see himself as definitively placed above the simian horde—which is, in his case, not just some cowering division or restive troupe of gladiators but his own planet's entire population. As he would presume himself in every way superior to the protomen of eons back, so does he presume himself—and of course the Council, which he represents—far superior to his fellow beings way back "down" (as he persists in putting it) on Earth. Those masses, he argues, need to be protected from the jarring news that there might be another thinking species out there—hence "the need for absolute secrecy in this": "I'm sure you're all aware of the extremely grave potential for cultural shock and social disorientation contained in this present situation," he tells the staff at Clavius, "if the facts were suddenly made public without adequate preparation and conditioning." That last proviso makes it clear that Dr. Floyd is, in fact, ideologically a close relation to those other, creepier doctors at the Ludovico Institute; the whole euphemistic warning of "potential cultural shock" betrays his full membership of that cold, invisible elite who run the show in nearly all Kubrick's films, concerned with nothing but the preservation of their own power. Surely, what the bureaucrat imagines happening "if the facts were suddenly made public" would be uncannily like what we have already seen back at "the Dawn of Man": everybody terrified at first, and then, perhaps, the smart ones putting two and two together and moving, quickly, to knock off those bullying others who have monopolized what everybody needs— "the facts" having instantly subverted those others' ancient claims to absolute supremacy (a revolutionary possibility that Kubrick, for his part, seems unlikely to have entertained).

The film itself is thus subversive, indirectly questioning the doctor's representative "humanity" through satiric contrast with his grunting antecedents. At first, the safe and slumbering Heywood Floyd seems merely antithetical to the ready, raging apes. Whereas those primates—once they have tasted meat, then blood—were all potential, standing taut and upright at the water hole, their leader fiercely beckoning them forward, Dr. Floyd is placid, sacked out, slack; as smooth of face as they were rough and hairy, as still as they were noisy and frenetic, as fully dressed (zipped up and buckled in) as they were bare—and, above or underneath it all, as soft as they were hard. If they were the first exemplars of the new and savage species *Homo occidens* (and only secondarily, if at all, fit to be titled *Homo sapiens*), the scientist, unconscious in his perfect chair, exemplifies the old and ravaged species *Homo sedens*. As he dozes comfortably, his weightless arm bobs slow and flaccid at this side, his hand hangs lax, while his sophisticated pen floats like a mini-spacecraft in the air beside him. It is a comic image of advanced detumescence, effective castration—as opposed (or so it seems) to the heroic shots of Moon-Watcher triumphing in "his" new knowledge of the deadly and yet death-defying instrument; his sinewy arm raised high, his grip tight, his tool in place, he seems to roar in ecstasy as he pulverizes the bones lying all around him ("Death, thou shalt die!"), and the pigs crash lifeless to the ground, as limp as Dr. Floyd looks minutes later.

Although seemingly so different from the simians, however, the doctor is not only their enfeebled scion but also, deep down, their brother in aggressiveness; a relation only gradually perceptible in his various muted repetitions of the apes' outright behaviors. As his subdued showdown with the Soviets recalls the frenzied action at the water hole, so does his mystified authority recall Moon-Watcher's balder primacy, the scientist relying not, of course, on screaming violence to best his enemies and rally his subordinates but on certain quiet managerial techniques (body language, tactical displays of informality, and so on). His inferiors are just as abject

toward him as Moon-Watcher's were toward that head monkey, although
the later entities display their deference toward the manager not, certainly,
by crouching next to him and combing through his hair for nits, but just
by sucking up to him, placating him with nervous, eager smiles, and stroking
him with witless praises, "Y'know, that was an excellent speech you gave
us, Heywood!" "It certainly was!" "I'm sure it beefed up morale a helluva
lot!" In such dim echoes of the apes' harsh ur-society we can discern the
lingering note of their belligerence—just as we can still perceive their war-
like attitude throughout the antiseptic world of their descendants, who are
still cooped up in virtual fortresses and still locked into an arrangement at
once rigidly hierarchical and numbingly conformist, the clean men as difficult to tell apart as were their hunched hairy forebears.

Thus is the primal animus still here; indeed, it is now more dangerous
than ever, warfare having evolved from heated manual combat to the cool
deployment of orbiting atomic weapons (one of which sails gently by as
The Blue Danube begins). Yet while the animus has taken on apocalyptic
force, its expression among human beings is (paradoxically, perhaps) oblique,
suppressed, symbolic, offering none even of that crude delight that the near-
anhedonic simians had known: the thrill of victory (as the sportscasters
often put it), and, inextricable from that, the base kinetic entertainment of
(as Alex often puts it) "the old ultra-violence." Such overt and bestial pleasures have been eliminated from the computerized supraworld of the
Council and its employees (although not from life back "down" on Earth,
as *A Clockwork Orange* will, from its very opening shot, remind us). Just as
the animal appetite has been, in those white spaces, ruthlessly denied, so
have all other pleasures, which in Kubrick's universe (as in Nietzsche's and
in Freud's) derive straight from that ferocious source. In the world of Dr.
Heywood Floyd, it is only the machines that dance and couple, man having had even his desires absorbed into the apparatus that we thought was
meant to gratify them.

As *The Blue Danube* starts to play, its old, elegant cadences rising and
falling so oddly and charmingly against this sudden massive earthrise, the
various spacecraft floating by as if in heavenly tranquility, there is, of course,
no human figure in the game—nor should there be, for in this "machine
ballet" (as Kubrick has called it) live men and women have no place. Out
here, and at this terminal moment, all human suppleness, agility, and
lightness, all our bodily allure, have somehow been transferred to those
exquisite gadgets. Thus the hypnotic circularity of Strauss's waltz applies
not to the euphoric roundabout of any dancing couple but to the even

wheeling of that big space station. And thus, while those transcendent items sail through the void with the supernal grace of seraphim, the stewardess attending Dr. Floyd staggers down the aisle as if she's had a stroke, the zero gravity and her smart "grip shoes" giving her solicitous approach the absurd look of inept ballet.

Her image connotes not only an aesthetic decline (Kubrick had idealized the ballerina-as-artist in his early *Killer's Kiss*) but a pervasive sexual repression. With the machines doing all the dancing, bodies are erotically dysfunctional—an incapacity suggested by Kubrick's travesties of dance. In *A Clockwork Orange,* he would again present a gross parody of ballet, in the scene at the derelict casino, where Billy-boy's droogs, getting ready to gang-rape the "weepy young devotchka," sway and wrestle with her on the stage, their ugly unity and her pale struggle in their midst suggesting a balletic climax turned to nightmare: Eros is negated crudely by male violence. In *2001,* the mock ballet implies no mere assault on the erotic but its virtual extirpation, its near-superannuation in the world of the machine. Here, every pleasurable impulse must be channeled into the efficient maintenance of that machine, which therefore exerts as inhibitive an influence as any fierce religion. Stumbling down the aisle, the stewardess—in her stiff white pantsuit and round white padded hat designed to cushion blows against the ceiling—looks like a sort of corporate nun, all female attributes well hidden. And so it is appropriate that, as she descends on the unconscious Dr. Floyd, her slow approach does not recall, say, Venus coming down on her Adonis, but suggests instead a porter checking on a loose piece of cargo as she grabs his floating pen and reattaches it to his oblivious trunk.

The stewardess dances not a fantasy of some delightful respite from the waking world, but only further service to, and preparation for, that world. Likewise, *The Blue Danube* refers not to the old sexual exhilaration of (to quote Lord Byron) the "seductive waltz," but only to the smooth congress of immense machines. As Dr. Floyd slumps in his chair, the flight attendant reattaching his loose implement, the very craft that holds them both (a slender, pointed shuttle named *Orion*) is itself approaching, then slides with absolute precision into, the great bright slit at the perfect center of the circular space station, the vehicles commingling as they do throughout the film—and as the living characters do not, as far as we can see. *Orion* having finally "docked," the waltz comes to its triumphant close—and Kubrick cuts on that last note, to an off-white plastic grid, an automatic portal sliding open with a long dull whirr. There first appears, seated stiffly in the circular compartment, another stewardess, a shapely and impassive blonde dressed all in pink and manning the controls; and then, two seats away from her, there again is Dr. Floyd, now wide awake and holding his big briefcase up across his lap like a protective shield. He zips it shut. "Here you are, sir" she says politely (and ambiguously). "Main level, please." "All right" he answers, getting up. "See you on the way back."

The human characters are thus maintained—through their very posture and deportment, the layout of the chill interiors, their meaningless reflexive courtesies—in total separation from each other, within (and for the sake of) their machines, which meanwhile interpenetrate as freely as Miltonic angels. And yet there is a deeply buried hint that even up in these hermetic spaces, people are still sneaking off to do the deed. "A blue, lady's cashmere sweater has been found in the restroom," a robotic female voice announces, twice, over the space station's PA system just after Dr. Floyd's arrival. That abandoned sweater may well be the evidence of the same sort of furtive quickie that takes place in General Turgidson's motel room in *Dr Strangelove,* or that, in *A Clockwork Orange,* a doctor and nurse enjoy behind the curtains of a hospital bed while Alex lies half-dead nearby. Given Kubrick's penchant for self-reference, it may be that, in conceiving that aside about the cashmere sweater, he had in mind the moment in *Lolita* when Charlotte Haze, speaking to her wayward daughter on the telephone (the nymphet having been exiled for the summer to Camp Climax), querulously echoes this suspicious news: "You lost your new sweater? . . . In the woods?"

Such details reveal yet another crucial similarity between the simian and human worlds of *2001.* For all the naturalness of their state before the monolith, we never see the apes attempting sex, although we see them trying to find food, to get some sleep, to fight their enemies. That gap in Kubrick's overview of their condition is surely not a consequence of prudishness (no longer a big problem by the mid-1960s), but would appear deliberate—a negative revelation of the thorough harshness of the simians' existence. The apes are simply too hungry, and too scared, to be thinking about sex, which would presumably occur among them only intermittently, in nervous one-shot bursts—much as in the world of Dr. Floyd, where everyone is much too busy for anything other than a quick bang now and then, and where there's not a decent place to do it anyway, just as there wasn't at the dawn of man.

Dr. Floyd's deprivation is not merely genital, however. If, in his asexual state he is no worse off than his simian forebears, in his continuous singleness he is far more deprived than they. For all their misery, those creatures had at least the warmth and nearness of one another—huddling in the night, there was for them at least that palpable and vivid solace. For that bond—too basic even to be called "love"—there can be no substitute, nor can it be transcended: "There are very few things in this world that have an unquestionable importance in and of themselves and are not susceptible to debate and rational argument, but the family is one of them," Kubrick once said. If man "is going to stay sane throughout (his) voyage, he must have someone to care about, something that is more important than himself."[1]

Sacked out on the shuttle, Dr. Floyd is the sole passenger aboard that special flight: literally a sign of his status and the importance of his mission, yet the image conveys not prominence but isolation. The man in the chair has only empty chairs around him, with no company other than the tottering stewardess who briefly comes to grab his pen and, on the television screen before him, another faceless couple in another smart conveyance, the two engaging in some mute love-chat (Dr. Floyd is wearing headphones) while the viewer sleeps and the living woman comes and goes. Here too the machine appears to have absorbed the very longings of the personnel who seemingly control it—for even those two mannequins, jabbering theatrically at each other's faces, have more in common with the huddling apes than does Dr. Floyd or any of his colleagues.

Whereas the apes had feared and fed together, here everyone is on the job alone. Efficient service to the state requires that parents and children, wives and husbands all stay away from one another, sometimes forever, the separation vaguely eased, or merely veiled, by the compensatory glimpses now and then available (at great expense) by telephone. For this professional class, the family is no sturdier within the "free world" than it had been under Soviet domination. "He's been doing some underwater research in the Baltic, so, uh, I'm afraid we don't get a chance to see very much of each other these days!" laughs the Russian scientist Irina, a little ruefully, when Floyd asks after her husband. Although (the unseen) Mrs. Floyd is, by contrast, still a wife and mother first and foremost, with Heywood the only wage-slave in the family, their all-American household is just as atomized as the oppressed Irina's. As we learn from Floyd's perfunctory phone chat with his daughter ("Squirt," he calls her), the members of his upscale ménage are all off doing exactly the same things that the apes had done millennia earlier, although, again, the simians did those things collectively, whereas Floyd's "home" is merely one more empty module. Mrs. Floyd, Squirt tells her father, is "gone to shopping" (charged, like Mrs. Moon-Watcher, with the feeding of her young), while Floyd himself, of course, is very far away, at work (squaring off against the nation's foes, as Moon-Watcher had done). Meanwhile, "Rachel," the woman hired to mind the daughter in their absence, is "gone to the bathroom" (that fundamental business having long since been relegated to its own spotless cell), and Squirt herself, she says, is "playing" (just as the little monkeys had been doing, except that Squirt—like her father—is alone).

Every human need is thus indirectly and laboriously served by a vast complex of arrangements—material, social, psychological—that not only takes up everybody's time but also takes us all away from one another, even as it seems to keep us all "communicating." In the adlike tableau of Dr. Floyd's brief conversation with the television image of his little girl, there is a poignancy that he cannot perceive any more than he can grasp the value of his coming home, in person, for her birthday party. "I'm very sorry about it, but I can't." he tells her evenly. "I'm gonna send you a very nice present, though." In offering her a gift to compensate her for his absence, Floyd betrays the same managerial approach to family relations that enables him to carry on, with his usual equanimity, this whole dis-embodied conversation in the first place: as far as he's concerned, that "very nice present" will make up completely for his being away, just as his mere image on the family telescreen ought to be the same thing as his being there. She, however, still appreciates the difference. When he asks what present she would like, with a child's acuity she names the only thing that might produce him for her, since it seems to be the sole means whereby he checks in at home: "A telephone." For all its underlying sadness, the scene is fraught with absurdist comedy; for that telephone is inescapable. It is not just the bright tool through which the family "communicates" but also the banal content of that "communication." Here the medium is indeed the message—and there's nothing to it. "Listen, sweetheart," says the father, having changed the subject, or so he thinks:

"I want you to tell Mummy something for me. Will you remember?"
"Yes."
"Tell Mummy that I telephoned. Okay?"
"Yes."
"And that I'll try to telephone again tomorrow. Now will you tell her that?"

(The sense of profound emptiness arising from this Pinteresque exchange persists throughout the film, but—once the story shifts to the *Discovery*—in a tone less satiric, more elegiac. The mood now becomes deeply melancholy, as the two astronauts—a pair identical and yet dissociated, like a man and his reflection—eat and sleep and exercise in absolute apartness, both from one another and from all humankind, each one as perfectly shut off within his own routine and within that mammoth twinkling orb as any of their three refrigerated crew-mates. Aboard that sad craft, every seeming dialogue—save one—is in fact a solitudinous encounter with the Mechanism: either a one-way transmission from earth, belatedly and passively received, or a "communication" prerecorded, or a sinister audience with the soft-spoken HAL, who, it seems, is always on the lookout for "his" chance to eliminate, once and for all, what Dr. Strangelove calls "unnecessary human meddling." That opportunity arises when the astronauts finally sit down, in private [or so they think], and for the first and only time talk face-to-face: an actual conversation, independent of technology and therefore a regressive move that HAL appears to punish, fittingly, by disconnecting his entire human crew—one sent careening helpless through the deeps, the three "sleeping beauties" each neatly "terminated" in his separate coffin, and the last denied readmittance to the relative warmth and safety of the mother ship. Thus HAL fulfills the paradoxical dynamic of the telephone: seeming to keep everyone "in touch," yet finally cutting everybody off.)

Too busy for erotic pleasure, as the apes had been too wretched for it, and much lonelier than those primal ancestors, Dr. Floyd is also much less sensitive than they—a being incapable of wonder, as opposed to the wild-eyed monkey-men. This human incapacity becomes apparent as the scientist very slowly, very calmly strokes—once (and with his whole self closed off in its efficient glove)—the lustrous ebon surface of the monolith, thereby both repeating and inverting the abject obeisance of his astounded forebears, crouched and screaming at its solid base, and touching at its face again and again, hands jerking back repeatedly in terror at its alienness. The men's profound insensitivity is already apparent in that first satiric tableau of the unconscious scientist, who in his (surely dreamless) slumber is as indifferent to the great sublimity around him as the tense simians were heartened by its distant lights and stirred by its expanses. Whereas the most adventurous among those older creatures might sometimes have looked beyond their own familiar niche (as Clarke's epithet "Moon-Watcher" implies), those now in charge take that "beyond" for granted, watching nothing but the little television screens before them.

On the phone to Squirt, Dr. Floyd pays no attention to the great home planet wheeling weirdly in the background, just outside the window. Here, as everywhere in *2001*, the cool man-made apparatus has lulled its passengers into a necessary unawareness of the infinite, keeping them equilibrated, calm, their heads and stomachs filled, in order to ensure that they stay poised to keep the apparatus, and themselves, on the usual blind belligerent course. Thus boxed in, they calculate, kiss ass, crack feeble jokes about the lousy food, and never think to glance outside. As the moon bus glides above the spectral crags and gullies of the lunar night, and seems to glide on past the low and ponderous pale-blue Earth, three-quarters full, the atmosphere sings eerily, exquisitely, in dissonant and breathless ululation. That is until the point of view shifts from the enormous night into the bus's close interior, with a dizzying handheld shot that slowly takes us back from the red-lit cockpit and back into the blue-lit cabin, where one of Floyd's subordinates first fetches a big bulky ice-blue "refreshment" carrier (himself in a bulky ice-blue spacesuit), then heaves it slowly back to where the head man (likewise suited) sits in regal solitude, perusing documents with Halvorsen, his second-in-command (who's dressed the same). As this shot settles us well into that snug artificial space, the atonal shrilling of the quasi-angels gradually gives way to the tranquillizing beeps and soporific whoosh of the smart bus itself, and to the stupid conversation of its passengers.

Within that ultimate cocoon, those wry little men are disinclined to think on what had come before them, or on what might lie ahead of them, but concentrate instead on their own tribal enterprise and on their own careers (and, at some length, on those sandwiches), trading bluff banalities as to the mystery awaiting them. "Heh heh. Don't suppose you have any idea what the damn thing is?" "Heh heh. Wish to hell we did. Heh heh." Such complacency endures until their instrument, the hapless "Bowman," is yanked out of their cloistral world of white and goes on his wild psychedelic ride "beyond the infinite," ending up immured again but only temporarily—and in a state promising some sort of deliverance from the human fix. At first shattered unto madness, as opposed to the others' blank composure, and then quickly wrinkled, turning white, as opposed to their uniform boyish smoothness, he finally, from his sudden death bed, reaches up and out toward, then merges with, the great dark monolith, thereby undergoing an ambiguous "rebirth."

"John Wayne, is that you?"

Living out his natural life in this cold suite, the ex-astronaut is still oblivious to his imprisonment—and to the enigmatic shrilling of those spectral entities who watch him in the cosmic zoo, or halfway house, where he has somehow ended up. Inexplicably diverted by his mere doings in that Earth-like habitat, those watchers are an audience at once reflective of, and yet also immeasurably beyond, the movie's audience, whatever year the latter did or do assemble. That spectatorial presence marks the first such audience-surrogate in Kubrick's oeuvre—although his films had all along reflected darkly on spectatorship, from *Killer's Kiss* to *Paths of Glory, Spartacus, Lolita.* The disembodied viewers at the end of *2001,* in some way taken by the human being's primitive behaviors, recur—albeit with a difference—in the malevolent ghosts who fasten on Jack Torrance in *The Shining,* chittering and whooping at the prospect of his feeding their bloodlust (and thereby giving them new life) by murdering his family. The masked voyeurs in *Eyes Wide Shut,* gathering in darkened rooms to savor the infernal spectacle of purchased beauties undergoing bestial violation, also appear as mean relations to the entities who so mysteriously gaze on Bowman in his cell. And of course there is a similar degraded hint of that unearthly viewership in *A Clockwork Orange* and *Barry Lyndon,* with their respective worlds of eminent spectators looking down upon an atavistic nastiness that they both hate and long to emulate. (Although the killers in *Full Metal Jacket* are related closely to the murderous Alex and to Redmond Barry "with his wild Irish ways," the soldiers' violence—a crucial state resource—inspires no choruses of moral condemnation.)

From *Paths of Glory* to *Eyes Wide Shut,* the human audience-within-the-film reflects uncannily on those who sit and watch the film itself, the fictive gazers mirroring the actual viewers' regressive fascination with vicarious release. And yet that superhuman audience "beyond the infinite" does not, in the end, reflect on gaping humankind—*Homo spectans*—in that subversive way. Alone among Kubrick's films, *2001,* for all its devastating satire, finally offers us a glimpse, or sense, of something other—better—than the long primordial rut of men at war, whether they have fought with clublike bones or space-based weaponry. Evolved unto the status of pure spirit, if not "God," those supernal viewers at the end of the "space odyssey" are well beyond the fray that we have always known. They have long since transcended the gratuitous aggression that drives human history, and therefore have no need for any simian underlings to do their dirty work for them, nor any backward hunger for the picturesque death-matches of low proxies. Such advancement has necessarily purged spectatorship of its age-old bad faith. Because they have no buried urge to emulate their catch, no secret wish to have him act out their desires, their gaze expresses no ferocious, guilty disapproval of his savagery. In that gaze, rather, there is something wholly new, yet also disconcertingly familiar—the sublime amusement of unprecedented gods, who laugh at mere humanity, with which they feel no empathy at all; and yet they laugh without a trace of anger or contempt, and even with a sort of glad indulgence that recalls the primal warmth and all-too-human expectation of parental love.

This Nietzschean projection may refer not just to an imagined distant future but could be taken also as a tacit invitation to a new kind of spectatorship right here on Earth. Back when the film was still big news, Kubrick talked about that worldly possibility, noting his attempt "to create a visual experience, one that bypasses verbalized pigeonholing and directly penetrates the subconscious with an emotional and philosophic content."[2] The director sought, in other words, to make a film that would reach viewers in extraordinary ways, shattering the blinkers forged by verbal formulae and abstract notions generally. In that avant-gardist effort Kubrick, although peerless, was experimenting in unconscious harmony with other cinematic geniuses at work for Hollywood. From the late sixties through the seventies—that is, between the breakdown of the studio system and the rise of the Blockbuster Era—the best American filmmakers were taking heady liberties with Hollywood's generic heritage. Thus what Stanley Kubrick did for the space opera was roughly similar to Sam Peckinpah's subversive renderings of the western, and it also looked ahead to *Chinatown*, which fractures the detective story, and to the three-part *Godfather* saga, which took the gangster film into uncharted territory, and to *Nashville*, that off-key, downbeat musical. Throughout that dazzling interim, moreover, the movies were not just generically unstable but stylistically adventurous as well. Such works variously asked us to surrender all our cinematic expectations and accept, from Hollywood, films that looked and sounded "foreign" in their structural ambitiousness, their sometime technical obscurity (Robert Altman's dense soundtracks, John Cassavetes' grainy, lurching style), their moral ambiguity, their sly self-reference, and the frequent darkness of their resolution.

In urging viewers beyond cliché, however, those films were soliciting an open-mindedness far more inclusive and momentous, than just a broadened taste in movies. The old sway of pat narratives obtained, of course, not only in the movie theaters but throughout the culture, blocking mass awareness of our nation's history and easing public acquiescence in those bloody worldwide interventions ordered by the managers of U.S. foreign policy. To move beyond the patriotic comfort of the movie mainstream was, therefore, also to open up one's eyes to the realities of history itself—and thereby to grow into real Americans, as undeluded by reactionary myth as Paine and Jefferson demanded that we be, in their enlightened efforts against "every form of tyranny over the mind of man."

At the time that skeptical imperative appeared to shed its cold light everywhere, exploding many potent myths that had for years been propagated in the schools, by government, and by the media. The jut-jawed image of the FBI—long burnished to a blinding sheen by Hoover's endless propaganda strokes (including many Cold War movies of the fifties, then ABC's *The FBI*)—was finally dented by the revelations that the bureau had played very dirty against Martin Luther King, the Black Panthers, and countless other activists both black and white. Likewise, the cowboy glamour of the CIA—concocted by the agency itself and heightened by innumerable spy novels (and also, indirectly, by the works of Ian Fleming) as well as CBS's *Mission: Impossible*—was devastated by the ugly memoirs of Phillip Agee, Frank McGehee, Joseph B. Smith, and John Stockwell, among other ravaged veterans, and also by the findings of the Church and Pike Committees in the U.S. Congress. Such bureaucratic disrepute was deeply troubling, and yet it was far less upsetting than the giant blot that Richard Nixon left upon the U.S. presidency. The tawdry contents of his secret tapes (and, later, a slow flood of memoirs, diaries, memos, still more tapes) gave the culture an iconoclastic jolt that is still shaking us. For, aside from wrecking Nixon's own laborious persona, that distasteful glimpse behind the curtain also lowered the standing of the presidency overall, by leading millions to believe that Nixon only did the sort of thing that every other president had done. (From the seventies, such mass cynicism was fed also by an avalanche of books and movies luridly debunking the idyllic fantasy of "Camelot.") And as the White House was demystified by Watergate, so was the old myth of American uprightness and benevolence blown all to hell by what was happening on the ground in southeast Asia. The myth that "we" were like the cavalry in *Stagecoach,* riding hard to save the innocent from hordes of savages, was copiously pitched by scores of politicians, military officers, and academic opportunists (and in movies like John Wayne's *The Green Berets* and John Ford's *Vietnam! Vietnam!*). In time that flattering gloss was rubbed away, to some extent by the occasional disturbing shot on television or in *Life,* but mainly by the tens of thousands of American dead, the ever-growing number of survivors suffering losses that could not be talked away. The gross discrepancy between the generals' optimistic spin and all those deaths exerted a great disenchanting power—a power augmented by the *New York Times*'s publication of the Pentagon Papers, which starkly contradicted the official line, making very clear that even those who had been hyping our impressive progress toward a smashing victory did not themselves believe a word of it. Thus, by the time the curtain fell on the makeshift "Republic of Vietnam," the war had painfully enlightened millions of Americans as to the utter groundlessness of fictions that they had believed in all their lives.

The most important films of that disorienting epoch were complex reflections on (what we might call) this great awakening. Those concerned most closely with the dark condition of America per se were duly haunted by the specter of the scheming Nixon, whose vast abuse of power inspired those matchless allegories of political corruption, *Godfather II* (Michael Corleone, Francis Coppola has said, was in fact Richard Nixon) and the terrifying *Chinatown*. More generally, the movies of that period, profoundly influenced by the pervasive sense of disappointment in official claims and dated genres, comprised a bracing visual meditation on the dismal truth behind the cracked façade. Beyond revising the heroic version of America's past and present (in films like *Soldier Blue, McCabe and Mrs. Miller, Bound for Glory, Three Days of the Condor, All the President's Men, Buffalo Bill and the Indians, Reds, The Parallax View, Who'll Stop the Rain?*), the movies challenged the well-packaged spectacle of U.S. politics (*The Candidate*), the feminine ideal sold by the advertising agencies (*The Stepford Wives*), the masculine ideal promoted by the culture overall (*Deliverance, Carnal Knowledge, Scarecrow, Alice Doesn't Live Here Anymore*), the manly theater of professional sports (*Slap Shot, North Dallas Forty*), the true-blue image of the military establishment (*The Last Detail*), the stalwart public face of the police (*The French Connection, Serpico, The Border, Cruising, Magnum Force*), the comforting PR of business corporations (*Blue Collar, Norma Rae, The China Syndrome, Coma, Silkwood*), Hollywood's own knack for glamorizing criminality (*The Panic in Needle Park, The Friends of Eddie Coyle, Klute, Mean Streets, Straight Time, Night Moves, Mikey and Nicky, Dog Day Afternoon, The Anderson Tapes, Sorcerer*), Hollywood's own history of romanticizing war (*The Wild Bunch*, the remake of *The Charge of the Light Brigade, Bring Me the Head of Alfredo Garcia, Taxi Driver, Apocalypse Now*), and finally the sunny myth of Hollywood itself, and the narcotic sway of entertainment generally (*Shampoo, The Last Tycoon, Network, Nashville, Cabaret, Rollerball*).

The shock of disillusionment that all such films reflected and expressed was something very healthy for a democratic nation of adults; but it was also an excruciating jolt, because those living through that time were not just watchful citizens of a distressed republic but also lifelong moviegoers, well-seasoned TV-viewers, and hardened veterans of the Cold War class-room. Thus they had grown up quite comfortably immersed in the regres-sive ideology of (what we might call) straight America. To be jerked up out of those dreamy depths, to have one's favorite bedtime stories traves-tied or merely complicated, is naturally traumatic—a deep rupture in one's very sense of what things mean, of where one lives, of who one is. We do not simply take in all the propaganda tales and lessons that amuse and guide us from the start, nor do they simply take us in. They function, finally, not as arguments with which one might agree or disagree completely or in part but as the monolithic building blocks of an alluring mythologic structure, which hails you inescapably with this smart pitch, or ultimatum: "Come on in, and warm yourself with everybody else, or just stay out there in the cold." We are, in short, urged to inhabit, psychologically, the tidy moral universe of propaganda; and it is not a bogus invitation, for in that place you're always in good company, and there is never any disappoint-ing news. So cozy is that mental paradise that any effort to bring down its walls can drive its inmates mad with rage.

Thus Kubrick was the most subversive filmmaker—perhaps the most subversive artist—of that epoch, although his films did not reflect directly on the dark scene of contemporary politics. Or, to be more accurate, his works were finally too subversive to re-echo the essentially political lament that resonated through so many of the other films made during that tor-mented interim. Although his vision of the power elite can certainly ac-commodate a strong political critique, Kubrick's longer, larger, and more fatalistic view of humankind is always less political than anthropological—even in *Paths of Glory, Dr. Strangelove,* and *Full Metal Jacket,* which, while dealing with atrocities that might be deemed politically preventable, imply that all of this has happened many times before, and will take place again, and yet again. In Kubrick's universe, the soldiers executed as examples, the global shower of H-bombs, and the doomed grunts in Vietnam point only secondarily to specific economic and/or sociopolitical arrangements—which, by contrast, are the tacit focus of more conventional protest movies, such as *Gallipoli, Fail-Safe,* and *Platoon.* In their various ways, Kubrick's stories all reflect primarily on the human plight as he perceives it. That plight seems impervious to revolution or reform; for either of those remedies presumes that progress is a possibility, whereas Kubrick appears to see it as just one more myth that mankind uses to screen out the void. Remini-scent of the pessimist philosophies of Burckhardt, Nietzsche, and Ortega, the director's baleful view of progress is (of course) as threatening to progressives as it is to the anti- or nonleftist teleologies of Christian doctrine, Hegel, Tocqueville, Henry Ford, Bruce Barton, Ronald Reagan, Bill Gates, and George W. Bush. Likewise, Kubrick's view of man holds little comfort for believers or for humanists, for Marxists or reactionaries, his films depicting that anomalous entity as neither bestial nor heroic but as a being part ape (by nature) and (by social inclination) part machine, yet also capable of beauty, if the animal within is free to yawp (and not trained by the power elite to murder on command). Nor does Kubrick see much promise in the works of man, which tend, in his films, not so much to better life as to absorb and mute it. Having come of age during World War II, he had observed—along with Orwell, Horkheimer, and Adorno, among others—the absolute perversion of man's gifts for grand accomplishment and rational precision in such ingenious systems as the death camp, the modern propaganda state, and the atomic bomb. That perception may have given rise to, or encouraged, Kubrick's vision of man's most imposing structures—the War Room, the *Discovery*, the Ludovico Institute, the Lyndon "home," the Overlook, the cavernous retreats in *Eyes Wide Shut*—as gleaming monuments of death. Sepuchral in themselves, and as majestic as the busy men inside them are affectless, bland, and hard to tell apart, those edifices seem to have grown powerful by sucking all the life from their inhabitants.

And so, however grim the endings of *Godfather II, The Stepford Wives, Nashville, The Last Detail,* and *Chinatown,* such nightmare visions of political surrender are less troubling than the deeper, darker questions raised by Kubrick's films in general, and by *2001* in particular: What is "man," anyway? A being really capable of change? Can we—and should we—finally rise above the animal within? Can anything made by us really make things better for us? Especially in a nation based on the Enlightenment ideal of endless progress, smitten by the mythos of heroic individualism, and largely certain that all problems can be solved by gadgets, drugs, or other goods, such questions finally cut too deep. Only from the late sixties through the seventies, that strange interlude of national skepticism, could such a movie as *2001* inspire the sort of general euphoria that greeted its release. As that period wound down, giving way to a protracted countermovement (still ongoing) of political and cultural reaction, *2001* lost much of its disquieting allure, in part because it had become an object of oblique revision by filmmakers inclined not to unsettle viewers but to comfort them, in service to the mammoth entertainment industry then starting to take shape.

That revision was but one expression of the Great Lurch Backward promoted by the Reagan Era—a broad reaction that first became apparent during (and, in part, against) the Carter presidency. Especially from 1980, mass
disapproval of the war in Vietnam was bitterly contested by reactionary
fantasists. That nostalgic reassertion of old myth came up in, for example,
Reagan's public utterances (he called the war "a noble cause" from 1980
on); and in the revanchist furor sparked in 1982 by Maya Lin's antitrium-
phalist war memorial (which outcry led to the addition, near the site, of
Frederick Hart's "Three Soldiers," a more traditional heroic sculpture);
and in movies like *Missing in Action* (1984), starring Chuck Norris, karate
master to the stars, and *Rambo: First Blood II* (1985), in which Sylvester
Stallone—having asked, "Do we get to win this time?"—goes back and
refights the war all by himself and does sort of win it, thereby both negat-
ing that war's actual history and repudiating all those somber and tor-
mented films that came before. And as such stirring propaganda quickly
overcame, in many minds, the queasy memories of My Lai, Kim Phuc, and
the Tet Offensive, the media too seemed imperceptibly to back away from
its brief show of adversary coverage (which was in fact an early aberration
in the history of American journalism). Where it had—temporarily—been
probing, it was now, once more, applauding, thereby ensuring that there
would be no more Vietnams or Watergates, however grave the latest scandal or gratuitous the latest war. Thus the invasions of Grenada and of
Panama, and then Iraq, were strenuously hailed from start to finish, and
in each case the lethal accidents and errors—and, in the Gulf, war crimes—
were misreported, underplayed, or whited out. And thus the Iran/contra
scandal, although more serious by far than Watergate, was only casually in-
vestigated by reporters (and the Democrats), who had also overlooked
the early crimes of Reagan/Bush ("debategate," "the October Surprise").
Thus did the press, as if badly rattled by the recent surge of mass icono-
clasm, now appear to reconfirm, whenever possible, the old mythology
of U.S. national goodness, special presidential wisdom, and the rightness
and efficiency (and, most absurdly, the infrequency) of U.S. military actions
overseas.

Hollywood too joined in the general retreat. Especially from the 1980s
(and the trend continues still), the movies sought to reconfirm the propaganda verities of yesteryear, by lightening up the tragic and satiric movies
of the past. Film after film came out as an ostensible homage to some troubling classic, only to reveal itself as a slick negation of the prior film, its very

adaptation merely a nostalgic gimmick, and with the memorable climax of the hard original replaced with a preposterous happy ending. Thus *Chinatown* (1974) was gigglingly revised as *Who Framed Roger Rabbit?* (1988), and Woody Allen's bleak *Manhattan* (1979) was scrupulously bowdlerized by Rob Reiner for his sugary romantic would-be comedy *When Harry Met Sally . . .* (1989), and Alfred Hitchcock's tense homoerotic thriller *Strangers on a Train* (1951) was straightened up into the funny and unthreatening *Throw Momma from the Train* (1987), and Jean Renoir's wry *Boudu Saved from Drowning* (1932) was sentimentalized as Paul Mazursky's cuddly *Down and Out in Beverly Hills* (1986), and Nicholas Ray's despairing *Rebel Without a Cause* (1955) was pumped up with amphetamines and made to dance as *Footloose* (1984), and Robert Rossen's downbeat parable *The Hustler* (1961) was optimistically revisited, its moral pith removed, as Martin Scorsese's *The Color of Money* (1986), which ends as a mere comeback allegory for old movie stars. Throughout that epoch of revision there was— is—nothing sacred in the history of cinema. Even the Odessa Steps sequence in Eisenstein's *Potemkin* (1925), still a hellish vision of authoritarian atrocity, recurs as a cute bit in *The Untouchables* (1987), with the baby in the runaway perambulator rescued by the government police; and, throughout this long regressive era, the matchless *Psycho,* Hitchcock's hardest challenge to his audience, has been made viewer-friendly time and time again, either in films— like *Silence of the Lambs* (1991) and *Hannibal* (2001)—that subtly glamorize the serial killer, or those—like *Psycho II* (1983), *Psycho III* (1986), and countless other semicomic slasher films—that frankly ironize the horror, keeping us protected from it by permitting us to squeal at it as of it were some great gut-wrenching theme-park ride.

This weakling climate is especially inhospitable to Kubrick's tough worldview. Of late his works have been disarmingly repackaged for us, their essential sting removed. Thus *Independence Day* (1996) alludes to the apocalyptic climax (both literal and narrative) of *Dr. Strangelove;* but the moment turns that most subversive shot into a dose of patriotic sedative. Major Kong's orgasmic ride down to annihilation—the Texas flyboy blissfully astride the great H-bomb as if it were the ultimate wild bronco, or a huge prosthetic hard-on—is an image capturing unforgettably the auto-destruct mechanism built deep into the vast and intricate machine of "national security." In Fox's sci-fi blockbuster, that shot recurs as a mere trite salute to soldierly self-sacrifice—the alcoholic pilot flying his atomic megapayload down into the aliens' mother ship, to save the world from devastation (and, of course, redeem himself). Similarly, in 1997 ABC-TV came out with Stephen King's own very long and wholly uncompelling version of *The Shining*, which straightens out the movie's cryptic narrative design, and does away with Kubrick's dark reflections—on the viewers, on human-kind, on Western history—in favor of eye-popping effects and much ham-handed psychologizing. Then there was Adrian Lyne's regressive, overhyped *Lolita* (1997). Kubrick's sly retelling of Nabokov's story ventures bravely onto sacred ground, scoring the conformist ethic, the hypocrisy of moral expertise, the dangers of canned fantasy, and other features of America, ca. 1962 (and, indeed, ca. 2006). Far from pointing back at us, Lyne's film is intently crammed with passé period detail, its every frame invoking an "America" that's heavily—and therefore safely—dated. And while its look is ultra-1947, the movie's sexual theatrics are pure nineties, its lithe little Lo a perfectly postmodern hot pants, eager to hump Hum, chew fiercely on his tongue, and give him head. Where Kubrick had at once idealized and eroticized Sue Lyon, portraying her Lolita as a sort of cinematic icon in the hero's humdrum life, Lyne uses Dominique Swain primarily to titil-late, and so devised, for all its "literary" gloss, a piece of porn.

And yet this retrospective drive to soften Kubrick's difficult world-view is not a recent thing, for it had started at an earlier moment in the epoch of revision. Indeed, this epoch more or less began with a high-profile effort to white out the disconcerting parts of Kubrick's vision. Soon after *Jaws* came out in 1975, demonstrating the colossal benefits of blockbuster mar-keting, Hollywood released a careful range of formulaic crowd-pleasers, which spelled the end of the extraordinary cinematic interval that had, from the late sixties, jolted and informed the culture. What those big new releases had in common was a blatant bid to take their viewers back into those happy days that had allegedly predated Dealey Plaza and the Beatles. There was *Superman* (1978), which, while gently ironizing that best-loved comic-book superhero, still left him with enough charisma to sustain a franchise well into the Reagan years. *Rocky* (1976) tapped the same nostal-gic impulse, its winning fable of the Little Ethnic Who Could also power-ing many sequels up to 1990. (With its jubilant finale and bright view of boxing as a sport remarkably untainted by corruption, like croquet, Rocky is itself a syrupy revision of such gray parables as *Body and Soul*, *Champion*, *Requiem for a Heavyweight*; the boxing genre having always been the gloomiest of sports films—and long before the sixties). And then there were those luminous sci-fi cartoons that, more than any other movies, marked the onset of the Great Retreat: George Lucas's *Star Wars* (1976) and Stephen Spielberg's *Close Encounters of the Third Kind* (1977). Those epoch-making fantasies are haunted by the memory of Kubrick's masterpiece, and both attempt to exorcise it.

George Lucas was at once bedazzled and befuddled by *2001* —"in awe of Kubrick's technical craftsmanship, but the movie was too obscure and downbeat for his tastes," notes biographer Dale Pollock. *Star Wars* was Lucas's anti-*2001*—a fond throwback to the ripping "space operas" of prewar Hollywood. In Lucas's universe, "deep space" is not the infinite disorienting void—"gravity all nonsense now"—that Kubrick had evoked so vividly. The spaces cruised by the Millennium Falcon seem cozier and warmer, like the precincts of a large nocturnal neighborhood; nor is the interplanetary night of *Star Wars* crazed by relativity but has an Up and Down as uniform and stable as on Earth. And as it reasserts premodern cosmology, *Star Wars*—also contra *2001*—reconfirms the pre-Darwinian view of Man as ontologically unique, the most exalted of all living creatures. Here the human characters are a class totally and reassuringly apart from the film's nonhuman characters, both bestial and mechanical. Kubrick's ape-man, in his cravings and initiative, is all too recognizably our father, or our brother, underneath the matted hair. Although a dead ringer for that uncanny creature, Chewbacca the Wookie—Han Solo's shaggy second—is a mere comic sidekick in the feets-do-yo'-stuff tradition of Sancho Panza, the Cowardly Lion, and Leo Carillo in "The Cisco Kid." That tame simian, in short, bears no disquieting resemblance to the film's organic characters who rule the roost as his unquestionable betters. Likewise, *Star Wars* dispels the strangeness of the all-too-human HAL by replacing "him" with the wee beeping, clanking droids—cute mechanisms, flagrantly subordinate, and therefore posing no threat to Man's place as master of the universe. Such domestication was essential to the inexhaustible success of Lucas's franchise. Whereas, in Kubrick's "odyssey," the striving ape-men and the tactful HAL diminish the heroic status of the blank, intrepid astronauts, the plucky leads in *Star Wars* lord it over all creation, like children towering over pets and toys.

NOTES

An earlier version of this essay appeared in *Sight and Sound* 4 (1994): 18–25.

1. *Stanley Kubrick: Interviews,* ed. Gene D. Phillips (Jackson: University Press of Mississippi, 2001), 67.

2. Ibid., 47.

Deviant Subjects in Foucault and *A Clockwork Orange*

Criminological Constructions of Subjectivity

━━━▶◆◀━━━

PAT J. GEHRKE

The clockwork metaphor has long been a tradition of Western sciences, both physical and social. Dreams of predicting and controlling human behavior have provoked nightmares of social control and behavior modification. The development of these models in behavioral and social sciences provided the context in 1962 for Anthony Burgess's best known work, *A Clockwork Orange*.[1] In 1972, Stanley Kubrick released his film adaptation of Burgess's novel in Europe and the United States. Meanwhile, Michel Foucault published a series of related texts, including *Madness and Civilization, The Order of Things,* and *An Archeology of Knowledge*.[2] Three years after the release of Kubrick's film, Foucault published one of his most popular books, *Discipline and Punish*.[3] During the same period, behavior modification techniques such as aversion therapy were booming.[4]

This essay examines how Foucault's writings and Kubrick's film lay out congruent critiques of social scientific and criminological attempts to define and constitute subjectivity. Foucault's theoretical insights rarely have been elaborated in relation to popular texts of his time, often obscuring the historical position of his writing. By situating Foucault in relation to a popular text of his time, this analysis begins to uncover how the discursive formations of the epoch gave rise to resistances to social scientific and criminological constructions of subjectivity.

This examination begins with a brief discussion of Foucault's pertinence to communication studies and a basic review of his writings. Following is a summary of the film version of *A Clockwork Orange* and a discussion of its centrality to European and American understandings of criminal deviancy. Next, the film is analyzed through application of relevant sections of Foucault's writings. The essay concludes with a discussion of the implications of this analysis for critical studies and for modern construction and management of deviancy.

Michel Foucault: Critic and Critical Tool

Foucault's work is especially important to studies of film and history because he offers methods of investigating knowledge and power as well as the role of discourse in the generation of truths and the construction of subjectivities. Foucault's work focuses heavily on these themes, especially in *The Order of Things, Archeology of Knowledge,* and *Discipline and Punish.* As Foucault isolates the ways that the sciences define what it means to be human—the subject that science creates—he also elucidates the practice of science itself. Works by Bogard and others spring from *Discipline and Punish* and expand Foucault's analyses to include more recent dissuasion and disinclination methods.[5] Foucault also provides insights in his extensive work on mental illness and deviancy that parallel the visions Kubrick presents to us in *Orange.*

   This essay begins from the question of the subject, using investigations of power, knowledge, and rules as tools to uncover how the subject is constituted and constitutes itself. In Foucault's work we often find a structure that leads us through history by way of discussions of subjectivity and the changes subjectivity undergoes. Hence, in *Madness and Civilization* Foucault takes us from the subject-position of the doctor in the Hospital General of seventeenth-century France to the subject-position of the modern psychiatrist. In *Discipline and Punish* he takes us from the subject-position of the slave to a violent discipline upon the body and, finally, to the subject-position of the modern convict. In this way we are shown the changes in subjectivity, and the discourses and practices that construct these subjectivities, as well as the implications of both for the interplay of power and knowledge.

   We hit near the mark by recognizing the interrelation of these elements and the centrality of subjectivity to Foucault's analysis. We should be careful to avoid treating subjectivity as merely another aspect of analysis, rather than the critical question. Foucault argues that the investigation of the ways that subjects are constituted socially and individually is the central focus of his work:

So it was that I was led to pose the problem of knowledge/power, which is not for me the fundamental problem but an instrument allowing the analysis—in a way that seems to me to be the most exact—of the problem of relationships between subjects and games of truth.[6]

Thus, in the study of discipline we find that "the elements are interchangeable, since each is defined by the place it occupies in a series, and by the gap that separates it from the others."[7] From this perspective, our analysis does not concern the specifics of certain individuals, places, acts, or statements. Rather, this analysis focuses on the subject-positions within a discursive formation, or as Foucault wrote, "the *rank*: the place one occupies in a classification."[8]

A Clockwork Orange: An Overview

Similar to much of Foucault's work, a central message in *A Clockwork Orange* is a warning against accepting science or the state as unimpeachable guardians of our civilization.[9] A central question today is how much we can or should place our faith in the behavioral sciences in light of how many progressive dreams of control and improvement of humanity have turned into nightmares.[10]

When Anthony Burgess published *A Clockwork Orange* in 1962, both critics and the market reacted unfavorably.[11] It remained relatively obscure until Stanley Kubrick converted the American release of the book into a film. Upon release in 1971 the movie received rave reviews, garnered three Academy Award nominations, and won the New York Film Critics' Best Picture Award.[12] Kubrick made the movie in Britain at a time when street violence in Britain had reached crisis proportions.[13] Less than two years after the film was released the movie was pulled from British cinemas, and only after Kubrick's death in 1999 was it again shown in Britain.

The movie's story follows the escapades of Alex (Malcolm McDowell), a reasonably intelligent young criminal and his three gang members, Pete, Georgie, and Dim. As they drink milk laced with drugs and spend their evenings entertaining themselves with what they call the "ultra-violent," Alex shocks us with his nonchalant brutality. We watch as the gang of youths taunts and then savagely beats a homeless man. Then we see them involved in a fight with another group of youths who were engaged in "a bit of the old in-out," Alex's euphemism for rape. To top off their evening they decide to play "surprise visit" and enter an author's home, tie him up, gag him, beat him, and rape his wife. All the while Alex sings "Singin' in the Rain," smiling and happy.

After a conflict with his gang Alex is betrayed and caught by the authorities. He goes to prison on a forty-year sentence, but after two years he enters a voluntary experiment in behavior modification. This conditioning through association makes him incapable of tolerating violence or sex. The doctors convert Alex into a model member of society—a "clockwork orange." He is sweet, bright, and delicious on the outside, but on the inside he is just a wind-up toy for some God, or Descartes's evil genius, or the nearly ubiquitous modern replacements for both: science and the state.

Upon release Alex finds himself incapable of coping with the everyday world's violence and brutality, and he is especially vulnerable to the societal retribution that awaits him. As a perfect citizen he also becomes the perfect victim, and those that he previously victimized soon exact their vengeance. Eventually the author, whose wife died shortly after Alex raped her, psychologically tortures Alex until it drives him to attempt suicide. Waking in a hospital bed Alex finds he has become a pawn in a power struggle between two political parties. Political officials promise to take care of him and compensate him for the damage.

Here is the definitive departure that Kubrick made from Burgess's book. When Burgess originally wrote the book it was twenty-one chapters long and ended with Alex escaping the effects of behavior modification, outgrowing his lust for violence, and yearning for peace, a wife, and a baby. Editors persuaded Burgess to cut the last chapter of the book for the American release. Kubrick, completely unaware of the discrepancy between the two versions, wrote his screenplay from the shorter American edition.[14]

Burgess saw significant differences between the book and the film. Although he was well disposed toward the movie, he also expressed dissatisfaction: "A vindication of free will had become an exaltation of the urge to sin."[15] This radical transformation is not merely the result of a missing chapter. The powerful critique presented in Kubrick's film is unique to the screenplay and its film adaptation. Some of *Orange*'s most vivid images, such as Alex bellowing out "Singing in the Rain" and the sarcastic closing moments, are not present in Burgess's original novel. Burgess penned a book that vindicated free will, an editor cut off the last chapter, and Kubrick used it as the groundwork for a screenplay and a movie. Such a situation troubles any assignation of authorship and seems especially appropriate given Foucault's skepticism of authorial intention.[16] What is most important about this phenomenon is that we should not consider the film to be simply an extension or mere adaptation of Burgess's book. Rather, this film is as unique (or as imitative) as any text. Nor is *A Clockwork Orange* simply a reflection of the mind or philosophy of Kubrick himself. In studying the operation of the film and its relation to surrounding discourses of the period, we are not assessing Kubrick's stance on scientific constructions of subjectivity or the status of humanism but, rather, watching how discourses come together at a particular moment to make certain critiques possible.

There are many reasons why *A Clockwork Orange* deserves our attention. During the two years the film was shown in Britain, it developed a strong cult following and is believed to have inspired copycat crimes.[17] In November of 1973 a seventeen-year-old girl was raped by a gang of youths imitating Alex with "Singin' in the Rain." A few months earlier a sixteen-year-old boy obsessed with Kubrick's film kicked a sixty-year-old homeless person to death. Another group of sixteen-year-olds dressed as Alex and his gang beat a younger boy almost to death.[18] The film also became a metaphor for other acts of violence. Incidents of animalistic violence in New York City's Central Park, called "wilding," were discussed by some reporters in relation to Kubrick's film.[19]

When one thinks of social control and behavior modification, Kubrick's film often springs to mind as a definition of the unacceptable. Newspaper writers compared Russian artists' experiences with brainwashing to Alex and his own modification.[20] A British intelligence operation code-named "Clockwork Orange" was designed to stifle political deviancy by using modern psychological techniques.[21] Crime, deviancy, and our methods of managing them are still high on the agenda and, for better or for worse, Kubrick's *Orange* is tied up in that discussion.

For well over three decades we have simultaneously been questioning the human sciences and rushing headlong into them. In the early 1980s, popular publications (even conservative publications) were asking the question "Is social science a god that failed?"[22] One of the primary movements in the humanities has been the examination of this dilemma by such thinkers as Foucault. He approaches this problem differently than many other scholars through his narrative and genealogical style, as well as his focus on the centrality of the subject.

Foucault and *Orange*: Congruent Critiques

A Clockwork Orange is a narrative about an individual (Alex) who transits through at least four subject-positions. In the transition between these positions, Alex is exposed (as are we) to different relations of power and knowledge. Following Alex from the life of his gang, through his stay in prison, his treatment at the psychology institute, and his release back into society, we see him constructed as a subject in at least four different ways. The elements of Alex that remain stable are relatively irrelevant to his shifting subjectivity. We could imagine a duller or more spiteful character walking the same path, though we may not be as interested in watching that story. For *A Clockwork Orange* it is not only the positions themselves but, more importantly, the ways that subjectivity is constructed differently at different points in the story that shape the narrative.

Whether set in the 1950s (nearer such films as *The Manchurian Candidate*) or set in the far future (nearer such films as *Brazil*), Alex's story could remain the same. As Alex narrates us through the story it is not important where Alex is, or when. It is what he is, as constituted by the rules and norms of his society, that interests us and makes the film powerful. Thus, we can focus on his shifting subjectivity in Kubrick's narrative read against the writings of Michel Foucault to reveal their congruent critiques of scientific methods of constructing and managing deviancy. The four positions examined here are criminal, convict, patient, and citizen.

ALEX AS CRIMINAL

That Alex ever abandons his desire for violence is doubtful, but only in the first third of the film do we see him acting out physically. There are a number of differences that set apart and define Alex in this section of the film, and the most striking is the high level of physical violence. Alex and his gang relate with others in the most shockingly violent ways, and that violence is not allocated randomly. Alex, as leader of the gang, is key to choosing their targets. These people have somehow struck Alex as appropriate targets for the violence they receive. For example, a homeless man is drunk and bellowing out songs, so Alex and his gang beat him nearly to death. Alex explains to us that he cannot stand to see such a filthy slob screaming so loudly about such nonsense.

In *Discipline and Punish*, Foucault explains that before the advent of the modern prison the primary method of dealing with deviancy was to exact pain upon the offender's body.[23] Such mechanisms of discipline are again manifest in the conflict between Alex and his gang. While at the milk bar they hear a woman at another table sing a section of Beethoven (for which Alex has an almost fanatical fondness). One gang member, Dim, makes a derisive flatulent noise toward her. Alex strikes him, telling him he has no

manners and should behave better. Their argument becomes an exchange
of threats of violence. The next day, the gang announces that they are re-
belling against Alex and that Georgie is their new leader. Alex initially is
compliant but, catching Dim and Georgie by surprise, he hits Georgie,
pushes him into a river, and slices the back of Dim's hand. Afterward they
are reunited and again become a gang. Alex describes, through narration,
his actions as necessary discipline for his gang.

This exchange displays Foucault's argument that power relations were
not univocal when punishment focused upon the body but rather always
involved multiple points of confrontation.[24] These types of confrontations
make up the micropolitics of the gang in *Orange* and become the means
of succession as well as maintaining dominance. In the end, Alex loses
out to Georgie when the gang leaves him wounded at a crime scene to be
apprehended by the police. Yet, even in this situation the method is overt
physical violence, as he smashes a glass bottle of milk across Alex's face,
leaving him temporarily blind and wounded at the scene of the crime.

This mirrors Foucault's analysis of the political investment of the body
and the microphysics of power:

> Now, the study of this microphysics presupposes that the power exercised on
> the body is conceived not as property but as strategy; that its effects of dom-
> ination are attributed not to "appropriation," but to dispositions, maneuvers,
> tactics, techniques, functionings; that one should decipher in it a network of
> relations, constantly in tension, in activity, rather than a privilege that one
> might possess; that one should take as its model a perpetual battle, rather
> than a contract regulating a transaction or the conquest of a territory.[25]

However, *Orange* further shows the politics of the body in the ways that
the agents of the state use such tools. Mr. Deltoid, a probation officer from
the corrective school Alex previously attended, chastises Alex, verbally abuses
him, and threatens him with sanction, all to little effect. The only thing
Mr. Deltoid can do that has any effect on Alex is to strike him in the genitals. Similarly, when the police catch Alex they proceed to interrogate him.
This involves some minor physical violence followed by a full-scale beating.
Even here we can see the instability of a power relationship focused on the
body, since Alex can strike back and injure one of the police officers. Of
course, he loses this struggle in the end, as he is overwhelmed to such a
radical degree as to make reversal of the relationship impossible. Once in
the hands of the authorities power relationships become more stable and

univocal. This marks the end of Alex's period as a criminal. A judge gives him a forty-year sentence, reconstructing him into a new subjectivity: the convict.

ALEX AS CONVICT

Foucault describes discipline as the control of the human machine.[26] Alex narrates the horror of going to prison as we see an aerial view of a prison somewhat similar to a panopticon, Jeremy Bentham's model for the ideal prison. Alex's new home contains a large tower in the center that can easily keep all six wings extending from the tower under surveillance. This is the first aerial view of the film, showing the entire institution from high above. Before this shot, the camera stayed at eye level and predominantly close in. There were frequent shots tightly focused on just the face, especially Alex's and the author's. These scenes were personal and passionately violent. Now, the camera reproduces the panoptic and impersonal gaze of the institution as it peers down on the gray stone prison. Throughout Alex's stay in prison the camera keeps a greater distance.

Alex's discipline begins the moment of his arrival. He is instructed to refer to all the guards and wardens as "sir" and told that his name will be "655321." Guards tell him to stand with his toes on a white line, put things down properly, strip, and get dressed. Alex obeys all orders without hesitation because an overwhelming violence is explicitly ready to step in if he should disobey. Alex learns the detailed regimen and order of prison life, in sharp contrast to the disorder and spontaneity of his life as a criminal. He adapts well to the role of the convict and takes on the clockwork discipline of the prison, though his changes are only behavioral. He appears to be a model prisoner.

This domination places Alex in a position that requires he submit to the order of the prison. This order appears calm and looks peaceful because the domination is so complete that it precludes the opportunity for Alex to resist physically. The guards and wardens do not hide the violence that underlies this order but justify it through Alex's position as criminal. Foucault studied the prison in part because of this overt threat of violence justified through order:

What is fascinating about prisons is that, for once, power doesn't hide or mask itself; it reveals itself as tyranny pursued into the tiniest details; it is cynical and at the same time pure and entirely "justified," because its practice can be totally formulated within the framework of morality. Its brutal tyranny consequently appears as the serene domination of Good over Evil, of order over disorder.[27]

Alex helps the prison pastor prepare sermons and leads the hymns during services. He soon has the faith of the pastor and is reading the Bible regularly, though with an alternative interpretation. Alex explains, in voice-over narration, that he most liked the first half of the book where people were killing each other and having sex, though he was much less interested in all the preachy stuff that came later. He sees himself as one of the Roman guards whipping Jesus along the street to his crucifixion or enjoying multiple mistresses attending to his every desire. Alex's fantasies about the violence and sex that his jailers will not permit are a subtle and personal form of resistance. These are the only scenes in this portion of the film where a guard, warden, or prison pastor do not accompany Alex. At every other moment that we see Alex, there is some official watching over him, from a corner of the screen or right in the center of the scene. He resists this panoptic gaze through his imaginative interpretations of the Old Testament. Here, he is the guard, passionately engaged in his violent work.

According to Foucault, discipline, to be meaningful, has to be self-sustaining.[28] It is less corporeal than a politics of the body and should have more of an effect upon the mind. However, Alex's experience in the prison had little such effect. Foucault notes such failures of the prison system, explaining how the very model of the prison causes recidivism.[29] These failures of the prison system are echoed not only by modern criminologists but also by *Orange*'s Minister of the Interior, who comes to Alex's prison. Alex breaks his rigid institutional training to strategically step out of line, speak out of turn, and state that he agrees with the Minister. This leads the Minister to choose Alex for an experimental new treatment that he expects will cure Alex of his criminal tendencies, much to the chagrin of the warden and guards. In the strict confines of the prison system Alex demonstrates that tactics of resistance are possible.

ALEX AS PATIENT

The transition in the film from the discipline and training model of the prison to the medical model is likewise paralleled by trends in modern mechanisms for diminishing deviancy and crime. Foucault explains that in the twentieth century there came to be a belief that to solve crime requires that we solve the psychology of crime.[30] The view came to be that criminals, rather than being evil or forced by social circumstances to commit crimes, are somehow sick or insane. This shift in the nature of the criminal subject came in part through the recognition of the failure of the classical prison model and in part through the promise of scientific and sociological solutions. *A Clockwork Orange* imagines the failure of the basic psychological methods as well. Foucault primarily discusses the panopticon and the methods of observation as means of reproducing power through discipline upon the mind. However, these tools for creating and managing deviancy were further developed by scientists and policy makers viewing deviancy and crime as psychological aberrations to be cured.

The guards take Alex to an institute where the doctors treat him like a child. They bring him his meals and speak to him in vague and reassuring tones. Alex's treatment requires that the doctors strap him into a chair and force him to watch films of graphic violence and sex. When he observes the films he is injected with a drug that makes him horribly ill. He is ill enough to wish to die. Eventually, just as Pavlov's bell would cause his dogs to salivate even without the presence of food, so do the acts depicted in the films cause Alex to become deathly ill even without the presence of the drug. Any time Alex encounters experiences that remind him of the film he is immobilized with pain and sickness. Unfortunately, the score for the films is all Beethoven, so that too becomes a stimulus for the illness. This classical conditioning removes from Alex the capacity for criminal action, though it cannot affect the drive.

Foucault notes that the doctor had little or no role in the incarceration of the insane in the classical prison model, but he became an essential figure in the asylum.[31] The doctors in *Orange,* like the doctors Foucault describes, become fathers and mothers, judging and executing as necessary, justifying the process through kindness and love rather than punishment. They attempt to reinforce in Alex that he was sick and that he is now getting better. There is a morbid irony in the fact that Alex's mental health requires his physical illness. In order to become a good citizen Alex has to be trained to be physically repulsed by the sight of violence or sex.

This connection between violence and sex is also comparable to the later works of Foucault. In volume one of *History of Sexuality* Foucault discusses the ways that sex moved from a common element of everyday life—discussed and practiced openly—to a crime or a sin.[32] That Alex's disinclination training not only focuses upon violence but also upon sex is a particularly modern association of sex with sin or crime.

Through this conditioning Alex ceases to have the ability to react, or even to really choose to act. He becomes an automaton, his actions ruled by his conditioning. The treatment and the effects are almost mystical, unexplainable, and Alex can find no way to resist them. He speaks in disbelief and horror at the power that is now wielded over him. Foucault noted the tendency for doctors to be transformed into magicians when psychiatry came under the sway of positivism.[33] This is further reinforced in *Orange* by the public demonstration of Alex's condition, providing empirical verification of his cure.

Alex is brought out onto a stage before an audience of wardens and government officials. First, a man walks onto stage, insults and slaps Alex, then pushes him to the ground. The violence triggers his incredible sickness, making him gag and wretch. The man takes a bow as he walks off stage. Next, a woman wearing nothing but a pair of briefs walks up to Alex. He reaches out to touch her, but the sickness again takes hold of him and sends him to the floor. She also leaves stage with a series of bows. The audience applauds after each trick the doctors perform through Alex. The next day, the doctors release Alex, and the newspaper headlines read "Murderer Freed: Science has the Cure."

The doctors have achieved the intended effect of the treatment; Alex can no longer act in criminal ways. He is incapable of acting violently or sexually toward anyone, no matter what the circumstances. He also can never listen to Beethoven again. However, as the prison pastor notes, Alex's incapacity for these actions does not arise from a moral choice, or really from any kind of choice. Rather, he is ruled by his new conditioning. For Alex, a certain element of his character has been reduced to a pure stimulus-response activity—a single-celled *ethos*. This inflexible and simple moral structure renders Alex incapable of dealing with the fluidity and complexity of social life.

ALEX AS CITIZEN

Alex's conditioning has transformed him from a subject acting with and upon others to a slave or object for others to act upon. Whereas the world was once his playpen, Alex is now a pawn, manipulated by the sciences and the state in the name of peace and public safety. Alex is as constrained and forced in his actions as the brainwashed soldiers in *The Manchurian Candidate* or the lobotomized Randall P. McMurphy of *One Flew Over the Cuckoo's Nest*.

For Alex, politics no longer resides in the body but in the mind, which has been stripped of significant choice, and hence no longer belongs to the subject it inhabits. However, unlike the characters from *Manchurian*

Candidate or *Cuckoo's Nest* Alex is both completely aware of his actions and able to know they are not his own. He has been manipulated and molded and keeps full knowledge of both his former state and his current state.

Alex becomes a focal point for the violence and anger of the everyday. Since Alex is unable to fight back, he makes an ideal target. Alex is turned away by his parents, beaten by the homeless man he previously assaulted, almost drowned by his former gang members (who are now working as police officers), and finally tortured by the author whose wife he raped. We come to see that no matter what cure or therapy has been exacted upon Alex, his world is a place closer to Hobbes's state of nature, where life is nasty, brutish, and short.

Oddly, it does not seem that these acts are retributive justice but are acts of passionate violence and anger, free from the cool rationality of institutional punishments. These are romantic acts of violence exercised upon both Alex's body and mind—first upon his body through the violence itself, and second upon the mind by the conditioning to which Alex has been prey. The camera returns to the occasional tight shot of only the face, but now it is the faces of the homeless people as they beat Alex and the face of the author as he tortures Alex. The passion and pleasure of their violence is expressed in their faces. As the ideal citizen, Alex is their ideal victim.

Alex finds no way to resist in this power relationship. He finds himself incapable of asserting influence and is subjected to the whims of those he encounters. He still has some space for action, but he cannot yet locate any means by which to make it an effective resistance. Alex is unable to defend either body or mind as points of politics. The conditioning enhances his torture and terror because it adds deathly sickness to his pain and abuse. The conditioning also opens new points for others to exercise violence through Alex. The author has no need to physically abuse Alex but need only expose him to a stimulus that produces his illness—he need only play Beethoven loudly—eventually to drive Alex to attempt suicide.

Alex is reborn through his attempted suicide into a highly politicized creature. His suicide is a public political issue, embarrassing the government and the doctors who "cured" him. When the Minister of the Interior comes to apologize to Alex and promise restitution for his pain, Alex can make the Minister feed him his hospital dinner. Of course, this also requires that Alex be willing to eat from the Minister's hand. Alex seems to have reestablished some position as a subject and regained some of his previously subverted will. However, he has not completely freed himself from his conditioning. Such escape seems impossible. His new choices are adaptations to his new subjectivity, and Alex now finds new avenues for his violence. He has in-corporated each new discourse and practice as he was incorporated into it, but in so doing he has found new ways to please his desires. In the end, the modern goal of disciplining or curing violence simply succeeds in open-ing new pathways to new forms of violence.

Aberrances and deviancies are the norm and *Orange* presents a story of how attempts to eliminate those norms only alter their expressions and shift the locations and tactics of violence. As the film closes with Alex's smiling face, surrounded by politicians, a happy crowd of hospital staff, and his now conciliatory family, Alex gives us the sly and heavily sarcastic commentary that he is cured. However, there is no less criminal, convict, patient, or citizen in him at this point than at the beginning of the film. We can be reasonably certain that he will simply find new ways to express his desires within new subject-positions.

Everyday Violence and Clockwork Subjects

Although we continue to strive for homogenizing treatments to create the perfect citizen through behavior modification, drugs, surgery, therapy ses-sions, or institutionalization, we are also increasingly realizing the violence and futility of these methods. In the United States, we can look to the mani-festations of the behavioral and social sciences in the "war on crime." In Florida we experiment with aversion therapy to train sex offenders (like Alex) to get ill and almost vomit when they witness a reenactment of a rape or child molestation.[34] The scientists in these processes call it "mind-bending." In the 1970s, two California prisons carried out a program "stunningly rem-iniscent of *A Clockwork Orange*."[35] When criticized about the dehumaniza-tion of the people being experimented upon, the doctors responded that the treatment was effective—the patient can no longer commit the act—and that the program is voluntary. Fundamentally, aversion therapy and similar models of behavior modification are justified through their "suc-cesses."[36] As *Orange*'s Minister of the Interior says, "These are subtleties. We're not concerned with motives or higher ethics. We are concerned only with cutting down crime." Meanwhile, the prisoners volunteering for the program parrot back Alex's words as he campaigned to be admitted to his behavior modification. It is as if someone with a script ran a giant per-formance of the film in the California and Florida prison systems.

Even assuming a society where heinous acts of violence such as murder, rape, and brutal assault were impossible because of disinclination therapies, we should be prepared for power relationships and violence simply to manifest differently. Instead, these tendencies might take the form of institutionally or socially sanctioned violence. Both law and behavior modification rely upon violence as a part of their operation. This violence is both figural and literal.[37] It is the representation of law as the orderly alternative to violence that masks the ways that legal action and discourse, and the criminological system, "inscribe themselves upon bodies."[38] As Robert Cover wrote, "Legal interpretive acts signal and occasion the imposition of violence upon others: A judge articulates her understanding of a text, and as a result, somebody loses his freedom, his property, his children, even his life."[39] It is the acceptance of this violence as legitimate that allows it to go unrecognized as violence.

We are shocked and outraged when we see "citizens" victimized by "criminals," but we are shocked far less by everyday violence. Foucault recognized that this separation legitimates certain forms of violence while casting others as illegitimate or evil:

> This was Genet's emphasis with relation to the judge at the Soledad trial or the plane hijacked by the Palestinians in Jordan; the newspapers decried the fate of the judge and the poor tourists being held in the middle of the desert for no apparent reason. Genet, for his part, was saying: "But is the judge innocent, and what of an American lady who can afford to be a tourist in this way?"[40]

The point here is not that we should cast American indulgences as evil, but that the distinction between the criminal and the citizen is not one of violence but of the capacity to conform that violence to accepted methods. To recast this violence as somehow order's "other or as outside of what is naturally right," is to fall prey to the illusion of a progressive dream for humanity. Foucault refuses the belief that a new set of rules or institutions can somehow free us from violence or power:

> Humanity does not gradually progress from combat to combat until it arrives at universal reciprocity, where the rule of law finally replaces warfare; humanity installs each of its violences in a system of rules and thus proceeds from domination to domination.[41]

Similarly, the violence of aversion therapy tactics, such as executed upon Alex, have become a means of enforcing social norms that extend beyond the legally inscribed. In the 1970s, doctors used aversion therapy, usually involving painful electric shocks, as a method to train people not to smoke, not to drink, to be faithful in their marriages, and to avoid overeating.[42] Pressures manifest in discourses and institutions drove individuals to desire conformity and avoid social stigma or discrimination. Aversion therapy became a means to surrender the self to science in order to affect a "cure." In such circumstances, anything socially unacceptable can be defined as an illness needing to be cured. For example, Sansweet discussed the use of aversion therapy to "cure" homosexuality. He described the case of Martin, a homosexual male who was discriminated against and pressured enough that he sought out a doctor to "cure" him of his sexual orientation.[43] The doctor showed Martin slides of athletic nude men, and for as long as he looked at them he received an intense electric shock to the inside of one thigh. Upon switching to a picture of an attractive nude woman, the shock would cease, only to resume as soon as another nude male appeared. Doctors conditioned him to be unable to have a homosexual relationship, though they could not change his sexual preference. Anything socially perceived as deviant can become an illness subject to the legitimacy and authority of scientific cure.

Although Foucault and Kubrick recognize the violence of the law and the economy, they are uniquely troubled by the power of behavioral sciences to preclude choice on the part of subjects. In Alex's world as a violent criminal, or even as prisoner, the broken body "restored the order of the body politic and became a human sacrifice."[44] Alex accomplished this through the violent discipline of his gang, as did the wardens and guards through constant threats and occasional uses of violence. However, as a patient and as a citizen it is no longer the broken body but the broken mind that restores the body politic. This restoration is not completed through fear or sacrifice, but rather through faith in the sciences and the state as guardians of society's progressive projects. Politics moves from the body to the mind, and Alex moves from subject to object, until he can re-politicize his new subjectivity.

This description of the subject as object, a media-saturated, norm-regulated, pseudo-free and yet sentient being, describes the shift in contemporary culture outlined by Kenneth Gergen.[45] In accepting the conditions of being (post)modern citizens—media-subjects—we also become perfect victims. Alex's final reaction to his conditioning is to take a leap from a window and dive headfirst (headlong) into the blacktop. He is reborn on the other side, not as reincarnation or resurrection but in the final surrendering of the self. In the surrender of life itself one again finds ways to renew a position as subject and agent in the world. Rather than fight his conditioning, Alex embraces it as the limits of a new subjectivity and a new politics. Alex's desires are similar, though mutated with his subjectivity. That he exerts his violence through political and economic channels rather than with a fist or knife only seems a cure because we are dull to the everyday violence of our politics and economy.

Kubrick's film makes plain to us, through the narrative of a single subject, the instability of the lines between criminal, convict, patient, and citizen. Likewise, Foucault sought to destabilize our common distinctions between these positions. As a political activist Foucault sought to "question the social and moral distinction between the innocent and the guilty."[46] Blurring the lines between these roles, as Foucault and Kubrick do, destabilizes the acceptance of the violence in law, science, economics, and politics as uniquely legitimate. It also opens new ways of thinking about ourselves as subjects and the politics of (post)modern subjectivity.

Power itself is not bad, and its omnipresence marks it as an intrinsic part of social existence. However, a fixed relationship of domination is contrary to what Foucault perceives as a necessary prerequisite for ethics: choice.[47] Foucault notes that many relationships in contemporary society increasingly approach a state of domination, which he defined as when the power relationship becomes invariable, radically restricting any possible effective resistance.[48] Foucault describes the role of the intellectual and the goal of discourse in general as the minimization of domination and the opening of the game of truth to as many voices as possible.[49] The focus on the subject is critical to this project for Foucault and for Kubrick. Just as Kubrick gives us the direct voice of Alex, through voice-over, so does Foucault seek to open spaces where the silenced might speak. For example, his work with the Information Group on Prisons was not a humanist call for better prison conditions but sought to include the voices of the prisoners themselves in the discourse of prison policies.[50]

In the 1960s and 1970s, these projects were just beginning points of resistance against the dominating influence of behavioral sciences. It is important to remember that in roughly the same period as Foucault's work on madness and discipline and Kubrick's *Orange*, aversion therapy went from being an obscure and unpopular field to one of the most popular elements of psychology. In 1960 it was unheard of, but between 1965 and 1975 hundreds of aversion therapy studies were printed in psychological and medical journals.[51] Both Foucault and Kubrick were articulations of this historical moment. Today we still confront these issues. Yet, when we invoke scholars such as Foucault we often do not consider their relationship to events and texts contemporary to their work. This essay only begins to consider how artifacts of the period manifest similar critiques of the social sciences. It opens an avenue, however, for research into the poststructural movements of the 1960s and 1970s as articulations of and resistances to discourses and practices of that epoch. Similarly, we might articulate the continuation of critiques such as Foucault's and Kubrick's as indicative of a continued relation of power and a relation between power and truth in the construction of deviant and criminal subjects.

Foucault's texts and Kubrick's film ask us to remember the violence of our everyday existence and recognize our modern nightmares as portents of what lie along this same path we have followed. Rather than applaud both the violence and the nightmares as elements of some great progressive humanist project, perhaps these critics give us much needed visions to invoke fits of shaking and sweating, disturbing our dreams of predicting and controlling the norm of deviancy.

NOTES

An earlier version of this essay appeared in *Critical Studies in Media Communication* 18 (2001): 270–84. Used by permission of the National Communication Association.

1. Anthony Burgess, *A Clockwork Orange* (New York: Ballantine Books, 1963).

2. Michel Foucault, *Madness and Civilization: A History of Insanity in the Age of Reason,* trans. Richard Howard (New York: Vintage Books, 1965); Michel Foucault, *The Order of Things: An Archeology of the Human Sciences,* trans. unidentified (New York: Pantheon Books, 1970); and Michel Foucault, *The Archaeology of Knowledge and the Discourse on Language,* trans. A. M. Sheridan Smith (New York: Pantheon Books, 1972). Many of Foucault's works were not translated into English until many years after their original publication in French. For example, these texts were originally published in 1961, 1966, and 1971 respectively.

3. Michel Foucault, *Discipline and Punish: The Birth of the Prison,* trans. Alan Sheridan (New York: Vintage Books, 1977). This work was originally published in 1975.

4. Stephen Sansweet, *The Punishment Cure: How Aversion Therapy Is Being Used to Eliminate Smoking, Obesity, Homosexuality . . . and Practically Anything Else* (New York: Mason/Charter, 1975), 4.

5. For example, see William Bogard, "Discipline and Deterrence: Rethinking Foucault on the Question of Power in Contemporary Society," *Social Science Journal* 28 (1991): 325–46.

6. Michel Foucault, "The Ethic of Care for the Self as a Practice of Freedom: An Interview with Michel Foucault on January 20, 1984," trans. J. D. Gauthier, *The Final Foucault,* ed. James Bernauer and David Rasmussen (Cambridge, MA: MIT Press, 1987), 10.

7. Foucault, *Discipline and Punish*, 145.

8. Ibid., 146 (emphasis in original).

9. Mark C. Smith, "Video Discovery: A Less Important but Still Sick *Clockwork Orange*," *Los Angeles Times*, Jan. 10, 1991.

10. George E. Jones and Carey W. English, "Social Sciences: Why Doubts Are Spreading Now," *U.S. News & World Report*, May 31, 1982, 70.

11. Tony Parsons, "Forbidden Fruit," *Times* (London), Jan. 30, 1993, 30.

12. Burt A. Folkart, "Anthony Burgess, Prolific Novelist, Linguist," *Los Angeles Times*, Nov. 26, 1993, A44.

13. Parsons, "Forbidden Fruit," 30.

14. Ibid.

15. Ibid.

16. Michel Foucault, "What Is an Author?" trans. Josue V. Harari, *Aesthetics, Method, Epistemology* vol. 2 of *The Essential Works of Michel Foucault, 1954–1984*, ed. James D. Faubion (New York: New Press, 1998), 205–22.

17. Matthew Norman, "Arthouse of Horror," *Evening Standard* (London), Oct. 27, 1993, 51.

18. Parsons, "Forbidden Fruit," 30.

19. Erica Goode et al., "*A Clockwork Orange* in Central Park," *U.S. News & World Report*, May 8, 1989, 10.

20. Victoria Finlay, "Brush with Oppression," *South China Morning Post* (Tai Po), May 11, 1995, Feature section, 23.

21. "John Deverell (Great Britain)," *Intelligence Newsletter* no. 243 (June 23, 1994): Who's Who section.

22. Jones and English, "Social Sciences," 70.

23. Foucault, *Discipline and Punish*, 24–25.

24. Ibid., 26–27.

25. Ibid., 26.

26. Ibid., 138.

27. Michel Foucault and Gilles Deleuze, "Intellectuals and Power: A Conversation between Michel Foucault and Gilles Deleuze," in *Language, Counter-Memory, Practice: Selected Essays and Interviews by Michel Foucault*, ed. Donald F. Bouchard, trans. Donald F. Bouchard and Sherry Simon (Ithaca, NY: Cornell University Press, 1977), 210.

28. Foucault, *Discipline and Punish*, 176–77.

29. Ibid., 264–71.

30. Ibid., 251–52.

31. Foucault, *Madness and Civilization*, 269–70.

32. Michel Foucault, *An Introduction*, vol. 1 of *The History of Sexuality*, trans. Robert Hurley (New York: Vintage Books, 1978).

33. Foucault, *Madness and Civilization*, 275.

34. Cynthia Mayer, "Aversion to Crime to Treat Sex Offenders," *St. Petersburg Times*, Feb. 9, 1987, 1B.

35. Sansweet, *Punishment Cure*, 2.

36. Ibid., 11.

37. Austin Sarat and Thomas R. Kearns, *Law's Violence* (Ann Arbor: University of Michigan Press, 1992), 1.

38. Ibid., 3.

39. Robert M. Cover, "Violence and the Word," in *Narrative, Violence, and the Law: The Essays of Robert Cover,* ed. Martha Minow, Michael Ryan, and Austin Sarat (Ann Arbor: University of Michigan Press, 1992), 203.

40. Michel Foucault, "Revolutionary Action: 'Until now,'" in Bouchard, *Language, Counter-Memory, Practice,* 227.

41. Michel Foucault, "Nietzsche, Genealogy, History," in Bouchard, *Language, Counter-Memory, Practice,* 151.

42. Sansweet, *Punishment Cure.*

43. Ibid., 63–64.

44. Foucault, *Discipline and Punish,* 47–48.

45. Kenneth J. Gergen, *The Saturated Self: Dilemmas of Identity in Contemporary Life* (New York: Basic Books, 1991).

46. Foucault, "Revolutionary Action," 227.

47. Foucault, *An Introduction,* 18.

48. Ibid., 3.

49. Ibid., 19–20.

50. Foucault, "Revolutionary Action," 227–28.

51. Sansweet, *Punishment Cure,* 4.

Pictures, Plurality, and Puns

A Visual Approach to
Barry Lyndon

BILLE WICKRE

The visual splendor of *Barry Lyndon*, Stanley Kubrick's 1975 adaptation of William Makepeace Thackeray's novel, echoes the lavish spectacle of eighteenth-century art. It is indisputable that Kubrick studied this art in preparation for the film, and he alludes to his study in a scene in which Barry wanders through a picture gallery, perusing the array of paintings before him. Paintings by Joshua Reynolds, Thomas Gainsborough, William Hogarth, George Stubbs, Antoine Watteau, Jean-Baptiste Simeon Chardin, Jean-Baptiste Greuze, Joseph Wright of Derby, and others are readily identifiable as sources of inspiration, as are a variety of sculptures, stately homes, and public buildings. Art adorns the interiors of Wilton House, Corsham Court, and Glenum, where Kubrick filmed on location.[1] Scholars have been unsuccessful in identifying specific examples of eighteenth-century art in the film, but paintings and sculptures from preceding centuries and works that resemble eighteenth-century works abound. In addition to the inclusion of the objects within scenes, the cinematography mimics the appearance of eighteenth-century paintings. The cinematography functions like a montage of still photos or paintings because of the static nature of the shots, with many scenes filmed directly from the front or held for long periods of time. The filming of candlelit scenes produce a particularly two-dimensional painterly effect. The static nature of the scenes is enhanced by characters within the scenes who do not move or move very slowly.[2] Frank Cossa has suggested that the "still compositions linger so long on the screen that even the casual viewer may turn art historian for lack of anything better to do."[3] The air of permanence and stasis created within the film bespeaks the order and decorum of the age and reflects the elegance

165

and control of the period's art. Kubrick's allusions to and evocations of eighteenth-century art contribute to more than historical verisimilitude. The visual qualities in this film are as important as any other form of narration in the film and should be understood to provide a visual text running parallel to, but not duplicating, the action of the story and the voice-over commentary of the unidentified third-person narrator.

Kubrick's allusions to and inclusion of art in *Barry Lyndon* create a mood, provide an authentic context for the story, focus the viewer on the act of looking, and constitute a visual narrative in their own right. The creation of a visual text is the standard fare of filmmaking, accomplished by framing, composition, lighting, color, tonality, point of view, cutting from scene to scene, and all of the other visual effects available to the filmmaker. In *Barry Lyndon* a visual subtext is created through the juxtaposition of images, references to works of art outside of the film, and the inclusion of works of art within scenes. Functioning as subtext, these strategies may work to support or amplify the dominant narrative, they may resist or contradict one or more of the other forms of narration, or they may provide ironic commentary on the dominant texts. The development of a visual subtext throughout the film is crucial because *Barry Lyndon*'s meaning depends on intricately linked levels of narration: the narrator as the third-person voice-over; the story line presented through the action and dialogue of the characters; the visual text and the visual subtext as counterpoints to the other narratives. While the voice-over offers a conventional picaresque tale of an unheroic protagonist, the story line often tells a more complicated tale, while the visual text and subtext often thwart or subvert these narratives and allow a sympathetic identification with Barry.[4] In addition, the visuals vie with the voice-over in providing ironic commentary on the story and creating friction between the multiple levels of meaning. While the visual text and subtext may contrast sharply with the commentary and may suggest the unreliability of the narrator, the narrator never comments upon the visual text, lending an air of truth to the visuals. Such intricate layering of narrative strategies marks all of Kubrick's filmmaking. In *Barry Lyndon* meaning resides in the interaction and the slippages between the verbal and the visual.

Eighteenth-century artists were adroit at such layering of narrative, using works of art within works to amplify meanings, create tension, or to insert wry commentary. For instance, English painter and printmaker William Hogarth was especially adept at weaving complex meanings into the myriad details of his works, creating multiple subtexts for the moral tales

that so intrigued him. A frequent commenter on the lives of the aristocracy, Hogarth was a rich source for Kubrick, and references to Hogarth appear
in *Barry Lyndon*. French artist Antoine Watteau was perhaps more subtle
but no less effective at creating multiple levels of meaning within a single
work. Painted during the artist's final months of life, *Gersaint's Shopsign* sums
up Watteau's life as an artist (fig. 1). This seemingly simple depiction of an
art dealer's shop has been interpreted as a statement on the artifice of the
artistic and aristocratic classes who are engaged in the pleasures of looking
at erotic imagery while maintaining a false decorum. Their vanity is hinted
at by the mirror to the right, behind which we see a painted scene of an
Adoration, the juxtaposition providing a comment on self-love. There is
further commentary on the worship of stylized and unnatural beauty. The
beauty admired by this group is not that of nature but of nature ordered
by art. Actual landscapes are no match for the controlled gardens and vis-
tas of the artist.[5] On a human level, the men examine the beauty of the
painted women while their own female companions are ignored. Such reflections on the manners and morals of the aristocratic classes with their
emphasis on orderliness and artifice characterize the life of Barry Lyndon
that Kubrick creates.

   Barry Lyndon tells the story of the rise and fall of Redmond Barry in the
ranks of the English aristocracy in the latter half of the eighteenth century.

Fig. 1. Watteau, *Gersaint's Shopsign*, 1721, Charlottenburg Palace, Berlin

Critics have referred to this film as a documentary about the manners and
mores of eighteenth-century court life, so intent is Kubrick to capture
every detail of an aristocracy and a way of life on the brink of extinction.
The world Kubrick (re)created in the film is one in which human passions
are constrained by an elaborate social code instantiated and enforced
within the institution of the family. Family is an institution from which
Barry is alienated but for which he strives throughout the film. Dispos-
sessed by the death of his father in the opening scene, Barry spends much
of the first half of the film trying to regain the security, status, and discipline that a father and mentor would afford him. Through a series of mis-
fortunes and his own naiveté Barry is expelled from his home, robbed of
his inheritance, and forced by finances to join the English army. Later he
is forced into the Prussian army and recruited as a spy to inform on a stylish gambler and suspected spy, the Chevalier de Balibari. Throughout the
first part of the film, Barry seeks connection with a succession of father
figures, all of whom fail or reject him in some way until he meets the Chevalier de Balibari, a master of deception who frequents the gaming tables
of the fashionable spas and courts of Europe. Rejecting his role as a spy at
the mere sight of the splendid Chevalier, Barry becomes his assistant and
apprentice. The Chevalier teaches Barry social conventions, modeling for
him the ways to project an illusion of calm and ordered splendor. In the
second part of the film, Barry trades his identity for the name, title, and
wealth of his bride, the widowed Lady Lyndon. Assuming the identity Barry
Lyndon, he masquerades among the aristocracy, attempting to assume their
habits; but beneath the surface of the identity he has adopted, the passions
and foibles of Redmond Barry reside. Despite his pursuit of a peerage
through bribery, lavish spending, and entertaining, Barry is unable to gain
the status he desires because he fails repeatedly to control his emotions.
He cannot control his lust for servants and prostitutes. His stepson Lord
Bullingdon goads him into a physical display of fury before an assembled
group of aristocrats. His excessive love of his son Bryan leads Barry to in-
dulge the boy with a horse that throws the child to his death. Challenged
to a duel by Bullingdon, Barry spares the young man's life after Bullingdon's gun misfires. By firing his own pistol into the ground, Barry demonstrates his remaining compassion. His impetuous nature and spontaneous
eruptions of emotion render him unable to live within social conventions
and thus unworthy of admittance to an aristocratic family. Eventually, they
will cause his downfall. While Barry struggles to live in the aristocratic world
of order, there is a disorder within him that subverts his plans and ultimately
results in tragedy. When the conventions of social order are broken there

is chaos, and eventually Barry himself is broken by convention. During the duel with Bullingdon, Barry acts in a noble but unconventional fashion when he refuses to kill his opponent, but rigid adherence to convention allows Bullingdon a second shot. That shot wounds Barry and causes the amputation of his leg. Barry's defeat in the duel gives Bullingdon an upper hand that finally allows him to exile Barry from the Lyndon home.

The rigid structures of the social order and Barry's increasing involvement with it are reflected in the visual approaches Kubrick takes to the film. In the first part of the film, numerous shots of expansive landscapes recall the paintings of Gainsborough and other landscape artists, and cozy domestic interiors echo the genre scenes of seventeenth- and eighteenth-century painters such as Chardin. As Barry is increasingly drawn into the aristocratic world and its conventions, scenes are more often located indoors, classical and neoclassical art appears more frequently, and outdoor scenes take place in geometrically sculpted gardens rather than bucolic expanses. After the marriage of Barry and Lady Lyndon, imagery resembling the aristocratic portraiture of Gainsborough and Reynolds is increasingly common. Hogarthian settings, compositions, and poses mark the dissolution of the marriage and the decay of Barry's character. A return to the simplicity and intimacy of a Chardinesque grouping signals a reemergence of honest emotion.

Kubrick's use of visual texts and subtexts varies in complexity and meaning throughout the film. There is, on one hand, a generalized usage of the visual that recurs throughout; on the other hand, there is a coded series of images that tell a sequential narrative. At a basic level, then, Kubrick used paintings, sculpture, and architecture to reflect the habits, modes of dress, behaviors, expressions, and manners of the age. Some of the compositions, lighting, framing, and other visual effects visible in the film derive in part from paintings. The genres of portraiture, scenes of daily life, and landscapes gained greater acceptance and popularity in the eighteenth century and are reflected in the film in ways that are suggestive of the spirit of the age. One might pause at almost any moment in the film and find a corresponding painting that echoes the composition, poses, coloring, and tonalities of the shot. For example, Lady Lyndon's preparations for an outing with her children reflect the activities, styles, and manners carefully recorded in Gainsborough's portraits. The costume, wig, and mannerisms of Lady Lyndon might have been modeled on Gainsborough's *Morning Walk* of 1785. The melancholy mood of the age is also reflected in Gainsborough's portraits and finds a resonance in many of Kubrick's close-ups of the Lady Lyndon.

Similarities with eighteenth-century paintings can also establish a mood within a scene, insert or reveal information within a scene, or suggest the emotional tenor of the scene. The moist atmospheric qualities, glowing expanses, and distant views of the landscape in the first half of the film set the mood of nostalgic bucolic reverie that is shared by eighteenth-century paintings such as Watteau's *Pilgrimage to Cythera* of 1718 (fig. 2). The inclusion of an art object in a scene can insert or reveal information in a single moment that will be suggested by the plot line over time. Early in the film, Barry has a romantic encounter with his cousin Nora. As the scene opens an image of a chubby child sculpted in stone fills the frame (fig. 3). The camera pulls back slowly to include the image of Nora and Barry playing cards. When Nora attempts to entice Barry to seek the ribbon she has hidden in her bodice, his shyness and awkwardness reveal him to be every bit the child that was suggested by the close-up of the statue. As the drama of Barry's infatuation with Nora unfolds, she dismisses him as "just a boy." In his efforts to prove his manhood, he challenges Nora's suitor to a duel and thus embarks on the episode that begins his life journey. The size and closeness of the initial shot of the child suggests the importance of Barry's childlike qualities in the events that followed immediately.

Fig. 2. Watteau, *Pilgrimage to Cythera*, 1717, Charlottenburg Palace, Berlin

Similarities to particular types of art may suggest the emotional tenor of a scene. For example, the glowing gold lighting, the painterly quality of the washes of color, and the composition of the shot of Redmond Barry with the German girl and her child have an affinity with the genre scenes that became popular in the eighteenth century (fig. 4). The candlelight scenes, shot with a special lens, demonstrate the dramatic tenebrism and halolike effects also found in Chardin or the dramatically lamp-lit paintings of Wright of Derby. For Wright of Derby, light is often associated with enlightenment or knowledge. In this scene the German girl seems to have insight into Barry's deception as she asks his name in a way that suggests that she wishes to know his first name, not only in the sense of his Christian name but also in terms of his former name and identity. Within the film these types of domestic shots recur, usually in the context of a scene of domestic harmony and simple emotion that will soon be set aside. In contrast, scenes that feature classical or neoclassical art are often those that are the most steeped in artifice or suggest false emotion or motives.

The loving relationship between Barry and his good and devoted mother is established early in the film through the voice-over that tells us that the mother lived for her son, eschewing the attentions of other men throughout her widowhood. The strength of the mother-son bond is restated throughout the story line of the film and is reinforced in scenes of their

Fig. 3. Carved stone sculpture of a boy

interactions. A particularly clear visual statement occurs in the scene when Redmond Barry returns to his mother's home after his duel with Nora's fiancé, John Quin (fig. 5). This scene is especially marked by its similarity to the genre scenes of Chardin such as *The Benediction* (fig. 6). Chardin was known for his moralizing scenes of wholesome and virtuous middle-class families, which were often accompanied by Bible verses or proverbs. In this case, the visual similarities include the earthen and silvery tonalities, the simple composition that focuses on the domestic interior and simple domestic acts, light that is softly diffused off the whitewashed walls, the loving attention devoted to the simple still-life objects such as kettles, dishes, the coarse bread, and blue-and-white china. However, this simple reading is subverted when we recall that Chardin also often accompanied his paintings with text that commented on the hidden misdeeds or potential for them of the pictured family. Barry has just committed a grave misdeed against the family in arguing and then dueling with Quin, Nora's suitor and the family's hope for financial salvation. In the scenes immediately following, Barry receives his mother's savings and his father's sword and pistols, and flees to Dublin, losing his inheritance to highwaymen along the road.

In some cases, the inclusion of a piece of architecture or art in the scene amplifies meaning in subtle ways that require a degree of detective work.

Fig. 4. Barry with the German girl

A view of cityscape with a neoclassical temple facade appears in a scene immediately following Barry's assent to becoming a spy for the Prussians (fig. 7). Subsequently he reveals himself to the Chevalier, the man he has been sent to monitor, and Barry finds in him a father figure he has lacked in his own life. At one level the temple facade suggests the stability and order of the society, yet it is but a facade, a false front, an imitation of the real temple, like the false Barry who pretends to be something he is not. If this building is the based on the Parthenon, a Greek temple model with a great deal of visual currency in the eighteenth century, the scene takes on additional meanings. The Parthenon is a masterpiece of engineering, the functional purpose of which was to create the optical illusion of stability and truth, as Barry's identity engineering was to do. In addition, the Parthenon was dedicated to the worship of Athena in her virgin manifestation. In this form, Athena is the protector of young women at a most vulnerable time of their lives, when they have outgrown girlhood and thus the protection of their fathers, and before they marry and come under the aegis of their husbands. Like Barry, they have lost their father's protection and must seek the assistance of another man to help them assume a place in society.

Kubrick draws upon the classical world again in order to enhance the meaning of the scene of Barry and Lady Lyndon's first illicit encounter (fig. 8). Marble sculptures of women in classical garb are set into niches behind

Fig. 5. Barry at his mother's table immediately after the duel with John Quin

Fig. 6. Chardin, *The Benediction*, 1740, Louvre, Paris

the couple. The sculptures represent Venus, the goddess of love, who urges the lovers on through the turn of her head and gesture of her arms. The inclusion of Venus figures in eighteenth-century paintings was a sign of erotic desire, if not sexual dalliance. The statues in this scene may suggest a more chaste love because of the way the position of the arms and the drapery screen the body. The pose imitates a modest gesture well known in antiquity. In eighteenth-century painting, the inclusion of Venus figures was common and usually suggests the divine sanction of the love affair and the inevitability of the romance. Within the film inclusion of Venus figures creates a visual narrative that resists one or both of the other narrative strategies or creates tension in the story. Once the viewer's expectations have been set up to welcome the tender love symbolized by the Venus in the early love scenes between Barry and Lady Lyndon, Kubrick subverts those expectations by using a similar symbol for a different symbolic purpose in later scenes. The Venus who encouraged the love between Barry and Lady Lyndon is echoed later in the film when Barry has a sexual encounter with one of the house servants (fig. 9). Prominently displayed to the left of the lovers is a Venus figure in a less modest pose. The shift in the moral tone is suggested by the bared breast, which may denote sexual intimacy. Later, when Barry solemnly comes to apologize to his wife, Kubrick mocks his character by the inclusion of the painted image that

Fig. 7. Scene with Neoclassical temple façade

appears in the scene (fig. 10). As Barry approaches his wife, who is now as cold, white, and sculptural as the Venus who betrayed her, a painting of a nude woman (perhaps Venus) engaged in an act of flirtation becomes visible between and behind the couple. The sincerity and solemnity of Barry's apology is thoroughly undermined by the image of the flirting couple.

In other instances the visual text departs from the narration in significant ways that underscore the irony of the narrator's voice. In a series of rapid cuts accompanied by narration, Kubrick creates two parallel but quite different commentaries on the lives of Barry and Lady Lyndon after the birth of their son. The narrator notes the birth of the child and intones the shift of responsibilities for both husband and wife, with Barry assuming the social obligations and Lady Lyndon retiring to a quiet life to enjoy her role as mother. In a series of three shots, each containing three figures arranged in a pyramidal composition, Kubrick suggests the profound irony of the narrative line. In the first shot, the new parents are shown together holding the newborn Bryan. Lady Lyndon, dressed in a simple white gown with her hair flowing over her shoulders, leans into Barry as they gaze adoringly at the child (fig. 11). This long shot promises a happy future for the loving couple, but those hopes are dashed by the cut to the next scene in which Barry embraces two partially nude prostitutes in a candlelit brothel (fig. 12). The next cut shows Lady Lyndon, beautifully

Fig. 8. Barry with Venus, the kiss

Fig. 9. Barry kissing maid

Fig. 10. Lady Lyndon in the bath

adorned, flanked by her children (fig. 13). One arm is draped around her
elder son, Lord Bullingdon, while the other dangles listlessly in the cradle
of Bryan. Mother and son are the embodiment of misery, a visual contradiction to the happy mother suggested by the voice-over. The narrator
reports that Lady Lyndon is a good mother who adores her children and
is adored by them in return. Even though the narrator tells us that Barry
believed his wife would enjoy the role of mother dandling the infant Bryan,
the image suggests that the construction of the happy mother is but a thin
tissue of lies. Once again the viewer's expectations are subverted to further
the emotional complexities of the film.

Among the recurrent themes in the film is Barry's desire to create a family, presumably to fulfill the longing for the father he lost as a child, and the
closeness he experienced as the only child of a doting mother. Beyond his
emotional quest there is the quest for status and wealth that his marriage
to Lady Lyndon tenuously offers him. Because his status is almost entirely
dependent on his wife, Barry sets out to gain a title of his own, largely
through the influence of corrupt aristocracy who for the right price agree
to lobby on his behalf. Barry meets with Lord Wendover, who virtually
guarantees him a title for a price exacted in cash and lavish behavior. Wendover's head is positioned between two paintings, to the left what seems
to be a classical arcadia peopled with nymphs at their baths, to the right a

Fig. 11. Barry and Lady Lyndon with Bryan

Fig. 12. Barry at the brothel.

Fig. 13. Lady Lyndon with her sons

scene of children and adults, very much like the family portraits that were so popular at the time (fig. 14). These portraits were not only statements of family pride but also served as documents of inheritance and traced family lineage. Both paintings ask us to question the morality and the feasibility of Wendover's actions. The scene that immediately follows is a humorous aside to the attentive viewer. As if to comment on the effort that will be required to accomplish the task of securing Barry a peerage, Kubrick thrusts an enormous statue of Atlas supporting the world into the frame (fig. 15).

In one of the most poignant scenes in the film, the impossibility of Barry's quest for family and heirs is confirmed (fig. 16). Even without the drone of the narrator's predictions of doom concerning Barry's project, the meaning of the scene is clear. Seated in front of and beneath an enormous family portrait, which has made several appearances in the hall of the Lyndon family home, Barry and his son Bryan are dwarfed by its size and presence in the cinematic frame.[6] The enormous physical and visual weight of the painting suggests the moral and cultural weight of family lineage. Their sun-bathed curvilinear forms are no challenge to the superiority of the ancient painting and the family it symbolizes. The prediction suggested in this scene and stated bluntly by the narrator is tragically borne out with the death of Bryan.

Fig. 14. Lord Wendover

Fig. 15. Atlas

Fig. 16. Anthony Van Dyck, *Philip, 4th Earl of Pembroke*, and his Family, 1630s, in the hall of Wilton House

After the death of Bryan, Barry falls into a deep depression, characterized by constant drunkenness. In one scene Mrs. Barry enters a darkened
room with two servants to carry the unconscious Barry to his bed. Barry's
pose is similar to the pose of the dissolute husband in Hogarth's print *The
Morning After*, from the series *Marriage Ala Mode* (fig. 17). Toward the end
of the film, we again find Barry in the same pose, this time having passed
out at his club (fig. 18). As he slumbers, Lord Bullingdon strides purpose-
fully through the club intent on finding his stepfather in order to challenge
him to a duel and defend his family honor. As he passes through the club
he walks beneath several portraits of aristocratic gentlemen, a visual statement of Bullingdon's pedigree and his right to inhabit these halls. Bullingdon believes, rightly, that Barry has insulted the family, dishonored the
Lyndon name, abused Lady Lyndon, and squandered the young lord's
inheritance. Bullingdon has long harbored hatred for the man who married his mother for the sake of wealth and title, with little love evident in
the union. *Marriage Ala Mode* was a series of paintings and prints that condemned the practice of loveless marriages for financial or social gain. The
inclusion of a pose and in the later case a similar setting, which was almost
a direct quotation from the eighteenth-century work, is intended to reinforce visually both the story line and the voiced narration.

At the end of the film Barry has been sent away from England, Lord
Bullingdon has reclaimed his ancestral home and what is left of his fortune,
and Lady Lyndon lives in quiet seclusion. In a kind of symmetry Bullingdon has assumed the position of only son to a solitary mother that Barry
occupied at the beginning of the film, and Barry has once again become
dependent on his mother. In the final scene, Lady Lyndon sits at a large
table beneath the family portrait, a sad reminder of the child who last
occupied that position in the cinematic world. As in the prior scene, the
portrait hangs in rebuke of the family that has fallen so low. They seem
frail and small in comparison to the painted figures behind them, an un-
spoken prediction of the future of the aristocracy and their way of life. As
Bullingdon hands Lady Lyndon a check to sign, she pauses to read the
inscription to Redmond Barry and to stare mournfully at nothing in particular. The date on the check is December 1789.

NOTES

I am grateful to my colleagues Leslie Cavell, Adam Lutzker, Sally Jordan, and Jim
Diedrick for discussion of ideas contained in this essay.

Fig. 17. Hogarth, *Marriage Ala Mode: The Morning After*, 1743–45, National Gallery, London

Fig. 18. Barry slumped in his chair at his club

1. Vincent LoBrutto, *Stanley Kubrick: A Biography* (New York: Donald I. Fine, 1997), 382; www.wiltonhouse.com/tours/double_cube_rm.html; www.corsham-court. co.uk, August 12, 2002.

2. John Engell, "Barry Lyndon, a Picture of Irony," *Eighteenth Century Life* 19 (May 1995): 84–86. It is interesting to note that Kubrick designated John Alcott as "photographer" rather than as cinematographer or director of photography.

3. Frank Cossa, "Images of Perfection: Life Imitates Art in Kubrick's Barry Lyndon," *Eighteenth Century Life* 19 (May 1995): 79.

4. These ideas have been explored by Mark Crispin Miller in "Barry Lyndon Reconsidered," *Georgia Review* 30, no. 4 (Winter, 1976): 827–53, and "Kubrick's Anti-Reading of the Luck of Barry Lyndon," *MLN* 91, no. 6 (December 1976): 1360–79; and by Willem Hesling, "Kubrick, Thackeray, and the Memoirs of Barry Lyndon, Esq.," *Literature/Film Quarterly* 29, no. 4 (2001): 264–78.

5. Cossa, "Images of Perfection," 79.

6. Anthony Van Dyck, *Philip, 4th Earl of Pembroke, and His Family,* 1630s.

Death by Typewriter

Stanley Kubrick, the Holocaust, and *The Shining*

GEOFFREY COCKS

It is one of the most unsettling scenes in all of cinema. A medium shot of two sets of red elevator doors flanked by vaguely *moderne* armchairs. Ominous music—Penderecki's *The Awakening of Jacob*—on the soundtrack. One of the elevator doors slides open, and in slow motion a thick torrent of what we know must be blood pours into the corridor. The livid purple-black flow bursts into a lurid red spray upon the floor and walls. The flood languidly carries the furniture toward the camera—toward *us*—then the blood itself washes up the camera lens and the screen goes black.[1] A long version of this scene from Stanley Kubrick's adaptation of Stephen King's horror novel *The Shining* was the first released to the public—at Christmas 1979—as the advertising trailer for the film. Such a scene appears nowhere in King's book and is thus another instance of Kubrick's inveterate shaping of his sources to his own vision.[2] Some reviewers complained upon the release of the film over the Memorial Day weekend in 1980 that the elevator scene was "suspended in the movie without meaning."[3] According to that line of reasoning, the image seems fit only as a marketing device, which it certainly must have been on the part of both Kubrick and Warner Brothers. But a close reading of Kubrick's life and work suggests that the ocean of blood flowing from the elevator in *The Shining* is the blood of centuries, the blood of millions, and, in particular, the blood of war and genocide in Kubrick's own century.

It is generally acknowledged that Kubrick's films display a deeply pessimistic outlook on the human condition. But little attention has been paid to the specific historical contexts and the specific contents of the books and films that inspired him. This essay argues that Kubrick's outlook was

decisively shaped by shattering world events as reflected in film and literature from the 1930s on. It also posits that the Holocaust was a central
influence on Kubrick's development as a person and as a filmmaker. Such
a dark outlook was appropriate for someone who took great interest in
modern history. Kubrick saw worldly powers at their worst in the modern
post-Napoleonic age of states newly energized by bureaucracy, science,
mass armies, and the xenophobic nationalism that reached its cruelest
expression in the fascism of the 1930s and 1940s. This perspective opened
him up to criticism for the lack of character portrayal and development
integral to conventional literature and film. For Kubrick, however, fine words
and traditional characterization were trivial compared to the power of images
as a means to address larger historical and cultural issues. All of his films
display a basic taxonomy: (1) violence; (2) systems of control; and (3) inherent human evil. Kubrick was not a cynic or a misanthrope, however. He
was a realistic and skeptical modernist who believed in the power of art to
draw attention to, and perhaps aid in mitigating, a dangerous world. Perhaps art could even provide balm and instruction for the twentieth century's greatest tragedy, the Holocaust, although Kubrick himself would
find it impossible to deal with this subject directly in his films.[4]

Part of Kubrick's reluctance to deal with the Holocaust directly in his
work had to do with the aesthetic problem of bringing art to bear on such
a subject. The appalling horror of the Holocaust made it a particularly
difficult subject for a satirist like Kubrick. The Holocaust was also a threatening topic not only because Kubrick was Jewish but because of the particular nature of some of his social, philosophical and historical concerns.
Unlike the rational systems whose *breakdown* Kubrick habitually contem-
plates in his films, the Nazis' Final Solution was not a rational system gone
wrong, it was a rationalized *system* gone *horribly right*. Moreover, the Holocaust at its black core is a horrible mystery of *irrational* evil that has in new
and extremely powerful ways thrown the nature and even the existence of
civilization and God into question. Kubrick searched for years for a book
on the Holocaust on which to base a film, but he never filmed the only
screenplay, "Aryan Papers," he wrote on the subject. After his death in 1999
Kubrick's wife reported that Kubrick was terribly depressed the entire time
he worked on that project.[5] For personal as well as aesthetic reasons, therefore, he was able to treat the subject only indirectly in *The Shining*. As
such, that film is the prime example in Kubrick's oeuvre of a curious, con-
flicted, and yet also creative approach-avoidance syndrome with regard to
the modern history of Germans, Jews, and the Holocaust. In the film there

is a deeply laid—and problematically obscure—subtext that positions the Holocaust as the veiled benchmark of evil in the modern world.

It has been correctly observed that Kubrick's films represent "a dispassionate, even antiseptic study of a found world."[6] It is this "found world" of great terror and danger that the Overlook Hotel represents in *The Shining* and whose horrors are witnessed by Danny, a young boy with the ability to see ("shine") into the past and future. Danny in this sense is a representation of Kubrick himself. Kubrick's directing style—many long takes and emphasis on actor interpretation to magnify emotional content—made him an "audience" as much as a "director,"[7] another indication of his ongoing desire to observe the world. Moreover, his fabled attention to detail in the preparation of his films and the composition of their images was driven by a desire for control and discipline over a threatening world very unlike the ordered chessboards over which he expertly pored. The human will to power was also something Kubrick felt within himself, symbolized by the names of birds of prey that he used for his production companies (Hawk Films, Harrier Films, Hobby Films, Eagle Films, and Peregrine Productions) and manifested in his lifelong fascination with the military, war, the Nazis, and his identification with Napoleon. Kubrick thus strove to sublimate antisocial drives into imperial artistic control of a world he found wanting and dangerous.[8]

Kubrick believed that film must attempt to rouse the audience to reflection instead of reconfirming comfortable assumptions in service to entertainment and commerce. His films—at least since *2001: A Space Odyssey* (1968)—employ an "open narrative" that requires the audience to derive meaning actively rather than being passively instructed, entertained, and manipulated. For the same reason Kubrick would never "explain" his films. As he put it early in his career: "I think for a movie or a play to say anything really truthful about life, it has to do so very obliquely, so as to avoid all pat conclusions and neatly tied-up ideas."[9] It is this same principle of critically examining ideas and phenomena that underlies Kubrick's postmodern interrogation of the film genres he adopts. He does this by making their constructions reflexive rather than transparent. For example, in *The Shining*, Kubrick parodies the "startle effect" by having the audience see Jack sneaking up on Wendy. Instead of our jumping in fright, only Wendy does. The film in this way works to have the audience understand, through both affect and intellect, the feelings of the characters as well as the larger historical issues it explores. The properly attentive audience will also think about how horror films and their audiences exploit the subject of human violence, fear, and suffering for purposes of commerce and diversion. *The Shining* thereby links enjoyment of fictional horror to repression of factual horror, a dynamic also represented in the deep burial—in plain sight—of visual references to the Holocaust. The result is not the "good scare" of a conventional movie of terror, but a lingering and informed sadness at the horrors of life as well as a deep unease at the human condition—an existential horror.

The choice of the medium of a horror film might seem to trivialize the Holocaust, but the very indirection of Kubrick's approach arguably coincides with doubts raised about the ability and appropriateness of art to represent the Holocaust.[10] According to this view, art, like Perseus viewing Medusa through a mirror, can approach such horror only by indirection and even then only with great difficulty. Kubrick's interests generally and the presentation of his dark view of the world also ran the artistic and ethical risk of making evil attractive, further complicating the aesthetic problems in representing the Holocaust.[11] Using a horror film, however, could be a means of attracting viewers and then engaging their interest—and their (eventual?) reflection—through a skillful mix of convention and artistry. This was particularly so in the case of *The Shining,* since it engaged contemporaneous cultural discourses that could heighten audience receptiveness to Kubrick's concerns. In Kubrick's hands *The Shining* was a self-consciously critical instance of a larger cultural phenomenon in the 1970s that saw a boom in horror films that registered crises within the American polity and patriarchy. And its historical trajectory was a response to the growth in the 1960s and 1970s of public interest in the Holocaust and Nazi Germany.

Given Kubrick's own serious intentions, the action of powerful contemporaneous discourses, and the "audience participation" that his style encouraged, any number of insights that occur to a thoughtful and observant viewer of *The Shining* almost certainly occurred to the obsessively meticulous Kubrick at one level of historical, psychological, or cultural consciousness or another. Any intertextuality between text and reader (and other texts) independent of the artist's intentions must therefore be complemented by a study of the convergence of *contexts* that influenced Kubrick's own concerns and choices.[12] More than anything else, *The Shining* displays a deep despair about the world after Auschwitz in line with a larger postmodern critique of the Enlightenment faith in reason and progress. It is thus a powerful example of art taking account of the Holocaust, and of a struggle within Kubrick and the surrounding culture to come to grips with its black legacy. A study of the history, structure, and content of *The Shining* reveals not just a convergence of evidence of Kubrick's struggle — and Kubrick's achievement — but a flood.

A Jewish Past

Born in the garment district of Manhattan in 1928, Kubrick spent most of his early life in the Bronx. He was the son of Jacob — or, as his father called himself, Jacques or Jack — and Gertrude Kubrick. Kubrick's father was a homeopathic physician who introduced his son to reading, chess, and photography. Both sides of the family had emigrated from the Austro-Hungarian Empire before World War I.[13] Like Sigmund Freud, one of the Central European intellectuals and artists who decisively influenced his view of the world, Kubrick was descended from the Eastern European Jews (*Ostjuden*) who would be the principal victims of the Final Solution. As a Jew in a Gentile world, Kubrick would — like Freud — use his position as an outsider with a deep sensitivity to social injustice to expose the dark underside of society. Because, again like Freud, Kubrick was distrustful of aspects of the human personality, he was also suspicious of enthusiasms and in particular of political attempts to improve humanity. Born into a world of growing nativist antisemitism and ethnic prejudice, he still regarded democracy as the least dangerous system of governance.[14] Even more important for Kubrick's developing outlook was the world of power, violence, and war dominated by men like Hitler in Europe, reflected, among other places, in the unceasing parade of movies and films Kubrick watched from the 1930s on. The deep distrust of the human personality shared by Kubrick and Freud stemmed in great part from consciousness of the precarious position of Jews in particular within a Christian society now afflicted with even more radical "racial" notions of Gentile superiority. As Kubrick once put it, "Gentiles don't know how to worry."[15]

Thus a great problem in Kubrick's films is the power that hypermasculine elites wield over the rest of humanity. His professed affinity for Carl Jung's concept of what Private Joker in *Full Metal Jacket* (1987) calls "the duality of man" was secondary to his Freudian view that good and evil are inextricably entwined within each of us and within society. Kubrick's interest in Jung's search for greater synthetic truths in the human unconscious served only as a thin defensive wish. As novelist Diane Johnson, who co-wrote the screenplay for *The Shining*, observed: "His pessimism seems to have arisen from his idealism, an outraged yearning for a better order, a

wish to impose perfection on the chaotic materials of reality."[16] In this world
the unconscious is not the repository, as Jung would have it, of supernatural or archetypal forms but the source of the duplicity of human expression whereby words do not reveal suprahuman truths but hide and
distort human motives. This psychoanalytic idea, like the dreams Kubrick
said his films resembled, animated his increased conviction from 1968 on
that film must argue and convince through the use of visual space and
image rather than through dialogue.[17]

Kubrick's position as a suspicious outsider was manifested and reinforced in the independence he won from the Hollywood studio system.
The original Hollywood moguls of the 1920s too were Eastern European
Jews, but they made movies that stressed assimilation and avoidance of conflict with the Gentile establishment. While the Russian and Polish pogroms
they had fled were sometimes reflected in their stories about the American
West, their movies molded the American Dream as happy escape for the
individual and generic common man.[18] Kubrick, like Freud and the moguls
a nonreligious Jew, would likewise concentrate on Gentiles in his films.
But Kubrick—eventually from the island of Britain anchored safely off the
Continent—also looked back across to Europe and at the world in light of
the fires of Auschwitz. The Kubrick homeland of Galicia had long been a
place of national conflict and contention, with the Jews there regularly victimized by Austrians, Poles, Russians, and Ukranians. The name Kubrick
itself is derived from the Ukrainian words *kubryk,* a small barrel, and *kubrak,*
a beggar or poor man.[19] In 1942 the transport of millions of Jews to the
extermination camps in Poland began. On October 4/5 the Jews of Buczacz
and the villages east of the town were subjected to "resettlement" operations. In the Kubrick hometown of Probużna on October 4, the Jewish
holiday of Simchat Torah, eight hundred Jews were sent to the extermination camp at Bełżec and the work camp at Lemberg-Janowska. Soon
after, the rest of the population of fifteen hundred Jews were sent to the
ghetto in Kopyczyne, which was liquidated in June 1943.[20]

We do not know how closely the Kubrick family followed events in
Eastern Europe during the war. But word of the exterminations had reached
America by 1942, and New York City was the center of Jewish-American
activity in response to the killings. Kubrick's wife, Christiane, has said that
Stanley knew of extended family members murdered by the Nazis.[21] Before
and during the war, however, Stanley spent much of his time at the movies,
watching double features twice a week at Bronx theaters like the Loew's
Paradise and the RKO Fordham, where between 1936 and 1946 more than
165 films were shown that dealt with World War II or the Nazis. One of

these, *Hotel Berlin* (1945), was unique for the time in that it even mentions the Birkenau camp at Auschwitz where "we can exterminate six thousand in twenty-four hours." During the war, Kubrick also indulged his passion for photojournalism. He sold his first photograph—of a downcast newsstand dealer surrounded by headlines announcing the death of President Roosevelt in April 1945—to *Look* magazine, which published it on June 26, 1945.[22] Only the month before, both *Look* and *Life* had published photographs taken in Nazi concentration camps. The effect of these photographs on the public was profound: "Images had shown themselves capable of conveying the very horror that had incapacitated words [and] helped turn collective disbelief into the shock and horror of recognition."[23] Thus from an early age Kubrick became convinced of the power of images. In connection with his view of a dangerous world run by dangerous men, it is no accident, for instance, that the walls of the evil Overlook Hotel in *The Shining* display countless black-and-white photographs of the powerful men who built and patronized it.

Kubrick's camera, however, was not only a way to record the world but also to distance it.[24] He never confronted antisemitism directly in his films and created only a handful of minor Jewish characters. Much of this, it is true, had to do with reasons of commerce and narrative economy, as when he wrote Jewish characters out of the screenplays of six of the sources he filmed, Humphrey Cobb's *Paths of Glory* (1935), Lionel White's *Clean Break* (1955), Anthony Burgess's *A Clockwork Orange* (1962), William Makepeace Thackeray's *The Memoirs of Barry Lyndon, Esq.* (1844), Gustav Hasford's *The Short-Timers* (1979), and Arthur Schnitzler's *Dream Story* (1926). In *Eyes Wide Shut* (1999), his adaptation of the Schnitzler novella, Kubrick even changed the protagonists from Jews to Gentiles, moved the location from Vienna to New York City, and changed a scene of street antisemitism to one of homophobia. But one of Kubrick's early ideas for *Eyes Wide Shut* had Woody Allen, in a dramatic and not a comedic role, playing a Manhattan Jewish doctor.[25] Beyond commerce and economy, Kubrick was clearly ambivalent about the portrayal of Jews and antisemitism on the screen. In—or near—the end, however, he found a way to deal with the Jewish people's greatest tragedy. But he did so in an extremely indirect fashion, meeting personal as well as artistic need.

A German Presence

Kubrick's life and career were characterized by a marked ambivalence about all things German. This had to do with the awful conjunction of beauty and horror he saw in German history that led him to observe: "I've never seen a history of Nazi Germany I didn't like."[26] But Kubrick's ambivalence also had to do with a certain psychological tension generated by the confluence of his Jewish background and his evolving relationship with the German world. Initially, this relationship grew within the confines of the Jewish community in New York. His first wife, high school sweetheart Toba Metz, was descended from a Latvian Jewish family; his second wife, dancer Ruth Sobotka, was a 1939 Jewish refugee from Vienna. His third wife, actress and painter Christiane Harlan, was a non-Jewish German he met while filming *Paths of Glory* in Germany in 1957. Suddenly, Kubrick was entangled in the "Aryan" side of Germanic Europe's recent past. Christiane's father, Fritz Harlan, was a musician who worked at the German Theatre in The Hague from 1942 to 1944 while living in confiscated Jewish housing.[27] Christiane was born in 1932 and, like most young Germans, spent some time in the Hitler Youth, once saw Hitler, recalls "that insane voice," and struggled with her family's contact in The Hague with direct evidence of the Final Solution.[28] From 1941 to 1945 she lived in Reihen, a small village near Heidelberg. She and her younger brother Jan had been evacuated from Karlsruhe to escape the Allied bombing raids. They lived on the grounds of a brick factory in Reihen and labored in the fields alongside other evacuees and forced laborers from France and Ukraine. One of her paintings, "The Brick Factory," portrays aspects of life in Reihen during the war: the harvesting of grain, the firing and stacking of bricks, children's games, the crash of an American bomber, and the air-raid bunker.[29] Christiane's uncle was Veit Harlan, the director of the infamous antisemitic film *Jew Süss* (1940), who was acquitted of war crimes in 1949. Kubrick met him in Munich in 1957 and wanted to make a film about him, Propaganda Minister Joseph Goebbels, and daily life in the Third Reich.[30] The Harlan family became an integral part of Kubrick's own artistic empire. Christiane contributed paintings to *A Clockwork Orange* and *Eyes Wide Shut;* Jan Harlan was executive producer for the last four films; Veit Harlan's daughter, Maria Körber, dubbed the psychiatrist's voice for the German release of *A Clockwork Orange;* and two younger Harlans, Manuel and Dominic, worked on *Eyes Wide Shut.*[31]

The style of Kubrick's films owed much to the work of German directors like Max Ophuls, G. W. Pabst, Erich von Stroheim, and Fritz Lang. Kubrick also displayed great familiarity with German classical music. While writing the screenplay for *2001,* for example, he and Arthur C. Clarke listened to Carl Orff's *Carmina Burana* (1937) and Kubrick even considered offering Orff a commission to write a score for the film. Kubrick also considered Mendelssohn and Mahler for the film and ended up using Richard Strauss's *Thus Spake Zarathustra* (1896) and Johann Strauss Jr.'s "Blue Danube Waltz" (1867).[32] In *A Clockwork Orange* he followed novelist Anthony Burgess in employing Beethoven's Symphony No. 9 (1824) as a leitmotif. Significantly, Kubrick never used the music of the antisemitic Richard Wagner, Hitler's favorite composer and scorer for much of the soundtrack to the Third Reich. Kubrick regarded the German-Jewish Franz Kafka as the greatest writer of the century because he thought Kafka unrivaled in placing the extraordinary in the ordinary world.[33] Kubrick also constantly considered German properties, including a World War II screenplay he wrote with Richard Adams titled "The German Lieutenant," which also features the "Blue Danube Waltz."[34]

But Kubrick also never approached the subject of Germany directly in his films, although odd features of almost all of his films before 1980 demonstrate uneasy engagement with the artifacts of the recent German past. *Fear and Desire* (1953), his first feature film, is a fable about war. The forest in which the story takes place is, the narrator tells us, "outside history." But the (mostly German) uniforms, weapons, and landscape tell us that the referent—save for a couple of scenes with ferns and palm trees that betoken the primeval and the Pacific—is Europe in World War II. Subsequent films betray the same small toying with the subject of Germany. *Killer's Kiss* (1955), a film noir shot in New York City, features a German Luger pistol. Film noir of the 1940s was itself a response to "the violence unleashed by the war," suggesting "that dangerous impulses resided in the souls of Americans themselves."[35] The Luger appears seemingly as a prize of war that marks the protagonist, fighter Davy Gordon, as a World War II veteran. Neither in film noir nor on the streets of the United States, however, was a Luger ever the weapon of choice; but the Luger was one of the most common symbols of Nazi brutality in American war films, having been a standard German army pistol since 1908 and exported in large numbers to America after World War I.[36] And the fight with and among mannequins in *Killer's Kiss,* which starts with a close-up—very similar to a shot in *Hotel Berlin*—of the Luger (fig. 19) dropped by the "dark beast" Vincent Rapallo, carries in its compositions disturbing associations with the photographs of bodies found stacked in Nazi concentration camps in 1945 (fig. 20).[37]

Four years later, Kubrick added a coda to *Paths of Glory* in which a young German girl (Christiane Harlan) sings of love and loss to French soldiers about to go back into the line against the Germans, while *Dr. Strangelove* (1964) rolls out the comic epitome of the mad Nazi scientist. In *A Clockwork Orange* (1971) a British street gang wears Nazi regalia; behavioral scientists use Nazi propaganda and combat footage to condition Alex; and one low-angle shot, taken from the point of view of a congregation of prisoners, consists of trusty prisoner Alex in black uniform and red armband à la SS, an officer with somewhat of a Hitler mustache and certainly a Hitler mien and posture, and the prison chaplain with his arm in the position of a Nazi salute (fig. 21).[38]

The Great Horror

Kubrick was not alone in his hesitation to confront the Holocaust. The Holocaust received little scholarly and even less public attention until the Adolf Eichmann trial in Jerusalem and the publication of Raul Hilberg's *The Destruction of the European Jews* in 1961, the appearance of Richard Rubenstein's *After Auschwitz: History, Theology, and Contemporary Judaism* in 1966, and the post-Vietnam American television series *Holocaust* in 1978.

Fig. 19. Luger

Fig. 20. Mannequins

Fig. 21. Nazi Troika

In 1962 Kubrick turned down an offer to make a film of the Holocaust novel *The Pawnbroker* (1961), but in 1975 he had Jan Harlan read Hilberg's book and sent Harlan to ask Isaac Bashevis Singer to help Kubrick write a screenplay for a Holocaust film. Singer refused, saying he didn't know anything about the Holocaust. Kubrick then sent a copy of the Hilberg book to Michael Herr in 1980, saying the book was "'*monumental*' [and] that, probably, what he most wanted to make was a film about the Holocaust, but good luck in putting all that into a two-hour movie."[39] In the early 1980s Kubrick even wrote Hilberg, asking for a recommendation of a book on which to base a Holocaust film. Hilberg suggested the diary of Warsaw ghetto leader Adam Czerniakow, published in English in 1979, but Kubrick rejected the idea, saying such a film would be antisemitic, presumably because of Czerniakow's role in carrying out Nazi deportation orders.[40]

Kubrick with obvious ambivalence was now pondering the film about the Holocaust he "probably . . . most wanted" to make. The outright Holocaust film Kubrick came closest to making—and even then not really close at all—was to be based on Louis Begley's *Wartime Lies* (1991) and which became the screenplay "Aryan Papers." The novel concerns a young Polish Jew—another child confronting a dark "found world"—who under the occupation is hidden as a Catholic. But Kubrick was distracted by another project (which became the posthumous production *A.I.* [2001]) and also apparently felt that Steven Spielberg's *Schindler's List* (1993) had beaten him to the punch.[41] Kubrick's approach-avoidance syndrome must have been engaged by young Maciek's first words in the novel: "I was born a few months after the burning of the Reichstag in T., a town of about forty thousand in a part of Poland that before the Great War had belonged to the Austro-Hungarian Empire. My father was T.'s leading physician. . . . My mother's older sister was . . . [of] the close world of wealthy Galician Jews."[42] T. by its population has to be Tarnopol, the only town of that size close to Buczacz and Probużna, while Kubrick's own father was a physician. Clearly, Begley's book was both attractive and threatening to Kubrick, certainly a reason he put it aside for other projects. It may also have been the case that *The Shining* had satisfied—and/or repelled—him at some subliminal level. *That* perhaps was as close as he felt he could come to the subject.

By the 1970s, in any case, in spite of his ambivalence and hesitation, Kubrick was beginning to bring his imaginative energies to bear on the Holocaust. This is apparent from a pattern of film plotting that developed in the period from *Dr. Strangelove* to *The Shining*. *Dr. Strangelove*, for example, has not one but two endings. There is the obvious nuclear destruction of the world by the Doomsday Machine, but that ending is only penultimate. It is only the means—an ultimate "Final Solution"—to clear the way for a Master Race selected by the Nazi Dr. Strangelove to survive underground. Kubrick's next film, *2001: A Space Odyssey*, in part an artifact of 1960s utopianism, constitutes a response of measured hope to *Dr. Strangelove*'s double end-of-the-world scenario. It does this by being a fairly scrupulous allegory of Nietzsche's ideal of the "overman" as a mor-ally—and not a racially—superior human being and ending with a "Star-Child" founding a new—not finding an old—world.[43] Kubrick, however, returned in the early 1970s to his usual grim outlook on humanity in *A Clockwork Orange*. In this he was responding to that decade's preoccupa-tion with a general disillusionment with American and Western institu-tions ranging from the military to the government to the family. *A Clock-work Orange* too addressed Kubrick's own growing preoccupation with the Holocaust, though faintly and indirectly. For example, Alex recalls his conditioning as including pictures of "concentration camps" when he—or at least the viewer—has, unlike in the novel, witnessed only Nazi leaders and German soldiers and weapons.[44]

A vignette from the filming of *A Clockwork Orange* might well be addi-tional evidence of Kubrick's mulling over of the Holocaust. In one scene there is a demonstration by the government of the conditioning of Alex to become physically ill whenever he feels anger or lust. He is insulted, struck, and pushed down by an "actor." Alex is incapacitated by nausea and, finally, flat on his back, is forced to lick the sole of the man's shoe. What is very odd about the scene (in an *Annie Hall* [1977] sort of way) is that the actor's enunciation of the line "You see that shoe?" sounds like "You see that, Jew?" John Clive, who played the part, recalls no discussion of the line, its enunciation, or any subtext. He even thinks he ad-libbed the line, a practice Kubrick encouraged. Clive also remembers that he was called back alone to do this particular (and common Kubrickian) shot, from Alex's point of view looking upward past the shoe into the actor's face: "Stanley decided that he wanted to shoot that himself. . . . So he took the camera and laid down on the floor at my feet. Something I'd never expected. . . . And I had to put my foot in front of his face and tell him to lick it. Like I said, right out of left field."[45]

It all went quite quickly, according to Clive, perhaps in a single take. Given Kubrick's fabled insistence on getting something he wanted no mat-ter how many takes it took, he was obviously satisfied. It is hardly far-fetched, therefore, to argue that at one level of consciousness or another

Kubrick, flat on his back with a camera in his hands and a foot in his face, found during filming and/or editing personal and artistic meaning in the sound of the words in terms of a recently heightened conscious and unconscious preoccupation with modern power, Jews, and the Holocaust. If valid, this interpretation gives even greater force to the shot, recreating as it does the historical reality of Jews—like other "Others"—under the boot of the powerful and the pitiless. It also presages the family in *The Shining* at the end of the decade of the 1970s, a family threatened from within as well as from without by contemporary forces of evil far greater than those faced by the destroyed family in the intervening *Barry Lyndon* (1975).

The Great Horror Film

The 1970s saw an explosion of horror films, a cultural discourse that reflected American struggles with unpleasant truths about its social and political order laid bare by recent changes and challenges. Kubrick, whose own *A Clockwork Orange, Barry Lyndon,* and plans to film Diane Johnson's novel *The Shadow Knows* (1974) reflected this culture's particular concern with the crisis of the patriarchal family, was predisposed to add a horror film to the genres he had already explored. The 1970s also saw "Hitler Wave" books, "Nazi-retro" films, and other events whereby "the Holocaust moved to the center of American culture."[46] Horror films were also attractive to Kubrick because their heritage was closely tied to German Expressionist cinema, whose "projection of emotional states by means of imagery" accurately describes the cinema of Kubrick, "the last Expressionist."[47]

Stephen King's *The Shining* (1977) is a supernatural thriller about a father, mother, and son—Jack, Wendy, and Danny Torrance—isolated by winter in the haunted mountaintop Overlook Hotel. Kubrick saw the book as a means to explode the horror genre and explore the violence inherent in human society. He hired Diane Johnson to help with the screenplay; not only was she an expert in the eighteenth- and nineteenth-century Gothic novel but also the Johnson novel Kubrick had read was about a woman whose mantra is "we are going to be murdered."[48] King's novel uses the Gothic tradition of "the terrible house" that was also the basis of a horror film Kubrick admired, Robert Wise's *The Haunting* (1963). But King's book also reflects the turn in the literature and cinema of horror toward replacing the old aristocratic haunted house with the modern hotel. Hotels—and, ever since Alfred Hitchcock's *Psycho* (1960), motels—are homes that are not homes, places of privacy but also of vulnerability, of collectivity but also of isolation. Vicki Baum's *Grand Hotel* (1932) is a site not only of romance but also of conspiracy, and physical and mental illness. Such characteristics reflect the fin-de-siècle change in Western hotels from a domestic environment to a commercial one, from a communal group to a collection of strangers.[49] The horrors in *The Shining,* as in *Psycho,* are Kafkaesque since they take place not in the gloomy shadows of an old private home but in the bright public rooms of modern life and activity.[50] In post-1945 film and literature, the hotel had become a literal and metaphorical extension of modern public violence and even specifically of Nazi state surveillance, as in Fritz Lang's *The 1000 Eyes of Dr. Mabuse* (1960), and persecution, as in Liliana Cavani's *The Night Porter* (1974), Aharon Appelfeld's *Badenheim 1939* (1980), D. M. Thomas's *The White Hotel* (1981), and the Coen Brothers homage to Kubrick, *Barton Fink* (1991). Kubrick was influenced in this association between hotels and inherent social evil not only by Lang and Hitchcock but also by James Agee's 1949 film script of Stephen Crane's short story, "The Blue Hotel" (1898). Crane's depiction—like Johnson's and film noir's—of the world as a place of danger and evil seemed particularly relevant after 1945.[51] Alain Resnais's early short documentary on the Final Solution, *Night and Fog* (1955), for its part, observed that a "concentration camp is built like a stadium or a big hotel."[52]

In an early treatment of the novel Kubrick creates a broader historical context by replacing King's musical and historical referents to America in 1945 with ones exclusively to Europe between the wars by means of 1930s British dance music and a New Year's Eve party of 1919.[53] But the Overlook Hotel most nearly resembles in its remoteness and attendant symbols the Berghof Sanitarium in Thomas Mann's *The Magic Mountain* (1924). As an artistic and philosophical response to the horrors of World War II, *The Shining* was modeled on Mann's artistic and philosophical response to the decline of European civilization to and through World War I. Kubrick was certainly familiar with Mann's novel, since he took literature classes at Columbia University from Lionel Trilling, who regularly taught it.[54] Unless one adopts the view that texts derive meaning only from other texts and not from their creators, there are too many parallels between Mann's novel and Kubrick's film not to assume at least some conscious as well as unconscious construction. It is consistent with Kubrick's avoidance of the established interpretations that accompany famous works that he never revealed this even to Diane Johnson or his family.[55] This was also a way of establishing his interpretation as a means of artistic and didactic control over the dangerous found world.

Kubrick surely was aware of the coincidence of the name of the sanitarium in Mann's novel and Hitler's own Berghof at Berchtesgaden, with its
"Eagle's Nest" above.[56] There are also strong overtones of Kafka's *The Castle* (1922) in the film, particularly in the association of eagles with malevolent hidden power. Kubrick was fascinated by coincidences and thus might
also have known that Kafka died in 1924 of tuberculosis, the very disease
Mann's sanitarium is dedicated to curing.[57] Mann, who was not Jewish
and had not yet witnessed the world after Auschwitz, retains at least some
faith in human reason to overcome the decline of civilization and the ten
million dead of the war of 1914–1918. *The Magic Mountain* is a bildungs-
roman; *The Shining* is a rueful contemplation of how history shows that
human beings learn nothing, or at least not enough to overcome the
malevolent forces that surround and inhabit them.

The Shining is also the most autobiographical of Kubrick's films, building upon a method of filmmaking centered within his family circle and
producing "a strange film that reveals much more about its maker than he
may have intended."[58] Like *Eyes Wide Shut*, the story focuses on a single-
family triad of husband, wife, and child without the usual Kubrick media-
tion of a narrator. Apart from Danny as another Kubrick child confronting
a dangerous world, the film focuses on the father, who is attempting to be
a writer. Even the typewriter Jack uses was one of Kubrick's own, and in
Vivian Kubrick's *Making The Shining* (1980) Kubrick himself is shown typing on a small yellow Adler.[59] Aside from Kubrick's habit of shooting his
films close to home, members of his family were, as usual or even more
than usual, a constant presence during the production of *The Shining*.
Whether causal or coincidental, their presence was a condition that joined
the personal with the historical over the long production schedule. It is
also significant that during the shooting of the film Kubrick allowed his
daughter Vivian to make the only formal record of him at work. *Making
The Shining* (1980) even shows Kubrick's parents, both of whom would die
in 1985, making an on-set visit to their son. Kubrick, in his usual realistic (though *not* naturalistic) manner, also eliminates many of the novel's
supernatural effects to focus on the internal and unconscious dynamics of
his characters that are the forces behind everyday "reality." The Grady girls,
who are a tiny part of the novel's narrative, assume a central role in the
film, reflecting not only Kubrick's own family ties but also the dark historical forces that threaten them. Kubrick admired King's book because it
fools the reader into thinking Jack is simply insane and then reveals the
supernatural forces at play in the hotel. On the symbolic level in *The Shining*,

however, Kubrick replaces the supernatural with the historical. The ghosts in the Overlook, after all, represent the hotel's—and humanity's—past. Ultimately, therefore, *The Shining* is not about ghosts; it is about death, that is, how people become the ghosts we imagine. And more specifically it is about murder, indeed, about mass murder, including the genocide of the Jews that Kubrick could not directly represent, in great measure because the threat was not only ruthless but personal and familial. As Kubrick himself revealingly commented on the virtues of the horror genre upon release of *The Shining*, "'we can see the dark side without having to confront it directly.'"[60]

The screenplay accordingly draws from Bruno Bettelheim's book *The Uses of Enchantment* (1976) and Freud's essay "The Uncanny" (1919).[61] Bettelheim argues that, unlike cartoons, fairy tales address the antisocial and aggressive drives basic to the human personality. While Danny watches Roadrunner and Wiley Coyote cartoons on television, Wendy makes reference to Hansel and Gretel, and Jack literally takes on the role of the Big Bad Wolf. All the quite naturalistic ovens in the film thus supplement the discourse on the timelessness of the fairytale witch's oven with a discourse on recent history. The image of a wolf, a popular cultural construction on the Nazis from the 1930s and 1940s, also links to World War II. A red Volkswagen—the Torrances drive a yellow VW—lies crushed under a jack-knifed (!) trailer rig, while a car radio reports on road conditions at the Eisenhower Tunnel, Red Mountain, and Wolf Creek. "Wolf" was Hitler's nickname, the Nazis building the town of Wolfsburg in honor of Hitler to produce Volkswagens.[62] And Eisenhower not only was the Supreme Allied Commander in Europe during World War II, he was the postwar president of Columbia University on whom Kubrick did two photo essays in the early 1950s. Freud's related idea is that what is most familiar is also the most sinister, all those repressed emotions "that which makes you feel uneasy in the world of your normal experience."[63] The uncanny has a long association with the horror genre and in the modern era has focused on the demonic in and as the world, particularly in the works of Kafka. In Kubrick, the uncanny is married to the grotesque, which in contrast to King's Gothic work "offers no resolution based on belief in a natural or moral order."[64] Kubrick's use of Paul Peel's painting of two naked children in front of a large fireplace, *After the Bath* (1890), thus creates the same critical and reflexive juxtaposition of cozy domesticity and historical horror as the same painting's appearance in Atom Egoyan's film about memory of the Armenian genocide of 1915, *Ararat* (2002). While the novel ends with the destruction of the evil Overlook Hotel, in Kubrick's film the hotel remains—eternally—open. *The Shining* is Kubrick's clearest expression of the contingency of human existence in a cold, silent, absurd universe—a hotel empty save for demons from history—devoid of purpose or meaning.[65]

Kubrick, much more than King, also emphasizes the history of racial persecution represented by the Overlook Hotel. Kubrick had treated race in his films before. In *Paths of Glory,* for example, a young French officer speaks in social Darwinian terms of "herd instinct" of men under shellfire as "a lower animal sort of thing."[66] Kubrick's hotel, like Mann's sanitarium and Kafka's castle, is the preserve of the social and political elite, "all the best people," the manager tells Jack and Wendy; and while the ghosts in the film are all white, consistent with Kubrick's preoccupation with per- petrators, the one actual victim of Jack's murderous rampage is, in the words of one of the ghosts, "a nigger cook."[67] Kubrick also invents the fact that the Overlook stands on "an old Indian burial ground," its interior trappings, copied from the Ahwahnee Hotel at Yosemite, based on Native American motifs.[68] There are other victims of the patriarchy as well: Danny has been abused by his father, while Wendy is another in a series of Kubrick women preyed upon by men. Unlike in the book, however, she, not Jack, takes care of the hotel and successfully resists Jack by means of both knife and baseball bat. Jack sits uselessly at his typewriter, hammering out the same sentence over and over. He is therefore another in a series of sitting Kubrick men who attempt to brutally manage the young and the female.[69] Jack is also one of those sad Kubrick functionaries who, very much in the Freudian language of anal aggression, do the "dirty work" for the masters, as reflected by Wendy's words in a dissolve from Jack "writing": "The loser has to keep America clean, how's that?"[70] This class perspective is power- fully informed by Kafka's "The Metamorphosis" (1916), a story about the alienation of self and family that comes from meaningless jobs in service to soulless authority. It has also been argued that there is a connection between the Volkswagen Beetle that Jack drives and Kafka's Gregor Samsa, who awakens one morning to find himself transformed into a beetle.[71]

But it is the Nazi devil more than anything else that lives in the details, so deeply in part because *The Shining* is structured in accord with Freud's dream theory. Kubrick systematically uses Freudian concepts to represent the repression and persistence of history. Because the Freudian uncon- scious exerts constant pressure on the conscious, signs and symbols in dreams are overdetermined, that is, they represent more than one mean- ing and they can also appear singularly and without apparent relevance to the immediate context. For example, the baseball bat with which Wendy slugs Jack bears the signature of Carl Yastrzemski.[72] This makes sense in that the Torrances are from Vermont, making them likely fans of Yastrzemski's team, the Boston Red Sox. But the fact that Yastrzemski is the only contemporaneous baseball star of Polish extraction also connects with the cultural geography of the film's Holocaust construction. A similarly indirect allusion to this particular dark past is Jack's typewriter. In one scene Kubrick dissolves from Jack's joking—and reflexive—reference to hotel ghosts and déjà vu (history as repetition) to a close-up of the typewriter flanked by a pack of Marlboro cigarettes (the rugged Western "Marlboro Man") and a smoking ashtray (fig. 22), the shot accompanied by a horrific booming on the soundtrack.[73] The typewriter is German, an *Adler*, or "eagle." An eagle also sits behind the desk of Overlook manager Stuart Ullman, whose initials transposed are U.S. and on whose desk—as over Jack's—is an American flag. Jack in the scene immediately before the dissolve to the close-up of the Adler wears a shirt emblazoned with an eagle and the words "Stovington Eagles." The eagle is a symbol of both the American and German state linked in the film as well through the persecution of Native Americans and Jews, respectively. In this construction, the Adler typewriter refers to the SS extermination bureaucracy detailed by Hilberg. Like Dr. Strangelove in his wheelchair, Jack is (part of) a machine, in Kubrick films always a sign of danger and a conflation Freud cites as an example of the uncanny. The opposition of the mechanical and the organic—the "mecha" vs. "orga" of *A.I.*—is a chillingly appropriate trope for the Holocaust, represented as well in the Torrances' Boulder apartment by a dark painting, *Horse and Train* (1954), and the sounds of a train on a television.[74] The typewriter thus is as central to Kubrick's film as typewriters are to Spielberg's *Schindler's List*. When the camera pulls back, up, and—frightened?—away from the close-up of the typewriter we see that Jack is hurling—and not tossing—a tennis ball again and again against a wall decorated with Native American designs. The direction of this sequence is into the past: from Jack in the present to the booming German death machine and back—with Jack's repeated throws symbolizing history as repetition—to European decimation of Native Americans.

The Shining follows *The Magic Mountain* in terms of two major symbols, the number seven and the color yellow. The number seven is the most culturally loaded of all numbers in the Western tradition and is often associated with the mysterious and the malevolent. *The Shining*, like *The Magic Mountain*, bulges with the number. Jack's liquor of choice is Jack Daniel's

Black Label No. 7; Jack drives to the Overlook from Boulder in three
and a half hours, a round-trip of seven hours; Sidewinder is twenty-five
($2+5=7$) miles from the hotel; cases of 7-Up are stacked in the kitchen corridors; Jack knocks seven times on the door to the bathroom in which
Wendy is hiding. Kubrick, however, uses seven most consistently with reference to history in fact and fiction. All of the dates mentioned in connection with the history of the Overlook Hotel are multiples of seven.
Construction on the Overlook began in 1907, the same year Mann's protagonist arrives for a seven-year stay at the Berghof. The former caretaker
at the Overlook killed his family in 1970, and the film ends with a photograph—one of twenty-one grouped on a wall—of eternal caretaker Jack at
a party in the seventh month of the year, on July 4, 1921. In *The Magic
Mountain* the pervasive pattern of permutations of the number seven has
most commonly been read as Mann's symbol of rational self-overcoming
of the fascination with evil and destruction. But Mann too had doubts about
the fate of the modern world. Even though Hans Castorp, whose name in
syllable, sound, and cadence resembles that of Jack Torrance, escapes freez-
ing in the snow like Jack, he dies in the war that breaks out in 1914.[75]

Fig. 22. Adler

But for Kubrick, the number seven is unambiguously the chronologi-
cal key to horrors past and present. This is clear from the most hidden
(though in plain sight and hearing) multiple of seven in *The Shining:* forty-
two. Television news reports a $42 million spending bill, and Wendy
watches the American home-front war movie *Summer of '42* (1971), in the
middle of winter. It is also the number on the sleeve of Danny's jersey early
in the film shown before and after his vision of the blood flowing from the
elevator (fig. 23).[76] In line with Kubrick's Gothic recourse to doubles (and
mirrors) in the film to characterize the hidden and dangerous side of
human nature, forty-two is twenty-one doubled. It is also the product of
the three digits in 237, the number of the double-doored room of mystery
and murder that embodies the dark past of the Overlook.[77] (Perhaps coin-
cidentally and perhaps not, Freud's discussion in "The 'Uncanny'" of the
recurrence of the number sixty-two appears on page 237 of *The Standard
Edition* of his works.) The awful historical significance of the year 1942
in the context of the years marking the history of the hotel in *The Shining*
lies in the fact that it was on January 20, 1942, in the middle of winter,
that the Nazis organized the Final Solution at the Wannsee Conference in

Fig. 23. 42

Berlin. This was also the year during which more Jews died in the Holocaust—2.7 million—including most of the Jews of Probużna—than in any
other year.[78] It is for this reason that Kubrick shows Wendy in the cold,
cavernous kitchen of the hotel as her attention is caught by a television
news report about the disappearance of a twenty-four-year-old woman on
a hunting trip with her husband, an ominous and derisive mirroring of the
black number forty-two in the year of publication of *The Magic Mountain*
that underlines the difference between the scale of horror contemplated by
Mann and Kubrick.[79] Mann after all was writing in 1924, while Kubrick
would be born only in 1928—fourteen years after the outbreak of the First
World War in 1914 and fourteen years before the full fury of the Holocaust
in 1942.

　　Kubrick's use of the number seven is not unique to *The Shining* but
builds upon the use of that number in previous films to symbolize war and
military organization. Kubrick thus centers war and violence in human
history through the number most closely identified with the Western tradition from Pythagoras through Judeo-Christianity. In *Paths of Glory*,
Kubrick changes the unit numbers from the novel into ones all dominated
by the number seven and displays them prominently in several shots. The
regiment number of the men condemned to be shot is 710, that of the
members of the firing squad 701, that of the officers of the court martial
727, and the execution itself occurs at seven in the morning. Kubrick also
uses seven in connection with criminal violence in *The Killing* (1956). The
shooting of a racehorse occurs during the seventh race by a World War II
veteran (played by Timothy Carey, one of the condemned men in *Paths of
Glory*), behind whom as he sets up to shoot (and is subsequently shot himself) is a car whose license plate displays four sevens. Kubrick's last war
film, *Full Metal Jacket* (1987), features the drill instructor in the first shot
of the opening scene in the Marine barracks with a sign on the wall behind
him showing a white seven on a red field.[80] It is thus in line with the association of seven with organized war and violence that Kubrick in *The Shining* centers the frame in one extended shot on the stock numbers on a box
behind Jack in the storeroom as Grady shames him into promising to murder his family: 01439, recalling the years of the outbreak of the two world
wars, and 39000, reiterating the Second World War and its horrors, especially those associated in the rest of the film with the year 1942.[81]

　　The color yellow in *The Shining* is another direct link with *The Magic
Mountain* and with the Final Solution. For Mann, yellow denotes the
tuberculosis consuming the lives in the sanitarium. Kubrick, like Mann,

also uses blue in association with cold, isolation, and death as well as red
for violence and murder, but it is yellow—for Kubrick as well as Mann—
that is the predominant color. In *The Shining,* yellow is initially informed
by its modern vehicular meaning as the color of caution and warning.
Under the opening credits, Jack drives a yellow—in King's novel, red—
Volkswagen (Hitler's "people's car") to his job interview at the Overlook.
Later he and his family arrive at the hotel in the same car, just as Hans Castorp arrives at the Berghof in a yellow cabriolet. More important, Kubrick
uses yellow in its historical associations with sin, jealousy, cowardice,
treachery, disease, and institutionalized antisemitism in the West. Medieval
Christians, like modern Nazis, used yellow cloth to mark Jews. In the 1942
essay "Color and Meaning" by Sergei Eisenstein that Kubrick, a fanatic
about color, knew very well, the Russian director stresses consistency in
the use of color to harmonize image and idea. And in that essay he focuses
on yellow, referring to wartime "Nazi revivals of medieval darkness."[82] The
Nazis also associated Jews with typhus—which they called *Judenfieber*—
and, following the practice of a yellow flag indicating quarantine for
typhus, deployed yellow warning signs around the ghettos.[83] Everywhere
in the Overlook yellow warns of murder. Yellow light bathes Jack's typing
paper as well as the bathroom door through which he is chopping with an
ax in order to murder his wife. The tennis ball Jack angrily hurls and which
mysteriously reappears to lead Danny into danger in Room 237 is yellow.
Wendy pours yellow fruit cocktail into a bowl as she learns of the woman's
disappearance. Grady spills the yellow liqueur Advocaat ("lawyer") on
Jack's dark red jacket, just as Nazi law marked Jews, saying, "I'm afraid it's
Advocaat, sir. It tends to stain." In line with the displacement and con-
densation of meanings in dreams, the perpetrator (who, like Grady, will take
the fall for his masters) is marked with the sign of the victim just as Grady
is marked as Jack pats him on the back with a stained hand. Advocaat,
which originated in the Netherlands, also forges a link with the German
literature of the uncanny and the grotesque through E. T. A. Hoffmann's
story, "The Sandman" (1817), in which the lawyer (*Advokat*) Coppelius is
a demonic being with "an ochre-yellow face" who spreads anguish and
disaster.[84]

Kubrick also links cold blue with yellow in a vision of Danny's that has
curious and compelling historical resonance. Kubrick and Mann both use
blue in its traditional associations with the ethereal, the transcendent,
and—for Kubrick—ghosts and death. They both also make much of blue
as the color of cold, natural, emotional, and—for Kubrick—hierarchical

power. In one scene, foreshadowed by a shot within Danny's first elevator vision, the Grady girls stand in light blue dresses in a hallway papered with blue flowers (forget-me-nots?) against yellow woodwork (fig. 24). This composition was certainly influenced by the eerie Diane Arbus photograph *Identical Twins* (1967) since Kubrick had studied photography with Arbus. But the composition goes even further back into Kubrick's past, for in 1948 he himself had photographed two girls for *Look* who had been rescued from carbon monoxide poisoning (fig. 25). Just like the doubles in *The Shining* they "stand side by side, wearing similar dresses, arms fully extended downward as they hold hands."[85] While this construction was probably a conscious one, it seems likely that there was also a largely or fully unconscious aspect of it as well having to do with associations connected with the Holocaust. Kubrick had two natural daughters of his own (who, like the Arbus, Grady [played by sisters], and *Look* girls, were not twins). Kubrick knew from reading Hilberg that at Bełżec, where the Jews of Probużna died, carbon monoxide gassing left bodies blue. Hilberg also describes the switch to hydrogen cyanide (prussic acid), which too killed by asphyxiation and even blued the walls of gas chambers. There is, moreover, a shot in *Barry Lyndon* in which the "Prussian army marches toward us, completely fills the screen, we see no breath [*Hauch*] of nature or sky . . . a foreboding of . . . modern . . . mechanized war."[86] The uniforms suffocating the screen in this shot were colored by the same "Prussian blue" dye discovered in Berlin in 1704 that served as the chemical basis for the Nazis' Zyklon B gas. It is possible that the subtle permeation of blue in these two films (and the light blue Volkswagen run off the road in *A Clockwork Orange?*) was an un/conscious creative association streaming from this troubling intersection of Kubrick's worldview, art, and family history. The cold blue light and air filling the Overlook like a gas is in accord with the claustrophobia effected through a progressive compression of space and time in the labyrinthine Overlook that mimics *The Magic Mountain* (over seven years) and *The Castle* (over seven days).[87]

The music, too, in *The Shining* bears the heavy weight of the Holocaust. Kubrick selected music whose sound fit the mood of a particular scene or sequence. But mood is not independent of the music's intent or context and Kubrick knew European music as well as he knew European history. The film opens by joining medieval and modern Europe through an electronic rendering of the *Dies Irae,* which begins "The day of wrath, that day / which will reduce the world to ashes." Kubrick here eschews German music in favor of twentieth-century Central and Eastern European compositions that echo the Holocaust. Before and subsequently, Kubrick has displayed a penchant for the non-German music of Central and Eastern Europe. In *2001* the adagio from Armenian Aram Khachaturian's *Gayane Ballet* (1942) expresses the cold loneliness of space travel, but that music was meant to convey the anxiety of a Soviet collective farm on the eve of the Nazi invasion.[88] And in *Eyes Wide Shut*, Kubrick uses as the title theme a waltz by Dmitri Shostakovich written in 1938 under the influence of the Nazi annexation of Austria, music that Michael Herr has characterized as a "rose with a canker in it."[89]

In *The Shining* the prewar music of Hungarian Béla Bartók and the postwar music of Pole Krzysztof Penderecki predominate. Kubrick includes only one Bartók piece, again an apprehensive Adagio: the "night music" of the third movement of *Music for Strings, Percussion, and Celesta* (1936), a composition written partly in protest against fascism. Bartók refused to play in Germany after the Nazis came to power in 1933, performing there for the last time seven days before Hitler became chancellor and, in 1937, forbade the broadcast of his own works in Germany and Italy.[90] Kubrick plays over nine minutes of the Adagio, which like the 1930s quivers with

Fig. 24. Sisters

SAVED TWO LITTLE GIRLS Phyllis, 5 years old, and Barbara, 8, were overcome by carbon monoxide. Henry F. and Edward B., trained in life saving methods, rushed over in time to save two precious lives.

Fig. 25. Rescued (courtesy Jan Harlan)

dread at the horror to come. It also plays under the first of only two scenes in which we see and hear Jack typing, a "relentlessly mechanical sound . . . echo[ing] down the corridors" in contrast to "King's howling wind as the hotel's menacing voice" that underscores Kubrick's portrayal of horror as immanent and banal rather than supernatural and spectacular.[91] Kubrick also twists the historical blade for the alert viewer by highlighting in the end credits details of the recording: on Deutsche Grammophon with the Berlin Philharmonic under the direction of Herbert von Karajan. Karajan (1908–89) joined the Nazi party in his native Austria in 1933 and supported the Nazi regime by "conducting orchestras for party functions, playing in occupied Paris, [and] performing for Hitler's birthday."[92] This fusion of anti-Nazi composer and Nazi conductor is another dreamlike construction from Kubrick's Freudian conviction that good and evil, beauty and horror, are inextricably woven together in human character and history.

Penderecki's music accompanies the actual horrors of the Overlook Hotel past and present. This is significant, for Penderecki's own father was a lawyer during World War II when the Nazis killed 70 percent of the lawyers in Poland. Born in 1933, Penderecki watched Jews being taken away by the Germans and devoted his musical career to the exploration of tolerance and intolerance.[93] He has most often done this in works based on Christian scripture and liturgy, two of which Kubrick uses in *The Shining* to link Christianity, Judaism, and Poland into a cinematically reproduced locus for contemplation of the Holocaust. As Danny envisions the elevator gushing blood and Jack dreams of murder, on the soundtrack is Penderecki's *The Awakening of Jacob* (1974). Jacob, aside from being the name of Kubrick's father, is he in the Bible who is renamed Israel and whose sons are the ancestors of the twelve tribes. The text is Genesis 28:16, "And Jacob awaked out of his sleep, and he said, 'Surely the Lord is in this place; and I knew *it* not.'" In twentieth-century Christian and Nazi Poland the descendants of Jacob would awaken, not to salvation, like the biblical Jacob, but to slaughter. In Kubrick's Holocaust construction, moreover, this passage suggests the question of the presence of God in light of the Holocaust. Kubrick similarly utilizes Penderecki's *Utrenja* ("Morning Prayer," 1969–70) from the Eastern Orthodox liturgy for Christ's entombment and resurrection to underscore savagely the hotel's final manifestation of its accumulated horrors. These concluding sequences include a reprise, witnessed this time by Wendy, of the disgorgement of blood from the hotel's elevator, a modern mechanical companion to Jack's murderous typewriter. With respect to all this mixing of music and history, it is perhaps subliminally revealing that one reviewer of the film upon its release mistakenly identified these latter passages as Penderecki's similar choral lament, the *Dies Irae* of 1967, also known as the *Auschwitz Oratorio*.[94] The invocation of the religious here also connects *The Shining* with another aspect of the literature and cinema of the uncanny, what Rudolf Otto in *The Idea of the Holy* (1917) called the *mysterium tremendum,* the coincidence of the fearsome and the divine as expressed by Jacob: "How dreadful is this place! This is none other but the house of God and this is the gate of heaven." This is the inextricability of good and evil in its highest cosmic sense, the source for Kubrick of the uncanny nature of existence, of human "dis-ease" in the "awe-ful" world.

Fade to Black

The Shining can be appreciated and criticized on many levels. As a horror film, it can be read as subversive of the social order, supportive of it, or exploitative of its worst violence. As a map of the male psyche, it can be read as an Oedipal fantasy of paternal violence; actual patriarchal violence within family, society, and culture; as misogyny; or as male fear and desire of return to the womb of the original caretaker.[95] But *The Shining* can most trenchantly be seen as the creative result of the action of a complex set of historical influences, especially the Holocaust, on Kubrick's life and work. Whatever the merits of his response in *The Shining*, he follows it to the very end of the film, concluding the soundtrack near the close of white credits on a black screen—when everyone will have left the cinema—with the crackle of applause and drone of conversation following a 1932 British dance tune. Dance in Kubrick's films is often a symbol of the dangerous coupling or opposition of power and desire, but the Holocaust is too dark a subject for such a sedate symbol. In *The Shining* we view dancing only once, barely, far in the background of two shots of Jack. At the very end of the film the dance is over.[96] The message is clear as well as—ironically—unheard: We are that audience, in our century, the century of genocide.

NOTES

Portions of this essay have appeared in Geoffrey Cocks, *The Wolf at the Door: Stanley Kubrick, History, and the Holocaust* (New York: Peter Lang, 2004).

1. *The Shining,* DVD (Warner Bros., 1999, 2001), scene 4, 11.43–12.07; Geoffrey Cocks, "Stanley Kubrick's Dream Machine: Psychoanalysis, Film, and

History," *Annual of Psychoanalysis* 30 (2003): 35–45; Geoffrey Cocks, *The Wolf at the Door: Stanley Kubrick, History, and the Holocaust* (New York: Peter Lang, 2004).

2. William Wilson, "Riding the Crest of the Horror Wave," *New York Times Magazine,* May 11, 1980, 63.

3. See, for example, David Denby, "Death Warmed Over," *New York,* June 9, 1980, 61.

4. Frederic Raphael, *Eyes Wide Open: A Memoir of Stanley Kubrick* (New York: Ballantine, 1999), 151.

5. Christiane Kubrick, personal communication, Nov. 20, 2002; Jan Harlan, *Stanley Kubrick: A Life in Pictures,* DVD (Warner Bros., 2001), scene 22, 1:56.31– 1:57; see also 1:56.11–17.

6. Dana Pollan, "Materiality and Sociality in *Killer's Kiss,"* in *Perspectives on Stanley Kubrick,* ed. Mario Falsetto (New York: Greenwood, 1996), 97.

7. Harlan, *Stanley Kubrick,,* DVD, scene 12, 42.28–35; Rick Lyman, "A Perfectionist's Pupil with a Major in Creepy," *New York Times,* Feb. 22, 2002, B7.

8. Anthony Lane, "The Last Emperor," *New Yorker,* March 22, 1999, 120–23.

9. Stanley Kubrick, "Words and Movies," *Sight and Sound* 30 (Winter 1960/ 61): 14.

10. *Probing the Limits of Representation: Nazism and the "Final Solution,"* ed. Saul Friedlander (Cambridge, MA: Harvard University Press, 1992).

11. Andrew Kelly, "The Brutality of Military Incompetence: 'Paths of Glory' (1957)," *Historical Journal of Film, Radio, and Television* 13.2 (1993): 223.

12. On intention, context, and critical reading, see Walter Metz, "A Very Notorious Ranch, Indeed: Fritz Lang, Allegory, and the Holocaust," *Journal of Contemporary Thought* 13 (Summer 2001): 71–86.

13. Vincent LoBrutto, *Stanley Kubrick: A Biography* (New York: Donald I. Fine, 1997), 5–10; Probezhna Jewish Community, Births, USC Archive, Warsaw, Poland.

14. Beth S. Wenger, *New York Jews and the Great Depression: Uncertain Promise* (New Haven: Yale University Press, 1996), 91–92, 197–201; Gene D. Phillips, *Stanley Kubrick: Interviews* (Jackson: University of Mississippi Press, 2001), 71.

15. Quoted in Michael Herr, *Kubrick* (New York: Grove Press, 2000), 53.

16. Diane Johnson, "Stanley Kubrick (1928–1999)," *New York Review of Books,* April 22, 1999, 28.

17. Joseph Gelmis, "Stanley Kubrick," in Gelmis, *The Film Director as Superstar* (Garden City, NY: Doubleday, 1970), 302–3; Gene D. Phillips, *Stanley Kubrick: A Film Odyssey* (New York: Popular Library, 1975), 137; Herr, *Kubrick,* 84.

18. *Hollywood: An Empire of Their Own* (Canadian Broadcasting Corporation, 1998).

19. Alexander Beider, *A Dictionary of Jewish Surnames from the Russian Empire* (Teaneck, NJ: Avotaynu, 1993), 347; Pages of Testimony, Hall of Names, Yad Vashem, Jerusalem.

20. Verhandlungsniederschrift, Oct. 31, 1966, sheet 3345, AR-Z 239/59, vol. 9:3161–3487, Bundesarchiv, Aussenstelle Ludwigsburg, Germany.

21. Christiane Kubrick, personal communication, Nov. 22, 2002; David S. Wyman, *The Abandonment of the Jews: America and the Holocaust, 1941–1945* (New York: Pantheon, 1984), 79–91.

22. LoBrutto, *Stanley Kubrick*, 14–15, 19–20, 57; Harlan, *Stanley Kubrick*, DVD, scene 3, 7.54–58.

23. Barbie Zelizer, *Remembering to Forget: Holocaust Memory Through the Camera's Eye* (Chicago: University of Chicago Press, 1998), 139, 138.

24. Raphael, *Eyes Wide Open*, 107–8; Geoffrey Cocks, "Kubrick Confronted Holocaust—Indirectly," *Los Angeles Times*, March 12, 1999, B9.

25. "Er war einfach schüchtern," *Der Spiegel*, Aug. 30, 1999, 198.

26. Quoted in Anthony Frewin, "Writers, Writing, Reading," in *The Stanley Kubrick Archives*, ed. Alison Castle (Cologne: Taschen, 2005), 518; Michel Ciment, *Kubrick: The Definitive Edition*, trans. Gilbert Adair (New York: Faber and Faber, 2001), 92, 105, 156, 163, 264–65.

27. Christiane Kubrick, personal communication, November 20, 2002; *Niederländisch-Deutschen Kulturgemeinschaft* (May 1943): 22, (Jan. 1944): 20, Haags Gemeentearchief, The Hague, Netherlands; NB 90834, 90835, 90837, Algemeen Rijksarchief, The Hague; I. B. van Creveld, personal communication, Nov. 10, 2000; Frank Noack, personal communication, July 25, 1998.

28. Ann Morrow, "Christiane Kubrick: Flowers and Violent Images," *Times* (London), Feb. 5, 1973, 10; Christiane Kubrick, personal communication, Nov. 20, 2002; Ortsgruppenkartei, National Archives, College Park, Maryland.

29. Christiane Kubrick, *Paintings* (New York: Warner, 1990); Marina Vaizey, "Christiane Kubrick: An Art of Life," in Kubrick, *Paintings*, 7, 11.

30. "Er war einfach schüchtern," 198; Raphael, *Eyes Wide Open*, 60.

31. Stanley Kubrick and Frederic Raphael, *Eyes Wide Shut* (New York: Warner, 1999), 168, 169; Christoph Hummel et al., *Stanley Kubrick* (Munich: Carl Hanser, 1984), 294; Frank Noack, personal communication, June 7, 1998; Frank Noack, *Veit Harlan: Des Teufels Regisseur* (Munich: Belleville, 2000), 35–36.

32. John Baxter, *Stanley Kubrick: A Biography* (New York: Carroll and Graf, 1997), 225–26.

33. Herr, *Kubrick*, 12–13. Kubrick listened to Wagner, however: Katharina Kubrick Hobbs FAQ, 1.14, http://www.visual-memory.co.uk/faq/kckh.html, August 18, 2000.

34. Richard Adams and Stanley Kubrick, "The German Lieutenant," screenplay (1956–57), Box 22, folder 2, Department of Defense Film Collection, Special Collections, Georgetown University Library, Washington, DC.

35. John Bodnar, "*Saving Private Ryan* and Postwar Memory in America," *American Historical Review* 106 (2001): 812.

36. See the illustration from *Hitler's Madmen* (1943), in Bernard F. Dick, *The Star-Spangled Screen: The American World War II Film* (Lexington: University Press of Kentucky, 1985), 194.

37. *Killer's Kiss*, DVD (MGM, 1999), scene 18, 59.46–47, 1:02.12; see also scene 15, 52.57–58.

38. *A Clockwork Orange*, DVD (Warner Bros., 1999, 2001), scene 17, 54.31. I am grateful to Mark Crispin Miller for drawing my attention to this tableau.

39. Herr, *Kubrick*, 10, 7–8, emphasis in original. Leonard J. Leff, "Hollywood and the Holocaust: Remembering *The Pawnbroker*," *American Jewish History* 84 (1996): 361; Jan Harlan, personal communications, Dec. 9, 2002, Oct. 6, 2003.

40. Raul Hilberg, personal communications, June 4, 1991, and April 15, 1999.

41. LoBrutto, *Stanley Kubrick*, 496–99; Baxter, *Stanley Kubrick*, 360–61.

42. Louis Begley, *Wartime Lies* (New York: Ivy, 1991), 5.

43. Leonard F. Wheat, *Kubrick's 2001: A Triple Allegory* (Lanham, MD: Scarecrow, 2000), 87–138.

44. *A Clockwork Orange*, DVD, scene 36, 1:56.30; cf. Anthony Burgess, *A Clockwork Orange* (New York: Norton, 1963), 119.

45. John Clive, personal communication, Sept. 27, 1999; *A Clockwork Orange*, DVD, scene 23, 1:22.54.

46. Peter Novick, *The Holocaust in American Life* (Boston: Houghton Mifflin, 1999), 112; Susan Sontag, "Fascinating Fascism" [1974], in Sontag, *Under the Sign of Saturn* (New York: Farrar, Straus, Giroux, 1983), 73–105; Saul Friedländer, *Reflections of Nazism: An Essay on Kitsch and Death,* trans. Thomas Weyr (New York: Harper & Row, 1984).

47. Cédric Anger, "Le dernier expressioniste," *Cahiers du cinema* 534 (April 1999): 28–29; Robin Wood, "*Written on the Wind,*" in *Film Studies: Critical Approaches,* ed. John Hill and Pamela Church Gibson (Oxford: Oxford University Press, 2000), 22.

48. Diane Johnson, *The Shadow Knows* (New York: Plume, 1974), 185.

49. Catherine Cocks, *Doing the Town: The Rise of Urban Tourism in the United States, 1850–1915* (Berkeley: University of California Press, 2001), 73, 81, 85, 86, 96–98.

50. Charles Derry, *Dark Dreams: A Psychological History of the Modern Horror Film* (New York: A. S. Barnes, 1977), 24.

51. James Agee, "The Blue Hotel," in Agee, *On Film, Volume Two: Five Film Scripts by James Agee* (New York: Beacon, 1967), 393–488; Baxter, *Stanley Kubrick,* 52, 306. See also Jan Kadar's *The Blue Hotel* (1977).

52. Jean Cayrol, "Night and Fog," in *Film: Book 2,* ed. Robert Hughes (New York: Grove Press, 1962), 235.

53. [Stanley Kubrick], "The Shining" [n.d.], James Boyle Collection 135/S, Warner Bros. Archives, School of Cinema and Television, University of Southern California, Los Angeles; Diane Johnson, personal communication, July 15, 2002.

54. Alexander Walker, *Stanley Kubrick, Director* (New York: Norton), 12; *Kubrick Interviews,* 165, 186; Lionel Trilling, *Beyond Culture: Essays on Literature and Learning* (New York: Viking, 1965), 28. I am grateful to Peter Loewenberg for first pointing out the similarity between *The Shining* and *The Magic Mountain.*

55. Diane Johnson, personal communication, July 1, 2002; Frank Noack, personal communication, Feb. 17, 2002, from an interview with Christiane and Jan Harlan.

56. Brita Bajer, "Hitler's Collapse Held Still Remote," *New York Times,* Nov. 11, 1943, 17.

57. LoBrutto, *Stanley Kubrick,* 481.

58. Walker, *Stanley Kubrick,* 271; Diane Johnson, "Writing *The Shining,*" page 57 in this volume.

59. Alan Bowker, Stanley's Room, http:www.bowkera.com/stanleys_room.htm, Jan. 3, 2001; *Making The Shining,* DVD (Warner Bros., 2001), 10.50–11.29.

60. Quoted in Jack Kroll, "Stanley Kubrick's Horror Show," *Newsweek,* May 26, 1999, 99. *Making The Shining,* DVD, 10.50–11.29.

61. Denis Barbier, "Entretien avec Diane Johnson," *Positif* 238 (Jan. 1981): 22.

62. Hans-Jörg Wohlfromm and Gisela Wohlfromm, *Deckname Wolf: Hitlers Letzter Sieg* (Berlin: edition q,2001); LoBrutto, *Stanley Kubrick,* 40, 51.

63. Siegbert Prawer, *Caligari's Children: The Film as Tale of Terror* (Oxford: Oxford University Press, 1980), 111.

64. Geoffrey Cocks, "Bringing the Holocaust Home: The Freudian Dynamics of Kubrick's *The Shining,*" *Psychoanalytic Review* 78 (1991): 108.

65. *The Shining,* DVD, scenes 16, 22, 38; Michael James Emery, "U.S. Horror: Gothicism in the Work of William Faulkner, Thomas Pynchon, and Stanley Kubrick," PhD diss., SUNY Binghamton, 1989, 24, 25, 113, 115–16, 159.

66. Norman Kagan, *The Cinema of Stanley Kubrick* (New York: Continuum, 1997), 49.

67. *The Shining,* DVD, scene 8, 21.22–23; scene 24, 1:29.26–28.

68. Flo Leibowitz and Lynn Jeffress, "The Shining," *Film Quarterly* 34.3 (1981): 45–51; Bill Blakemore, "The Family of Man," *San Francisco Chronicle,* July 29, 1987.

69. Mark Crispin Miller, "Kubrick's Anti-Reading of the Luck of Barry Lyndon," *Modern Language Notes* 91 (1976): 1373.

70. *The Shining,* DVD, scene 11, 37.59–38.02.

71. Mark J. Madigan, "'Orders from the House': Kubrick's *The Shining* and Kafka's 'Metamorphosis,'" in *The Shining Reader,* ed. Anthony Magistrale (Mercer Island, WA: Starmont, 1990), 214.

72. *The Shining,* DVD, scene 29, 1:44.30. King's Red Sox referent is Carlton Fisk.

73. *The Shining,* DVD, scene 11, 37.31. A huge eagle sits behind the director's desk in Matthew Chapman's *Stranger's Kiss* (1983), a fictionalization of the making of *Killer's Kiss. The Shining* was a Peregrine Film made by Hawk Films, and the production company for *Making The Shining* was Eagle Films.

74. *The Shining,* DVD, scene 6, 14.34, scene 2, 4.48; Helen J. Dow, *The Art of Alex Colville* (Toronto: McGraw-Hill Ryerson, 1992), 41.

75. Christiana Pritzlaff, "Die 7 im 'Zauberberg,'" in Pritzlaff, *Die Zahlensymbolik bei Thomas Mann* (Hamburg: Helmut Buske, 1972), 27–42; Norman Mailer, *The Naked and the Dead* [1948] (New York: Henry Holt, 1998), 342; Stephen Dowden, "Mann's Ethical Style," in *A Companion to Mann's Magic Mountain,* ed. Dowden (Columbia, SC: Camden House, 1999), 35–36.

76. *The Shining,* DVD, scenes 4 and 5.

77. The management of the Timberline Lodge on Oregon's Mount Hood, used for exterior shots, asked Kubrick to change the number 217 used in the novel. The Timberline has rooms 217 and 227 but not 237. Walker, *Stanley Kubrick,* 296; Timberline Lodge, personal communication, March 20, 2000.

78. Raul Hilberg, *The Destruction of the European Jews,* rev. ed. (New York: Holmes & Meier, 1984), 3:1220.

79. *The Shining,* DVD, scene 12, 40.41–51.

80. *Full Metal Jacket,* DVD (Warner Bros., 1999, 2001), scene 2; *The Killing,* DVD (MGM, 1999), scene 25; *Paths of Glory,* DVD (MGM, 1999), scenes 7, 15, 21.

81. *The Shining,* DVD, scene 31, 1:55.52–1:57.43.

82. Sergei Eisenstein, "Color and Meaning," in Eisenstein, *The Film Sense* [1942], *Film Form: Essays in Film Theory and The Film Sense,* ed. and trans. Jay Leyda (Cleveland: World, 1967), 136; Walker, *Stanley Kubrick,* 233; Gelmis, "Stanley Kubrick," 315.

83. Paul Weindling, *Epidemics and Genocide in Eastern Europe, 1890–1945* (Oxford: Oxford University Press, 2000), 104, 273–74.

84. *Selected Writings of E. T. A. Hoffmann,* ed. and trans. Leonard J. Kent and

Elizabeth C. Knight (Chicago: University of Chicago Press, 1969), 1:140; Prawer, *Caligari's Children*, 117, 131; Sigmund Freud, "The 'Uncanny,'" in *The Standard Edition of the Complete Psychological Works of Sigmund Freud*, ed. James Strachey (London: Hogarth, 1955), 17:227–33; *The Shining*, DVD, scene 23, 1:24.53–56.

85. LoBrutto, *Stanley Kubrick*, 445; *The Shining*, DVD, scene 15, 42.42.

86. Georg Seesslen and Fernand Jung, *Stanley Kubrick und seine Filme* (Marburg: Schüren, 1999), 216; *Barry Lyndon*, DVD (Warner Bros., 2001) scene 20, 1:05.07–21, 33–48; Hilberg, *Destruction of the European Jews*, 565, 627–28; William Gass, *On Being Blue: A Philosophical Inquiry* (Boston: David R. Godine, 1976), 11, 75–76; Eisenstein, "Color and Meaning," 137; *Goethe's Color Theory*, ed. Rupprecht Matthei and trans. Herb Aach (New York: Van Norstrand Reinhold, 1971), 170; Elie Wiesel, "Never Shall I Forget," in *Holocaust Poetry*, ed. Hilda Schiff (New York: St. Martin's, 1995), 42. Holocaust denial has stained the controversy over the color of the corpses, but the scientific evidence seems to be that they would have been either blue or pink depending on the concentration of carbon monoxide: Charles D. Provan, "The Blue Color of the Jewish Victims at Belzec Death Camp—and Carbon Monoxide Poisoning," *The Revisionist* 2.2 (2004): 159–64.

87. Ciment, *Kubrick*, 135; Nelson, *Kubrick*, 211; *A Clockwork Orange*, DVD, scene 5, 8.28–30.

88. Victor Yuzefovich, *Aram Khachaturian*, trans. Nicholas Kournikoff and Vladimir Bobrov (New York: Sphinx, 1985), 84.

89. Herr, *Kubrick*, 84; Paul Griffiths, "Music That Switches Its Gaze, from Future to Past," *New York Times*, July 21, 2002.

90. Bence Szabolcsi, *Béla Bartók: His Life in Pictures*, ed. Ferenc Bónis (London: Boosey & Hawkes, 1964), 52; *Béla Bartók Essays*, ed. Benjamin Suchoff (Lincoln: University of Nebraska Press, 1976), 423.

91. Jeff Smith, "Careening Through Kubrick's Space," *Chicago Review* 33.1 (Summer 1981), 65; *The Shining*, DVD, scene 12.

92. Michael H. Kater, *The Twisted Muse: Musicians and Their Music in the Third Reich* (New York: Oxford University Press, 1997), 60.

93. Wolfram Schwinger, *Krzysztof Penderecki: His Life and Work*, trans. William Mann (London: Schott, 1989), 214.

94. Paul Mayersberg, "The Overlook Hotel," *Sight and Sound* 50 (Winter 1980/81): 57.

95. James Hala, "Kubrick's *The Shining*: The Specter and the Critics," in *Shining Reader*, 209–11; Vivian Sobchack, "Child/Alien/Father: Patriarchal Crisis and Generic Exchange," *Camera Obscura* 15 (1986): 13–15; William Paul, *Laughing, Screaming: Modern Hollywood Comedy and Horror* (New York: Columbia University Press, 1994), 341–44; Dennis Bingham, *Acting Male: Masculinities in the Films of James Stewart, Jack Nicholson, and Clint Eastwood* (New Brunswick, NJ: Rutgers University Press, 1994), 143–45.

96. *The Shining*, DVD, scenes 23, 1:22.13–23.06, 1:24.26–25.11; 40, 2:22.53–2:23.35.

Full-Metal-Jacketing, or Masculinity in the Making

⟹◦⟸

PAULA WILLOQUET-MARICONDI

You reach maturity in fighting, you reach maturity in smoke and fire.

—National Front for the Liberation of Vietnam motto

Loren Baritz's *Backfire,* a provocative study of American involvement in Vietnam, opens with the assertion that the Vietnam war worked as a "magnifying glass that enlarged aspects of some of the ways we, as Americans, think and act."[1] Like the war it portrays, Stanley Kubrick's *Full Metal Jacket* (1987) also works as a magnifying glass, enlarging one aspect of American culture in particular: the making of the American man and war hero. Like Baritz, Kubrick explores the reasons behind American involvement in Vietnam. He does so, however, by focusing our attention primarily on the cultural conditioning of the men who fought in the war. Kubrick's film reveals the profound analogies between the making of the marine and the making of masculinity in general, and in doing so unmasks the true meaning of patriarchy and its motivations. The film shows that the standards of manhood required and promulgated by the military apparatus permeate the rest of American society and are broadcast by its institutions.

In her 1989 study, *The Remasculinization of America,* Susan Jeffords argues that the 1980s ushered the revival of manhood in contemporary American culture through the cinematic portrayal of Vietnam veterans as victims, as what she calls "emblems of an unjustly discriminated masculinity." This revival of manhood, Jeffords further notes, was achieved by means of a "rejection of the feminine." According to Jeffords's analysis, *Full Metal Jacket* exemplifies this shift, between 1979 and 1987, toward the remasculinization of the American male defined in opposition to a feminine enemy. Jeffords's analysis is rooted in a comparison of Kubrick's film and Gustav Hasford's novel *The Short-Timers,* on which the film is based, and focuses on three particular scenes to show that "the film shuts down the novel's ambiguity and reinstates a clarified rejection of the feminine and restitution of the masculine." The principal locus of that rejection, she shows, is the killing of the female sniper. Jeffords thus reads the film as essentially a battle between a "purified masculine" and a "castrating feminine," who is ultimately silenced.[2]

Although Jeffords convincingly argues that in Hasford's novel "neither the masculine nor the feminine 'survives' as soldiers in this Vietnam," her analysis fails to credit Kubrick's film with a similar message. While *Full Metal Jacket* was indeed released during the period Jeffords defines as "the culmination of a masculine regeneration," exemplified by the *First Blood* (1982) and *Missing in Action* (1984) series, I will argue here that Kubrick cannot be said to be endorsing the masculinization process he portrays and analyzes.[3] Moreover, as others have argued since the original publication of the present essay, his revision of the sniper incident does not constitute an instance of misogyny on his part.[4]

Jeffords concludes her study of the remasculinization process with a warning worth restating:

Because constructions of masculinity and femininity are being used in American mass culture to repress awareness of other forms of patriarchal dominance, it is methodologically *important to maintain a distinction between patriarchy and masculinity.* Masculinity is the primary mechanism for the articulation, institutionalization, and maintenance of the gendered system on which patriarchy is based . . . It is itself constructed and manipulated by interests other than those defined by gender.[5]

Taking heed of this warning, I propose to look at how Kubrick stages this masculinization process to show that the myth of masculinity is bound to another central myth that forms the basis of American nationalism: the myth of "the city on a hill" that manifests itself through the belief in American idealism and technological invincibility.[6]

Vietnam movies produced after John Wayne's *The Green Berets* (1968) have been divided into two waves. The first wave, films made in the late 1970s, includes films like *The Deer Hunter* (1978) and *Apocalypse Now* (1979) that portray the Vietnam experience as shattering and apocalyptic. The second wave, in the late 1980s, is seen as a celebration of military life and, as such, as support for the "prolonged and concerted effort on the part of official America to reverse the old verdict on Vietnam." To this second wave belong, according to John Stevenson's study of Vietnam films, *Platoon* (1986), *Gardens of Stone* (1987), and *Full Metal Jacket*. Although Stevenson recognizes that *Full Metal Jacket* breaks in many ways with traditional Vietnam narratives, he argues that the film's second half "degenerates into clichés," encouraging audience identification with traditional combat films and consequently rejoining the mainstream ideology about Vietnam reflected in movies of the late eighties.[7]

Stevenson's reason for placing *Full Metal Jacket* within the second wave of Vietnam movies is, like Jeffords's, centered on the sniper incident. Although Stevenson does not interpret the killing of the female sniper in exactly the same terms as Jeffords does, he does agree with her that it represents a final and unquestionable statement about Joker's masculinity, about his bravery in battle. In killing the sniper, Joker proves he *is* a man, and in doing so he legitimates his presence in the war.

While agreeing with both Jeffords and Stevenson that the sniper incident is crucial in the film, I would argue that rather than endorsing the dominant patriarchal ideology that turns boys into men through a display of bravery in the face of death, Kubrick criticizes the whole process of masculinization by showing that it involves not only the defeat of an "other" (female, or otherwise) but, more fundamentally, the defeat of the very self. Both Jeffords and Stevenson are too quick to disregard the whole first half of the film, which lasts a full fifty minutes and, as Thomas Doherty notes, "outpoint[s] combat footage in both running time and emotional investment." It is in these first fifty minutes that the key to understanding Kubrick's criticism of the myths of masculinity and American idealism is to be found. As Doherty puts it, after Parris Island, "Vietnam is redundant."[8]

Films inspired by or directly dealing with the Vietnam war have tended to address similar issues, from the reasons for and the responses to the war, to the war's effects on the veterans and on American society. In "Charlie Don't Surf," David Desser contends that although the films made about Vietnam since 1978 do not present a unified, coherent vision, they all share the same view of the war "as a problem within American culture." In this respect, *Full Metal Jacket* does not break with the pattern established by these films. The ways in which Kubrick's film does depart from the conventions, however, are very telling for they help illuminate the more profound message conveyed by the film's adherence to the tradition of portraying the war "in specifically American terms."[9]

An obvious way in which *Full Metal Jacket* breaks with one of the Vietnam genre's conventions is by staging the combat in a city rather than in the jungle. In doing this, Kubrick places the action within a very specific and important historical moment: the Hué battle during the Tet offensive of 1968. Practical considerations may have been a factor in Kubrick's choice of setting: it enabled him to shoot the war in London, where he lived, by blowing up an abandoned gas works on the Thames and turning it into the dilapidated Hué City. But the setting also helps generalize the reference: it reflects Hué as well as any other city in dereliction, Vietnam as well as any other war. To be "in a world of shit," a phrase often used in the movie, is not only to be in war but, as Michael Pursell points out, it is also to be in "a strictly man-made world."[10] The ubiquity of this "world" is a reflection of its cultural dimension. In Kubrick's film, the true nature of the war is no longer camouflaged by the natural wild jungle setting. The war space is clearly a man-made environment, and the war itself is a man-made, unnatural disaster—an act of Man.

The battle of Hué also represents a turning point in the way Americans in Vietnam and at home viewed the war. For the first time, serious doubts about the United States' ability to win the war were raised. Walter Cronkite's remark, "What the hell is going on, I thought we were winning this war,"[11] is referenced in the film by Lieutenant Lockhart's report during a meeting with his newspaper staff in Da Nang base:

> Charlie has hit every major military target in Vietnam, and hit 'em hard. In Saigon, the United States Embassy has been overrun by suicide squads. Khe Sanh is standing by to be overrun. We also have reports that a division of N.V.A. has occupied all of the city of Hué south of the Perfume River. In strategic terms, Charlie's cut the country in half . . . the civilian press are about to wet their pants and we've heard even Cronkite's going to say the war is now unwinnable.[12]

Although the Communist forces were finally defeated in Hué after twenty-six days of battle, the determination of the North Vietnamese and Viet Cong armies could no longer be doubted. Furthermore, the United States' technological and "masculine" power as well as its status as the "redeemer nation" were seriously put into question. By choosing Hué as his setting and by building into his representation of 1968 consequences and responses that only became clear later, Kubrick poses again, in 1987, questions about American supremacy, power, and good intentions. He forces his audience to reexamine the myths behind the United States' involvement in this and other wars and, indeed, to see more clearly the central myths that continue to define "America" by defining masculinity.

One of these myths dates back to early colonial days when John Winthrop, perhaps inadvertently, helped establish the image of America as "a city on a hill" by declaring that "we must consider that we shall be as a city upon a Hill, the eyes of all people are upon US."[13] This myth continued to make itself manifest in the settling of the West and was extended beyond America's Pacific borders to Asia: "Americans have perceived themselves as having a world destiny intertwined with the fate of Asia," remarks John Hellmann in *American Myth and the Legacy of Vietnam.* The missionary presence in China, for example, helped foster the view Americans had of themselves as bestowers of light to a dark landscape. China was perceived as a frontier and was portrayed as such in films and literature of the early and mid-twenties, until it was "lost" to Communism. The further threat of Communism to French dominance of Indochina revitalized the American frontier myth: "When they thought about Indochina, Americans generally saw themselves entering yet another frontier, once again 'western pilgrims' on a mission of protection and progress."[14]

America's frontier heritage was evoked in the mid-fifties by two works which appeared within months of each other: Tom Dooley's *Deliver Us from Evil* (1956), which promoted the frontier mentality, and Graham Greene's *The Quiet American* (1955), which put it into question.[15] *Full Metal Jacket* can be seen as referring to the historical period and the critical message reflected by the latter. The film's marine recruit, Leonard Lawrence—dubbed Gomer Pyle by Hartman, the drill instructor, and subsequently simply called Pyle—constitutes a double allusion. Critics have noted that this nickname is a reference to the 1960s television show starring the alleged homosexual Jim Nabors.[16] The nickname Pyle, however, is also an invitation to connect Kubrick's film with Greene's book. *The Quiet American* features a naïve American agent whose last name is also Pyle. Greene's Alden Pyle, fully absorbed in "the dilemmas of Democracy and the responsibilities of the West," goes to Vietnam determined to fight the evil forces of Communism and to bring democracy and God to a people who, he says, "won't be allowed to think for themselves" under Communism.[17] In *Full Metal Jacket,* Alden Pyle's idealism is reflected in the words of the marine colonel who questions Joker's peace button: "We are here to help the Vietnamese, because inside every gook there is an American trying to get out" (72). This statement takes us back to the origins of American involvement in Vietnam evoked in *The Quiet American,* and thus to the myths that motivated that involvement.

A third book of the early period of American involvement in Vietnam also often cited as having played an important role in rehabilitating the frontier myth is William Lederer and Eugene Burdick's *The Ugly American* (1958), made into a film in 1963. *The Ugly American* was an appeal for the return of the true traditional American hero. President John F. Kennedy's deployment of four hundred Green Berets to the jungles of South Vietnam in 1961, in violation of the 1954 Geneva agreements, is said to have been a response to the call of *The Ugly American*. As John Hellmann notes, "they were real men going into a real country, but they were also symbolic heroes entering a symbolic landscape—a landscape of American memory redrawn in *The Ugly American*."[18]

In January of that same year, President Kennedy defined the American mission to defend freedom and "those human rights to which this nation has always been committed, and to which we are committed today at home and around the world" as a divine mission: "God's work."[19] The Green Berets, or Special Forces, were, one might say, the agents of God. Originally organized in the early 1950s as guerilla experts, the Green Berets became the leading symbol of Kennedy's "New Frontier" and the reincarnation of the western hero. The Green Berets' original image of toughness and prowess, promulgated by Kennedy, found its expression in Robin Moore's *The Green Berets* (1965), written in response to Kennedy's expressed desire for a book that would celebrate the Special Forces. Moore's best-selling novel had a tremendous impact on the youth of the time, inducing many enlistments of young men hoping to become Green Berets. Even after the Special Forces ceased to be an important factor in the war, they remained an important symbol, continuing to be celebrated in songs and films. John Wayne's *The Green Berets*, for example, took as its primary subject the combat in Southeast Asia. Through the image of John Wayne, *The Green Berets* tied the Vietnam War to previous wars fought by the United States and depicted in American films staring John Wayne, as well as to the western frontier myth. *The Green Berets,* notes Michael Anderegg, is "filled with characters and motifs self-consciously borrowed from westerns."[20]

Full Metal Jacket's numerous references to John Wayne constitute another of the film's historical and cultural connections. By invoking John Wayne, the star of so many war and western films, Kubrick refers his audience back to America's early involvement in Vietnam, as well as to its involvement in previous wars and in the settling of the West. By associating the image of John Wayne with the character known as Joker, however, Kubrick may be intimating that the war and western hero, incarnated in the characters played by John Wayne, is "simultaneously a potent symbol of toughness and bravery and a grim joke."[21]

The New Frontier mentality promoted by Kennedy and exemplified by the Green Berets found its expression in the creation of programs such as the Space Program, the Council on Physical Fitness, and the Peace Corps. Domestic emphasis on physical fitness and on international leadership helped reawaken the traditional American virtues of hardiness and self-sacrifice. In the words of John Hellmann, "the Peace Corps man and the soldier were symbolic links to the nation's frontier heritage."[22] The "Born to Kill" slogan on Joker's helmet and the peace button on his jacket may be seen as representing the common motives behind both the Peace Corps and the Special Forces. Placing these two signs on the same individual suggests that the "duality of man," as Joker calls it, is the final illusion hiding the underlying unity of American motives. Kubrick collapses the boundaries around particular and distinct events to show that they are parts of a broader, comprehensive cultural agenda.

Through explicit references to the tradition promulgated by the western genre, *Full Metal Jacket* reflects the classic western's obsession with masculinity and its technological extensions, and critiques it. The first and most obvious reference to the western is the one to John Wayne in the first few minutes of the film. As Sergeant Hartman is walking down the row of recruits, insulting them in his masculine and tough posture, Joker murmurs in an imitation of John Wayne's voice, but loud enough for the sergeant to hear: "Is that you, John Wayne? Is this me?" (4). The image of the masculine western and war hero conjured up by the reference to John Wayne is, however, immediately put into question by the references to Communism and homosexuality in Hartman's rant: "Who's the slimy little communist shit twinkle-toed cocksucker down here, who just signed his own death warrant?" (4). It is at the end of this particular exchange, when Joker admits to being the culprit, that he is "baptized" "Joker" by Hartman. The juxtaposition of John Wayne, Communism, and homosexuality with the image evoked by the nickname "Joker" work to undermine the concept of heroism underlying the reference to John Wayne.

The first half of the film closes with another reference to John Wayne, which may not have come across as strongly as intended in the film but which is explicit in the screenplay. In the latrine scene where Pyle is about to commit suicide and Hartman, played by Lee Ermey, is trying to persuade Pyle to drop his gun, the screenplay directs the actor to put "all his considerable powers of intimidation into his best John-Wayne-on-Suribachi voice" (46). The significance of the reference is twofold: Mount Suribachi is the mountain on Iwo Jima where the American flag was planted by marines—an image which remains the most familiar icon of the Marine Corps in World War II. Suribachi is, of course, also a reference to the 1949 film *Sands of Iwo Jima,* starring John Wayne as Sergeant Stryker. This reference to the film is important because *Sands of Iwo Jima* had an inspiring effect on the authors of a number of memoirs and novels about Vietnam, some of which became movies. William Turner Huggetts's *Body Count* (1973), Ron Kovic's *Born on the Fourth of July* (1976), and Philip Caputo's *Rumor of War* (1977) all recount their protagonists' fascination with *Sands of Iwo Jima* and the John Wayne character.[23] Philip Caputo, for instance, recalls picturing himself as a young marine second lieutenant "charging up some distant beachhead, like John Wayne in *Sands of Iwo Jima.*"[24] In explaining his motivation for joining the Corps, Caputo also admits to having been "swept up in the patriotic tide of the Kennedy era."[25] Michael Herr and Gustav Hasford themselves, who co-authored the screenplay with Kubrick, included numerous references to John Wayne in their accounts, *Dispatches* and *The Short-Timers.* In the scene that closes the first half of Kubrick's film, however, the western and war hero/icon is mocked once again just as he is being evoked. As we know, Pyle shoots Hartman in the chest, killing him. He then shoots himself through the mouth.

Interestingly, by first linking the hero of *Sands of Iwo Jima* and Hartman, and then immediately killing Hartman, Kubrick refers us to another message, a more subversive one, underlying *Sands of Iwo Jima:* as Michael Anderegg notes, the 1949 film also "strongly condemns those very qualities—toughness, adherence to a simple code, self-enclosure—that would make for a clear-cut hero. In fact, the film ultimately shows that these character traits are a masquerade, hiding deep emotional wounds."[26] In killing Hartman, *Full Metal Jacket* joins *Sands of Iwo Jima* in this condemnation and shows that the wounds referred to by Anderegg are those inflicted by the masculinization process itself, represented in the boot camp section of the film. The first half of *Full Metal Jacket,* which describes the making of masculinity, is thus structured by two references that unmake the masculine hero just as he is being made.

Toward the beginning of the second half of the film, during a discussion with fellow marines, Joker uses his John Wayne voice once again. After expressing his desire to be "back in the shit," he says to them: "Listen up, pilgrim. A day without blood is like a day without sunshine" (60). Joker's words are a reference both to the blood of modern wars and to the blood shed during the settlement of the American continent. The term "pilgrim," used by John Wayne in *The Man Who Shot Liberty Valance* (1962), evokes the brave, embattled colonists who, upon arrival on this continent, found themselves surrounded by what they perceived to be a hostile environment inhabited by the "Wild" Other.[27] The discussion among the marines then escalates into an argument over who's been "in the shit" and who hasn't, until Joker suggests that Payback is trying to appropriate the John Wayne role for himself: "Don't listen to any of Payback's bullshit, Rafterman. Sometimes he thinks *he's* John Wayne" (60). In the next scene, "they are startled by the dull boom of mortar shells outside" (61). Once again, the hero is evoked and immediately threatened. Later, when Joker meets his Parris Island friend Cowboy in a pagoda courtyard, he calls him "Lone Ranger." This identification with the celebrated hero is undermined when Cowboy is mortally wounded by the sniper near the end of the film.

The correlation between the film, its subject matter, and American culture in general reaches its apogee in a scene where the platoon, under fire in the outskirts of Hué City, is hunched down behind a low wall as a three-man TV crew moves past them, filming. Joker reiterates his "is that you John Wayne? Is this me?" (75) as the camera shows us the crew zeroing in on the marines to "shoot" them. As the cameramen in the film begin filming, the soldiers seem to retreat back against the wall behind which they are hiding, as if under attack by the cameras. What follows is a multidimensional commentary on war and its representation in the media. Cowboy cries out, "This is 'Vietnam—the Movie!'" as each soldier is given a part: Joker, of course, will play John Wayne; T. H. E. Rock will be Ann-Margaret; Animal Mother, a rabid buffalo; Crazy Earl, General Custer; and the "gooks play the Indians" (81). This allusion to the Vietnam War *as a movie* had already been made by Herr and Hasford in their own works.[28]

This sequence serves to establish a direct link between the Vietnam War and its various media portrayals: as a "tragic serial drama" on TV during the war period and in films dating from after the war.[29] It also explicitly links this particular war with the wars fought against the Indians in the colonization process. As Tony Williams notes, "Kubrick is conscious of Vietnam literature's use of the western as a mythic-interpretative device. . . . The Vietnam generation was conditioned by westerns from puberty, so it was an easy transition to view the Viet Cong as Native Americans."[30] To reinforce this reference, in the next scene Kubrick shows us the men negotiating with a Vietnamese prostitute while seated outside a movie theater advertising *The Lone Ranger* and displaying a poster of a Native American.

The juxtaposition of the Vietnamese prostitute and the image of the Native American in the same scene reflects the Americans' attitude toward the "other" and suggests that history is repeating itself.

The next scene depicts the platoon moving through a bombed factory in Hué City. One of the men, Crazy Earl, picks up a stuffed toy that triggers a booby trap and kills him. This scene works as a "payback" for the degradation of the Vietnamese in the previous scene in two ways. First, it restores to the VC a certain power undermined earlier by the associations Vietnamese/Indian/Female. David Desser remarks that the "image of the VC-as-woman, the ubiquity of women who are VC, is a near-hysterical reaction to the shock to the (masculine) American psyche that this physically smaller, technologically inferior race could defeat the hypermasculinized, hypertechnologized American soldier."[31] Second, the death of Crazy Earl—a character who earlier had been "assigned" the role of Custer—also references the early settlement days by simultaneously evoking the death of General George Armstrong Custer in 1876 in the Battle of the Little Bighorn and the victory over the Americans by the Indian chief Crazy Horse. Crazy Horse and General Custer are fused into one in the character of Crazy Earl, thus suggesting the inescapable inner battle unfolding within the self, who, in being an instrument of oppression, is himself oppressed. Kubrick suggests that self and enemy are the same and, thus, that all war deaths are in fact suicides. Pyle's death at the end of the first half foreshadows and exemplifies this convergence of self and enemy.[32]

In *A Certain Tendency of the Hollywood Cinema*, Robert Ray recalls Richard Schickel's observation that the Vietnam War was an attempt to "externalize" the frontier no longer available in America. Ray adds that "the word 'frontier' could have replaced 'war' without losing the meaning of the marine general's notorious 'It's not a good war, but it's the only war we've got.'"[33] The definition of masculinity embraced by the western and war heroes in American popular culture and deconstructed by Kubrick in this film is inextricably linked to the need for a frontier—a space to be colonized and a combat zone.

Kubrick's deconstruction of the masculinization process in the Parris Island portion of the film shows that the first space that must be colonized before all others is the very self. The self becomes, in fact, a combat zone where the unity of being is shattered. The drill instructor's mission is explicitly to "sweep and clear" what he identifies as "enemy" in the core of the marines' selves. Hartman's goal is akin to that of the troops he is training. He subjects them to the same treatment they are expected to inflict on the

enemy. As his own name suggests, he is to win "hearts," that is, the symbolic locus of the self, as well as "minds." As Christopher Sharrett points
out, the film's major theme is "the fate of men at the hands of other men."[34]

The "enemy" that must be overcome within the self is an "other" that
does not conform to the definition of masculinity defined and exemplified
by the war and western heroes. *Full Metal Jacket* sets up an opposition
between this masculinity and that which is feminine and infantile. Masculinity is shown to be a one-dimensional identity formation that denies
ambiguities or plurality. Furthermore, masculinity must be won and preserved, for it can be lost. As Frank Lentricchia puts it, "If you're male,"
social engenderment demands "that you must police yourself for traces of
femininity."[35] Thus, masculinization is an ongoing, never-ending process
that is only truly completed, and thus immune to being challenged, with
the *de facto* death of the self.

The making of manhood also involves a sexual rhetoric of dominance
of females and of the feminine within. Soldiers who, for whatever reasons,
did not want to engage in (violent) sexual talk or action would have their
masculinity questioned. Loren Baritz recounts the story of an American
GI who declined his sergeant's invitation to rape a young Vietnamese
woman and as a result was accused of betraying his manhood as well as his
buddies who had participated in the rape.[36] What Susan Jeffords calls the
"clarified rejection of the feminine"[37] is not a simple "restitution" of the
masculine, but a necessary condition for the *creation* of the masculine. *Full
Metal Jacket* exposes the process of dominance of the feminine within by
defining this feminine as the enemy, by exteriorizing it so it can be seen,
attacked, and eliminated, and by linking sexuality with violence.

This process of exteriorization of the feminine begins with an allusion
to the recruits' masculinity that simultaneously puts into question the "purity" of that masculinity: "Sound off like you got a pair," says Hartman, and,
immediately afterward, "If you ladies leave my island, if you survive recruit
training . . ." (3). The marines must prove that they have "a pair," and until
they do so, they are "ladies." The masculine is shown to be contaminated
by an "other" defined as feminine by expressions such as "ladies" and
"sweetheart," or as homosexual: "Only steers and queers come from Texas,"
"Only faggots and sailors are called Lawrence," "Do you suck dicks? Are
you a peter-puffer?" The recruit training program is thus one of purification.
This "purification" of the military forces from homosexual "contamina-
tion" has been, at various points in history, considered a national security issue, particularly during the Cold War years,[38] and continues to be a

contentious issue. In *Full Metal Jacket,* the purification of the recruits involves rituals, chants, prayers, and sacrifices. The sergeant himself draws the analogy between this cleansing process and religion when he orders Joker and Cowboy to clean the head and make it so sanitary that the "Virgin Mary herself would be proud to go in there and take a dump!"(23).[39]

Furthermore, the marines' mission to bring freedom and democracy to the rest of the world is explicitly defined as a religious one, much like that of missionaries: "you will be a minister of death, praying for war," says Hartman in the first few minutes of the film. And, as the first part of the film nears its conclusion, Hartman reiterates the same message: "Today . . . is Christmas! There will be a magic show at zero-nine-thirty! Chaplain Charlie will tell you about how the free world *will* conquer Communism with the aid of God and a few marines" (40). In the scene immediately following this one, perhaps that same Christmas night, we see Pyle talking to his rifle as he cleans and oils it, an indication that he has begun his deadly rebirth into manhood. Interestingly, Pyle's resurrection as a *man* on Christmas night coincides with that of Christ himself who, according to David Gilmore's study *Manhood in the Making,* was portrayed in turn-of-the-century pamphlets as "the supremely manly man."[40] The following scene confirms Pyle's rebirth by showing him successfully shooting at targets and earning the drill sergeant's commendations that he is "definitely born again" (41). These references to religion can also be understood as evocations of a statement made by President Woodrow Wilson in which he conjures the image of the Christian soldier, armed to the teeth, bringing democracy to the "pagan" world: "When men take up arms to set other men free, there is something sacred and holy in the warfare."[41]

The quasi-religious *conversion* of boys into men, through the suppression of the feminine within and through the identification of sex with violence, is facilitated by the technological power represented by the recruits' guns, which have become sacred objects. As Loren Baritz points out, "the power of technology . . . to bestow potency on the weak, caused many young American males to think of machinery and sex as the same thing."[42] Hartman explicitly invites the recruits to do so by ordering them to give a girl's name to their rifles and to sleep with them "because this is the only pussy you people are going to get! . . . You're married to this piece, this weapon of iron and wood! And you will be faithful! Port . . . hut! Prepare to mount! Mount!" (13). The command to "mount" the bunks carries a double connotation: it refers to both the sexual act and to the image of the western hero mounting his horse.

Soon after, the recruits are seen marching inside the barracks, their rifles in their right hands and their left hands clutching their genitals, chanting, "This is my rifle! This is my gun!" "This is for fighting! This is for fun!" (18). As Baritz shows, many GIs in Vietnam admitted to the excitement induced by their powerful weapons: "To some people," explains one GI, "carrying a gun was like having a permanent hard-on. It was a pure sexual trip every time you got to pull the trigger." A pilot for the navy describes the feeling of entering an airplane as being "the pre-orgasmic mindset of the military person" and the firing of a rocket and watching it hit its target as an "orgasm."[43]

This identification between sexual and technological power and prowess is illustrated in the film by the juxtaposition of four seemingly unrelated scenes. The first scene shows Pyle tenderly talking to and cleaning his "beautiful" and "smooth" rifle, Charlene—the feminine and diminutive of Charlie, which is both a man's name and the name used by the marines to refer to the enemy Vietnamese. This scene dissolves into a brief depiction of Pyle and a few other recruits mopping the barracks floor, a transition to a third scene showing Joker and Cowboy talking while cleaning the latrine. The obvious links among these three scenes are the fact that they all involve cleaning and that Pyle is either present on the scene or evoked in the other characters' conversation (in the sequence's third scene, Joker tells Cowboy about Pyle's habit of talking to his rifle). The more subtle link is created when, immediately following the discussion about Pyle, Joker tells Cowboy that he wants "to slip my tubesteak into your sister" (41). The sexual act referred to by Joker is tied to the image of Pyle cleaning his "feminized" rifle. The suggestion is that the evocation of Pyle's relationship with his rifle is arousing to Joker. The fourth and final scene where Pyle is successfully shooting his M-14 constitutes a symbolic climax, one that will be echoed later when Pyle shoots his gun into his own mouth—a sexual metaphor. As the sound of the shots fired by Pyle echo in the distance, we hear Hartman's comment that "we've finally found something that you do well!" (41). The identification between sexual and military performance in these scenes that culminate in the climactic firing of the M-14 is a preamble to Pyle's suicide—another symbolic as well as literal climax in the film. As Pyle brings the M-14 loaded with full-metal-jacketed bullets to his mouth in a deadly quasi-sexual embrace and pulls the trigger, he achieves complete unity with his gun. This is a fatal and infertile unity between man and machine, one that substitutes for the fertile and pleasurable sexual unity between two people.

The masculinization process portrayed by the boot camp portion of the film has run its course to its logical conclusion, a logic that is suicidal. According to this logic, a real man, that is, a "*man*-made" man, is figuratively and literally a dead marine whose masculinity can never be threatened nor put into question again. Masculinity constructed in opposition to a threatening feminine is a feat of military engineering and ingenuity, engendered by Mother Green. The unity described above is shown to be so complete that the marines themselves have been refashioned into technological tools, machine-hard, penetrating and penetrated full metal jackets: "you will be a weapon," says Hartman (3), a deadly weapon: "the deadliest weapon in the world is a marine and his rifle" (28).

Another kind of unity forged by the boot camp training program is the unity between the Marine Corps and its recruits, or, as the film states it, between "Mother Green" and her "killing machine" (85). As Thomas Doherty puts it, "Kubrick renders the visceral appeal of being a working cog in a well-oiled machine, of enveloping the private self in a full metal jacket."[44] Moreover, the original unity between mother and child, which according to post-Freudian ego psychology constitutes that child's primary identity, is now replaced by the unity between the reborn masculine recruit and the patriarchal mother.[45] As Joker puts it in Hasford's *The Short-Timers*, the body or the marine (his "corps"/core) and that of the Marine Corps are one and the same: they are "parts of the same body."[46]

In opposition to Freudian theory that constitutes the male infant as already having a male identity, post-Freudian theorists argue that all infants—male and female—establish a primary identity and a social bond with the nurturing parent, in most cases the mother. During the separation/individuation stage, the child becomes receptive to social demands for gender-appropriate behavior, and the male child is forced to embrace masculinity as a category of self-identity that is distinct from femininity. This stage is more problematic for boys than for girls because, while the girl's femininity is reinforced by her original symbiotic unity with her mother, the boy's masculinity demands that he overcome the previous sense of unity with the mother "in order to achieve an independent identity defined by his culture as masculine."[47] In *Full Metal Jacket*, the oneness with the mother that the boy must reject in order to become a man and a marine is replaced by the oneness with the *Corps*, the "body" of the Marine Corps and the brotherhood of marines. Masculinity is thus shown to be a reductive process that involves a symbolic castration. In severing his identification with the mother, the male child is also severing a part of himself. The Marine Corps exploits this lack by seeming to replace the lost mother.

This notion of "manhood" as a state that must be won is, according to

David Gilmore, shared by most, but not all cultures: "Ideas and anxieties about masculinity as a special status category of achievement are widespread in societies around the world, being expressed to varying degrees, but they do not seem to be absolutely universal."[48] Gilmore's study shows that in most cultures that subscribe to this definition of masculinity, the candidate for manhood is subjected to rituals of humiliation and self-mutilation, or mutilation by others. In order to maintain a manly image, and to earn his manhood, he is asked to undergo painful ordeals, not show fear, take risks with his life, and display contempt for death. Often, he must undergo this initiation away from his family, in an isolated place. All of *Full Metal Jacket,* and in particular the Parris Island portion of the film, brilliantly illustrates these rituals.

The first mutilation—initially a symbolic one—occurs in the film's opening scene. With Tom T. Hall's country-western "Hello Vietnam" playing on the sound track, the marine recruits are seen having their heads shaved at the barbershop of the Parris Island Marine Base—an isolated locale, as the word "island" indicates.[49] This constitutes the first phase of their training and of the shattering of their identities. This shaving ritual establishes the recruits' identities as boys rather than men, or rather, as babies: with their heads shaven, they resemble infants. This image is reinforced in later scenes when they appear in white underwear and T-shirt: they look like babies in diapers. Their neatly lined up bunks are reminiscent of incubators in a hospital nursery. These "babies" are not yet fully "born" into the world of war where they will become real men. The recruits also resemble one another. They are, or will soon become, clones of each other, as illustrated in the inspection scene where the inductees stand at attention on top of their footlockers, in their white undergarments, erect, arms stretched out, like naïve, inert robots.

The men's identities are further broken down by humiliating insults: their mouths are "sewers," their bodies are "maggots" (3), they are "equally worthless," "amphibian shit" (4). Their sexuality as well as their patriotism are put into question in the same breath: they are described as "communist cocksucker[s]" (4).

What follows is the rebuilding of their identities that begins with a renaming process designed to emphasize the one-dimensionality of their new selves: the Texan is named "Cowboy," the funny guy is "Joker," the black recruit is "Snowball," and the overweight and clumsy boy is "Gomer Pyle." They undergo arduous physical training to which they must submit stoically. The Marine Corps wants "indestructible men, men without fear"

(42). This training is designed to give them a tough inner and outer core, much like that of a metal-jacketed bullet. "It is your hard heart that kills," says Hartman, the incarnation of a "hard heart." The very spelling of his name suggests both the words "heart" and "hard."

The marines' actions too must be one-dimensional: they are told to have a "war face," which they must rehearse and perfect. To stamp out all differences, they are subjected to self-mutilation and mutual mutilation. As Joker puts it, the recruits "are ready to eat their own guts and ask for seconds" (42). Pyle, whose initial nonconformity represents a threat to the unity of the Corps, is ordered to "lean forward and choke" himself on the hand of the drill sergeant (11). When this proves to be of no avail, the other recruits are summoned to participate in his conversion. One scene shows Pyle, in football-style helmet, being beaten to the ground by another recruit while the rest cheer. Joker becomes Pyle's surrogate mother and is given the responsible of teaching him "everything": from disassembling an M-14 rifle to properly lacing his boots and making his bed. When Pyle is struggling over the "confidence climb," Joker coaxes him along with encouraging cheers: "That'a boy. That's it" (28). Pyle is continuously portrayed as a child, sucking his thumb, marching behind the platoon with his pants down around his ankles, eating a jelly doughnut, while the rest of the platoon does push-ups. Pyle's infantilism is stressed by the fact that he has to be taught the most fundamental tasks: Joker will "teach you how to pee," Hartman tells him, further emphasizing Joker's role as mother and Pyle's infantile state (23). As the recruits themselves acknowledge in one of their chants, they are all given a new identity during boot camp: "I love working for Uncle Sam! Let's me know just *who I am!*" (my emphasis). Pyle's infantilism also serves to hide from the other recruits the fact that they too are being infantilized, feminized, humiliated, and mutilated.

Pyle remains "unconverted" until the night when all the recruits execute a massive assault on him while he sleeps. This is the film's—and the Marine Corps'—version of male bonding. Pyle is held secure to his bed and beaten with soap bars wrapped in towels by the entire platoon, while his cries are muffled by a gag in his mouth. When Pyle is next seen, he is staring blankly ahead, as if he already had the "thousand-yard stare" that, we later learn, is characteristic of marines who have been in combat. What these scenes suggest is that the first combat the marine must undergo before he is sent to war is a combat against his own self.

Kubrick shows, however, that the masculinization process does not end with boot camp. The war is itself another testing ground for masculinity.

Tony Williams comments on the fact that "war's function as an act of ritual cleansing whereby man can purify his masculinity and disavow his feminine side," is widely recognized. The soldier must not only take risks with his life, he must welcome such risks and have the courage to look death in the face. He must continue to kill whatever is not purely masculine in him. The killing of the female sniper, for instance, is but another phase of Joker's rebirth as a man. "The Vietcong sniper symbolizes Joker's earlier comments about Jungian duality," adds Williams,[50] and therefore she must not only be female but must be killed in precisely the way that she is. That she represents the feminine, and that Joker is the one to deliver the blow that finally kills her, invites us to read her death as emblematic of Joker's progress toward self-mutilation and, therefore, toward masculinization.

However, the female sniper is a soldier in addition to being female, and this fact also invites further scrutiny of the incident. In their study of the Viet Cong and North Vietnamese armies, Michael Lee Lanning and Dan Cragg explain that women revolutionaries not only played a part in the recruiting and indoctrination of soldiers but also actively participated in guerilla units and in combat operations. Only young and unmarried women—like the sniper herself—were recruited. In North Vietnam, female students took pledges of loyalty and dedication to the Motherland that included serving in combat when necessary. Kubrick seems to have intended for us to see the sniper *as a soldier* as well as a woman. As the script indicates, the face she turns toward the camera as she tries to get a shot at Joker is that of a "grunt": "With the hard eyes of a grunt, the SNIPER fires her AK-47 rifle" (113). Joker's killing of the sniper is not just an act of self-mutilation, that is, of the annihilation of the feminine within. It is also, metaphorically, a suicidal act—the killing of a soldier like himself. The sniper incident enables us to see self-mutilation as, in effect, suicidal.

Once again, Kubrick reveals that the other is always the self because the oppositional duality between masculine and feminine dictated by the masculinization process described here is a false one. Masculinity and femininity are shown to be cultural constructs, symbolic scripts, and the masculine is not to be confused with the male. As Jeffords's remark cited in the opening pages of this essay reminds us, it is crucial to our understanding of the social construction of gender—both male and female—that patriarchy and masculinity be differentiated. Not only does patriarchal oppression operate on men and on women, but, I would argue, it operates *first* on men. As Frank Lentricchia succinctly puts it: "It is in the patriarchal interest that the two terms (masculine and male) stay thoroughly confused."[51] Kubrick's

Full Metal Jacket is an attempt to disentangle this confusion by showing that women too can be grunts and by exposing the process through which the masculinization (of males and females) is enacted.

This gendering process illustrated by *Full Metal Jacket* and described here has found expression in other films of the late 1980s to the present and is not limited to Vietnam War films. Andrew Ross's analysis of *Aliens* (1979) shows that this film too already offered a typically western showdown, this time between a good mother and an evil mother. Ripley appears empowered by a Rambo style of masculinity and weaponry that gives her a "recognizably national identity." Like the marine recruits in Kubrick's film, she is assimilated into a "western-masculinist posture." Ross concludes by saying that "in fact, Ripley's story shows some of the moves by which women can be, and increasingly will be, presented as accomplices, unwilling or not, in the particular national tradition of engendering men."[52] What Kubrick does is to show us how men themselves have been made into accomplices, victims, and perpetuators of this engendering process.

Full Metal Jacket closes with the disentanglement of another confusion encouraged by the patriarchal order. The process described by *Full Metal Jacket* and analyzed here is only delusively one of maturation. As the platoon marches through the city of Hué against the background of smoke and fire, singing the "Mickey Mouse Club" song, two things are made clear. The first is the marines' infantilism, which returns us to the opening segment of the film. This scene represents a return to childhood that puts into question the process of maturation and masculinization we have just witnessed. In terms of post-Freudian theory, it also represents the powerful urge back toward childhood that the child's struggle for masculinity is designed to suppress or mask. The scene reminds us that masculinization is a continuous unfinished "battle against these regressive wishes and fantasies, a hard-fought renunciation of the longings for the prelapsarian idyll of childhood."[53]

Second, the Mickey Mouse episode shows that boot camp and war are continuous with the rest of American popular culture. The "Vietnam generation" was the first generation to grow up with television, and the "Mickey Mouse Club" was a popular program during the time the members of that generation were growing up. War is thus shown to be the logical conclusion of a process that begins with the Mickey Mouse Club, the Boy Scouts, the high school football team. Peter Davis, in his Academy Award–winning 1974 documentary *Hearts and Minds,* explicitly draws the analogy between the rhetoric of sports, of war, and of religion in a scene showing a pep talk given before an important game to a high school foot-ball team in Niles, Ohio. The speaker himself invokes war, God, and the victory of the team in his exaltation of the making of masculinity:

> When you go forth to war against your enemies, and see horses and chari-ots, and an army larger than your own, you shall not be afraid. Now, let's not anybody be so naïve as to think that we're here, in any way, to worship football. Nor are we here, as I am sure many people believe, to pray for a vic-tory. We believe in victory, we believe it will come to the team that's best pre-pared. This is serious business that we are involved in, and that's religious, and God cares. There are going to be men made tonight. And that's religious, and God cares about that.

In choosing the Mickey Mouse Club anthem to close the film, Kubrick once again calls attention to the fact that the process depicted here is one that calls for the participation of all members of society, male and female. As the song goes: "Boys and girls from far and near you're as welcome as can be" (120). Furthermore, the process described by the words of the Mickey Mouse Club anthem is an accurate summary of the process illus-trated by the film: "Here we go a-marching and a-shouting merrily . . . We play fair and we work hard and we're in harmony . . . Who is marching coast to coast and far across the sea? . . . Come along and sing this song and join our family." More importantly, however, these words also refer to the process of colonization in general.

The making of *Full Metal Jacket* dates back to when Stanley Kubrick and Michael Herr first met at Kubrick's house in London, in the spring of 1980, to discuss war and movies. According to Herr, Kubrick "had a strong feeling about a particular kind of war movie that he wanted to make, but he didn't have a story."[54] Gustav Hasford's *The Short-Timers* provided Kubrick with the story he needed. In adapting Hasford's novel, Kubrick enlarged considerably the Parris Island episode, which occupies only 10 percent of the novel, thus departing from most Vietnam genre films that focus pri-marily on combat. In choosing to depict the Vietnam war in particular, Kubrick directs our attention to the fact that, in the words of the editors of *The Vietnam War and American Culture,* "our part in the wars fought to subjugate the Vietnamese people to various colonial rulers was merely the latest chapter in a long history. Our responsibility for 'that war' con-nected us to the ugly history of Western colonization."[55] This coloniza-tion, Kubrick shows, was, and sadly continues to be, foremost one of hearts and minds before and long after it is a colonization of territory. If the recent resurgence and popularity of the war movie genre is any indication, we may still be "in a world of shit." But, are we still enjoying it?

This is the patent-age of new inventions
For killing bodies, and for saving souls,
All propagated with the best intentions.
—BYRON, *Don Juan* canto 1, 132[56]

NOTES

An earlier version of this essay appeared in *Cinema Journal* 33.2 (1994): 5–21. Copyright © 1994 by the University of Texas Press. All rights reserved.

1. Loren Baritz, *Backfire: A History of How American Culture Led Us into Vietnam and Made Us Fight the Way We Did* (New York: William Morrow and Company, 1985), 2.

2. Susan Jeffords, *The Remasculinization of America* (Bloomington: Indiana University Press, 1989), 116, 173, 176.

3. Ibid., 173.

4. Richard Rambuss, for instance, notes that not only is most of the violence in the film male-on-male violence, but the film's version of the killing of the woman sniper "empties the scene of male bravura" and thus of misogynistic overtones. Unlike in the film, Joker's killing of the sniper in the novel elicits a competitive response from one of the other marines, Animal Mother, who chops off the woman's head and brandishes it as a trophy. (Richard Rambuss, "Machinehead," *Camera Obscura* 14.42 (1999): 97–122). While Hartford's rendition of this incident can be read, as Rambuss does, as misogynistic, I argue in the present essay that it is also a metaphorical expression of the marines' violent but successful competition/cooperation with one another in killing the feminine within and as a celebration of that defeat.

The sniper incident continues to be a much discussed scene in the critical literature. Bruno Cornellier, in a recent essay on war and sexuality, takes issue with my reading of the film and sees the killing of the woman sniper as undermining the critique of the making of masculinity effected by the film in the first half that culminates with Gomer Pyle's suicide. While denouncing the masculinization process, the film offers no alternatives to it, according to Cornellier. (Bruno Cornellier, "Le sexe et la guerre: le meurtre de la femme et la construction de la masculinité dans *Full Metal Jacket* de Stanley Kubrick," *Cadrage: Revue de Cinéma*, Jan/Feb 2002, www.cadrage.net.) Here, I will argue that the killing of the sniper is a metaphorical reenactment of Pyle's suicide, and serves the same purpose. It is a testament to the richness of Kubrick's film that it does lend itself to multiple readings, depending on what complex of elements from the film one takes into account.

5. Jeffords, *Remasculinization*, 181, my emphasis.

6. For an excellent discussion of the technologization of the marines as killing machines, see Richard Rambuss's essay mentioned above.

7. John Stevenson, "Recent Vietnam Films," *Enclitic* 10 (1988): 41, 48.

8. Thomas Doherty, "Full Metal Genre: Kubrick's Vietnam Combat Movie," *Film Quarterly* 42 (1981): 27, 28.

9. David Desser, "Charlie Don't Surf: Race and Culture in the Vietnam War Films," in *Inventing Vietnam: The War in Film and Television,* ed. Michael Anderegg (Philadelphia: Temple University Press, 1991), 81.

10. Michael Pursell, "*Full Metal Jacket*: The Unravelling of Patriarchy," *Literature/Film Quarterly* 16 (1988): 221.

11. Quoted in Baritz, *Backfire,* 180.

12. Stanley Kubrick, Michael Herr, and Gustav Hasford, *Full Metal Jacket: The Screenplay* (New York: Alfred A. Knopf, 1987), 64. All quotations from *Full Metal Jacket* refer to the screenplay. Page numbers will be given in parentheses in the text.

13. Baritz, *Backfire,* 26.

14. John Hellmann, *American Myth and the Legacy of Vietnam* (New York: Columbia University Press, 1986), 6, 15.

15. *The Quiet American* was first adapted to the screen in 1958 and directed by Joseph Mankiewicz. A new screen adaptation, directed by the Australian Phillip Noyce, was released in early 2003 after having been shelved by Miramax for nearly a year. Noyce's version, more true to the tone and intent of Greene's novel than Mankiewicz's, was under postproduction when the September 11 attacks occurred. Miramax, the film's distributor, promptly decided to delay the release of the film because it would have been construed as too critical of American foreign policy. In an interview with Stephanie Bunburg for the Melbourne paper *The Age,* Noyce explained that when he first read *The Quiet American* in 1995 while traveling in Vietnam, he realized that this was "the great Vietnam war movie that hadn't been made." He called it, the "missing link," that "helps us to understand why we pursued that war so vehemently. And for the Vietnamese it is the same thing, because they would like to know why we rained hell on them for so long . . . So in that sense, I think this is the most important of the so-called Vietnam movies. Because it is not a film about fighting the war, so much as why we fought the war" (Jan. 19, 2003. Reprinted in http://www.kooriweb.org/foley/backroads/cast/story31.html.). It was a fateful coincidence that Noyce's film gained release precisely at a time when the United States, and the world, were engaged in renewed turbulent debates over another war, this time with Iraq. It was doubly poignant that Noyce's other tale of imperial atrocities, *The Rabbit-Proof Fence,* was also on release at the same time.

16. Susan White, for instance, points out that the TV show *Gomer Pyle, USMC,* portraying the relationship between the recruit Pyle and his sergeant, was at the height of its popularity in 1968. See Susan White, "Male Bonding, Hollywood Orientalism, and the Repression of the Feminine in Kubrick's *Full Metal Jacket*," *Arizona Quarterly* 44 (1988): 120–44.

17. Graham Greene, *The Quiet American* (London: William Heinemann Ltd., 1955), 13, 119.

18. Hellmann, *American Myth,* 38.

19. Baritz, *Backfire,* 42.

20. Michael Anderegg, "Hollywood and Vietnam: John Wayne and Jane Fonda as Discourse," in *Inventing Vietnam,* 24.

21. Ibid., 28.

22. Hellmann, *American Myth*, 44.

23. *Born on the Fourth of July*, directed by Oliver Stone, was released in 1989, and *Rumor of War*, directed by Richard T. Heffron, was shown as a two-part television program in 1980.

24. Cited in Anderegg, "Hollywood and Vietnam," 19.

25. Hellmann, *American Myth*, 106.

26. Anderegg, "Hollywood and Vietnam," 25.

27. See Hayden White, *Tropics of Discourse: Essays in Cultural Criticism* (Baltimore: Johns Hopkins University Press, 1978).

28. See Gustav Hasford, *The Short-Timers* (New York: Harper and Row, 1979), and Michael Herr, *Dispatches* (New York: Alfred A. Knopf, 1977).

29. Anderegg, *Inventing Vietnam*, 2.

30. Tony Williams, "Narrative Patterns and Mythic Trajectories in Mid-1980s Vietnam Movies," in *Inventing Vietnam*, 130.

31. Desser, "Charlie Don't Surf," 96.

32. An additional reference to western mythology worth noting in the prostitute sequence is a possible citation from a western revisionist film made in 1979. In response to the prostitute's contention that "soul brotha too boo-coo," Eightball responds: "This baby-san looks like she could suck the chrome off a trailer hitch." This line is also spoken by Willie Nelson in Sydney Pollack's *The Electric Horseman*, starring Robert Redford and Jane Fonda. If, in fact, this line is a citation, its significance is twofold. First of all, by referring us to a movie produced eleven years after the period portrayed in *Full Metal Jacket*, Kubrick generalizes his reference to the motivations behind American expansionism. *The Electric Horseman* shows American expansionism now at work through big business and advertisement. The colonization illustrated by this film is that of the minds of American consumers through the image of the western cowboy. The character played by Robert Redford is a defunct cowboy who now makes his living advertising cereal. Second, *The Electric Horseman* is an ironic commentary on the demise of the western hero and of the frontier. The only space left to be explored by the western cowboy is the space of billboards, television sets, and cereal boxes. The Wild West has been turned into a gambling strip in Las Vegas.

33. Robert Ray, *A Certain Tendency of the Hollywood Cinema, 1930–1980* (Princeton, NJ: Princeton University Press, 1985), 254.

34. Christopher Sharrett, "*Full Metal Jacket*," *Cineaste* 16 (1987): 64.

35. Frank Lentricchia, "Patriarchy Against Itself: The Young Manhood of Wallace Stevens," *Critical Inquiry* 13 (1987): 743.

36. Baritz, *Backfire*, 25. It is also worth noting that the GI mentioned by Baritz became the model for the Michael J. Fox character in *Casualties of War* (1989).

37. Jeffords, *Remasculinization*, 173.

38. John D'Emilio and Estelle B. Freedman, *Intimate Matters: A History of Sexuality in America* (New York: Harper and Row, 1988), 293. See also Richard Rambuss's discussion of the homophobic homoeroticism of the military.

39. Many of the key events and conversations, including Pyle's suicide, take place in the "head," calling attention to the word's multivalence. The term "head"

and Hartman's comment evoke simultaneously a place of defecation (of purging, cleansing), the body's orifice, and the minds of the recruits. This multiple association suggests a cleansing of body and of mind (and thus the insistence on sexual "purity") and also helps bring to the fore the scatological conflation of mouth and anus throughout the film discussed by Richard Rambuss.

40. David D. Gilmore, *Manhood in the Making: Cultural Concepts of Masculinity* (New Haven: Yale University Press, 1990), 19.

41. Baritz, *Backfire*, 37.

42. Ibid., 52.

43. Ibid., 53.

44. Doherty, "Full Metal Genre," 27.

45. Gilmore, *Manhood in the Making*, 26–29.

46. Hasford, *Short-Timers*, 72.

47. Gilmore, *Manhood in the Making*, 27.

48. Ibid., 4.

49. For an interesting study of the uses of rock music in Vietnam War films, see Douglas W. Reitinger's "Paint It Black: Rock Music and Vietnam War Film," *Journal of American Culture* 15.3 (1992): 53–59. The choice to use a country-western song in the film's opening already invites an analogy between the war and western heroes, and between Vietnam and the Western frontier. Reintinger observes that all the songs used in the film, with the exception of the Rolling Stones' "Paint It Black" that closes the film, predate the 1968 Tet Offensive. He also notes the relationship between sex and violence that is evoked by many of the songs. See also Thomas Doherty for a discussion of the film's S&M overtones in its use of Nancy Sinatra's "These Boots."

50. Williams, "Narrative Patterns," 129, 130.

51. Lentricchia, "Patriarchy Against Itself," 774.

52. Andrew Ross, "Cowboys, Cadillacs and Cosmonauts: Families, Film Genre, and Technocultures," in *Engendering Men: The Question of Male Feminist Criticism*, ed. Joseph A. Boone and Michael Cadden (New York: Routledge Press, 1990), 101. Examples of this complicity and of what Richard Rambuss calls the "military retooling of the female recruit" can be found in films that purport to give women equal standing and status in the military, the most notable example of which is Ridley Scott's *G.I. Jane* (1997).

53. Gilmore, *Manhood in the Making*, 29.

54. See Michael Herr's introduction in *Full Metal Jacket: The Screenplay*, v.

55. John Carlos Rowe and Rick Berg, eds., *The Vietnam War and American Culture* (New York: Columbia University Press, 1991), 1.

56. George Gordon Byron. *The Selected Poetry and Letters,* ed. Edward E. Bostetter (New York: Holt, Rinehart and Winston, Inc. 1961), 228. These lines served as the epigram for Graham Greene's *The Quiet American,* a fact noted by numerous reviewers of Phillip Noyce's filmic rendition of the novel. In his 18 February review of *The Quiet American* for the *Boston Globe,* James Carroll notes the prophetic relevance of Noyce's film to 2003, as the United States continues to push for war with Iraq, concluding that "Vietnam haunts our national spirit because America's violence was so well-motivated—destroying villages, yes, but only to

save them. Vietnam teaches that good intentions are not enough. In the patent age of new inventions, there must equally be the knowledge—we have it from Greene, but also from the American generation that fulfilled his prophecy—that saving souls by killing bodies is impossible. Beware a nation announcing its innocence en route to war."

Final Take

EYES WIDE SHUT

In Dreams Begin
Responsibilities

—⪧◆⪦—

JONATHAN ROSENBAUM

Writing about *Eyes Wide Shut* in *Time,* Richard Schickel had this to say about its source, Arthur Schnitzler's *Traumnovelle* (1926): "Like a lot of the novels on which good movies are based, it is an entertaining, erotically charged fiction of the second rank, in need of the vivifying physicalization of the screen and the kind of narrative focus a good director can bring to imperfect but provocative life—especially when he has been thinking about it as long as Kubrick had"—i.e., at least since 1968, when Kubrick asked his wife to read it.[1] This more or less matches the opinion of Frederic Raphael, Kubrick's credited co-writer, as expressed in his recent memoir, *Eyes Wide Open.*[2] But I would argue that *Traumnovelle* is a masterpiece worthy of resting alongside Poe's "The Masque of the Red Death" (1842), Kafka's *The Trial* (1925) and Sadegh Hedayat's *The Blind Owl* (1937). Like the Poe story, it features a phantasmal masked ball with dark and decadent undercurrents, and like the Kafka and Hedayat novels, it continually and ambiguously crosses back and forth between fantasy and waking reality. But it differs from all three in containing a development that might be described as therapeutic—Schnitzler, a doctor, was a contemporary of Freud—making *Eyes Wide Shut* a rare departure for Kubrick and concluding his career with the closest thing in his work to a happy ending. Moreover, the question about the novella is not whether Kubrick has "brought it to life"—it lives vibrantly without him, even if he has brought it to a lot of people's attention, including mine—but whether he's done it justice, a problem also raised by his films of *Lolita* (1962) and *A Clockwork Orange* (1971).

I read *Traumnovelle* before I saw the movie, which hindered as well as helped my first impressions. The last time I tried this with a Kubrick film was when I read Stephen King's *The Shining* (1977) before seeing the film and found that King's novel, whatever its literary limitations, was genuinely scary, whereas Kubrick's movie, for all its brilliance, generally was not. Yet practically all of Kubrick's films improve with age and repeated viewings, and scary or not, his version of *The Shining* (1980) fascinates me a lot more than King's. I cannot say the same about *Lolita;* Vladimir Nabokov's novel improves with rereading a lot more than Kubrick's film improves with reviewing. And *A Clockwork Orange* is a draw: I embrace the moral ambiguity of Anthony Burgess's novel and detest the morality of Kubrick's film, yet I would rather see the film again than reread the novel. In the case of *Eyes Wide Shut* I am inclined to think Kubrick has done Schnitzler's masterpiece justice. Allowing for all the differences between Vienna in the 1920s and New York in the 1990s and between Jews and WASPs, it is a remarkably faithful and ingenious adaptation. Kubrick made this movie convinced that relationships between couples have not significantly changed over the past seventy-odd years, and whether you find it a success probably depends a lot on whether you agree with him.

I will not attempt a full synopsis, but I have to outline chunks of the first two-thirds of the plot to make certain points. Bill Harford (Tom Cruise), a successful New York doctor, and his wife, Alice (Nicole Kidman), the former manager of a Soho art gallery, attend a fancy Christmas party at the town house of Victor Ziegler (played to perfection by Sydney Pollack), one of Bill's wealthy patients, where each engages in flirtation—Alice with a Hungarian lounge lizard, Bill with a couple of models. Bill recognizes the orchestra's pianist, Nick Nightingale (Todd Field), as a former classmate and chats with him briefly; later he is called upstairs by Ziegler to help revive a naked prostitute who has overdosed on drugs. Bill and Alice make love when they get home that night, clearly stimulated by their flirtations, but the following evening, after they smoke pot, Alice begins to challenge Bill's total confidence in her faithfulness by telling him a story that shocks him about her passionate attraction to a naval officer she glimpsed only briefly when they were at Cape Cod with their little girl the previous summer.

Called away by the death of a patient, Bill is haunted by images of Alice having sex with the officer, and his night and the following day and night turn into a string of adventures consisting of sexual temptations or provocations that come his way with and without his complicity—all of which prove abortive. The dreamlike interruptions and certain passing details share some of the same hallucinatory texture—as they do in Schnitzler's story—so that even waitresses glimpsed in a diner and coffeehouse and a gay hotel desk clerk suggest sexual possibilities. The daughter (Marie Richardson) of the man who has just died is engaged to be married soon, yet suddenly declares her love for Bill. Wandering the streets afterward, he is harassed by college kids who think he is gay (in *Traumnovelle* the hero is Jewish and the students anti-Semites), then picked up by a prostitute named Domino (Vinessa Shaw). He finally winds up at the Sonata Café, where Nick Nightingale is performing with a jazz quartet. Nick has a gig later that night as a blindfolded pianist at a costumed orgy in a country house on Long Island, and Bill, after discovering the password, persuades Nick to give him the address. He then proceeds to a costume-rental shop to acquire a tux, cloak, and mask, and takes a taxi to the house. Eventually exposed as an intruder, he fears for his life until a masked woman mysteriously offers to sacrifice herself for him.

When he finally arrives home he wakes Alice from a troubled dream involving the naval officer and an orgy in which she participates while laughing scornfully at Bill, which she recounts. It is one of the movie's many indications that the unclear separations of imagination and reality include many rhyme effects between Alice's dreams and fantasies and Bill's reality, as well as rhymes between her fantasies and his (such as her having sex with the naval officer). In fact, though the film initially appears to be mainly about Bill because it follows him around more than Alice, Alice's confession and dream are just as important as anything that happens to him; in some respects, thanks to Kubrick's and Schnitzler's careful calibrations in the storytelling, she makes an even stronger impression than he does, especially because she seems more in touch with her fantasy life than he is with his own—and because every other woman in the movie is in one way or another a doppelgänger for her. Some of the other rhyme effects create disquieting connections—between a sexual invitation at Ziegler's party ("Do you know where the rainbow ends?") and the name of the costume shop (Rainbow) and between the password to the orgy, "Fidelio," which suggests the Italian word for "faithful" and Bill's failure to betray her there. (Schnitzler's story is full of comparable echo effects: there the password to the orgy is "Denmark," which happens to be where the hero's wife was tempted to commit adultery.)

Eyes Wide Shut has a lot to say about the psychological accommodations of marriage—and has a sunnier view of human possibility than any other Kubrick film, in spite of all its dark moments. It depends on a sense of the shared mental reality of a couple that almost supersedes any sense of their shared physical reality, a strange emphasis that is probably the source of most of the confusion felt by everyone in the course of processing the story. (A similar sense of shared mental reality can be found in the title characters of Schnitzler's startling, almost equally masterful novella *Beatrice and Her Son* [1913]). A list of the things we never learn about the characters is at least as long as the list of things we know with any certainty. We remain in the dark about how the wife happens upon the mask worn by the husband at the orgy, about the accuracy of Ziegler's account of many of those same adventures, and even about whether they happen outside the husband's imagination. Yet there is never any doubt about what transpires emotionally between this husband and wife.

For years, two misleading adjectives have been used to describe Kubrick's work: "cold" and "perfectionist." "Cold" implies unemotional, and it simply is not true that Kubrick's films lack emotion. They are full of emotions, though most of them are so convoluted and elusive that you have to follow them as if through a maze—perhaps the major reason his films become richer with repeated viewing. He so strongly resists sentimentality that cynicism and derision often seem close at hand. One difficulty I had with *Eyes Wide Shut* the first time I saw it was accepting the caricatural side of Kubrick—his handling of Cruise's "normality" in the lead role as Dr. William Harford and the mincing mannerisms of the gay hotel desk-clerk— as something other than malicious. My memory of Kubrick's mocking inflation of Jack Nicholson's narcissism in the second half of *The Shining* made me think he was being equally diabolical here about Cruise's narcissism, but a second look at the movie has rid me of this impression. Maybe Steve Martin would have made a more interesting Harford; according to Michael Herr in *Vanity Fair,* Martin was Kubrick's first choice for the role twenty years ago. But using a real couple such as Cruise and Kidman had obvious advantages as well.[3]

   That Bill Harford lies to his wife about both his lust for the models at Ziegler's party and the reason Ziegler called him upstairs identifies him at the outset as a glib hypocrite who thinks privilege can get him anywhere— which differentiates him somewhat from Schnitzler's hero—but that does not mean Kubrick views him with contempt. The remainder of the story may undermine Harford's confidence, but Kubrick doesn't let us know whether his recounting of his nocturnal adventures to Alice near the end of the movie is fully or only partially honest—we don't hear any of it. All we know is that it brings them both to tears.

Ironically, the major difference between Kubrick and Schnitzler may be that Kubrick is more of a moralist, even if he is unusually subtle about it. The only important invented character in *Eyes Wide Shut*, Ziegler, is the only one I regard as unambiguously evil. But Ziegler's evil, unlike mad Jack Torrance's in *The Shining*, is wrapped in impeccable manners, so some viewers may misjudge him. His darker side emerges mainly in glancing hints, such as his momentary reluctance to wait an hour before sending home the hooker after she recovers from her drug-induced coma. He is a charming monster—a statement about class and power and a composite portrait of every Hollywood executive Kubrick ever had to contend with. In this respect, Ziegler is closely allied to the highly cultivated General Broulard (Adolphe Menjou) in *Paths of Glory* (1957)—the true villain of that film, in contrast to the more obvious and scapegoated villain, General Mireau (George Macready), who is openly hypocritical and malicious.

The climactic dialogue between Harford and Ziegler in Ziegler's huge town house—a remarkable scene that runs a little over thirteen minutes—has been getting some flak from reviewers who claim it explains too much. But it explains nothing conclusive, apart from Ziegler's Zeus-like access and power—in a billiards room that seems to belong on Mount Olympus, like the chateau in *Paths of Glory*—and Harford's ultimate remoteness from those reaches; Ziegler holds all the cards, and we and Harford hold none. Critic David Ehrenstein recently told me he thought *Barry Lyndon* (1975) was Kubrick's most Jewish movie in its depiction of social exclusion, but that was before he saw *Eyes Wide Shut*.

The second misleading label attached to Kubrick's work, "perfectionist," might be plausible if it were used to describe his choice of lenses, his ideas about décor, or his obsession with prints and projection. But usually it is used to describe his habit of demanding multiple drafts from writers and repeated takes from actors. Everyone seems to agree that such demands stemmed largely from Kubrick's not knowing what he wanted except through negative indirection, but this is a far cry from what is usually meant by perfectionism. His use of improvisation with actors to great effect—most famously Peter Sellers in *Lolita* and *Dr. Strangelove* (1964) but probably also Timothy Carey in *The Killing* (1955) and *Paths of Glory*, and Kidman in some stretches of *Eyes Wide Shut*—further complicates this notion of perfectionism, as does his use of handheld cameras for filming violence in movies as diverse as *The Killing* and *Barry Lyndon*, which involves a certain amount of chance and improvisation. Kubrick came of age artistically during the same period as action painting, and in his work classical notions of composing frames and telling stories vie with other aspects of the artistic process that are more random and less controllable. (Paradoxically, Kubrick's perfectionism in some areas prevented him from being a perfectionist in others. He would not allow the Venice film festival to show his films subtitled at a retrospective during the shooting of *Eyes Wide Shut* because he did not have enough time to check the prints, so the festival had to show dubbed versions he had already approved.)

Convoluted emotions and negative indirection are two ways Kubrick deliberately kept himself innocent of his own intentions, especially in his later movies. Positing himself as the ideal spectator of his own films, he wanted to be surprised by what his writers and actors did, and that entailed refusing to impose interpretations on his stories, striving to keep some particulars of his stories free from his intellect, and ultimately letting his unconscious do part of the work. (Jacques Rivette has used the same modus operandi in some of his own features, especially during the 1970s.)

This dialectic between control and lack of control eventually became not only Kubrick's method but part of his subject. As Gilles Deleuze noted in *Cinema 2: The Time-Image,* "In Kubrick, the world itself is a brain, there is an identity of brain and world"; Deleuze singles out such central images as the War Room in *Dr. Strangelove,* the computer housing HAL's circuits in *2001: A Space Odyssey* (1968), and the Overlook Hotel in *The Shining* as examples of what he meant, to which I would add the racetrack in *The Killing* and the training camp in *Full Metal Jacket* (1987). Moreover, Deleuze writes, the monolith in *2001* "presides over both cosmic states and cerebral stages: it is the soul of the three bodies, earth, sun, and moon, but also the seed of the three brains, animal, human, machine."[4] And in each film the brain, the world, and the system connecting the two start to break down from internal and external causes, resulting in some form of dissolution (*The Killing*), annihilation (of the world in *Dr. Strangelove* and HAL's brain in *2001*), mutilation (of the brain in *A Clockwork Orange* and the body in *Barry Lyndon*), or madness (*The Shining* and *Full Metal Jacket,* which also chart respectively the dissolution of a family and a fighting unit).

Building on Deleuze's insight, critic Bill Krohn has proposed, in the only plausible account I have read of the structure of *Full Metal Jacket,* that "the little world of the training camp . . . is portrayed as a brain made up of human cells thinking and feeling as one, until its functioning is wrecked first from within, when a single cell, Pyle, begins ruthlessly carrying out the directives of the death instinct that programs the organ as a whole, and then from without by the Tet offensive, the external representation of the same force." As a result, in the second part of the film "the narrative itself begins to malfunction" along with the group mind, exploding "the conventional notion of character" and drifting off in several different directions.[5]

There is no such narrative breakdown in *Eyes Wide Shut,* which proceeds in conventional linear fashion throughout—though interludes created by a fantasy and a dream Alice recounts are every bit as important as waking events. This time the "brain" belongs to neither a single character (like HAL) nor a group (like the soldiers in *Full Metal Jacket*) but to a happily married couple—to their shared experience and the world created between them—and the threat of a breakdown, which forms the narrative, is eventually overcome. In this case the "identity of brain and world" is more explicit, and negotiating a relationship between the two, between dreaming and waking, is what the movie is all about. Even the title tells you that.

"Among those I would call the 'younger generation,' Kubrick appears to me to be a giant," Orson Welles said in a *Cahiers du Cinéma* interview in the mid-1960s, after the release of his adaptation of Kafka's *The Trial* (1962). Stressing that *The Killing* was superior to *The Asphalt Jungle* (1950) and that Kubrick was a better director than John Huston, Welles added, "What I see in him is a talent not possessed by the great directors of the generation immediately preceding his, I mean [Nicholas] Ray, [Robert] Aldrich, etc. Perhaps this is because his temperament comes closer to mine." Both Welles and Kubrick started out in their early twenties, both died at the age of seventy, and both completed thirteen released features. Another significant parallel is that both ended up making all the films they completed after the 1950s in exile, which surely says something about the creative possibilities of American commercial filmmaking over the past four decades. But in other respects their careers proceeded in opposite directions: Welles entered the profession at the top when it came to studio resources and wound up shooting all his last pictures on a shoestring, without studio backing; Kubrick began with shoestring budgets and wound up with full studio backing and apparently all the resources he needed.

On this basis one could argue that Kubrick succeeded in working within the system while retaining his independence on every picture except *Spartacus* (1960), while Welles retained his independence sporadically, imperfectly, and ultimately at the price of working outside the system. Yet the price paid by Kubrick for his success—a sense of paranoid isolation that often seeped into his work and as few completed features as Welles—cannot be discounted. (By isolation I do not mean to endorse the "hermit" myth that the press always attaches to artists who are reluctant to speak to reporters—including Thomas Pynchon and J. D. Salinger as well as Kubrick—I mean his more general habits as a relatively sedentary control freak who spent a lot of time on the phone.)

Inside and outside, interiors and exteriors, form as important a dialectic in his work as control and lack of control, which is perhaps one reason the interiors in his films gradually seem to grow larger—from the dingy lairlike apartments of *The Killing* to the chateau in *Paths of Glory,* from the spaceship in *2001* to the hotel in *The Shining.* This culminates in the palatial interiors of *Eyes Wide Shut,* which contrast with the claustrophobic railroad flat shared by two women and the cluttered costume shop. The throwaway and sometimes artificial quality of the exteriors conforms to the same expressionist system, and if the overall spatial orientation of the interiors at times recalls Welles, it is the Welles who wound up alternating oversize and cramped interiors in *The Trial.* Many reviewers of *Eyes Wide Shut* have been citing Martin Scorsese's *After Hours* (1985)—a picture even more indebted to Welles's *The Trial* in its handling of paranoia—but Welles's influence on Scorsese can be taken as a filtered form of Kafka's influence. (Kafka's story, unlike Welles's, is set almost entirely in cramped spaces.) In Schnitzler's novella the two scenes in the costume shop are already pure Kafka, especially in the uncanny way the relationships of the characters shift between the hero's two visits, and Kubrick catches both the queasiness and the unhealthy sexuality of Kafka at least as effectively as Welles did. Perhaps significantly, this is the only scene in which Kubrick allows the story's Eastern European origins to come out, most noticeably in the accent and appearance of the shop owner (Rade Sherbedgia).

There are already signs that *Eyes Wide Shut* is dividing critics, sometimes along regional, even tribal lines. Most Chicago critics were enthusiastic—at least until a lack of public support for the film apparently caused a certain backlash—but a good many New York critics were not, apparently in part because the contemporary New York this movie conjures up—basically shot on sets in England, apart from a few stray second-unit shots of New York streets—is not their city. It is true that Kubrick—born and raised in the Bronx but for many years an expatriate who refused to fly—did not go near Manhattan in the 1990s, and the movie clearly reflects that. But given the highly stylized and even mannerist nature of his late work, I cannot see how this matters much. (There is some disagreement in the press about when he last visited New York. I am fairly certain I spotted him in Soho in 1980 around the time *The Shining* came out; he was sloppily dressed and was methodically tearing down a poster from a streetlamp advertising an interview with him in the *Soho News*.)

The kind of jazz played by Nick Nightingale in the Sonata Café seems a good two or three decades off, and the nightclub itself seems like an improbable throwback to the 1950s. It is even more out of date than the nightclub jazz in the second feature of Kubrick's former producer James B. Harris, *Some Call It Loving* (1973)—a fascinating cross-reference to *Eyes Wide Shut* in its treatment of erotic dreaming that deserves to be better known. But if we can accept the precise yet highly stylized city of Fritz Lang's *M* as early 1930s Berlin—and presumably Berliners of that period did—we shouldn't have any trouble accepting this paraphrase of 1990s Manhattan.

Other objections include the film's methodical slowness (especially apparent in the delivery of the dialogue and the dreamlike repetitions of various phrases), its failure to live up to the hype and rumors about its sexual content, and the stupid and tacky digital "enhancements" added to the orgy sequence to fulfill Kubrick's contractual agreement to deliver an R-rated film. The enhancements, by exposing the routine idiocy of the MPAA ratings, may help to foster some overdue reform. At the very least they show how American adult moviegoers are treated like children, unlike their European counterparts who can see *Eyes Wide Shut* without these digital fig leaves, basically for the sake of Warners' moneygrubbing, which allows for an eventual "director's cut" on video and DVD, generating more income while avoiding the risk of an NC-17 rating. Apparently corporate indifference to the public's understanding prevented most critics, including me, from seeing this movie until the last possible minute before writing their initial reviews. That Warners has also chosen to conceal the degree to which *Eyes Wide Shut* was unfinished when Kubrick died—he had not yet completed the sound mixing, which, as David Cronenberg pointed out, cannot be discounted as a creative part of the filmmaking process—clears the way for critics to complain that the public is being sold a bill of goods.

But Kubrick recut both *2001* and *The Shining* after they opened commercially, and a climactic pie-throwing free-for-all in the War Room in *Dr. Strangelove,* filmed in color, was cut shortly before the film opened. Obviously what constitutes a "finished" Kubrick film has long been somewhat tenuous. Undoubtedly he would have made a few slight adjustments in *Eyes Wide Shut* had he lived longer—he probably would have fixed the bumpy sound edit at the end of Bill and Alice's lovemaking scene and perhaps shortened the sequence in which Bill is followed by a generic bald man in a trench coat—which means that the released version is in some ways a rough cut. But I regard the opportunity to view a Kubrick rough cut as a privilege. What I resent is Warners' refusal to clarify which portions and aspects of the sound mix were completed by others and how this was carried out—and the only defense I can think of for that is the profit motive.

Most reviews of every Kubrick picture since *2001* have been mired in misapprehensions and underestimations—many of which are corrected years later without apology, one reason he apparently gave up on critics about thirty years ago. This does not necessarily mean he was always ahead of his time: one of the best things about *Eyes Wide Shut*—evident in such artisanal qualities as the old-fashioned sound track, the grainy photography, and the exquisite color balances (such as the dark blue lighting of a bathroom behind one of Kidman's monologues)—is that it is not a film of the 1990s in most respects but something closer to what movies at their best used to be. (One might even argue that the film has something substantial to say about virtually every decade of the twentieth century *except for* the 1990s.) The Harfords' apartment calls to mind an Otto Preminger noir film of the 1940s or 1950s, and the costume orgy hearkens all the way back to silent cinema—not to mention Georges Franju's *Judex* (1963)—in its ceremonial intensity. The film credits a lighting cameraman but no director of photography, which has led critic Kent Jones to surmise correctly that Kubrick shot most of it himself. This is personal filmmaking as well as dream poetry of the kind most movie commerce has ground underfoot, and it is bound to survive a good deal longer than most of its detractors.

NOTES

This is a revised, expanded version of an essay that originally appeared in the *Chicago Reader* on July 23, 1999.

1. Richard Schickel, "All Eyes on Them," *Time,* July 15, 1999, 68.
2. Frederic Raphael, *Eyes Wide Open: A Memoir of Stanley Kubrick* (New York: Ballantine, 1999).
3. Michael Herr, "Kubrick," *Vanity Fair,* August 1999, 137–50, 184–89.
4. Gilles Deleuze, *Cinema 2: The Time-Image,* trans. Hugh Tomlinson and Robert Galeta (Minneapolis: University of Minnesota Press, 1989), 205–6.
5. Bill Krohn, *"Full Metal Jacket,"* in *Incorporations* (*Zone* 6), ed. Jonathan Crary and Sanford Kwinter (New York: Urzone, 1992), 430–31.

Freud, Schnitzler, and *Eyes Wide Shut*

⟹•◆•⟸

PETER LOEWENBERG

—all diese Ordnung, all dies Gleichmass, all diese Sicherheit seines Daseins
nur Schein und Lüge zu bedeuten hatten.

[—all this order, this regularity, all this security of his existence, was nothing
but illusion and lies.]

—ARTHUR SCHNITZLER

Things have changed a lot between men and women since Schnitzler's time.

—FREDERIC RAPHAEL

Have they? I don't think they have.

—STANLEY KUBRICK

Stanley Kubrick's film *Eyes Wide Shut* was inspired by Arthur Schnitzler's
novel *Dream Story* [*Traumnovelle*] (1926), set in the Vienna of the 1890s.
Freud's relationship to Schnitzler (1862–1931), the Viennese dramatist,
novelist, and physician, was one of kindred spirits.[1] Indeed, Freud feared
that he had such an intimate affinity with Schnitzler that he avoided personal contact, a need in himself that he would analyze. Schnitzler's stories,
novels, and plays laid bare the interplay of fantasy and reality, of dreams
and waking life, in the inner and outer lives of his characters.[2] He wrote:

Dreams are carnal cravings without courage,
Insolent wishes which the light of day
Chases back into the corners of our soul.
Only by night do they dare creep out.[3]

In the "Dora" case (1905) Freud cited Schnitzler's play *Paracelsus* as "very correctly" expressing understanding about patients who resist giving up their symptoms.[4] This was the occasion of his first letter to Schnitzler in which Freud wrote:

> For many years I have been conscious of the far-reaching agreement existing between your conceptions and mine on many psychological and erotic problems; and recently I even found the courage to expressly emphasize this conformity ["Fragment of an Analysis of a Case of Hysteria," 1905]. I have often asked myself in wonder how you came by this or that piece of secret knowledge which I had gained by painstaking research of the subject, and I finally came to the point of envying the author whom I had otherwise admired.
>
> Now you may imagine how pleased and elated I felt on reading that you too have derived inspiration from my writings. I am almost bitter to think that I had to reach the age of fifty before hearing something so flattering.
>
> Yours with esteem[5]

Freud had many personal connections to the Schnitzler family. In ways involving class, social, and professional networks, Vienna was and still is a *dorf*—a small town. Schnitzler's brother Julius was a prominent Viennese surgeon, a close family friend, and a regular partner in Freud's Saturday afternoon card games.[6] Schnitzler's sister Gisela married Marcus Hajek, the surgeon who in 1923 performed the disastrous first operation on Freud's cancer of the upper palate.[7] Freud referred to Schnitzler and his physician father in his 1905 book *Jokes and Their Relation to the Unconscious*.[8] Freud used Schnitzler's short story "Das Schicksal des Freiherrn von Leisenbogh" as an example of the dynamics of his "Taboo of Virginity" (1918).[9] Freud congratulated Schnitzler on his fiftieth birthday in 1912 with an expression of how much he had always been certain of Schnitzler's

> sympathy and understanding for his works even though I have never been in a position to exchange a word with you. Likewise I have always counted myself among those who can understand and enjoy your beautiful and genuine poetic creations to a very special degree. Yes, I imagine that a reflex of the adolescent and wicked underestimation which people today allow for the erotic has also fallen upon your works, and that therefore you may be especially important to me.[10]

Freud also congratulated Schnitzler on the occasion of his sixtieth birthday in 1922 with the gift of an intimate disclosure:

> I shall make you a confession . . . which you will kindly, in consideration of me, keep to yourself and not share with either friend or stranger. I have been struggling with the question of why I have never, in all these years, made any effort to meet you and to talk with you (not considering, at that point, whether you on your part would have wanted such acquaintance).
>
> The answer to this question contains what appears to me as too intimate a confession. I think I have avoided you out of a kind of fear of finding my own double [*Doppelgänger Scheu*]. Not that I otherwise tend to identify easily with others, or that I should wish to ignore the difference in talent which separates me from you; it is rather that when I read one of your beautiful works I seem to encounter again and again, behind the poetic fiction, the presumptions, interests, and conclusions so well known to me from my own thoughts. Your determinism as well as skepticism—what is generally called pessimism—your ability to be deeply moved by the truths of the unconscious, by the instinctual nature of man, and to analyze the accepted cultural-conventional "verities," the recurrence of your thoughts to the polarity of love and death—all of this had for me an uncanny familiarity. (In a little book of 1920, *Beyond the Pleasure Principle,* I have tried to present Eros and the Death Instinct as the basic forces whose interplay dominates all the riddles of life.) I have thus gained the impression that you have learned through intuition—though actually as a result of sensitive introspection—everything that I have had to unearth by laborious work on other persons. I even believe that basically you are yourself an explorer of psychological depths, as honestly unbiased and courageous a one as ever was; and if you were not that, then your artistic skill, the beauty of your style and your imaginativeness would have had free play and would have made you into a writer of far more popular appeal. I, of course, tend to prefer to be the researcher. But forgive me that I strayed into analysis, that is all I know. Except that I know that analysis is no way to become popular.
>
> With heartfelt devotion
> Freud[11]

The two men at last met in 1922. Three weeks after the *Doppelgänger* letter, Freud invited Schnitzler to an evening supper at his home with his wife and daughter Anna "so that we may have a lengthy talk as long as

there is still time, as you suggest. I am happy in anticipation without planning an agenda for these hours. . . . No other person will be there." Freud
offered three dates.[12] Schnitzler chose 16 June 1922 to spend the evening
in Freud's home. As he left Freud presented Schnitzler with a new edition
of his *Introductory Lectures on Psychoanalysis*. Then, as he occasionally did
with special friends, Freud late at night walked Schnitzler to his home at
the Sternwartestrasse 71, in Währing, which is in the eighteenth district of
Vienna, northwesterly from the Berggasse, a walk of close to an hour. Two
months later, on 16 August 1922, Schnitzler visited Freud during his summer holiday in Berchtesgaden.[13]

Freud developed cardiac symptoms in the spring of 1926 and spent
some weeks in the Cottage Sanitarium, a private clinic on the Sternwartestrasse, just a few minutes from Schnitzler's home.[14] He wrote to Schnitzler from the hospital saying: "I have never been so close to you. I am in
a Sanitarium on your street." He thanked Schnitzler for two gifts, one of
which was probably the *Dream Story* which had just been published.[15] Freud
sent Schnitzler a copy of *Inhibitions, Symptoms and Anxiety*, which he describes as "my last publication, perhaps in all meanings of the word—other
than that it is quite uninteresting and for you unimportant. Take comfort
in the fact that you neither need to read it nor need to deliver an opinion
on it."[16] Schnitzler visited Freud at the sanitarium on 12 March 1926.[17] He
later tried in vain to visit, to which Freud, describing it as "a Magic Mountain or magic cavern" [Zauberberg oder dieser Zauberhöhle], responded
with an invitation to visit that same evening.[18] The visit took place two
nights later on 26 March 1926.[19]

Freud's international and Viennese colleagues and friends celebrated
his seventieth birthday on 6 May 1926.[20] Vienna's "official circles," that is,
the medical society (*Gesellschaft der Ärzte*), the academy, the university,
ignored the occasion. The socialist Lord-Mayor of Vienna, Karl Seitz, and
the Municipal Councillor for Health and Social Welfare, Professor Julius
Tandler, popularly known as "the medical Pope of Social Democracy,"[21]
personally presented to Freud the certificate of the freedom of the City of
Vienna (*Bürgerrecht*). Freud's B'nai Brith Lodge held a festival meeting in
his honor addressed by Freud's cardiologist Ludwig Braun and Eduard
Hitschmann and published a commemoration issue of their periodical
B'nai Brith Mitteilungen.[22] Freud expressed his reactions to these varied
receptions in a letter to Schnitzler:

Above all I am grateful for the honest abstention of the official circles. (Among which, of course, the socialist Vienna Commune is not included.) The Jews have with enthusiasm seized my person from all sides and all places as though I were a great God-fearing Rabbi. I have nothing against this as I have unambiguously made my position toward religion clear. Judaism still means a great deal to me emotionally.

Freud added a postscript, which is written evidence of his reading of Schnitzler's *Dream Story,* published that year: "I have some thoughts about your *Traumnovelle.*"[23]

Schnitzler, who was one of the very few readers of the first edition of *Die Traumdeutung,* respected Freud's "greatness," termed him a "genius" [English in the original].[24] Yet Schnitzler had reservations about what he viewed as the one-sidedness of the psychoanalytic method, particularly as practiced by Freud's followers.[25] The psychoanalyst and close associate of Freud, Theodor Reik (1888–1969), wrote a book on *Arthur Schnitzler as a Psychologist* in 1913. On the final day of that last year of peace Schnitzler wrote to Reik:

You have especially seen, observed, recognized, relationships in my works that went right past most professional critics. And where you stay with consciousness, I often follow you. However, about my unconscious, let us better say my half-conscious—, I still know more than you do. There are more paths into the dark depths of the soul, I feel this ever more strongly, than the psychoanalysts permit themselves to dream of (and dream interpret). And in fact, often a trail leads through the center of the illuminated inner world, even though they—and you—believe all too soon that you have to turn off into the dark realm of shadows.[26]

During World War I Schnitzler ironically questions Freud's categorical certainties when he records a "dream that the Russians are completely surrounded. (Freud would doubt that I meant the Russians)."[27] He is implicitly inviting the psychoanalysts to construct a wider range of interpretations and potentialities than the current psychoanalytic concepts and techniques of interpretation provided.

During the summer of 1922 Schnitzler visited Freud, who was on holiday with his family in the Pension Moritz on the Ober-Salzberg.[28] He took the midday meal with ten of the extended Freud family, then the two

friends talked psychoanalysis and other things on the windy veranda while
the young people cleaned wild mushrooms, which Freud and his family
enjoyed collecting in the forest. Schnitzler declined the mushrooms "in
order not to give rise to a later literary-historical anecdote: that he died of
mushroom poisoning from Freud's kitchen."[29]

II.

Schnitzler's *Traumnovelle*, which went through thirty editions, explores the
erotic fantasies of a socially successful Viennese doctor, Fridolin, and his
wife, Albertine. On the day after a *Redoute,* a public masked ball, where
she flirted with a Pole, and Fridolin flirted with two women dressed in red
dominos, "the missed opportunities take on a painful and magical glow"
(12). Both Albertine and Fridolin are aware that "the breath of freedom,
adventure, and danger," had touched them, and both sense that the other
is being less than fully honest, so they felt slightly vengeful (13). Fearfully,
with self-torment and unfair curiosity, each tries to entice confessions from
the other. Albertine, who was the first to find the courage to candidly
share, relates her fantasy of going off with an officer they had observed at
a seaside resort in Denmark and of "being prepared to give up you, the
child, my future" (14). She coaxes Fridolin to tell of a morning stroll on
the beach seeing a nude adolescent girl with loose blond hair hanging over
her shoulders and delicate breasts who smiled marvelously. "Her eyes wel-
comed me, beckoned to me." In *Traumnovelle,* just as the flirtations and
the fantasies are mutual, the sharing of confessions is symmetrical.

Notwithstanding that the Schnitzler *Traumnovelle* fantasies are symmetrical, Fridolin regards Albertine's fantasy as a personal betrayal and
a humiliation. He makes no moral distinction between dream, fantasy,
and behavior; indeed, he draws an emotional equivalence. "It was no different," he thinks to himself, "than if she had been his lover. Even worse."
[Es war ja doch nicht anders, als wenn sie seine Geliebte gewesen wäre.
Schlimmer noch] (29). He felt "she had revealed herself as she really was,
faithless, cruel and treacherous, and whom he at this moment hated more
than he had ever loved her" [Dieser Frau, die sich in ihrem Traum enthüllt
hatte als die, die sie war, treulos, grausam und verräterisch, und die er in
diesem Augenblick tiefer zu hassen glaubte, als er sie jemals geliebt hatte]
(67). He imagines taking "revenge for the bitter and shameful things
she had perpetrated against him in a dream" by having sinful amorous
affairs and coolly confessing all of them to her (Um so Vergeltung zu üben

für das, was sie ihm in einem Traume bitteres und Schmachvolles angetan hatte) (78).

The quotidian surface dialogue conceals the uncanny (*Unheimlich*) terrors ahead. The uncanny, said Freud: "[i]s that class of the frightening which leads back to what is known of old and long familiar."[30] He postulates that the *unheimlich* is what was once *heimlich-heimisch*, familiar; the prefix *un* is a token of repression, and has returned from it (17:245). When something in our lives happens that appears to confirm the early repressed primitive magical beliefs, we get the feeling of uncanny (17:247–48). In "The Uncanny" (1919) Freud draws on Schnitzler's story *Die Weissagung* ["The Prophecy"] (1904), a tale about a Polish Jew who could foresee future events, including personal calamities. Freud uses Schnitzler as an example of authors who play with us by:

> betraying us to the superstitiousness which we have ostensibly surmounted. . . . We retain a feeling of dissatisfaction, a kind of grudge against attempted deceit. I have noticed this particularly after reading Schnitzler's *Die Weissagung* and similar stories which flirt with the supernatural. . . . He can keep us in the dark for a long time about the precise nature of the presuppositions on which the world he writes about is based.[31]

III.

Kubrick was obsessed by Schnitzler's *Traumnovelle* and wished to make a movie of it for decades—it seasoned nearly thirty years in his mind.[32] This may be Kubrick's rehearsal of Freud's attraction/inhibition toward Schnitzler. Kubrick said of Schnitzler: "It's difficult to find any writer who understands the human soul more truly and who had a more profound insight into the way people think, act and are."[33] In 1980 Kubrick sent the novel to screenwriter Michael Herr who called it:

> The full, excruciating flowering of a voluptuous and self-consciously decadent time and place, a shocking and dangerous story about sex and sexual obsession and the suffering of sex. In its pitiless view of love, marriage, and desire, made all the more disturbing by the suggestion that either all of it, or maybe some of it, or possibly none of it is a dream, it intrudes on the concealed roots of Western erotic life like a laser, suggesting discreetly, from behind its dream cover, things that are seldom even privately acknowledged, and *never* spoken of in daylight.[34]

The transposition/translation of novel to film is always a challenge. It is virtually impossible to make a film from a fine piece of literature without making radical alterations—as Kubrick did. Converting the verbal to the visual is a translation to an entirely different medium. So much cannot be described. Much has to be compressed. Many monologues are suppressed so the film will not be talky or stagy. The camera's eye is the observer of all that is seen; it follows the screen writer's point of view, but it narrates from omniscient heights.

Freud is a presence as producer/director Stanley Kubrick and writer Frederic Raphael work on the script. On first reading the script Raphael found the dreams unconvincing, speculating, "I wonder what Sigmund would have thought of them. Not a lot, I would guess. . . . The author has to have read Freud, doesn't he?" Kubrick responds: "Freud and Arthur knew each other."[35] Raphael suggested "the Freudian background of Bill's character." This "was soon axed" (121). Raphael says to Kubrick: "It's a story that deals with the unconscious. I may as well tap into my own, which I don't find easy to do in public" (40). When Raphael is speculating on the origins of Kubrick's inner compulsion, he writes: "Freud, thou shouldst be living" (60).

In *Eyes Wide Shut* Dr. William Harford (Tom Cruise) is on top of the world. He has a prestigious medical practice in Manhattan, a beautiful trophy wife, Alice (Nicole Kidman), and a lovely child (Helena). Kubrick and Raphael moved the setting from Vienna to Manhattan and the summer locale from Denmark to Cape Cod. Most importantly, they altered the emotional constellation of Schnitzler's plot by making the confession asymmetrical—only Alice tells Bill of her explicit erotic fantasy of the officer, making the interaction one of hostile revenge, aggressive and sadistic—she means to cause him suffering. Bill's smugness and self-satisfaction provoke his wife's taunting ridicule. In 1996 Kubrick wanted Herr to do a "fix-up" rewrite (this is termed "a wash and a rinse" in the industry) of the Frederic Raphael script, to "colloquialize" the dialogue to Manhattan idioms, "like when someone says 'Hello' it should read 'Hi.'" Herr was unable at the time to drop everything and go to London to do it.[36]

The film opens with a brief shot of Kidman undressing to the theme of Dimitri Shostakovich *Jazz Suite; Walzer II* that blends the music of America with that of Vienna. This shot sets the theme of the film—tantalizing sexuality abruptly seized away—a prelude to the frustrations of attraction, allurement, seduction, and lack of consummation to come. Kubrick blurs the boundary between reality and dream by presenting us with an intimate and friendly comfort, which conceals the uncanny *Unheimlich* frightening terror to follow that hovers beneath the surface "reality." The first scene—*Heimlich*—is an upscale Manhattan couple at home, "running a little late," getting dressed to go out to a holiday party. Bill picks up his keys, cell phone, opens a drawer to take out a handkerchief, asks his wife where his wallet is. Alice, sitting on the toilet, asks him: "How do I look?" "Perfect" he answers without looking at Alice as he fusses in the mirror checking his bow tie. "Is my hair OK?" she asks. "It's great," he says as she drops the toilet paper in the bowl and flushes. She says: "You're not even looking at it." The couple take care of the final arrangements with the babysitter: phone and pager numbers on the fridge, food in the kitchen, permitted television programs (*The Nutcracker*), bedtime, and cab home.[37]

The character Victor Ziegler, Bill's millionaire patient, does not exist in *Traumnovelle;* he is new in *Eyes Wide Shut.* Ziegler is a Kubrick invention, the name of Frederic Raphael's sometime agent in California.[38] In Schnitzler, the couple attend their first ball of the year just before the end of the carnival season, instead of an opulent Christmas party in the Ziegler midtown Manhattan mansion. At the Zieglers' palace the trivial party chatter between the Harfords and Ziegler and his wife Ilona (Ziegler: "Merry Christmas! How good to see the both of you. Thanks so much for coming." Alice: "We wouldn't have missed it for the world.") and the big band era background songs, "It Had to be You" (1924), "I'm in the Mood for Love" (1935) and "I Only Have Eyes for You" (1934), ironically mirror Mandy, the overdosed and comatose prostitute upstairs.[39] The foreigner with a Polish accent merits a single brief mention in *Traumnovelle* as an unnamed man who fascinated, then offended, Albertine at the ball. In the film he becomes a distinctive seductive Hungarian playboy, Sandor Szavost.

Each of Bill's and Alice's sexual adventures is unconsummated. *Eyes Wide Shut* is a paean to desired but anxiously feared and postponed sex, which always remains unaccomplished and unfulfilled. Kubrick teases us, repeatedly building expectation of realized sexual contact, holding us in suspense, then frustrating us, letting us down from anticipated sexual consummation. The film is full of unconscious symptomatic acts, especially "opportune"/"inopportune" interruptions. Bill is picked up at Ziegler's party by two beautiful models who invite him "to where the rainbow ends." They are interrupted by Ziegler's personal assistant (the script calls for "a tall good looking man") to call Bill to Ziegler's private quarters. Alice, who has been invited upstairs by Szavost, ends their flirtation "because I'm married."[40] Bill and Alice's intense confessional bedroom dialogue, perhaps the most important of their relationship, is allowed to be interrupted by the repeated ringing of the telephone calling Bill to the Nathanson home where his patient has just died. People who wish to complete a profoundly important conversation do not pick up the telephone. The late patient's beautiful daughter, Marion, professes her intense love for Bill and this is interrupted by the arrival of her fiancé. At the point of copulation with the prostitute, Domino, Bill's cell phone rings—and he takes the call. People who wish to have undisturbed sex turn off their cell phones. At the orgy, just as Bill talks with the mysterious woman they are interrupted by a tall masked butler who escorts Bill away.[41] *Eyes Wide Shut* is a study in delay and repression, not in the sense of any known manual of sexual pleasure, but in the way virtually every scene has to do with sexual desire and the self-creation of obstacles to its realization.

The chateau scene invokes the Viennese masked balls, as in *Der Rosenkavalier* (1911) and *Die Fledermaus* (1874), where identities are confused and identifications are suspended, where deception, intrigue, and extramarital adventures may take place. Orgies in country houses is the European cultural equivalent to the colonial world of Joseph Conrad's *Heart of Darkness* (1902), a world where the rules of "moral" society do not hold, a world without superego, without conventional interdictions, where the realization of bizarre and perverse fantasies is possible. This is the world without law, of uncontrolled impulses, of the late Italian Fascist potentates pictured by Pier Paolo Passolini in *Salo: 120 Days of Sodom* (1975).

In the orgy of *Traumnovelle,* sixteen to twenty people are dressed in religious costumes, monks and nuns, and Italian church music is playing. The manor scene is a Black Mass with threatening evocations of public humiliation and death, of the Inquisition and Torquemada. The secret password to the closed sexual orgy in *Traumnovelle* is *"Dänemark"*—the site of Fridolin and Albertine's holiday fantasies.[42] In *Eyes Wide Shut,* Bill Harford gains access to the world of libidinal pleasure in "Somerton," a great country house set in parklike grounds, through the password "Fidelio." Kubrick's irony is pointed—the secret entry code to lascivious infidelity is the title of Beethoven's only opera, which valorizes faithfulness and loyalty, and uses costume and disguise to overcome all obstacles and achieve marital reunion with Florestan. The original libretto bears the title "Leonora, or the Triumph of Wedded Love."[43]

The ritualized orgy presided over by a high priest wearing a red cape and waiving an incense censer in one hand and sporting a staff in the other, surrounded by a chanting crowd in black cloaks and masks who kneel and prostrate themselves before him, is evocative of a Black Mass. This turns into a terrifying nightmare of Inquisition when Bill is literally unmasked, exposed as an outsider, identified as the "other," and threatened with public undressing, rape, humiliation, and death—a modern *auto-da-fé*, the medieval ceremony of the public torture and burning of heretics. His virility is compromised, and he is rescued by the sacrifice of a woman.

IV.

Late in the film Alice has a dream that reinforces the theme of mocking and humiliating Bill. He returns home in the dawn to find Alice hysterically laughing in a deep sleep. He awakens her. She relates her dream:

> We . . . we were . . . we were in a deserted city and . . . our clothes were gone. We were naked, and . . . I was terrified, and I . . . I felt ashamed Oh, God! And . . . I was angry because I felt it was your fault. You . . . you rushed away to try to find our clothes for us. As soon as you were gone it was completely different. I . . . felt wonderful. Then I was lying in a . . . in a beautiful garden, stretched out naked in the sunlight, and a man walked out of the woods, he was . . . he was the man from the hotel, the one I told you about . . . the naval officer. He . . . he stared at me and then he just laughed . . . he just laughed at me.

Alice buries her face crying in her pillow. Bill urges her on: "That's not the end, is it?"

ALICE: No.
BILL: Why don't you tell me the rest of it?
ALICE: It's . . . it's too awful.
BILL: It's only a dream.
ALICE: He . . . he was kissing me, and then . . . then we were making love. Then there were all these other people around us . . . hundreds of them, everywhere. Everyone was fucking, and then I . . . I was fucking other men, so many . . . I don't know how many I was with. And I knew you could see me in the arms of all these men, just fucking all these men, and I . . . I wanted to make fun of you, to laugh in your face. And so I laughed as loud as I could. And that must have been when you woke me up.[44]

Alice's intense rage is expressed by the manifest content of this dream of Bill's demeaning humiliation. Schnitzler's original version of Albertine's dream in *Traumnovelle* is even more intensely sexual and sadistic:

> I was lying stretched out on the meadow in the sunshine,—looking much more beautiful than in real life, and as I lay there a gentleman stepped out of the forest, a young man in a light fashionable suit, looking, I now realize, very like the Dane I told you about yesterday. . . . I laughed seductively, more so than ever in my life before, but when he stretched out his arms toward me I wanted to fly yet failed to do so,—and he lay down with me on the meadow. . . . [I]t would be. . . . hard to conceive of anything in normal conscious life that could equal the freedom, the abandon, the sheer bliss I experienced in that dream.[45]

Albertine's anger and sadism toward Fridolin is also more pronounced in *Traumnovelle* where he is "chastised with whips . . . the blood flowed from you in streams. . . . your body was covered with welts. . . . I found your conduct utterly ludicrous and pointless and felt tempted to laugh in your face with scorn."[46] Albertine, in what must be Schnitzler's most acute fantasy of humiliation, an Oedipal enactment—having his wife, embraced in her lover's arms, watch him tied naked, flayed, mocked, and killed, relates her dream:

> You were to be executed. I knew this without pity, without horror, with complete detachment. They led you out into a sort of castle courtyard. There you stood, your hands tied behind your back and naked. And just as I could see you even though elsewhere, you too could see me together with the man who held me in his arms, and all the other couples in that unending tide of nakedness which surged around me, in which I and the man embracing me represented but a single wave.[47]

Fridolin's images of women are split between the kind prostitute, his maternal rescuer who has sacrificed her life for him, and the cruel woman who dreams of his punishment, whipping, humiliation, and death as she stands watching in the arms of her lover.

Fridolin's quest for vengeance against Albertine involves seeking out Marianne, a relationship in which "the betrayal of a bridegroom, which might have given others pause, was for him merely an additional inducement."[48] He is in a state of fragmentation and identity dissolution, his most intimate anchors to the world are gone: "He felt helpless and inept and everything seemed to be slipping from his grasp; everything was becoming increasingly unreal, even his home, his wife, his child, his profession, his very identity as he trudged on mechanically through the evening streets turning things over in his mind."[49]

V.

Nick Nightingale, the piano player, is Bill's "double" (as Schnitzler was to Freud), who pursued the path not taken—he dropped out of medical school and lives an apparently exciting bohemian life. Bill follows him and wants to taste that erotic frisson. Jewish identities are explicit in *Traumnovelle*. The Jewish musician Nachtigall (Nightingale in *Eyes Wide Shut*) is a homeless wanderer with a wife and four children in Lemberg, Austrian East Galician Poland. He lives in a miserable boardinghouse smelling of unaired beds, stale fat, and chicory ersatz coffee in the Leopoldstadt.[50] Though he may be insulting in his provocative behavior, he is willing to serve as a blindfolded flunkey. He speaks German with a soft Polish accent and a slight Jewish undertone (polnisch weichem Akzent mit mässigem jüdischen Beiklang) (34). He is the son of a Jewish bar owner in a tiny, miserable, godforsaken Polish village (Sohn eines jüdischen Branntweinschenkers in einem polnischen Nest) (35). Once, when Nachtigall played at a dance in the home of a Jewish bank director, he got into an altercation with the director who snarled a Jewish insult in his face (dieser, empört, fauchte, obwohl selbst Jude, dem Pianisten ein landesübliches Schimpfwort ins Gesicht . . .). Nachtigall responded by giving the director a powerful box on the ears, an act that thereafter closed the better houses of the town to him (36).

Schnitzler had earlier developed the theme of a Galician Jewish ambiance in his story *Die Weissagung,* which Freud enjoyed and used in his essay on "The Uncanny" (1919). The story is told from the perspective of an Austrian army officer whose regiment is posted an hour from the nearest city, which is filled with Jews, including the hotel owner, the café owner, and the shoemaker. The soldiers resented the Jews because a prince, who had been assigned to the regiment as a major, was particularly polite toward them and to the regimental doctor, who was of Jewish extraction. The story concerns an actor and soothsayer, dressed with laughable elegance, who is the son of a Jewish distillery owner, a *Branntweinjude,*[51] which evokes associations to *Nachtigall*-Nightingale, the son of a Jewish bar owner (*Branntweinschenker*) in a tiny Polish Jewish village. The shtetl soothsayer predicts the death of a colonel in marked Yiddish syntax: "Ich seh nur, dass Sie im Herbst sein werden ein toter Mann."[52]

Kubrick and his screenwriter Frederic Raphael disagreed on the level of Jewish identification to leave in the script. Jews are not featured in any of Kubrick's films. His family came from Austria-Hungary, the world of Schnitzler and Freud, and he is quoted as saying he was not really a Jew, he just happened to have two Jewish parents.[53] Yet he was obsessed by the Holocaust and questioned whether it could be the subject of a movie. The deep cynicism of his judgment of *Schindler's List* bears quoting: "That was about success, wasn't it? The Holocaust is about six million people who get killed. *Schindler's List* was about six hundred who don't." Kubrick insisted that the New York doctor in *Eyes Wide Shut* not be Jewish: "Give some name that doesn't . . . identify him, okay? It could be Robinson, but . . . we don't want him to be Jewish."[54] Raphael pointed out that "transferring the story to New York seemed to me to offer an opportunity for keeping the Jewish aspect of the story, however it might be modernized. Kubrick was firmly opposed to this; he wanted Fridolin to be a Harrison Fordish goy and forbade any reference to Jews." Kubrick gave Fridolin the name Harford, "which—with Freudian neatness—does not sound very different from Hertford(shire), the county in which Stanley lived (or indeed from Harrison Ford)."[55]

VI.

Homosexuality and homoerotism are not single nosological entities; in fact there are a multiplicity of "homosexualities" and defenses against homoerotism. There are three varieties of homoerotism in *Eyes Wide Shut*. The first is the conscious homosexuality of the hotel clerk. He was introduced by Kubrick, who transformed the "evil looking" hotel portier of *Traumnovelle* into a specifically gay hotel clerk called for in the script of *Eyes Wide Shut*.[56] For a recognition of the unconscious forms of homosexuality and defenses against it, we are indebted to psychoanalysis, which illuminates the defensive, projective, and reaction formative quality of the humiliation and persecution of minorities as aggressive denial of parts of the self. As he prowls Vienna's central city just off of the Rathausplatz, Fridolin in *Traumnovelle* encounters a group of six or eight *Couleurstudenten,* students whom he recognizes by their blue colors as belonging to the anti-Semitic dueling fraternity *Alemannen.* The last one deliberately bumps Fridolin with his elbow, evoking fantasies of confrontations, duels, wounds, and honor.[57] Kubrick turns these anti-Semitic Austrian *corps* students into gay-bashing Yalies in Greenwich Village who bump Bill into a parked car and hurl homophobic insults at him.

Schnitzler is reputed to have engaged in numerous sexual affairs, including group sex, during his military service.[58] According to his diaries, from 1887 to 1889 Schnitzler made love with his mistress Anna Heeger 583 times. Peter Gay deftly interprets the defensive quality of Schnitzler's sexual book-keeping, the periodic compiling of balances of sexual encounters, both by an exaggeration and an absence. He notes the prodigious record as

> a symptom more than an achievement. . . . His meticulously registered orgasms intimate that he was driven to prove something to himself, inviting the conjecture . . . that his heroic exhibitions of virility were ways of drowning out homoerotic impulses. . . . Schnitzler's near silence about such desires, except for a handful of casual jokes, suggests a deep-seated need for denial.[59]

Bill's most graphically intense fantasies are of Alice fornicating with her imagined lover. He is obsessed by the fantasy of the handsome officer having passionate sex with his wife even though it is clear that nothing happened between Alice and the officer; it was all her fantasy, and it became his with a compulsively driven force. Bill's erotic fantasy appears five times in the film as a sexually exciting, even pornographic, fantasy shown in blue-tinted black and white in a color film. Alice keeps her (phallic) high heels on during the sex scenes.[60]

Bill's fantasy of Alice's sexual ardor with another man enables him to identify with the other man, with Alice who is penetrated, and with the woman who is shared by the two men. The unconscious homosexuality of Fridolin/Bill is demonstrated by his paranoid focus on the other man who is omnipresent in his day dreams. The handsome officer is not only Albertine and Alice's fantasy, he is Fridolin and Bill's. Fridolin expresses violent hatred for the Danish officer: he fantasies meeting him, facing him, and killing him. His focus is on the details of the officer's face and hair as on a beloved object: "Yes, I would like to encounter him. Oh, it would be a true ecstasy to meet him somewhere in a forest glade and aim a pistol at the smoothly combed blond hair of his forehead." For Bill the handsome officer of his obsessions is a narcissistic object—a male such as he would like to be himself and have for himself, and be adored by his woman. In his essay of 1922, "Some Neurotic Mechanisms in Jealousy, Paranoia, and

Homosexuality," Freud defined three grades of jealousy: normal or competitive; projected; and delusional jealousy.[61] He attributed the latter to a
paranoid defense against unconscious homosexuality as in the formula: "*I*
do not love him, *she* loves him."[62] Freud describes a clinical case like that
of Bill/Fridolin, in which a "jealous husband perceived his wife's unfaith-
fulness instead of his own; by becoming conscious of hers and magnifying
it enormously he succeeded in keeping his own unconscious."[63]

VII.

Schnitzler's abusive jealousy of his mistresses represents a striking confluence of personal dynamics and artistic creation. He wished them to be vir-
gins and was furious when they were not. He would press them for their
erotic history of sexual affairs, then would suffer agonies of jealousy as he
pictured his mistresses in the arms of their lovers. The twenty-eight-year-
old Schnitzler wrote his former patient and mistress, the Viennese actress
Marie Glümer, of his fantasies of jealousy of her former lovers as a reason
why he could not marry her:

> Let us say I marry you and I introduce you into a social world. A society
> where it can with certainty happen that in a salon where you are introduced
> as my wife, there is a man who has held you in his arms, who was in your
> home, while your mother was in the kitchen, threw you on the divan and
> possessed you, a man who, when we leave the salon, can smile to himself and
> think—I too enjoyed her—before him—and I was also not the first![64]

The meaning of this fantasy is that he expected her to never have had a
man before—to be a virgin—that he should be the first! Cruel Viennese
social class snobbery is exhibited in Schnitzler's attitude toward Marie. She
was of modest background and in the bohemian world of the theater, suitable to be his mistress, but not his wife. She could be accepted neither by
his upper bourgeois family nor in the sophisticated cultural salons of his
social circle. He affirms that "if his family knew of her past, and they would
learn of it, they would never consent" (100). Yet the underlying dynamic
is his obsession with her former lovers. Schnitzler freely enters into their
minds and constructs the fantasies of her previous lovers and the contempt
they feel toward him. He asks her to understand:

> what all it means to encounter the previous lover of your wife. . . . I am
> ashamed to cross the street arm in arm with you when there are whispers

behind me: "She is the wife of S, the former lover of Misters F. and G." . . .
There are people who go around with their memories—who look at you and
remember you in the beauty of your body, in the ecstasy of your lovemaking
that they created and have shared. . . . Others than I have heard your sighs
in lovemaking, have feasted on your charms [deine Liebesseufzer gehört und
haben in deinen Reizen geschwelgt.] And when I think of it . . . the enormous loathing [ungeheure Ekel] that fills me in these moments is not to be
overcome. (100–102)

Schnitzler manifestly had the fantasy that this Viennese actress should
have had no previous sexual relationships—she should be a virgin. He
heaped abuse on Marie when he learned of her "disloyalty" with another
man. He accused her of "being the lowest creature under the Sun" [der
niedrigsten Creatur unter der Sonne] (180), "my disgust for you is more
than my love ever was" (181). He charged that she had a whore's nature,
that she was common, which left him paralyzed with horror:

it could have happened to me to feel the *touch of a kiss* from *your lover's well
known mistress* on my lips [einen Kuss von seiner stadtbekannten Maitresse
auf meinen Lippen zu spüren] and allow myself to be bewitched by your
charms, and the sighs, to hear the love sighs. . . . Are there words?—No,
no!—Disgust, Loathing, Revulsion! [Ekel, Ekel, Ekel!—Du hast mich
besudelt, wie nie ein Mann besudelt worden ist.] You have besmirched me
as no man has ever been besmirched. (181–82, emphasis mine)

What matters is the touch of the lover's lips on his own via the "lover's well
known mistress."

He accused her of being "the prostitute of a rag-tag scoundrel," of per-
petrating "the most outrageous meanness that a woman is capable of"
(194). She was "the most depraved creature under the Sun" (196).

It is not the fantasy of sex, it is the fantasy of the other men having sex
with his woman that provides the emotional torque that captured Schnitzler and Kubrick and that drives their creatures Fridolin/Bill in their obses-
sional jealousy.

VIII.

Homosexuality is now a media staple. Kubrick had to cloud out the les-
bianism, the cunnilingus, and the anal sex from the orgy scene and make
editing concessions in order to avoid an NC-17 rating and settle for an R

rating: "for strong sexual content, nudity, language and some drug-related material." Too explicit or too graphic sex is an American media taboo, although allusive representations are entirely permissible. However, child sex and physical love of the dead are, in our culture, an absolute taboo in film (as distinguished from prose).

The erotic attraction to childlike nubile pubescent girls (I will not call it pedophilia, which I take to refer to children) and sexual arousal by the dead are prominent themes in both Schnitzler and Kubrick. Three decades prior to Vladimir Nabokov's *Lolita* (1955), the girl who aroused Fridolin on the Danish coast was:

> a very young, possibly fifteen year old girl with loose blond hair which fell over her shoulders and on one side over her tender breast. . . . Suddenly she smiled, a wonderful smile; it was a greeting, a twinkle in her eyes-and at the same time a quiet mockery. . . . Then she stretched her young slim body, enjoying her beauty and, as was easy to see, she felt proud and sweetly aroused by the intensity of my gaze. Thus we stood for perhaps ten seconds facing each with half open lips and flaming eyes. Involuntarily I stretched my arms out to her; her gaze was filled with joy and abandon.[65]

There are passages in *Traumnovelle* suggestive of Freud's self-observations at the effect of meeting one's own image unbidden and unexpected that he interprets as "a vestigial trace of the archaic reaction which feels the 'double' to be something uncanny." Freud relates:

> I was sitting alone in my *wagon-lits* compartment when a more than usually violent jolt of the train swung back the door of the adjoining washing-cabinet, and an elderly gentleman in a dressing gown and a travelling cap came in. I assumed that in leaving the washing cabinet which lay between the two compartments, he had taken the wrong direction and come into my compartment by mistake. Jumping up with the intention of putting him right, I at once realized to my dismay that the intruder was nothing but my own reflection in the looking-glass on the open door.[66]

In *Traumnovelle*, immediately after longingly seeing the nymphet, "white and delicate, stand at her door and sadly shake her head at him," Fridolin sees "a gaunt pilgrim in a large wall mirror who was none other than himself and wondered at the nature of such things" (44) Schnitzler's use of shock at the self-reflective image has an important erotic context, whereas no psychodynamic context is offered in Freud's example. Fridolin has just lusted for a young girl. His unrecognized haggard visage in the mirror is the shock of the truths of time and aging as irremediable and finite—the nymphet is no object for an old man.

The costume-shop owner, Mr. Milich (Gibiser in *Traumnovelle*), is a Mephisto who provides the means of transformation and promises to supply sex, to sell his daughter, and anything else Bill wishes. Schnitzler describes Fridolin's erotic arousal by:

> a delightful very young girl, almost still a child, . . . The child pressed herself on Fridolin as though he needed to protect her. Her small narrow face was powdered white and decorated with several beauty spots, the scent of roses and powder rose from her delicate breasts;—her eyes smiled with roguish lust. . . . What he would have preferred was to stay there or to have taken the girl away with him immediately, where did not matter—and regardless of the consequences. She gazed up at him child like and enticing, as if spellbound. (42)

When Fridolin/Bill discover that the nubile nymphet is supplying sex to the customers of the costume shop, her father offers his daughter for prostitution: "If Herr Doktor should have any further desires . . . It need not be a monk's habit" (71). Kubrick does not reproduce the level of ambiguous attraction, arousal, and return to control that Schnitzler evokes by making the reader cognizant of Fridolin's aged visage. Tom Cruise is no "haggard pilgrim."

The theme of necrophilia is stronger in *Traumnovelle* than in *Eyes Wide Shut*. When he hears that what he believes to be the mysterious woman who rescued him the night before died of suicide, Fridolin goes to the Pathology Institute, is taken to the morgue by an old fellow medical student who is working there in the middle of the night, and shown the corpse:

> Involuntarily, indeed as if driven by some unseen power, Fridolin touched the woman's brow, cheeks, arms and shoulders with both hands; then he intertwined his fingers with the dead woman's as if to fondle them, and, stiff as they were, they seemed to him to be trying to move and to take hold of his; indeed he thought he could detect a faint and distant gleam in the eyes beneath those half-closed lids, trying to make contact with his own; and as if drawn on by some enchantment he bent down over her.

Then suddenly he heard a whisper close behind him: "What do you think you are doing?" [Aber was treibst du denn?]

Here Kubrick softens and tones down Schnitzler's explicit bodily contact of the doctor with the "wonderful blooming" dead beauty who the night before had "filled him with tortured longing" and, he believes, had sacrificed herself for him (der wunderbare, blühende, gestern noch qualvoll ersehnte) (90). Bill places himself in the position of his "faithless" wife— he goes out to seek sexual encounters. He finds two "good" motherly prostitutes who insist that he not pay for unconsummated sex, who solicitously invite him to "sit down and have a cup of coffee." Beneath the surface is death by AIDS, a deadly epidemic that is Kubrick's modernization of what in *Traumnovelle* was the early twentieth-century highly infectious public health threat of tuberculosis.

IX.

Ziegler, Bill's *patron,* returns at the end of the film, providing narrative continuity and the Euripidean voice of common sense everyday rationality. He functions as a classic deus ex machina—a character who is improbably introduced to resolve a situation. He provides the alibis: he was there at the orgy, claims it was all staged, a charade, fake; Bill's humiliation during the masked ritual, his rescue by the sacrificing woman, the dispatch of Nick the piano player—he is on his way back to Seattle, to Mrs. Nick whom he is "now banging." Ziegler had Bill shadowed "for his own good."[67] The "hero" is rescued by a good self-sacrificing *mater.* She buys his life, and it is implied that she pays with her own. Was this for love or out of gratitude? Is Mandy the hooker's death by overdose a coincidence? Is Nick, the piano player, "on a plane to Seattle" as Ziegler, the paternal counselor of reassurance, wants Bill to believe, or is the hotel clerk's testimony of a bruise on his face an uncanny clue to brutality? Was it all "staged," a "charade," "fake" as Ziegler puts out?[68] Mandy's death from an overdose was an expectable (and deserved?) outcome for a hooker. Bill does not buy these self-serving alibis. He angrily challenges Ziegler: Nick had a bruise on his face; Mandy is in the morgue. "Well, Victor, maybe I'm . . . missing something here. You called it a fake, charade. Do you mind telling me what kind of fucking charade ends with somebody turning up dead?"[69]

Bill appeared to have the world in the palm of his hand, but he has learned that he has nothing. Beneath the cozy family life of arranging for the babysitter's taxi, saying good-bye to their daughter, Christmas shopping, is unconsummated sexual lust and orgy. Leaving his rented mask at home suggests that Bill wanted to be found out by his wife and to confess to her, include her, and he succeeded. He was Leonore of *Fidelio*–he was exquisitely loyal to Alice. What they both have realized is, in Schnitzler's words: "all this order, this regularity, all the security of his existence, was nothing but delusion and lies" [all diese Ordnung, all dies Gleichmass, all diese Sicherheit seines Daseins nur Schein und Lüge zu bedeuten hatten] (77).

The ending of *Traumnovelle* is romantic, ambiguous, and reassuring—life goes on in comfort and loyalty despite erotic desires and the tenuousness of love. Albertina says: "I think we should be grateful to fate that we have come out of all our adventures—the real ones and the dreamed ones—unharmed." "Are you quite sure of that?" he asked. "Just as sure as I sense that neither the reality of one night, nor even of a person's entire lifetime, is the sum of his innermost truth." "And no dream," Fridolin responds with a sigh, "is entirely a dream." She took his head in both hands and pillowed it on her breast. "And so they lay, both silent, dozing, dreamless, close to each other—until, as at seven every morning, there was a knock on the door and with the usual noises from the street, a triumphant ray of light through the opening of the curtain, and the clear laughter of a child from the next room, the new day began" (94–95). Schnitzler's title *Traumnovelle* suggests that whatever happens in the story may also be regarded as a dream. The ending is ambiguous—a knock on the bedroom door announcing a new day. If there is a cheerful note it is the laughter of a child, but this too implies social ties and cultural obligations. Schnitzler leaves us with a deliberate lack of closure—"life goes on," but with the skepticism about what is truth and what is fantasy, what is inner dream, what is outer reality, and what will happen in the new day.

Kubrick's title refers to the metaphorical ability to see, even with closed eyes. Eyes are closed in sleep, but dreams make another reality visible. Oedipus first "sees" after he has blinded himself. Kubrick's ending is uncharacteristically upbeat—the couple have transcended a traumatic rupture and are reunited in Christmas shopping with their little girl in a fancy toy department and presumably, in sex:

ALICE: But I do love you and you know there is something very important we need to do as soon as possible?
BILL: What's that?
ALICE: Fuck.[70]

Her intention is that sex be no longer displaced or postponed. However, Bill and Alice are in a toy store shopping with their child—they cannot do it then. The ambiguities of their individual lives and the unresolved issues of their relationship continue. Schnitzler in 1887 wrote what may serve as an epigram for Bill and Alice, for all relationships, and for our time: "Dream and waking, truth and lie flow into one another. Safety is nowhere."[71]

NOTES

An earlier version of this essay appeared as "Freud, Schnitzler und Eyes Wide Shut," in *Psyche* 12 (2004): 1156–81.

1. Frederick J. Beharriell, "Freud's 'Double': Arthur Schnitzler," *Journal of the American Psychoanalytic Association* 10 (1962): 722–30. The epigraphs to this chapter are taken from Arthur Schnitzler, *Traumnovelle* (1926; Frankfurt am Main: Fischer, 1999), 77, trans. J. M. Q. Davies as *Dream Story* (New York: Warner Books, 1999), 259, and Frederic Raphael, *Eyes Wide Open: A Memoir of Stanley Kubrick* (New York: Ballantine, 1999). Unless otherwise indicated the translations from the German are mine.

2. Peter Gay, *Schnitzler's Century* (New York: Norton, 2001), 64–65.

3. Arthur Schnitzler, *My Youth in Vienna* (New York: Holt, Rinehart and Winston, 1970), 129.

4. Freud, "Fragment of an Analysis of a Case of Hysteria" (1905), in *Standard Edition of the Complete Psychological Works,* ed. James Strachey et al. (London: Hogarth Press, 1953), 7:44 n.

5. Freud to Schnitzler, May 8, 1906, "*Sigmund Freud: Briefe an Arthur Schnitzler,*" *Neue Rundschau* (Frankfurt am Main: S. Fischer Verlag, 1955), 66: 97 [hereafter Freud-Schnitzler *Briefe*]. Also in *Letters of Sigmund Freud,* ed. Ernst Freud (New York: Basic Books, 1960), no. 123, 251. Unless otherwise noted the translations are mine.

6. Max Schur, *Freud: Living and Dying* (New York: International Universities Press, 1972), 337, n. 17. Schur considered Julius "a brilliant and very experienced diagnostician" (348).

7. Bruce Thompson, *Schnitzler's Vienna: Image of a Society* (London: Routledge, 1990), 191.

8. Freud, *Jokes and Their Relation to the Unconscious* (1905), in *Standard Edition,* 8:36–37.

9. Freud, "The Taboo of Virginity" (1918), in *Standard Edition,* 11:206–7, n. 2. See M. Katan, "Schnitzler's Das Schicksal des Freiherrn von Leisenbogh," *Journal of the American Psychoanalytic Association* 17 (1969): 904–26.

10. Freud to Schnitzler, May 14, 1912, Freud-Schnitzler *Briefe*, 95–96.

11. Freud to Schnitzler, May 14, 1922, Freud-Schnitzler *Briefe*, 97. Also in *Letters of Sigmund Freud,* no. 197, 339–40.

12. Freud to Schnitzler, June 8, 1922, Freud-Schnitzler *Briefe*, 98.

13. Freud-Schnitzler *Briefe*, 104.

14. Schur, *Freud*, 390–91. Freud had anginal pain and paroxysmal tachycardia in 1894–95. Schur (92, 133) infers that Freud suffered a mild coronary thrombosis or a myocarditis in 1894.

15. The opinion of Professor Henry Schnitzler, the author's son. Freud-Schnitzler *Briefe*, 105.

16. Freud to Schnitzler, March 8, 1926, Freud-Schnitzler *Briefe*, 99.

17. Based on Schnitzler's diary, Freud-Schnitzler *Briefe*, 105.

18. Freud to Schnitzler, March 24, 1926, Freud-Schnitzler *Briefe*, 99.

19. Freud-Schnitzler *Briefe*, 105.

20. For the American response, including Joseph Wood Crutch in the *New York Times*, see Peter Gay, *Freud: A Life for Our Time* (New York: W. W. Norton, 1988), 458–59.

21. Helmut Gruber, *Red Vienna: Experiment in Working-Class Culture, 1919–1934* (New York: Oxford University Press, 1991), 160.

22. Ernest Jones, *The Life and Work of Sigmund Freud: The Last Phase*, vol. 3 (New York: Basic Books, 1957), 123–24; Gay, *Freud*, 597.

23. Freud to Schnitzler, May 24, 1926, Freud-Schnitzler *Briefe*, 99–100.

24. Schnitzler to George Sylvester Viereck, March 29, 1928, *Arthur Schnitzler Briefe 1913–1931* (Frankfurt am Main: S. Fischer Verlag, 1984), 536–38. Schnitzler describes Viereck as "very lively, very vain, not entirely reliable" [nicht ganz verlässlich], 1020, n. 485.

25. Schnitzler to Lili Cappellini, October 29, 1927, *Schnitzler Briefe 1913–1931*, 501–3.

26. Schnitzler to Theodor Reik, December 31, 1913, *Schnitzler Briefe 1913–1931*, 35–36.

27. August 18, 1915, in Arthur Schnitzler, *Tagebuch 1931*, ed. Peter Michael Braunwarth (Vienna: Verlag der Österreichischen Akademie der Wissenschaften, 2000), as cited in Leo A. Lensing. "Schnitzler's Alphabet of Love," *Times Literary Supplement* 5089 (October 13, 2000), 5.

28. *Schnitzler Briefe 1913–1931*, 932, n. 12.

29. Arthur Schnitzler to Heinrich Schnitzler, August 19, 1922, *Schnitzler Briefe 1913–1931*, 284–85.

30. Freud, "The Uncanny" (1919), in *Standard Edition*, 17:220.

31. Ibid., 17:250–51. I am indebted to Donald J. Coleman for suggesting this citation to me.

32. Michael Herr, *Kubrick* (New York: Grove Press, 2000), 46. Also Michel Ciment, *Kubrick: The Definitive Edition*, trans. Gilbert Adair (New York: Faber & Faber, 2001), 259.

33. Herr, *Kubrick*, 46. Also Ciment, *Kubrick*, 259.

34. Herr, *Kubrick*, 8.

35. Raphael, *Eyes Wide Open*, 34.

36. Herr, *Kubrick*, 17–19.

37. Stanley Kubrick and Frederic Raphael, screenplay of *Eyes Wide Shut* (New York: Warner Books, 1999), 4–9. Hereafter *Eyes Wide Shut*.

38. Raphael in Ciment, *Kubrick*, 269.

39. *Eyes Wide Shut*, 11.

40. Ibid., 34.

41. Ibid.,106.

42. Schnitzler, *Traumnovelle*, 46.

43. Ernst Newman, *Stories of the Great Operas and Their Composers* (Philadelphia: Blakiston, 1930), 427.

44. *Eyes Wide Shut*, 112–14.

45. Schnitzler, *Dream Story*, 242–44.

46. Ibid., 245–46.

47. Ibid., 244.

48. Freud termed this "the precondition that there should be 'an injured third party'; it stipulates that the person in question shall never choose as his love object a woman who is disengaged—that is, an unmarried girl or an unattached married woman—but only one to whom another man can claim the right of possession as her husband, fiancé, or friend." "A Special Type of Choice of Object Made by Men" (1910), in *Standard Edition*, 11:164–75. The quotation is from 166.

49. Schnitzler, *Dream Story*, 263.

50. Schnitzler, *Traumnovelle*, 69. The Leopoldstadt was the poor Jewish immigrant district of prewar Vienna.

51. Schnitzler, "Die Weissagung" (1904), in *Stories and Plays* (Boston: D.C. Heath and Co., 1930), 66. The story is on 58–86.

52. "I see only that by autumn you'll be a dead man." Ibid., 68.

53. Raphael, *Eyes Wide Open*, 107–8.

54. Ibid., 90. See also 70 and 153.

55. Ibid., 59.

56. *Eyes Wide Shut*, 117.

57. Schnitzler, *Traumnovelle*, 27–28.

58. Herbert I. Kupper and Hilda S. Rollman-Branch, "Freud and Schnitzler– (*Doppelgänger*)," *Journal of the American Psychoanalytic Association* 7 (1959): 109–26. The reference is to 112.

59. Gay, *Schnitzler*, 64–65.

60. I am indebted to Alain J. J. Cohen for alerting me to this image.

61. Sigmund Freud, "Some Neurotic Mechanisms in Jealousy, Paranoia, and Homosexuality" (1922), in *Standard Edition*, 18:223.

62. Ibid., 18:225.

63. Ibid., 18:226.

64. Schnitzler to Marie Glümer, November 18, 1890, in Arthur Schnitzler, *Briefe 1875–1912*, ed. Therese Nickl and Heinrich Schnitzler (Frankfurt am Main: S. Fischer Verlag, 1981), 1:100.

65. Schnitzler, *Traumnovelle*, 15–16

66. Freud, "The Uncanny," 17:248, n. 1.

67. *Eyes Wide Shut*, 153.

68. Ibid., 156.

69. Ibid., 158. Egon Schwarz offers a different reading, suggesting that Bill

"seems to believe him." "Kubrick's 'Eyes Wide Shut' and Schnitzler's *'Traumnovelle,'* a Comparison." Paper presented to the conference Austria in the Heart of Europe, Center for Austrian Studies, University of Minnesota, April 5, 2001, 10. I am indebted to Professor Schwarz for sharing his prepublication manuscript with me.

70. *Eyes Wide Shut,* 165.

71. *Paracelsus,* as cited in Gay, *Schnitzler,* xxix.

Introducing Sociology

TIM KREIDER

So . . . do you . . . do you suppose we should . . . talk about money?

—DR. WILLIAM ("BILL") HARFORD

Critical disappointment with *Eyes Wide Shut* was almost unanimous, and the complaint was always the same: not sexy. The national reviewers sounded like a bunch of middle-school kids who'd snuck in to see the film and slunk out three hours later feeling horny, frustrated, and ripped off. Kubrick was old and out of touch with today's jaded sensibilities, they griped. The film's sexual mores and taboos, transplanted from Arthur Schnitzler's fin-de-siècle Vienna (jealousy over dreams and fantasies, guilt-ridden visits to prostitutes, a strained discussion of HIV that distantly echoes the old social terror of syphilis) seemed quaint and naive by the standards of 1999, year of the sordid Starr Report. One last time Stanley Kubrick had flouted genre expectations, and once again, as throughout his career, critics could only see what wasn't there.

The backlash against the film is now generally blamed on a cynical, miscalculated ad campaign. But why anyone who'd seen Kubrick's previous films believed the hype and actually expected it to be what *Entertainment Weekly* breathlessly anticipated as "the sexiest movie ever" is still unclear; the most erotic scenes he ever filmed were the bomber refueling in *Dr. Strangelove* and the spaceliner docking in *2001*. He mocks any prurient expectations in the very first shot of this movie; without prelude, Nicole Kidman, her back to the camera, shrugs off her dress and kicks it aside, standing matter-of-factly bare-assed before us for a moment before the screen goes black like a peepshow door sliding shut. Then the title appears like a rebuke, telling us that we're not really seeing what we're staring at. In other words, *Eyes Wide Shut* is not going to be about sex.

The real pornography in this film is in its lingering depiction of the

280

shameless, naked wealth of millennial Manhattan, and of the obscene effect of that wealth on our society, and on the soul. National reviewers' myopic focus on sex and the shallow psychologies of the film's central couple, the Harfords, at the expense of any other element of the film—its trappings of stupendous wealth, its references to fin-de-siècle Europe and other imperial periods, its Christmastime setting, the sum Dr. Harford spends on a single night out, let alone the unresolved mystery at its center—says more about the blindness of our elites to their own surroundings than it does about Kubrick's inadequacies as a pornographer. For those with their eyes open, there are plenty of money shots.

There is a moment in *Eyes Wide Shut,* as Bill Harford is lying to his wife over a cell phone from a prostitute's apartment, when we see a textbook in the foreground titled *Introducing Sociology.* The book's title is a dry caption to the action onscreen (like the slogan "Peace is our profession" looming over the battle at Burpelson Air Force Base in *Dr. Strangelove*), labeling prostitution as the most basic, defining transaction of our society. Almost everyone in this film prostitutes themselves, for various prices. But it is also a key to understanding the film, suggesting that we ought to interpret it sociologically—not as most reviewers insisted on doing, psychologically.

Michiko Kakutani of the *New York Times* tells us that Kubrick "never paid much attention to the psychology of characters, much less relationships between men and women," and in fact "spent his career ignoring (or avoiding) the inner lives of people, their private dreams and frustrations."[1] Unable to imagine what other subjects there could be, she, like so many critics before her, writes him off as obsessed with mere technique. She is, first of all, wrong; Kubrick examines his characters' inner lives through imagery, not dialogue; as he said, "scenes of people talking about themselves are often very dull."[2] (In fact, it could be argued that most of this film takes place inside Bill Harford's head.) Secondly, and more importantly, she misses the point: Kubrick's films are never only about individuals (and sometimes, as in the case of *2001,* they hardly contain any); they are always about Mankind, about human history and civilization. Even *The Shining,* until now the director's most intimate family drama, is not just about a family, as Bill Blakemore showed in his article "The Family of Man," but about the massacre of the American Indians and the recurring murderousness of Western civilization.[3]

Reviewers complained that the Harfords were ciphers, uncomplicated and dull; these reactions recall the befuddlement of critics who thought they were being clever by pointing out that the computer in *2001* was more human than the astronauts, but could only attribute this flaw (just four years after the unforgettable performances of *Dr. Strangelove*) to human error. Kubrick's choice of flawless Hollywood faces from the covers of glossy check-out-aisle magazines to play a conspicuously attractive high-society couple recalls the casting of handsome, bland-faced Ryan O'Neill to play the eighteenth-century social climber Redmond Barry. The Harfords may seem as naive and sheltered as, say, the Victorians in Galsworthy's *Forsyte Saga*, but to wish that the characters had been more complex or self-aware is misguided. To understand a film by this most thoughtful and painstaking of filmmakers, we should assume that this characterization is deliberate—that their shallowness and repression is the point. Think of Bill in the back of the cab, his face a sullen mask as he tortures himself by running the same black-and-white stag film of Alice's imagined infidelity over and over in his head. (Anyone who doubts that it is the character, rather than the actor, who lacks depth and expressiveness should watch Cruise in *Magnolia*.) Or of Alice giggling in her sleep, clearly relishing her dream about betraying and humiliating her husband, only to wake up in tears, saying that she had "a horrible dream"; her denial is as immediate and complete as Jack Torrance's in *The Shining* when he wakes up shouting from "the most terrible nightmare I ever had" about chopping up his family with an axe, about twelve hours before he tries to chop them up with one. The intensely staged vacuity of the Harford's inner lives should tell us to look elsewhere for the film's real focus.

One place to look is not at them but around them, at the places where they live and the things they own. Most of the film's sets, even the New York street scenes, were constructed on soundstages and backlots, just like the Overlook Hotel, which was almost as central to *The Shining* as its actors. Even the street sets (criticized by the uniquely provincial New York press as "inaccurate") are expressionistic dreamscapes, with confrontations summoned up by Bill's subconscious (the frat boys, the hooker) and newspaper headlines (LUCKY TO BE ALIVE) and neon signs (EROS) foreshadowing and commenting on the action. In Kubrick's mature work, nothing is incidental.

Stephen Hunter of the *Washington Post* mentions that the Harfords' apartment "must have cost $7 million," but only to make fun of Kubrick's apparent disconnect from contemporary America.[4] But the meticulously rendered setting of the film, the luxurious apartments and sumptuous mansions, are meant to raise our eyebrows. Kubrick and his collaborator, Frederic Raphael, discussed exactly how much money a New York doctor like Bill Harford must earn per year.[5] The Harfords' standard of living raises questions about their money, and where it comes from—from Bill's sparsely scheduled private practice, or the sorts of under-the-table services we see rendered upstairs at the party? Dr. Harford is on call to that class of person who can afford not to wait in emergency rooms or die in hospitals—people like his friend Victor Ziegler, whose name denotes him as one of the world's winners. Bill uncomfortably tries to compliment the prostitute Domino's apartment by calling it "cozy" (and her use of the standard joke "maid's day off" to excuse the leftovers and mess only draws further awkward attention to the class gulf between them), but his own place looks cramped and cluttered compared to Victor's. Ziegler's house is reminiscent of the Overlook Hotel, with its vast ballrooms and grand staircases, its mirrors and gilt, its bedroom-sized bathrooms. And even Ziegler's place seems modest compared to the opulent Moorish palace of Somerton, where the secret orgy takes place (in Schnitzler's novella it is "a one-story villa in a modest Empire style."[6])

To some extent, the fact that no critics recognized this as deliberate is excusable; we all overlook the fantastic affluence of the sets and wardrobe in most movies and TV shows, just as black audiences, for decades, had to put up with the oppressive, unanimous whiteness of everyone onscreen. But make no mistake: this is not a film about the "private dreams and frustrations" of what Victor condescendingly calls "ordinary people"; it is about really, really rich people, the kind that Lord Wendover in *Barry Lyndon* and Mr. Ullman in *The Shining* call "all the best people." And it shows us that these people are empty and amoral, using their social inferiors as thoughtlessly as if they were possessions, ultimately more concerned with social transgressions like infidelity than with crimes like murder—just as the film's audience is more interested in the sex it was supposed to be about than in the killing that is at its core.

Bill and Alice Harford may be what we think of, uncritically, as "nice" people—that is to say, attractive, well-educated, and upscale, a couple who collect fine art and listen to Shostakovich. But that's no reason to assume we're expected to empathize with them. (Kubrick once told Michael Herr he wanted to make a film about doctors because "everyone hates doctors.")[7] Evil among our elites is more often a matter of willful ignorance and passivity—of blindness—than of deliberate cruelty. And Kubrick has always emphasized that culture and erudition have nothing to do with goodness or depth of character (his great aesthetes, like Gen. Broulard, Humbert and

Quilty, and Alex de Large, are all decadent and depraved). In this film they
have everything to do with the exhibitionistic display of imperial wealth.

The paintings that cover the Harfords' walls from floor to ceiling (painted
by Kubrick's wife Christiane) almost all depict flowers or food, making
explicit the function of art in their environment as mere décor—art as conspicuous consumption. Most of them probably come from Alice's defunct
gallery, which brokered paintings like any other commodity. The Harfords
aren't the only art-lovers in the film; the apartment of Bill's patient Lou
Nathanson is decorated with even more expensive objets d'art (and his
bedroom, like the hall outside the Harford's apartment, is wallpapered
with imperial French fleurs-de-lis); Victor Ziegler has a famous collection,
including antique china arrayed in glass cases, a soaring winged statue of
Cupid and Psyche in his stairwell, and, reputedly, a gallery of Renaissance
bronzes upstairs; and the house in Somerton is hung with tapestries and
oil portraits of stern patriarchs, and decorated in appropriated imperial
styles from medieval Moorish to Venetian to Louis XIV. Like the trashed
mansion of the renowned playwright and pedophile Clare Quilty in *Lolita,*
these people's houses are tastefully stacked with the plundered treasures of
the world.

The film's elegant, antique appointments, its opening waltz, and its cast
full of European characters (Sandor Szavost, the models Gayle and Nuala,
the Nathansons, Milich, the maitre d' at the Sonata Café) all blur the distinction between millennial Manhattan and fin-de-siècle Vienna—another
corrupt and decadent high culture dancing at the brink of an abyss. In the
champagne haze of Victor's party the 1990s and 1890s become one, just as
the 1970s and the 1920s merged in one evening at the Overlook Hotel. But
the comparison is not only to the European capitals of the Gilded Age; a
broad sweep of references insinuates America's continuity with other previous imperial periods, all the way back to Rome. Sandor Szavost, Alice's
would-be seducer, inquires whether she has read Ovid's *Art of Love,* a reference fraught with sly implications. *Art of Love* is a satiric guide to the
etiquette of adultery, set among the elite classes of Augustus's Rome, full
of advice about bribing servants, buying gifts, and avoiding gold-diggers.
(Szavost's drinking from Alice's glass is a move lifted right out of Ovid's
pick-up manual.) And the fact that Ovid was an exile from his own center
of empire links him to the expatriate Hungarian. Szavost's extraordinary
skill at the Viennese waltz, and his offer to show Alice Ziegler's collection
of sculptures, extend the examples of imperially sponsored high art from
the Latin poetry of Rome to the ballroom dance of the Austro-Hungarian

Empire to the plastic arts of the Renaissance, bringing them all up to date in New York's gleaming, art-encrusted façade.

While Alice resists Szavost's courtly come-on, her husband is called away to the scene of a less classy assignation, where Kubrick shows us what lies behind that façade: unadorned exploitation and death. Behind the scenes at Ziegler's party, in an upstairs bathroom, Bill Harford finds the same thing Jack Torrance finds in the bathroom of room 237 of the Overlook: a woman's nude body. Banal, glittering dance music echoes from downstairs as we see the call girl Mandy sprawled naked in a narcotic stupor, while Victor hurriedly pulls up his pants, his use of her having been interrupted by an overdose. (Or has it?) After Bill brings her around, Victor impresses upon him that this near-scandal has to be kept "just between us"—but Kubrick, our own contemporary American artist-in-exile, in his own bitter *Art of Love,* tells all. With every detail and allusion he exposes the base, exploitative impulses behind imperial high culture: the erudite Szavost uses the classics, ballroom dance, and Renaissance sculpture as so many lines and props to seduce another man's wife, while Victor, looking distractedly down at Mandy as she lies naked and twitching, is framed by a painted nude. Asked about Alex's fondness for Ludwig Van in *A Clockwork Orange,* Kubrick answered, "I think this suggests the failure of culture to have any morally refining effect on society. Many top Nazis were cultured and sophisticated men, but it didn't do them, or anyone else, much good."[8] The point is reprised overtly in *Eyes Wide Shut* when we hear the title of Beethoven's opera, *Fidelio,* used as the password to an orgy.

As omnipresent as the art in the film's backgrounds are its Christmas decorations. It can't be incidental that the story is set at Christmastime; Schnitzler's book, which the script follows closely in most other particulars, is set "just before the end of carnival period."[9] Stanley Kubrick seems to have gotten seriously into the yuletide spirit in his last film. Hardly an interior in the film (except, of course, for the Satanic orgy) is without a baubled Christmas tree, and almost every set is suffused with the dreamlike, hazy glow of colored lights and tinsel. In the film's first scene, the Harfords' daughter, Helena, wants to stay up to watch *The Nutcracker* on TV, and its denouement takes place in the toy section of a decidedly upscale department store, where they've taken Helena Christmas shopping. *Eyes Wide Shut,* though it was released in summer, was *the* Christmas movie of 1999.

There is a thread of allusions to the Judeo-Christian fall-and-redemption myth woven throughout the film: Alice's allegorical dream about being

"naked," "terrified," and "ashamed," and fucking "in a beautiful garden";
the Harford's Edenic apartment, crammed with plants and paintings of
gardens; the two temptresses at Ziegler's party, twined and undulating like
serpents, practically molting out of their glittering skintight gowns; the
picture of an apple with a single, vaginal slice cut from it on the wall of
the prostitute's kitchen; the self-sacrificial "redemption" rite at the orgy.
This all seems like uncharacteristically old-world symbolism coming from
a director whose films—even his historical films—all take place in a modern,
godless universe. (The most memorable Christian imagery in Kubrick's previous work are Alex's ceramic chorus line of can-canning Jesuses and his
Hollywood-epic daydream about being a centurion who gets to flog him
in *A Clockwork Orange*. And in that film it's made clear that Christianity is
just a less efficient version of the sadistic, Skinnerian Ludovico treatment.)
But these biblical references only serve to show us how bankrupt the Christian ethic is in America by the end of the second millennium AD, how completely it's been co-opted and undermined by commerce. As Ziegler angrily
tells Bill in their final confrontation, "That whole play-acted 'take me' phony
sacrifice had absolutely nothing to do with her *real* death!" No, Mandy's
death had more to do with the cult of secrecy and power at the heart of
wealth—in other words, it was just business.

In *Eyes Wide Shut,* much as in the real world circa 1999, Christmas is less
a religious observance than an annual orgy of consumerism, the ecstatic
climax of the retail year. Merry Christmas banners hang in places of business alongside signs reading "No Checks Accepted and Thank You For
Your Custom." Rows of Christmas cards are on display in Bill's office below
a not particularly merry sign saying, "Payment is expected at the time of
treatment unless other arrangements have previously been made." These
juxtapositions undercut the supposed significance of the holiday and reveal
the real nature of the season, its ostensible warmth and sentimentality be-
lied by the bottom line. Even Milich, the Scroogelike owner of Rainbow
Costumes, calls holiday greetings to the two men with whom he has just
come to "another arrangement" concerning the use of his daughter. The
equation of Christmas with crass desire is made explicit in a song heard in
the Gillespie Diner: "I Want a Boy for Christmas." *The Nutcracker*, remember, is the story of a little girl whose new toy comes to life and turns into
a handsome prince.

The Harfords themselves, like most of the film's reviewers, don't really
see their surrounding mise-en-scene—the wealth, the art, the ubiquitous

Christmas glitz—preoccupied instead as they are with their own petty lusts and jealousies. But again and again Kubrick visually links his characters to their settings, indicting them as part of the rarefied world in which they live and move, through which his relentless Steadicam tracks them like an omniscient presence. At Ziegler's ball, the starburst pattern of lights on the walls is echoed by the lace edging of Alice's gown and by the blue stelliform ribbon on Szavost's lapel. Bill is haunted wherever he goes by the colors blue and gold, the color of the wallpaper outside his apartment. Domino first appears in a black-and-white striped fur coat, a pattern repeated in the zebra-skin stool at her dresser and the coat of the plush tiger on her bed. It's as though they're all just accessories coordinated to match the interiors. It seems to suggest that these people are as much commodities as the art and décor around them—that everyone can be had for a price. This implication is borne out by a close examination of the Harfords' characters; Alice is depicted as just another classy acquisition for display and Bill as a cocky consumer who learns, too late, that he's already been bought.

Alice Harford's obvious resentment of her husband, which she can only express when she's dreaming or high, is motivated by her unconscious recognition that she is a kept woman. We know Bill's supporting her, her art gallery having gone broke. She tells Szavost that she's looking for a job, but we don't see her looking; mostly we see her being looked at. Alice's role as a voyeuristic object is defined by her first breathtaking appearance and by her first onscreen line: "How do I look?" (And it rankles her that her husband doesn't see her anymore—he tells her her hair looks "perfect" without even looking, and asks her the babysitter's name about twenty seconds after she's told him.) Everyone she encounters in the first fifteen minutes of the film compliments her appearance; Bill dutifully tells her she always looks beautiful, the babysitter exclaims, "You look amazing, Mrs. Harford," and she's also flattered by such admirers of beauty as Victor Ziegler and Sandor Szavost. Ziegler tells her she looks "absolutely stunning—and I don't say that to all the women." "Oh, yes he does," retorts his wife—a jibe that resonates less funnily when we find out who "all the women" associated with Ziegler are.

Being beautiful *is* Alice's job, as much as it is the ex-beauty queen/call girl Mandy's or the hooker Domino's. During the quotidian-life-of-the-Harfords montage in which her husband examines patients at the office, we only see Alice tending to her toilette: brushing her daughter's hair, regally hooking on a brassiere, applying deodorant in front of the bathroom mirror. Hers is the daytime regimen of a courtesan (or an actress), devoted to the rigorous maintenance of her looks. She's associated, more than any other character, with mirrors; we see her giving herself a critical once-over before leaving for the party, and look of frank self-assessment in the medicine cabinet when she decides to get stoned. Her expression in the mirror as she watches her husband making love to her (the film's iconic image) begins as bemusement, giving way to fondness and arousal, but in the last seconds before the fade-out it becomes something more ambiguous, distracted, and self-conscious; this is her moment of clearest self-recognition, an uncomfortable glimpse of what she really is.

A series of insidious parallels throughout the film unmistakably suggest Alice's real status—the wife as prostitute. She's doubled, first of all, by the hooker Mandy; they're both tall redheads with a taste for numbing drugs, who we first see in compromising poses in bathrooms, and Mandy's last night on earth is distortedly echoed in Alice's dream about "being fucked by hundreds of men." Alice is also associated with the streetwalker Domino by the striking mauve of her sheets and of Domino's dress, and by their conspicuous dressing-table mirrors (the essential accoutrement of anyone who lives by her looks). Mandy and Domino are connected, as in Freud's dream-associations, by the identical consonants of their names, just as Alice is connected with Domino's roommate Sally (their names being aural anagrams). When Domino disappears, she's replaced by Sally the next day, just as in dream-logic one person may turn into another yet remain the same. In a sense, there is only one woman in this film. Lee Siegel sees the various prostitutes that Bill meets as different incarnations of his wife, the one woman he's really seeking all along.[10] But the similarities between them are more revealing (if less romantic) when read the other way—as implying that Alice is just another, higher-class whore. When we last see her in the film, in that toy store, she's surrounded by shelves full of stuffed tigers exactly like the one on Domino's bed. (Tiger and leopard-print patterns connote Charlotte Haze's predatory sexuality in *Lolita*.) Even in this scene, as she delivers the film's ostensible moral, Alice is visually linked to a doomed hooker.

She's also grooming her daughter, Helena, (named after the most beautiful woman in history) to become a high-ticket item like herself. During the montage of their day at home, we see Helena alongside her mother in almost every shot, holding the hairbrush while her mother gathers her hair into a ponytail, brushing her teeth at the mirror, learning to groom herself. When we overhear her doing word problems with her mother, she's learning how to calculate which boy has more money than the other. We hear her reading a bedtime story aloud, reciting the line, "before me when I jump into my bed." In this film, a line about "jumping into bed" isn't likely to be innocent. Her mother silently mouths it along with her, echoing and coaching her. At Bill's office, we see a photo of Helena in a purple dress, like the one worn by the girl her father paid for sex the night before.

Like his wife, Bill Harford is defined by his first line: "Honey, have you seen my wallet?" As she is a possession, he is a buyer. ("Doctor Bill," as both his wife and Domino call him, is a Swiftian pun, like Jack D. Ripper or Private Joker.) He flashes his professional credentials and hands out fifty- and hundred-dollar bills to charm, bribe, or intimidate cabbies, clerks, receptionists, and hookers—all members of the vast service economy on whom the enormous disparities of wealth in America are founded. Including unconsummated prostitution, costume rental, assorted bribes, and cab fare, his tab for a single illicit night out totals more than seven hundred dollars. He seems unfazed by the expenditure. His asking Domino "Should we talk about money?" his repeated insistence on paying her for services not quite rendered, his extended haggling with Milich and the cab driver— all these conversations about cash are too frequent and too drawn-out to be included in the interest of mundane verisimilitude. They do not occur in the novel. Doctor Bill even tears a hundred-dollar-bill in half with a wolfish, self-satisfied smirk.

Bill's nocturnal journey into illicit sexuality is, more importantly, a journey into invisible strata of wealth and power. Money is the subtext of sex from the very first temptation of Bill; the two models who flirtatiously draw him away from his wife at Ziegler's ball invite him enigmatically to follow them "Where the rainbow ends." At that moment he's called away, saying to them, "To be continued . . . ?" After he's gone, the two models exchange a cryptic, conspiratorial look. The exchange foreshadows Bill's finding himself at Rainbow Costume rentals in his effort to get admitted to an orgy ("to be continued," indeed). We never find out exactly what the models meant by the odd phrase, but everyone knows what lies at the end of the rainbow.

The colorful arc of Bill's adventure does lead him, finally, to the pot of gold—Somerton, the innermost sanctum of the ultrawealthy where the secret orgy is held. The orgy scenes in particular were singled out by reviewers for disappointment and derision. Listen to the groans of critical blueballs: David Denby called it "the most pompous orgy in the history of film."[11] "More ludicrous than provocative," said Michiko Kakutani, "more voyeuristic than scary."[12] "Whose idea of an orgy is this," demanded Stephen Hunter, "the Catholic Church's?"[13] Again they misunderstood Kubrick's artistic intentions, which are clearly not sensual. When Bill passes through the ornate portal past a beckoning golden-masked doorman, we should understand that we are entering the realm of myth and nightmare. This sequence is the clearest condemnation, in allegorical dream imagery, of elite society as corrupt, exploitative, and depraved—what they used to call, in a simpler time, evil. The pre-orgiastic rites are overtly satanic, a Black Mass complete with a high priest gowned in crimson, droning organ, and backward-masked Latin liturgy. What we see enacted is a ceremony in which faceless, interchangeable female bodies are doled out, fucked, and exchanged among black-cloaked figures, culminating in the ritual mass rape and sacrificial murder of a woman.

The haunted ambiance here recalls that of the film's other big exclusive party, Ziegler's; the opulent surroundings, the mannered, leaden dialogue, the camera afloat like the disembodied point of view in a dream. A ballroom full of naked, masked couples dancing to "Strangers in the Night" reminds us not only Ziegler's party but of the Overlook Hotel, whose ghosts also danced and coupled in costume. (Remember the quick, surreal zoom shot in *The Shining* of a man in a bestial costume fellating tuxedoed millionaire Horace Derwent in an upstairs room?) The two sequences are identical in length, mirror images of each other. The party and the orgy are conclusively linked in the back room of Rainbow Costumes, a sort of antechamber to Somerton, where we see a row of masked and costumed mannequins posed in front of the same cascade of glittering white lights that hung from the walls at Ziegler's.

The orgy makes the metaphor of sexual objectification visually literal. The prostitutes wear masks that render them anonymous and identical. Their nude bodies are unnaturally perfect, smooth and immaculate as mannequins, lit under a chilling white spotlight and photographed with that Kubrickian detachment that somehow desaturates them of any real eroticism. The ritualistic kisses exchanged are spooky and sterile, the sculpted white lips of one mask touching another's. The sex consists of static tableaus of spectators posed around mechanically rutting participants. A masked and tuxedoed valet on all fours serves as a platform for a fucking couple, a piece of human furniture like the tables at the Korova Milk Bar in *A Clockwork Orange*. One might remember, with a shudder, the Lugosian-toned Szavost inviting Alice to have casual sex upstairs, among the sculptures.

The masks worn by the revelers (Venetian—an allusion to another mercantile empire) serve a similar symbolic purpose: the transformation of the wearer into a soulless object. They certainly aren't expressive of ecstatic self-annihilation, as some critics suggested; they're creepy as hell. We see a bird with a scythelike beak, a cubist face fractured in half, contorted grimaces and leers, a frozen howl, painted tears, blindly gazing eyes. These revelers have "lost themselves" not in erotic abandon but in the same way that the recruits in *Full Metal Jacket* lose their selves, along with their hair and their names. The utterly still, silent shots of staring masks at Bill's "trial" are images of empty-eyed dehumanization, faces of death. Note that when Ziegler first sees Bill enter the ceremonial hall, even though they are both masked, he gives him a solemn, knowing nod. He *recognizes* him. Here at Somerton, the guests at Ziegler's party are unmasked for what they really are.

Masks and mannequins are a recurring motif in Kubrick's work: think of the fight with mannequins' limbs in *Killer's Kiss,* the anthropomorphic furniture at the Korova, the grotesque masks worn in *The Killing* and *A Clockwork Orange.* In *Eyes Wide Shut* we see them not only at the orgy but throughout the film, always as the attendants or harbingers of death. A stone Greek mask keeps vigil by Lou Nathanson's deathbed. African masks gaze down, like the masked spectators silently watching the sex acts at Somerton, at the bed where Bill has his interrupted trick with the HIV+ hooker Domino. A "domino" is itself a kind of mask.

They also serve as metaphors for women being treated like possessions. Costumed mannequins surround Bill and Milich in the back room at Rainbow Costumes. "Like life, eh?" says Milich, just before he catches his daughter consorting with two men in wigs and livid makeup. Milich's daughter, for all the coquettish depravity at play in her face, looks somehow as eerily inanimate as the Grady twins in *The Shining*—her skin is smooth and white as the mannequins' in the back room, her painted lips and glittering eyes flawless as a china doll's. In a carefully composed shot in the scene when Bill returns his costume, we see Milich and his daughter paired on the right side of the frame opposite Bill and one of the mannequins (seen through the door to the back room) paired on the left. "If Doctor Harford should ever need anything else," says Milich, hugging his daughter close beside the cash register, "Anything at all . . . it needn't be a costume." The line only reinforces the clear visual equation of the girl with the store's more legitimate merchandise. And the three times we see the prostitute Mandy her face is always a mask: in Ziegler's bedroom, her drug-dilated eyes are lit to look like empty black holes in her face; at the

orgy she is literally masked; and on the slab at the morgue her face is slack
and white, her eyes wide open but sightless.

Although Bill doesn't actually fuck or kill anyone himself, the film im-
plicates him in the exploitation and deaths of all of the women he encounters. He didn't give Domino HIV, but she contracted it servicing someone
like him. Milich alternates with hilarious aplomb between berating the men
he's caught with his daughter—"Will you please to be quiet! Can't you see
I am trying to serve a customer?"—and unctuous apologies to Harford,
conflating the two exchanges. (After all, Bill isn't just paying for a costume
but for the illicit opportunity it affords. Like the sign over the bar at the
Sonata Café says, "The customer is always wrong.") And, ultimately, does
it really make a difference whether Mandy was ceremonially executed by
some evil cabal or only allowed to O.D. after being gang-banged again?
Given Kubrick's penchant for blackly humorous literalism (think of "Gentlemen, you can't fight in here—this is the War Room!" or "I said, 'I'm not
gonna hurt you'—I'm just going to bash your brains in!"), when Ziegler
explains that Mandy wasn't murdered, she just "got her brains fucked
out," the contradiction should be obvious.

Bill learns about Mandy's overdose in a café whose walls are covered
with antique portraits of women, while Mozart's *Requiem* plays. The setting and the music make the moment timeless, universal. Kubrick's last
three films form a sort of thematic trilogy about our culture's hatred of the
female. In *The Shining,* Jack Torrance despises his wife and child and tries
to murder them, just as the previous "caretaker" murdered his own wife
and daughters. (We also hear, on a TV news bulletin, about a woman who's
mysteriously "disappeared while on a hunting trip with her husband.") In
Full Metal Jacket, the institutionalized misogyny of the Marine Corps is pervasive, and the absence of women (we see only two hookers and a sniper)
is so conspicuous it becomes a haunting presence. That film's climax is the
execution of a fifteen-year-old girl. The requiem in the Sonata Café plays
not just for Mandy but for all the anonymous, expendable women used
and disposed of by men of Harford's class throughout the ages.

For all his flaunting of his money and professional status, Bill Harford is
ultimately put back in his place as a member of the serving class. Recall
how he's summoned away from Ziegler's party in the same polite but perfunctory manner as his friend Nick, the pianist; like him, Bill is just hired
help, the party doctor, called on to mop up human messes like Mandy.
When he goes to his patient Lou Nathanson's apartment, he's met by their

housemaid, Rosa, who's also dressed in black with a white collar, in a perfectly symmetrical entry hall where every object is in a neatly matched pair. The shot makes the doctor and the maid doubles; regardless of their respective salaries or social status, they're equals here. When Bill tries to infiltrate the orgy, he's given away by telltale class markers—he shows up in a taxi rather than a limo, and has a costume rental slip in his pocket. His real status at Somerton, as an outsider and intruder, is spelled out for him the next day when he returns to the estate, only to be dismissed with a terse typed note handed him through the bars of the front gate by a tight-lipped servant. (This isn't the only time we see Bill through bars—he has to bribe his way past the grated door at Milich's.) When Ziegler finally calls him onto the carpet for his transgressions, he chuckles at Bill's refusal of a case of twenty-five-year-old Scotch (Bill's a Bud man), not just because this extravagance would be a trifle to him but because Bill's pretense of integrity is an empty gesture—he's already been bought. Bill may be able to buy, bribe, and command his own social inferiors, and he may own Alice, but he's Victor Ziegler's man.

Although Ziegler has a credible explanation for everything that's happened—Harford's harassment, Nick Nightingale's beating and disappearance, Mandy's death—we don't ever really know whether he's telling the truth or lying to cover up Mandy's murder. The script very carefully withholds any conclusive evidence that would let us feel comfortably certain either way. Ziegler does have suspiciously privileged access to details of the case: "The door was locked from the inside, the police are happy, end of story! [dismissive raspberry.]" He also claims to be dropping his façade and coming clean a few too many times to be believed: "I have to be completely frank," "Bill, please—no games," and finally, "All right, Bill, let's . . . let's . . . let's cut the bullshit, all right?" And notice how he introduces his explanation: "*Suppose* I were to tell you . . ." [emphasis mine]. He's not being "frank"; he's offering Bill an escape, a plausible, face-saving explanation for the girl's death to assuage his unexpectedly agitated conscience. And it's one of the few things in this film that Bill has a hard time buying—watch the way his hand adheres to his cheek and slowly slides off his face as he rises to his feet and walks dazedly across the room, trying to absorb the incredible coincidence Ziegler's asking him to believe. Ziegler's "no games" plea notwithstanding, this entire conversation is a game—a gentlemanly back-and-forth of challenges and evasions over a question of life and death, throughout which the two opponents circle each other uneasily around a billiards table the color of blood.

When Bill persists in his inquiries, Ziegler loses his temper and resorts
to intimidation and threats. He reminds him of their respective ranks as
master and man: "You've been way out of your depth for the last twenty-
four hours," he growls. Of his fellow revelers at Somerton, he says, "Who
do you think those people were? Those were not ordinary people there. If
I told you their names—I'm not going to tell you their names, but if I did,
you might not sleep so well." In other words, they're "all the best people,"
the sorts of supremely wealthy and powerful men who can buy and sell
"ordinary" men like Bill and Nick Nightingale, and fuck or kill women like
Mandy and Domino. The "you might not sleep so well" is a veiled threat,
and it isn't Ziegler's last. His final word of advice—"Life goes on. It always
does . . . until it doesn't. But you know that, don't you, Bill?"—proffered
with an avuncular, unpleasantly proprietary rub of the shoulders, sounds
like a reassurance but masks a warning. (We immediately cut from this
to a less friendly warning—the mask placed beside Alice on Bill's pillow.)
Bill's expression, in the foreground, is by now so tight and working with
suppressed and conflicting feelings that it's hard to read, but one of those
feelings is clearly fear for his life—he looks as though he might burst into
tears or hysterical laughter, and when Victor claps those patronizing hands
on his shoulders, he flinches. In the end, he accepts Victor's explanation
not because there's any evidence to confirm it, but because it's a convenient excuse to back down from the danger of any further investigation.
He finally understands that he, too, no less than a hooker or a hired musician, is expendable.

So the questions remain: *Did* Mandy just O.D., or was she murdered?
Was Bill's jeweled mask left on his pillow by Alice as an accusation, or by
Ziegler's friends as a third and final warning, a death threat like the horse's
head in the bed in *The Godfather*? These are crucial questions, ones that
Kubrick deliberately leaves unanswered. And yet most reviewers didn't
even seem to notice that they *were* questions, instead automatically pro-
jecting their own interpretations onto the story—most assuming that
Ziegler was providing redundant exposition, that Mandy's death was the
coincidence Ziegler claimed it to be, and that Alice put the mask there herself. (*Dream Story* does not even include the character of Ziegler, or any
final confrontation with a member of the secret society, and it also makes
clear that it was the protagonist's wife, Albertina, who placed the mask on
the bed.) But Kubrick bends over so far backward to preserve these ambiguities that they become glaring, demanding of us that we, like Bill, con-
sciously decide what we're going to believe. Bill's reaction when he sees

the mask in his bed could be interpreted either as shame and relief at having his lies exposed, or as the terrified realization that his wife and daughter could have been murdered in their sleep. When Alice wakes up to Bill's sobbing, her expression doesn't betray whether she's startled to see the mask beside her or already knows it's there. When we cut to her the next morning, her eyes swollen and red-rimmed from weeping, we don't know whether she's crying because her husband almost cheated on her or because he's endangered their family. And the final dialogue between Bill and Alice is so vague and allusive ("What should we do?" "Maybe we should be grateful,") that it could as easily refer to Mandy's murder and the implied threat to their lives as to Bill's indiscretions. If we choose to believe the former, then the Harfords aren't just reconciling over their imagined and attempted infidelities; they're agreeing to cover up a crime, to be accomplices after the fact to a homicide.

This is the film's final test—a projection test, like the ambiguous cartoons with blank word balloons shown to Alex at the end of *A Clockwork Orange* to determine whether his conditioning has been broken. His lewd and violent interpretations of the images proves that it has been. Has ours? The open-ended narrative forces us to ask ourselves what we're really seeing: is *Eyes Wide Shut* a movie about marriage, sex, and jealousy, or about money, whores, and murder? Before you make up your own mind, consider this: has there ever been even one Stanley Kubrick film in which someone *didn't* get murdered?

In the film's upbeat but dissonant denouement, the Harfords have taken their daughter, Helena, Christmas shopping (which turns out to mean letting her run around picking out items she wants for herself), but they respond to her wishes only politely, preoccupied instead with their own inner children. Like many reviewers, they're still wrapped up in psychology and sex, missing the sinister sociological implications of what's onscreen. As in so much of Kubrick's work, the dialogue is misdirection; the real story is told visually. As Helena flits anxiously from one display to the next (already an avid little consumer) every item she fondles associates her with the women who have been bought and discarded by her father and his circle. Helena's Christmas list includes a blue baby carriage (like the blue stroller seen twice outside Domino's apartment), an oversized teddy bear (right next to a rack of tigers like the one on Domino's bed) and a Barbie doll (reminiscent of Milich's daughter) dressed in a diaphanous angel costume just like the one Helena herself wore in the film's first scene. She herself has already become a doll, a thing to be dressed up and accessorized. Another toy, conspicuously displayed under a red ring of lights, is called "The Magic Circle"; the name is an allusion to the ring of ritual prostitutes at the orgy, and the bright red color of the box recalls the carpet on which they genuflected to the high priest, as well as the felt of the pool table over which Bill made his bargain with the devil. The subplot with Milich and his daughter is echoed here, in another place of business, as the Harfords casually pimp their own little angel out to the world of commerce.

ALICE: And, you know, there is something very important we have to do as soon as possible.
BILL: What's that?
ALICE: Fuck.

As *Eyes Wide Shut* closes, this final exchange between Bill and Alice suggests that all the dark adventures they've confessed ("whether they were real or only dreams"), and the crimes in which they may be complicit, have occasioned nothing more than another kinky turn-on, no more enlightening than the flirtations at the ball that inflamed their lovemaking when they got home. For all their talk about being "awake" now, their eyes are still wide shut. Reconciled, they plan to forget all this unpleasantness soon in the blissful oblivion of orgasm. (Try keeping your eyes open during orgasm.) Maybe, in the end, it is a film about sexual obsession after all: about sex as an all-consuming distraction from the ugly realities of wealth and power all around us; about audiences who strain their eyes for a glimpse of skin while the skull is staring them in the face. Maybe the customer is always wrong.

It's an exquisitely ambiguous ending to an enigmatic film. Perhaps, as some critics have speculated, there is some glimmer of hope or awakening here; certainly a subtler, more thoughtful psychological reading of the film than has yet been attempted would be possible. But to focus exclusively on the Harford's unexamined inner lives is to remain willfully blind to the profoundly visual filmic world that Stanley Kubrick devoted his career to creating. The vision of the world he tried to show us in his last—and, he believed, his best—work, the capital of the American empire at the end of the American Century, is one in which the wealthy, powerful, and privileged use the rest of us like throwaway products, covering up their crimes with pretty pictures, shiny surfaces, and murder, condemning their own children to lives of servitude and whoredom. The feel-good ending intimates, in Kubrick's very last word on this or any subject, that the Harfords' daughter is, just as they've resigned themselves to being, fucked.

NOTES

The hours I spent in conversation with Rob Content about this film were invaluable in developing my argument. Bart Taylor pointed out some of the Christian imagery in the film. I am indebted to Boyd White and to Ann Martin, editor of *Film Quarterly*, for their editorial acumen. An earlier version of this essay appeared in *Film Quarterly* 53.3 (2000): 41–48. Copyright © 2000 by the Regents of the University of California.

1. Michiko Kakutani, "A Connoisseur of Cool Tries to Raise the Temperature," *New York Times*, July 18, 1999, 22.

2. Michel Ciment, "Second Interview," in *Kubrick: The Definitive Edition*, trans. Gilbert Adair (New York: Holt, Reinhart, and Winston, 1980), 171.

3. Bill Blakemore, "The Family of Man," *San Francisco Chronicle*, July 29, 1987.

4. Stephen Hunter, "The Lust Picture Show: Stanley Kubrick Stumbled with His Eyes Wide Shut," *Washington Post*, July 16, 1999, C5.

5. Frederic Raphael, *Eyes Wide Open: A Memoir of Stanley Kubrick* (New York: Ballantine, 1999).

6. Arthur Schnitzler, *Dream Story,* trans. Otto P. Schinnerer (Los Angeles: Sun & Moon Press, 1995), 128.

7. Michael Herr, *Kubrick* (New York: Grove Press, 2000), 13.

8. Ciment, "First Interview" in *Kubrick*, 163.

9. Schnitzler, *Dream Story*, 4.

10. Lee Siegel, "Eyes Wide Shut: What the Critics Failed to See in Kubrick's Last Film," *Harper's Magazine,* October 1999, 76–83.

11. David Denby, "Last Waltz," *New Yorker*, July 26, 1999, 84.

12. Kakutani, "A Connoisseur of Cool," 22.

13. Hunter, "The Lust Picture Show," C5.

Filmography

Bibliography

Contributors

Index

Filmography

Day of the Fight (1950). Producer, director, writer: Stanley Kubrick. Distributor: RKO Radio. 16 minutes.

Flying Padre (1951). Producer, director, writer: Stanley Kubrick. Distributor: RKO Radio. 9 minutes.

The Seafarers (1953). Producer: Lester Cooper. Director: Stanley Kubrick. Writer: Will Chasen. Distributor: Seafarers International Union, Atlantic and Gulf Coast District, American Federation of Labor. 30 minutes.

Fear and Desire (1953). Producer, director, editor: Stanley Kubrick. Screenplay: Howard O. Sackler. Cast includes: Frank Silvera (Mac), Kenneth Harp (Corby), Paul Mazursky (Sidney). Distributor: Joseph Burstyn, Inc. 68 minutes.

Killer's Kiss (1955). Producers: Stanley Kubrick, Morris Rousel. Director, screenplay: Stanley Kubrick. Cast includes: Frank Silvera (Vincent Rapallo), Jamie Smith (Davey Gordon), Irene Kane (Gloria Price). Distributor: United Artists Release of Minotaur Production. 67 minutes.

The Killing (1956). Production company: Harris-Kubrick Productions. Producer: James B. Harris. Director: Stanley Kubrick. Screenplay: Stanley Kubrick from Lionel White's novel *Clean Break*. Cast includes: Sterling Hayden (Johnny Clay), Coleen Gray (Fay), Vince Edwards (Val Cannon), Jay C. Flippen (Marvin Unger), Marie Windsor (Sherry Peatty), Ted De Corsica (Randy Kennan), Elisha Cook (George Peatty), Joe Sawyer (Mike O'Reilley), Timothy Carey (Nikki). Distributor: United Artists. 83 minutes.

Paths of Glory (1957). Production company: Harris-Kubrick Productions. Producer: James B. Harris. Director: Stanley Kubrick. Screenplay: Stanley Kubrick, Calder Willingham, Jim Thompson, based on the novel by Humphrey Cobb. Cast includes: Kirk Douglas (Colonel Dax), Ralph Meeker (Corporal Paris), Adolphe Menjou (General Broulard), George Macready (General Mireau), Wayne Morris (Lieutenant Roget), Richard Anderson (Major Saint-Auban), Joseph Turkel (Private Arnaud), Timothy Carey (Private Ferol). Distributor: United Artists, presented by Bryna Productions. 86 minutes.

Spartacus (1960). Production company: Bryna Productions. Executive producer: Kirk Douglas. Producer: Edward Lewis. Director: Stanley Kubrick. Script: Dalton Trumbo, based on the novel by Howard Fast. Cast includes: Kirk Douglas (Spartacus), Laurence Olivier (Marcus Crassus), Jean Simmons (Varinia). Distributor: Universal Pictures. 196 minutes in original British release. Cut to 184 minutes for U.S. and international release.

Lolita (1962). Production company: Seven Arts/Anya/Transworld. Producer: James B. Harris. Director: Stanley Kubrick. Screenplay: Vladimir Nabokov, based on his novel. Cast includes: James Mason (Humbert Humbert), Sue Lyon (Lolita Haze), Shelley Winters (Charlotte Haze), Peter Sellers (Clare Quilty). Distributor: Metro-Goldwyn-Mayer. 153 minutes.

Dr. Strangelove, or How I Learned to Stop Worrying and Love the Bomb (1964). Production company: Hawk Films. Producer and director: Stanley Kubrick. Screenplay: Stanley Kubrick, Terry Southern, Peter George, based on the novel *Red Alert* by Peter George. Cast includes: Peter Sellers (Group Captain Lionel Mandrake, President Muffley, Dr. Strangelove), George C. Scott (General Buck Turgidson), Sterling Hayden (General Jack D. Ripper), Keenan Wynn (Colonel Bat Guano), Slim Pickens (Major T. J. "King" Kong). Distributor: Columbia Pictures. 94 minutes.

2001: A Space Odyssey (1968). Production company and distributor: Metro-Goldwyn-Mayer. Producer and director: Stanley Kubrick. Script: Stanley Kubrick, Arthur C. Clarke, based on Clarke's short story "The Sentinel." Cast includes: Keir Dullea (David Bowman), Gary Lockwood (Frank Poole), Douglas Rain (voice of HAL-9000). 141 minutes.

A Clockwork Orange (1971). Production company: Warner Brothers, Polaris Productions. Producer and director: Stanley Kubrick. Screenplay: Stanley Kubrick, based on the novel by Anthony Burgess. Cast includes: Malcolm McDowell (Alex DeLarge), Patrick Magee (Mr. Alexander), Adrienne Corri (Mrs. Alexander), Sheila Raynor (mother), Philip Stone (father), Anthony Sharp (minister). Distributor: Warner. 136 minutes.

Barry Lyndon (1975). Production company: Hawk/Peregrine, for Warner Brothers. Producer and director: Stanley Kubrick. Screenplay: Stanley Kubrick, from the novel by William Makepeace Thackeray. Cast includes: Ryan O'Neal (Barry Lyndon/Redmond Barry), Marisa Berenson (Lady Lyndon), Patrick Magee (Chevalier de Balibari), Hardy Kruger (Captain Potzdorf), Michael Hordern (narrator), Leon Vitali (Lord Bullingdon). Distributor: Warner. 187 minutes.

The Shining (1980). Production company: Hawk/Peregrine, for Warner Brothers. Producer and director: Stanley Kubrick. Screenplay: Stanley Kubrick and Diane Johnson from the novel by Stephen King. Executive producer: Jan Harlan. Cast includes: Jack Nicholson (Jack Torrance), Shelly Duvall (Wendy Torrance), Danny Lloyd (Danny), Scatman Crothers (Hallorann), Barry Nelson (Ullman), Philip Stone (Grady), Joe Turkel (Lloyd). Distributor: Warner. 146 minutes.

Full Metal Jacket (1987). Production company: Warner Brothers. Producer and director: Stanley Kubrick. Screenplay: Stanley Kubrick, Michel Herr and Gustav Hasford, based on Hasford's novel *The Short-Timers*. Cast includes: Matthew Modine (Joker), Adam Baldwin (Animal Mother), Vincent D'Onofrio

(Gomer Pyle), Lee Ermey (Sergeant Hartman), Dorian Harewood (Eightball), Arliss Howard (Cowboy), Kevyn Major Howard (Rafterman). Distributor: Warner. 116 minutes.

Eyes Wide Shut (1999). Production company: Warner Brothers. Producer and director: Stanley Kubrick. Screenplay: Stanley Kubrick and Frederic Raphael, based on the novella *Dream Story* by Arthur Schnitzler. Cast includes: Tom Cruise (Dr. William Harford), Nicole Kidman (Alice Harford), Syndey Pollack (Victor Ziegler), Marie Richardson (Marion), Todd Field (Nick Nightingale), Rade Sherbedgia (Milich), Vinessa Shaw (Domino), Fay Masterson (Sally), Alan Cummings (desk clerk), Sky Dumont (Sandor Szavost), Julienne Davis (Mandy). Distributor: Warner. 159 minutes.

Bibliography

Adams, Richard, and Stanley Kubrick. "The German Lieutenant: An Original Screenplay." 1956–57. Box 22, Folder 2, Department of Defense Film Collection, Special Collections, Georgetown University, Washington, DC.

Agee, James. "The Blue Hotel" [1949]. In *Agee on Film, Volume Two: Five Film Scripts by James Agee*, 393–486. New York: Grosset & Dunlap, 1967.

Agel, Jerome, ed. *The Making of Kubrick's 2001*. New York: NAL, 1967.

Anger, Cédric. "Le Dernier Expressioniste." *Cahiers du Cinema* 534 (Apr. 1999): 28–29.

Baxter, John. *Stanley Kubrick: A Biography*. New York: Carroll & Graf, 1997.

Baxter, Peter. "The One Woman." *Wide Angle* 6.1 (1984): 34–41.

Begley, Louis. *Wartime Lies*. New York: Alfred A. Knopf, 1991.

Bier, Jesse. "Cobb and Kubrick: Author and Auteur." *Virginia Quarterly Review* 61 (1985): 57–61.

Bizony, Piers. *2001: Filming the Future*. London: Aurum, 2000.

Blakemore, Bill. "The Family of Man." *San Francisco Chronicle*, July 29, 1987.

Bogdonavich, Peter. "What They Say About Stanley Kubrick." *New York Times Magazine*, July 4, 1999.

Burgess, Anthony. *A Clockwork Orange*. London: William Heinemann, 1962.

——. "A Clockwork Orange Resucked." In Burgess, *A Clockwork Orange*, v–xi. New York: W. W. Norton, 1986.

Castle, Alison, ed. *The Stanley Kubrick Archives*. Cologne: Taschen, 2005.

Chion, Michel. *Eyes Wide Shut*. Translated by Trista Selous. London: British Film Institute, 2002.

——. *Kubrick's Cinema Odyssey*. Translated by Claudia Gorbman. London: British Film Institute, 2001.

Ciment, Michel. *Kubrick: The Definitive Edition*. Translated by Gilbert Adair. New York: Faber & Faber, 2001.

Clarke, Arthur C. *2001: A Space Odyssey*. New York: NAL, 1999.

Cobb, Humphrey. *Paths of Glory*. New York: Grosset & Dunlap, 1935.

Cocks, Geoffrey. *The Wolf at the Door: Stanley Kubrick, History, and the Holocaust*. New York: Peter Lang, 2004.

Conrad, Joseph. *Heart of Darkness* [1902]. Mineola, NY: Dover, 1990.

Coyle, Wallace. *Stanley Kubrick: A Guide to Reference and Resources*. Boston: Hall, 1980.

Crane, Stephen. "The Blue Hotel [1898]." In Crane, *Maggie, Together with George's Mother and The Blue Hotel*. New York: Knopf, 1931.

Crone, Rainer. *Stanley Kubrick: Drama and Shadows*. New York: Phaidon, 2005.

Davis, Natalie Z. "Trumbo and Kubrick Argue History." *Raritan* 22 (2002): 173–90.

Eisenstein, Sergei. "Color and Meaning." In Eisenstein, *The Film Sense*. Edited and translated by Jay Leyda, 113–53. New York: Harcourt Brace, 1942.

Falsetto, Mario. *Stanley Kubrick: A Narrative and Stylistic Analysis*. Westport, CT: Greenwood, 1994.

———, ed. *Perspectives on Stanley Kubrick*. New York: Hall, 1996.

Fast, Howard. *Spartacus*. New York: Simon & Schuster, 2000.

George, Peter. *Dr. Strangelove: or How I Learned to Stop Worrying and Love the Bomb*. Oxford: Oxford University Press, 1988.

Griffiths, Paul. "Music That Switches Its Gaze, from Future to Past." *New York Times*, July 21, 2002.

Hasford, Gustav. *The Short-Timers*. New York: Harper & Row, 1979.

Herr, Michael. *Kubrick*. New York: Grove Press, 2000.

Howard, James. *Stanley Kubrick Companion*. London: Batsford, 1999.

Hughes, David. *The Complete Kubrick*. London: Virgin, 2000.

Hummel, Christoph, et al., *Stanley Kubrick*. Munich: Hauser, 1984.

James, Nick. "At Home with the Kubricks." *Sight and Sound* 9.9 (Sept. 1999): 12–18.

Jenkins, Greg. *Stanley Kubrick and the Art of Adaptation*. Jefferson, NC: McFarland, 1997.

Johnson, Diane. *The Shadow Knows*. New York: Knopf, 1974.

———. "Stanley Kubrick (1928–1999)." *New York Review of Books*, April 22, 1999.

Kafka, Franz. *The Castle* [1922]. Translated by Willa and Edwin Muir. New York: Knopf, 1992.

Kagan, Norman. *The Cinema of Stanley Kubrick*. 2nd ed. New York: Continuum, 1997.

Kelly, Andrew. "The Brutality of Military Incompetence: 'Paths of Glory' (1957)." *Historical Journal of Film, Radio, and Television* 13.2 (1993): 215–27.

King, Stephen. *The Shining*. New York: Doubleday, 1977.

Kirschmann, Kay. *Stanley Kubrick: Das Schweigen der Bilder*. Marburg: Hitzeroth, 1993.

Koestler, Arthur. *The Gladiators*. Translated by Edith Simon. New York: Macmillan, 1947.

Kolker, Robert. *A Cinema of Loneliness*. 3rd ed. Oxford: Oxford University Press, 2000.

Kubrick, Christiane. *Stanley Kubrick: A Life in Pictures*. Boston: Little, Brown, 2002.

Kubrick, Stanley. *A Clockwork Orange* [1972]. Southwold: Screenpress, 2000.

Kubrick, Stanley, Michael Herr, and Gustav Hasford. *Full Metal Jacket: The Screenplay*. New York: Alfred A. Knopf, 1987.

Kubrick, Stanley, and Frederic Raphael. *Eyes Wide Shut: A Screenplay.* New York: Warner, 1999.

LoBrutto, Vincent. "The Old Ultra-Violence." *American Cinematographer* 80.10 (Oct. 10, 1999): 52–60.

———. *Stanley Kubrick: A Biography.* New York: Donald I. Fine, 1997.

Magid, Ron. "Quest of Perfection." *American Cinematographer* 80.10 (Oct. 10, 1999): 40–51.

Magistrale, Anthony, ed. *The Shining Reader.* Mercer Island, WA: Starmont, 1991.

Mann, Thomas. *The Magic Mountain* [1924]. Translated by H. T. Lowe-Porter. New York: Knopf, 1955.

Modine, Matthew. *Full Metal Jacket Diary.* New York: Rugged Land, 2005.

Nabokov, Vladimir. *The Annotated Lolita.* Edited by Alfred Appel. New York: McGraw-Hill, 1970.

———. *Lolita: A Screenplay.* New York: McGraw-Hill, 1974.

Nelson, Thomas Allen. *Kubrick: Inside a Film Artist's Maze.* 2nd ed. Bloomington: Indiana University Press, 2000.

Phillips, Gene D. *Stanley Kubrick: A Film Odyssey.* New York: Popular Library, 1975.

———, ed. *Stanley Kubrick: Interviews.* Jackson: University of Mississippi Press, 2001.

Phillips, Gene D., and Rodney Hill, eds. *The Encyclopedia of Stanley Kubrick: From Day of the Fight to Eyes Wide Shut.* New York: Facts on File, 2002.

Pipolo, Tony. "The Modernist and the Misanthrope: The Cinema of Stanley Kubrick." *Cineaste* 27.2 (Spring 2002): 4–15, 49.

Pudovkin, Vsevolod. *Film Technique.* Translated by Ivor Montagu. London: Newness, 1933.

Raphael, Frederic. *Eyes Wide Open: A Memoir of Stanley Kubrick.* New York: Ballantine, 1999.

Schnitzler, Arthur. *Dream Story.* Translated by J. M. Q. Davies. New York: Warner, 1999.

Seesslen, Georg, and Fernand Jung. *Stanley Kubrick und seine Filme.* Marburg: Schüren, 1999.

Southern, Terry. "Strangelove Outtake: Notes from the War Room." *Grand Street* 13.1 (Summer 1994): 65–80.

Stanley Kubrick: A Life in Pictures. Produced and directed by Jan Harlan. 142 min. Burbank, CA: Warner Bros., 2001. DVD.

Thackeray, William Makepeace. *The Luck of Barry Lyndon* [1844]. Edited by Martin F. Anisman. New York: New York University Press, 1970.

Thissen, Rolf. *Stanley Kubrick: Der Regisseur als Architekt.* Munich: Heyne, 1999.

Walker, Alexander. "Inexactly Expressed Sentiments About the Most Private Person I Know." In Walker, *"It's Only a Movie, Ingrid": Encounters On and Off Screen.* London: Headline, 1988.

———. *Stanley Kubrick, Director.* New York: Norton, 2000.

White, Lionel. *Clean Break.* New York: E. P. Dutton, 1955.

White, Susan. "Male Bonding, Hollywood Orientalism, and the Repression of the Feminine in Kubrick's *Full Metal Jacket.*" *Arizona Quarterly* 44 (1988): 120–44.

Zweig, Stefan. *The Burning Secret.* London: Allen & Unwin, 1914.

Contributors

Geoffrey Cocks is Julian S. Rammelkamp Professor of History at Albion College in Albion, Michigan. He is the author of *Psychotherapy in the Third Reich: The Göring Institute* (1985, 1997) and *The Wolf at the Door: Stanley Kubrick, History, and the Holocaust* (2004).

James Diedrick is Associate Dean of the College at Agnes Scott College and the author of *Understanding Martin Amis* (1995, 2004).

G. L. Ercolini is a doctoral candidate in the department of communication arts and sciences at the Pennsylvania State University. Her research focuses on the history of rhetoric, rhetoric of the Enlightenment, and early modern period and contemporary rhetorical theory.

Pat J. Gehrke is assistant professor of speech communication at the University of South Carolina. He has published essays on film criticism, communication ethics, poststructural theory, and rhetoric in journals such as *Critical Studies in Media Communication, Philosophy and Rhetoric,* and *Argumentation and Advocacy*.

Novelist and screenwriter Diane Johnson is author of numerous works, including *The Shadow Knows* (1974) and *Le Divorce* (1997), which was a National Book Award finalist and won a California Book Award gold medal for fiction.

Tim Kreider's weekly cartoon, *The Pain—When Will It End?*, appears in the *Baltimore City Paper,* the *New York Press,* and online at www.thepain comics.com. Two collections of his cartoons, *The Pain—When Will It End?* (2004) and *Why Do They Kill Me?* (2005), are available from Fantagraphics Books. He has written critical essays for *Film Quarterly* and *The Comics Journal.*

Vincent LoBrutto is the author of nine books, including *Stanley Kubrick: A Biography* and *The Encyclopedia of American Independent Filmmaking.* He is the associate editor of *Cinemaeditor* magazine and a member of the faculty for the Department of Film, Video, and Animation at the School of Visual Arts in New York City.

Peter Loewenberg is professor of history and political psychology at the University of California, Los Angeles. He is a Training and Supervising Analyst and co-dean and co-chair of the Education Committee of the New Center for Psychoanalysis in Los Angeles. He is the author of *Decoding the Past: The Psychohistorical Approach* (1986) and *Fantasy and Reality in History* (1995).

Mark Crispin Miller is professor of media ecology in the Department of Culture and Communication at New York University. He is the author of *Boxed In: The Culture of TV* (1988), *Seeing Through Movies* (1990), and *The Bush Dyslexicon: Observations on a National Disorder* (2002).

Glenn Perusek is Royal G. Hall Professor of the Social Sciences at Albion College and a member of the editorial board of *New Politics.* He is co-editor of *Trade Union Politics: American Unions and Economic Change, 1960s–1990s* (1995).

Novelist and screenwriter Frederic Raphael is the author of numerous works, including the novels *Lindmann* (1963), *The Glittering Prizes* (1976), *A Double Life* (1993), and *Coast to Coast* (1999); the short story collections *Sleeps Six* (1979) and *Oxbridge Blues* (1980); and a recent translation of Petronius, *Satyrica* (2003). His other screenplays include *Darling* (1965), for which he won an Academy Award, and *Two for the Road* (1967).

Jonathan Rosenbaum is film critic of the *Chicago Reader* and author of several books, including *Greed* (1993), *Placing Movies* (1995), *Movies as Politics*

(1997), *Dead Man* (2000), *Movie Wars* (2000), *Essential Cinema: On the Necessity of Film Canons* (2004), and, as editor, *This Is Orson Welles* (1992).

Bille Wickre is associate professor of art history at Albion College, where she teaches courses in eighteenth- and nineteenth-century European art.

Paula Willoquet-Maricondi is associate professor of media arts at Marist College, where she teaches film history, theory, and criticism. She is editor of and contributor to *Peter Greenaway's Postmodern/Poststructuralist Cinema* (2001) and *Pedro Almodóvar: Interviews* (2004).

Index

Index note: Characters in films are listed under first name or military rank ("Alice Harford" rather than "Harford, Alice"). Illustrations are indicated with *italic* page numbers.

Abel, Marco, 102

Academy Awards: *A Clockwork Orange* nominated for, 148; *Dr. Strangelove* nominated for, 41; *2001* nominated for, 43

Adams, Richard, 193

adaptation of literature, 7; artistic license and deviation from originals, 14–16, 44–46, 69, 102, 144, 149, 162, 185, 191, 200–201, 236–37, 262–63, 289, 294; authorship of screenplays, 13–17

Adorno, Theodor, *v*, 5, 10, 25n11

Aesthetic Theory (Adorno), 10

Agel, Jerome, 123

agency, 108, 109, 111–18, 119

A.I. (2001), 11, 71, 196, 203; antihumanism in, 101; critical reception of, 101; screenwriting for, 15; selection of project, 48; Spielberg's involvement in, 49, 101

Aldiss, Brian, 48, 67

Alexander I, Tsar of Russia (character in *Napoleon*), 78–79

Alex de Large (character in *A Clockwork Orange*), 19, 108–9, 115–16, 118, 295; behavior modification or aversion therapy, 108–9, 149, 154–56, 158–60, 161–62, 194; Kubrick on, 44; mechanization of, 108–9, 153–56; subjectivities of, 148, 150–58

Alice Harford (character in *Eyes Wide Shut*), 24, 103, 111, 116–17, 254, 262, 263, 269, 281–82, 287–88, 295

Aliens (1979), 235

allegory: *Dr. Strangelove* as, 197; *Eyes Wide Shut* as, 106, 285–86, 290; *Fear and Desire* as, 7; films as political, 139; *2001* as, 197

ambiguity, 103, 137–38; in *2001*, 141; in *Eyes Wide Shut*, 294–95; lack of resolution and, 105, 107–8; open narrative and, 9–10; power and manipulation of, 25; in *The Short-Timers*, 219

American New Wave: Kubrick's influence on, 53

Anderegg, Michael, 225

Animal Mother (character in *Full Metal Jacket*), 92–93, 107

antihumanism, 101–2, 119

Apocalypse Now (1979), 55

"apparatus" theory of film, 21
Ararat (2002), 201
Arbus, Diane, 208
Arthur Schnitzler as a Psychologist
    (Reik), 259
artistic control: collaboration and, 49;
    of early projects, 32, 33; film indus-
    try and, 190, 251; improvisation
    and, 11, 15–16; of *Lolita,* 39–40;
    organic evolution of projects and,
    15–16, 57; over Clarke's novel, 43;
    "ownership" of screen stories and,
    36; of *The Shining,* 57; telling
    details, 281. *See also* collaboration;
    writing credits
artistic license, 7
Art of Love (Ovid), 284
"Aryan Papers," 186, 196
audience: alienation of, 7, 69, 114, 115;
    commercial films as transparent to,
    8; copycat crimes committed by,
    150; director as spectator, 187, 250;
    identification with characters,
    114–17, 150, 166, 220; MPAA and,
    253; narrative structures as obstacle
    to engagement of, 103–5; nonlinear
    construction and engagement of,
    36, 50–51n11; as privileged spectator,
    21; reception theory, 10–11; *The
    Shining* and, 114, 115, 187–88; spec-
    tatorship within the films, 136–37,
    153–54; *2001* and, 122–23, 141–42; as
    voyeurs, 21, 136
Auschwitz, 18, 188, 191
auteur theory, 8, 16–17; Kubrick as
    auteur, 41. *See also* artistic control
The Authentic Death of Hendry Jones
    (Neider), 38
aversion therapy. *See* behavior
    modification
The Awakening of Jacob (Penderecki),
    185, 211

Backfire (Baritz), 218
ballet, 129–30
Baritz, Loren, 218, 228, 229

Barry Lyndon (1975), 14, 56, 126, 191,
    282; allusion to art works in, 166,
    169–71, 171, 182, *183;* architecture as
    symbolic in, 173, *175;* Barry Lyndon
    as character in, 14, 45, 167–69; cine-
    matography of, 19–20, 169, 171;
    Classicism *vs.* genre paintings in,
    171–72; critical reception of, 19;
    eighteenth-century art and, 19–20,
    165–83; family in, 168, 172, 173, 178,
    180, *181,* 182; lighting and, 171;
    mechanization of man in, 208;
    Nora Brady in, 170–71; prostitution
    in, 168, 176; spectatorship in, 136;
    stills from, *171, 172, 173, 175, 176,
    177–81, 183;* Venus imagery in, 173,
    175, 176, *176;* visual puns in, 170
Barry Lyndon (a.k.a. Redmond Barry,
    character in *Barry Lyndon*), 14, 45,
    167–69
Bartók, Béla, 209–10
"Bat" Guano (character in *Dr. Strange-
    love*), 97, 100n18
Baudry, Jean-Louis, 21
Baum, Vicki, 199
Baxter, Peter, 22
Bazin, André, 3, 8
Beethoven, Ludwig, 264
Begley, Louis, 48, 196
behaviorism, 19
behavior modification: in *A Clockwork
    Orange,* 149, 154–56, 158–60, 161–62,
    194
The Benediction (Chardin), 172, *174*
Bentham, Jeremy, 153
Berenson, Marisa, 45
Beria, Levrentri, 64, 73n2
Bettelheim, Bruno, 40, 46, 201
Bill Harford (character in *Eyes Wide
    Shut*), 17, 24, 103, 104, 111, 113,
    116–17, 246–49, 263–64, 267, 268,
    274, 281–82, 289, 292–93
black comedy, 40, 41, 52n19, 292
blacklist, 38
Blade Runner (1982), 53n28
Blakemore, Bill, 281

Blue Danube Waltz (Strauss), 110,
  129
Blue Sky (1994), 22
Bobbitt, Philip, 67–68
body: in *Full Metal Jacket*, 234, 239–
  40n39; law as "inscribed" upon,
  159; mannequins and, 193, 290–91;
  Marine "corps "equated with, 231;
  politics of the, 152, 154, 156–57, 160;
  women as embodiment, 22
boxing films, 35, 144; *Day of the Fight*,
  32–33
Brecht, Bertolt, 7
Bryna Productions, 37–38, 40
Buchan, Alastair, 40
Bullingdon, Lord (character in *Barry
  Lyndon*), 168–69, 182
Burdick, Eugene, 223
Burgess, Anthony, 149; *A Clockwork
  Orange*, 44; on Kubrick's adapta-
  tion of his work, 14; *Napoleon
  Symphony*, 44
The Burning Secret (Zweig), 37
Byron, George Gordon, Lord, 237

The Cabinet of Dr. Caligari (1919), 11
Caligula, 62
capitalism, 5–6, 96–97
Carey, Timothy, 249
Carlyle, Thomas, 67
Carmina Burana (Orff), 192–93
Cartier, Walter, 32–33
casting, 57, 71–72, 104, 248, 282
censorship, 23–24, 39, 271–72
chance, in *Eyes Wide Shut*, 113
Chaplin, Charlie, 25n11
characterization: audience identification with characters, 114–16, 150,
  166; as caricature, 116, 248; casting
  and, 104, 282; Kidman on Kubrick's
  direction of actors, 12; Raphael on
  "puppetlike," 72; relationships
  between characters, 117, 281; strategic thought and power dynamic
  revealed through, 17; will and, 108.
  See also specific characters

Chardin, Jean-Baptiste Simeon, 20,
  165, 169, 171–72, *174*
Charlotte Haze (character in *Lolita*),
  131
Chasen, Will, 33
chess, 12, 31; strategic thinking and, 78,
  79–80, 86
children: in *Barry Lyndon*, 168, 176,
  180; Danny Torrance in *The Shining*, 58, 111, 115, 118, 187, 202; as
  erotic or sexual objects, 272–73;
  Grady girls in *The Shining*, 200;
  Helena Harford in *Eyes Wide Shut*,
  262, 285, 288–89, 295; infantilism in
  Full Metal Jacket, 228, 231, 232, 233,
  235; Squirt in *2001*, 132–33
Christmas, in *Eyes Wide Shut*, 285, 295
Ciment, Michel, 7, 17
Cinema 2: The Time-Image (Deleuze),
  250
cinematography: in *Barry Lyndon*,
  19–20, 165–66, 169, 171; in *A Clockwork Orange*, 153, 157, 197; depth of
  field, 3; dolly shots in early works,
  33; editing related to, 36; in *Eyes
  Wide Shut*, 254, 287; in *Full Metal
  Jacket*, 226; "painterly" effects,
  165–66; shifting point of view, 115;
  Steadicam and omniscient point of
  view, 24, 287
Clare Quilty (character in *Lolita*), 39,
  284
Clarke, Arthur C., 14; collaboration
  with, 14, 42–43; contract with
  Kubrick, 52–53n24; novelization of
  2001, 52–53n24, 124–25
class, social. *See* hierarchy
Claudius, 62–63
Clean Break (White), 13, 35–36, 191
Clive, John, 197
A Clockwork Orange (1971), 13, 119, 194,
  295; Alex de Large in, 19, 44,
  108–9, 115–16, 118, 149, 154–56,
  158–62, 194; awards nominations
  for, 148; comedic elements in, 33;
  conclusion of, 44–45, 149; critical

A Clockwork Orange (*continued*)
reception of, 148; deviations
from Burgess's work, 44–45, 149,
191; domination in, 151–52, 157;
Foucauldian analysis of, 19; human
nature in, 95; human relationships
in, 117; identification with characters in, 115; mechanization in,
108–9, 153–56; music in, 149, 150,
151, 155, 193, 285; politics of the body
in, 152, 154, 156–57, 160; rationality
in, 107; sex in, 130, 131, 148–49,
155–56; as social criticism, 19; spectatorship in, 136, 153–54; stills from,
195; violence in, 148–49, 150, 155–57;
will and subjection in, 18, 108–9,
110, 112, 156, 157–58
A Clockwork Orange (Burgess), 44;
critical reception of, 148
Cobb, Humphrey, 36
Cocks, Geoffrey: cited, 20–21, 59, 60;
introduction by, 3–25
Cold War, 22, 92
collaboration: with Adams, 193; with
Aldiss, 48, 67; with Clarke, 14, 42–43,
52–53n24, 124–25; on early works, 34–
35; with George, 40; with Hasford,
47; with Herr, 47, 261–62; improvisation and, 4, 11; with Johnson, 15–16,
46, 55–61, 189–90, 198; on *The
Killing,* 36; Kubrick's choice of
writers, 16; with Maitland, 48;
method and process of writing, 15,
46, 59–60; with Nabokov, 39–40;
with Raphael, 48, 60, 255, 261–62;
screenwriting and, 13–17; with Shaw,
48; with Singer, 32; with Southern,
14, 41, 52n21, 56; with Thompson,
36, 50n10, 51n13; with Watson, 48
Colonel Dax (character in *Paths of
Glory*), 17, 88–89, 91, 283
color, use of: blue, 135, 206, 207–8,
217n42, 254, 268, 269, 287; pink, 124,
131, 217n86; red, *195,* 201, 206, 207,
293, 296; in *The Shining,* 201, 203–7,
217n86; yellow, 201, 203–6, 287

comedy and comedic elements: black
comedy, 40–41, 52n19, 292; in *Dr.
Strangelove,* 40–41, 52n19, 100n18;
in *Full Metal Jacket,* 47; Kubrick as
both comic and pessimistic, 11; in
Lolita, 52n17; in *2001,* 133–34
commodification of human beings,
287, 294–95; "market-state" and, 24,
67–68
compassion, 89–91, 107; in *Barry
Lyndon,* 168; HAL as compassion-
ate, 107
consumer culture, 141; capitalism, 5–6,
96–97; Christmas as emblematic of,
286–87, 295–97; commodification of
human beings, 24, 67–68, 287,
294–95; *Eyes Wide Shut* as critique
of wealth and power, 280–97;
"market-state" and international
politics, 67–68; sex as commodity,
289, 291 (*see also* prostitution). *See
also* film industry
Content, Rob, 297
"continuity" style, 8
Coppola, Francis Ford, 55, 139
Cornellier, Bruno, 237n4
corruption, 119; in *Eyes Wide Shut,*
284–85, 290; in *Full Metal Jacket,*
95; in *Paths of Glory,* 78, 94–95, 178
Cossa, Frank, 165
costume, 57, 61, 124, 131, 176; in *Eyes
Wide Shut,* 288, 289; in *Lolita,* 288
Cowboy (character in *Full Metal
Jacket*), 226
Cragg, Dan, 234
Crazy Earl (character in *Full Metal
Jacket*), 227
critical reception of works, 11, 19, 64,
101–2, 111, 116, 148, 245, 250–52,
280–81, 289–90
Cronkite, Walter, 221
Cruise, Tom, 48, 71–72, 116–17, 248,
282
cultural criticism, 5; *Barry Lyndon* as,
45; evolution of human society, 20;
film industry as culture industry, 6;

films as critique of patriarchy, 110;
Kubrick and, 8–9; Kubrick's films as
operative critiques of society, 102;
Kubrick's films as political critiques,
140; of misogyny, 24, 292; political
consciousness and film, 137–39;
popular culture, 10
cynicism, 137–38, 140, 186, 197
Czerniakow, Adam, 196

dance, 129–30, 212
Danny Torrance (character in *The
Shining*), 58, 111, 115, 118, 202; as
representative of Kubrick, 187
Dave Bowman (character in *2001*), 107,
114–15
Davis, Peter, 235–36
Davy Gordon (character in *Killer's
Kiss*), 81–82, 86–87, 193
Day of the Fight (1950), 32–33, 50n3
deception: in *Barry Lyndon*, 171; in
Eyes Wide Shut, 103; by Josephine
of Napoleon, 79; marital infidelity,
23, 264, 266–67, 270–71
deep focus, 3
The Deer Hunter, 107
Delbert Grady (character in *The Shining*), 111, 132, 206–7
deleted scenes: pie-throwing scene in
Dr. Strangelove, 41, 253; "scrapbook" in *The Shining*, 58
Deleuze, Gilles, 250
Denby, David, 289
DePalma, Brian, 46
depth of field, 3
de Rochemont, Richard, 34
Desser, David, 220
dialogue: in *2001*, 43, 103, 133–34, 135;
collaboration and writing of, 36;
critics objections to "shallow"
nature of, 111; discrepancies
between image and, 12–13; in *Dr.
Strangelove*, 41, 98n8, 100n18; in
Eyes Wide Shut, 69, 111, 116, 265–66,
295–96; in *Full Metal Jacket*,
98–99n11; minimization of, 14, 43,

57–58, 103; as misdirection, 295–96;
in *Napoleon*, 79; narration as alternative to, 32; repetition in, 111; in
The Shining, 57
Diedrick, James: introduction by, 3–25
direction: improvisation by actors, 39;
Raphael on, 65; of *The Shining*, 187
Discipline and Punish (Foucault), 146,
147, 151
discipline as technology, 108–10
documentary films, 9, 32–33, 50n3, 168
Doherty, Thomas, 220, 231
domination, 90–91; by "alpha males,"
23; in *A Clockwork Orange*, 151–52,
197; in *Eyes Wide Shut*, 24–25,
292–94; gender and, 18, 21–22; of
the other, 190, 198; setting and, 23;
sexual violence and, 228; systems of
control, 186
Domino (character in *Eyes Wide Shut*),
104, 113, 264, 283, 288, 291, 294
doubling. See mirrors or doubling
Douglas, Kirk, 37, 38, 40
Downey, Sharon, 107
*Dr. Strangelove, or How I Learned to
Stop Worrying and Love the Bomb*
(1964), 40, 107, 119, 194; as adaptation of *Red Alert*, 14, 102; bikinied
women as embodiment in, 22; as
black comedy, 40–41; casting for,
104; conclusions of, 196–97; dialogue from, 98n8; dramatic tension
in, 83; gender politics in, 18; General Buck Turgidson in, 5, 82–83,
98n8, 126; General Jack D. Ripper
in, 78, 95–96; Group Captain
Lionel Mandrake in, 17–18, 97,
100n18; *Independence Day* and,
143–44; irony in, 97; music in, 22;
as political critique, 140; rationality
and madness in, 92; strategic thinking in, 77, 78, 82–83; violence in, 126
dreams: dreamlike quality of *Eyes Wide
Shut*, 60–61, 108, 262–63, 274–75; in
Eyes Wide Shut, 282; films as, 9; in
The Shining, 282

"Dream Story" (Schnitzler). *See Traumnovelle* "Dream Story" (Schnitzler)
Duvall, Shelly, 57

eagles, 187, 200, 203
editing: early films and, 50n4; of *Eyes Wide Shut,* 253; flashbacks, 36; Kubrick's approach to, 12; montage school and, 8. *See also* deleted scenes
Edwards, Douglas, 32
Egoyan, Atom, 201–2
Eisenstein, Sergei, 8, 12
Electric Horseman (1979), 239n32
elegiac mode: *Barry Lyndon* and, 20; *2001* and, 20
Engels, Friedrich, 99–100n16
Enlightenment, *v*, 18, 141
Ercolini, G. L.: cited, 18–19; on free will, 18; on subjectivity and *A Clockwork Orange,* 19
evil, 92, 186, 283, 290; difficulty in representing, 188; in *Eyes Wide Shut,* 249; Foucault on, 159; Holocaust as benchmark of human, 187; hotels as symbol of, 199; as inherent, 94, 99–100n16; in *The Shining,* 46, 199; Victor Ziegler as, 249
Existentialism, 32–33, 34–35
Expressionism, 9, 11, 12
Eyes Wide Open: A Memoir of Stanley Kubrick (Raphael), 16–17, 48–49
Eyes Wide Shut (1999): Alice Harford in, 24, 103, 111, 116–17, 254, 262, 263, 269, 281–82, 287–88, 295; as allegory, 106, 290; Bill Harford in, 17, 24, 103, 104, 111, 113, 116–17, 246–49, 262, 263–64, 267, 268, 274, 281–82, 289, 292–93; casting for, 71–72, 104, 248, 282; chance in, 113; collaboration with Raphael on, 48–49, 282–83; conclusion of, 245, 295–97; critical reception of, 64, 111, 116, 245, 252, 280–81; deception in, 103; deviation from Schnitzler's work, 69, 162, 191, 263, 289, 294;

dialogue in, 111, 116, 262, 263–64; Domino in, 113, 264, 283, 288, 291, 294; dreamlike quality of, 60–61, 108, 262–63, 274–75, 282, 288; Freudian theory and, 23, 262; Helena Harford in, 285, 288–89; identification with characters in, 115, 116; infidelity in, 264, 266–67, 270–71; Johnson on critical analysis of, 55; Kidman on, 12; Kubrick's career as context for, 23; Mandy in, 263, 285, 288, 291–94; music in, 117, 209, 253, 262, 263, 292; Nick Nightingale in, 113, 253, 267, 274, 293–94; pacing of, 253; as parallel to or reflection of *The Shining,* 23, 285, 290, 291; prostitution in, 246, 247, 264, 274, 281, 288, 289, 296; Raphael on collaboration with Kubrick, 16–17; sadism in, 162, 265–66; Schnitzler's *Traumnovelle* as literary source, 44, 245–46, 255; screenwriting for, 15; set in, 285; sex and sexuality in, 60, 71, 117, 253, 262–63, 264–66, 268–70, 269, 273–74, 274–75, 280; sociological analysis of, 24; sound track for, 253–54; spectatorship in, 136; subjection of will in, 18, 110, 111, 112–14; synopsis of, 246–48; telling details in, 24; title of, 275; truth as illusory in, 104–6, 113–14, 248, 274, 293; as "unbelievable," 60–61; Victor Ziegler in, 23, 25, 103, 104, 249, 263, 274, 283, 284, 287, 293; will as reactive rather than proactive, 112–13; women in, 22. *See also specific characters under this heading*

family: in *Barry Lyndon,* 168, 172, 173, 178, 180, *181,* 182; in *A Clockwork Orange,* 117, 197; in *Eyes Wide Shut,* 113, 262, 274; Holocaust and, 190–91; Kubrick's family life, 31, 57, 73n2, 192; in *The Shining,* 46, 198, 200; in *2001,* 132–33

Fast, Howard, 38
fatalism, 36, 140; in *Full Metal Jacket*, 92; in *Paths of Glory*, 77–78, 94
Fear and Desire (1953), 92, 193; collaboration on, 34–35; strategic thinking in, 77; war as subject in, 34
Fellini, Frederico, 65
film industry, 8, 65, 141–42; advertising campaigns for Kubrick films, 185, 280; blockbusters, 144; "Commercial Correctness," 68–69; as culture industry, 6; "director's cuts" as commercial ploy, 253; Kubrick's independence and, 190, 251; mythmaking and, 17; Raphael on, 67; ratings and, 39, 253; rejection of *Paths of Glory*, 37; and sentimental or humorous remakes of films, 142–43
film noir, 9, 193, 254; *Killer's Kiss* as, 35
flashbacks, 35–36
Flying Padre (1951), 33
Foucault, Michel, 5, 13, 146, 155; on domination, 153–54; Foucauldian analysis of *A Clockwork Orange*, 19, 146–62; on guilt and innocence, 159, 161; politics of the body, 152, 154, 156–57; on power, 152; on prisons, 153–54; on sex, 155; on violence, 155, 159
Frank Poole (character in *2001*), 107
French revolution, 93–94
Freud, Sigmund, 4, 5, 189, 257; on jealousy, 270; Schnitzler and, 23–24, 255–60; on the uncanny, 201, 261, 267
frontier mentality, 223–24, 226, 227, 239n32
Full Metal Jacket (1987), 119, 206; allusion to other war films in, 225; audience and, 104, 114; comedic elements in, 47; conclusion of, 105, 108, 235–36; Cowboy in, 226; Crazy Earl in, 227; critical reception of, 250–51; deviations from literary sources, 236–37; gender theory and,

21; Gomer Pyle / Leonard Lawrence in, 110, 118, 224–25, 225, 227, 229, 230, 233, 238n16; human relationships in, 117; infantilism in, 228, 231, 232, 233, 235; irony in, 97; isolation in, 117; masculinity in, 21–22, 110; mechanization of man in, 109, 229–30; military training as religious conversion, 228–29; misogyny in, 292; music in, 105, 232, 235–36; Parris Island scenes, 104, 109, 110, 224, 227–30, 232; Payback in, 226; as political critique, 140; prostitution in, 97, 226–27, 239n165; Rafterman in, 92–93, 226; rationality in, 92; ritual purification in, 228–29, 239–40n39; screenwriting for, 14–15, 225; self-referential elements in, 226; setting of, 220–22; sex in, 105, 107, 229–30 (*see also* prostitution *under this heading*); sniper scene in, 104, 115, 118, 219, 220, 226, 234, 237n4, 292; *stahlhartes Gehäuse* (steel-hardened casing), 5, 96; strategic thinking in, 77; subjection of will in, 18, 109, 110; technology of discipline in, 109; tone of, 104; as war film, 47

Gaffney, Robert, 50n5
Gainborough, Thomas, 169–70
Gay, Peter, 269
Gayane Ballet (Khachaturian), 209
gaze: Alice as voyeuristic object in *Eyes Wide Shut*, 287; male gaze and female subjectivity, 21; male gaze in Watteau, 167; spectatorship, 136–37
Gehrke, Pat: articles by, 101–19, 146–62; cited, 18–19; on free will, 18; on subjectivity and *A Clockwork Orange*, 19
gender: domination and power dynamics, 18; ideals challenged in films, 139; male "gaze" and female subjectivity, 21; misogyny, 24, 110, 212, 219, 237n4, 292; patriarchy and

gender (*continued*)
  constructions of, 231, 234–35;
  sexism, 110; in *2001*, 18. *See also*
  masculinity; women
General Broulard (character in *Paths
  of Glory*), 80, 87–89, 249
General Paul Mireau (character in
  Paths of Glory), 80, 87–88, 249
General Jack D. Ripper (character in
  Dr. Strangelove), 78, 95–96
General Buck Turgidson (character in
  Dr. Strangelove), 5, 82–83, 98n8, 126
genre, 3–4, 187–88; Kubrick's interro-
  gation and reinvention of, 21, 55,
  102–3, 137; undercut, 198
George, Peter, 14, 40, 102
Gergen, Kenneth, 160
German Expressionist filmmaking, 9,
  11, 12, 192, 198
"The German Lieutenant," 195
German singing girl in *Paths of Glory*,
  89, 95, 193
Gersaint's Shopsign (Watteau), 167, *167*
Gilmore, David, 229, 232
Gloria Price (character in *Killer's Kiss*),
  81–82
Goldman, William, 66
Gomer Pyle / Leonard Lawrence
  (character in *Full Metal Jacket*), 110,
  118, 224–25, 225, 227, 229, 230, 233,
  238n16
Grady girls in *The Shining*, 200, 208, *209*
Grand Hotel (1932), 199
Green Berets (1965), 138, 219, 223, 224
Group Captain Lionel Mandrake
  (character in *Dr. Strangelove*), 17–18,
  97, 100n18
Gunnery Sargeant Hartman (*Full
  Metal Jacket*), 104, 109, 116, 224,
  227–29, 231, 233

HAL (character in *2001*), 18, 106–7,
  134; droids in *Star Wars* contrasted
  with, 145
Hall, Tom T., 232
Harlan, Christiane, 192

Harlan, Jan, 192
Harlan, Veit, 192
Harris, James B., 13, 14, 35, 38, 39, 40,
  50n8, 253
Harris-Kubrick Pictures, 35, 50n8;
  Bryna Productions and, 37, 40;
  MGM and, 36–37
Harvey, Anthony, 41
Hasford, Gustav, 14–15, 47, 53–54n37,
  191, 218–19, 225
The Haunting (1963), 198
Hayden, Sterling, 51n11
Hearts and Minds (1974), 235–36
Heeger, Anna, 269
Heidegger, Martin, 64
Helena Harford (character in *Eyes
  Wide Shut*), 285, 288–89, 295
Hellman, John, 223
"Hello Vietnam" (Hall), 232
Herr, Michael, 12, 14, 47, 64, 196, 209,
  225, 236, 248, 261–62, 283
Heywood Floyd (character in *2001*), 18,
  124, 127–28, 131–34
hierarchy, v, 17–18; in *Barry Lyndon*,
  19–20, 126, 167, 168–69, 178, 283;
  blue and, 207–8; cinematography as
  expression of, 19–20; in *Eyes Wide
  Shut*, 116, 282, 292–93, 293–94;
  Foucauldian subject-position and,
  148; in *Killer's Kiss*, 86–87; in *The
  Killing*, 86; military organization
  and, 95–96; in *Paths of Glory*, 77–78,
  87–89; and power dynamics, 17–18,
  90–91, 189; in *The Shining*, 126,
  202, 283; systems of control, 186;
  technology as "elite" power, 127–29;
  threats to, 126; in *2001*, 116; in war
  films, 77. *See also* domination
Hilberg, Raul, 195, 196
history: historical contexts for films, 8,
  41, 138–40, 141, 142; Kubrick's
  interest in, 8
Hitchcock, Alfred, 11, 143, 198–99
Hogarth, William, 166–67, 182
Hollenbeck, Don, 33
Hollywood. *See* film industry

the Holocaust, 10, 141, 190; attention,
198, 199; in *A Clockwork Orange*,
190; as context, 188–89; as evidence
of human nature, 18; as film subject, 21, 48, 268; images of, 190–91;
193; Kubrick and, 20; Kubrick's personal connection to, 190–91; scholarly and public attention to, 194,
196; symbolism and allusions in *The
Shining*, 20–21, 59, 60, 205–6, 211–12
homosexuality or homoeroticism, 160,
224, 228, 232, 268–70, 271
Hooper, Tobe, 46
Horkheimer, Max: quoted, *v*
horror, 46, 143, 187–88; boom in
horror films, 198; coincidence of
the fearsome and the divine, 212; as
genre, 55; Kubrick's generic innovations, 102–3; *The Shining* as horror
film, 21, 187–88, 246
Horse and Train (Colville), 203
Hotel Berlin (1945), 191, 193
Hubbard, Faith, 31–32
Hué (Vietnam), as setting in *Full
Metal Jacket*, 220–22
humanism, 101, 140–41
human nature: apes as parallels in *2001*,
123–24, 126, 128–29, 132, 145; bestial
animus in, 18, 126, 129, 202; in *A
Clockwork Orange*, 95, 157; as corrupt, 95; evil inherent in, 46, 94,
99–100n16; in *Fear and Desire*, 35;
Foucauldian insight into, 147;
Kalberg on, 25n6; Kubrick's
pessimistic vision of, 140–41;
Rousseauian philosophy and, 18,
89–90; as subject of films, 281; in
2001, 18–19; as violent, 198
Hunter, Stephen, 282
Huston, John, 23, 37, 251

identity: audience and identification
with characters, 114–17, 150, 166,
220; in *Barry Lyndon*, 168, 171;
denial of, 114; in *Eyes Wide Shut*,
264, 290–91, 291; in *Full Metal

Jacket, 21–23, 231–33; masculine,
21–22, 231; masks, 264, 291; names
in *Full Metal Jacket* and, 224, 226,
232–33; otherness and, 18, 114, 127
improvisation: by actors, 39, 249–50;
artistic control and, 11, 15–16; in *A
Clockwork Orange*, 197
intellectualism, 59, 65–66
intermediaries, 17–18, 24–25
isolation: in *A Clockwork Orange*, 127;
in *Eyes Wide Shut*, 117; in *Full Metal
Jacket*, 232; Rousseau on, 89–90; in
The Shining, 198–99; in *2001*, 18,
132–34. *See also* social exclusion

Jack Torrance (character in *The
Shining*), 16, 111, 115, 136, 200, 202,
292
jealousy, 270
Jeffords, Susan, 218–19, 228
Johnny Clay (character in *The Killing*),
80
Johnson, Diane: cited, 11, 13, 15, 199;
collaboration with Kubrick, 15–16,
46, 55–61, 189–90, 198; on Kubrick,
11, 15; on screenwriting, 13
Joker / J. T. Davis (character in *Full
Metal Jacket*), 97, 98–99n11, 115, 118,
189, 223–24, 225–26, 230, 233, 234
Jones, Kent, 254
journalism, 142, 221, 226; photojournalism, 4–5, 31–33, 191, *210*
Judaism: Freud on, 259; Jewish characters "written out" of works, 191,
267–68; Jewish heritage of Kubrick,
48, 49, 69, 186, 189–91; social exclusion of the Jew, 23, 189, 207. *See also*
the Holocaust
Jung, Carl, 189–90
Jungian psychology, 224
Jungian theory, 189, 234

Kael, Pauline, 11
Kafka, Franz, 9, 193, 200, 202, 245
Kagan, Norman, 119
Kakutani, Michiko, 281, 289–90

Kauffmann, Stanley, 11
Kennedy, John F., 41, 223, 224
Khachaturian, Aram, 209
Khrushchev, Nikita, 65
Kidman, Nicole, 48, 71–72, 103, 116–17, 248, 254, 280; on Kubrick's direction of actors, 12
Killer's Kiss (1955), 35–36, 130, 193; Davy Gordon in, 81–82, 86–87, 193; stills from, *194, 195;* strategic thinking in, 77, 81–82, 83
The Killing (1956), 13, 206, 249; strategic thinking in, 77, 80, 83; women in, 22
King, Stephen, 14; adaptation of works to film, 46; television adaptation of, 53n36
Kolker, Robert, 102
Kozinski, Jerzy, 24
Kreider, Tim: cited, 23, 24
Krohn, Bill, 250
Kubrick, Stanley: biographical information, 31–32, 69, 73n2, 189–91; as cultural critic or social reformer, 18; death of, 7–8, 254; family life of, 31, 57, 73n2, 192; Jewish heritage of, 48, 49, 67, 69, 186, 189–91; as perfectionist, 66–67, 248, 249–50; as self-promoter, 67
Kubrick (Ciment), 7
Kubrick (Nelson), 7

Lacan, Jacques, 21
Lady Lyndon (character in *Barry Lyndon*), 168, 169, 175–76, 178, 182
Lanning, Michael Lee, 234
Lazar, Swifty, 38
Lederer, William, 223
length of films, 12
Lentricchia, Frank, 228, 234–35
Leonard Lawrence. *See* Gomer Pyle / Leonard Lawrence
Lewis, Edward, 38
Ligeti, Gyorgi, 114
lighting: in *Barry Lyndon*, 171
literary sources, 7; artistic license and

deviation during adaptation, 7, 14–15, 16, 44–45, 46, 69, 102, 144, 149, 162, 185, 191, 200–201, 262, 263, 289, 294; choice of controversial works, 13, 37, 39, 51n14; Kubrick as reader, 10–11, 15, 31–32; literary traditions as context for works, 23; neglected by critics, 185; Raphael on Kubrick as *charcutier,* 71; reliance on, 34; selection of, 37, 38, 44, 46, 48, 51n14, 55, 56, 186, 196, 236, 261. *See also* adaptation of literature; *specific works*
LoBrutto, Vincent: cited, 14, 15
Loewenberg, Peter: cited, 23, 215n54
Lolita (1962), 13, 14, 144; Clare Quilty in, 39, 284; comedic elements in, 33, 52n17; Humbert in, 284; selection of project, 37, 38, 51n14; sex in, 131; spectatorship in, 136
Lolita (Lyne film), 51–52n17, 144
Lolita (Nabokov), 7, 37, 38, 51n14, 272
Look (magazine), 31, 32, 191, 208, *210*
Lovecraft, H. P., 46
The Loved One (1964), 41, 52n21
Lucas, George, 144–45
Lynch, David, 53n28
Lyne, Adrian, 51–52n17, 144
Lynn, Vera, 22
Lyon, Sue, 144

machines. *See* mechanization of man
The Magic Mountain (Mann), 21, 199–200, 204, 206–7
Maitland, Sara, 48
The Making of Kubrick's 2001 (Agel), 123
The Manchurian Candidate (1962), 156–57
Mandelstam, Osip, 65
Mandy (character in *Eyes Wide Shut*), 263, 285, 288, 291–94
Mann, Anthony, 14
Mann, Thomas, 21, 199, 204, 206–7
mannequins, 35, 193, 195, 290–91
Marion, 111
Markham, Felix, 43

marriage: in *Barry Lyndon*, 176; casting of married couple in *Eyes Wide Shut*, 71–72; in *Eyes Wide Shut*, 263; Kubrick's marriages, 192

Marriage Ala Mode (Hogarth), 182, *183*

Martin, Steve, 248

Marvin Unger (character in *The Killing*), 86–87

Marxist criticism, 91–92

masculinity: in *A Clockwork Orange*, 116; in *Full Metal Jacket*, 22, 110, 189, 218–37; ideals challenged in films, 139; patriarchy differentiated from, 234–35; power and, 189; rejection or destruction of the feminine and, 220, 234; religion and American, 235–36; "remasculinization," 22, 218–19; westerns and construction of, 235

masks: in *Eyes Wide Shut*, 290–92, 294–95

Mattessich, Stefan, 106, 116–17

mazes (labyrinths), 17, 69–70

meaning: ambiguity and, 9–10; as construct *vs.* "truth," 105–6; films as texts, 10; *Full Metal Jacket* and lack of, 92–93, 105; Johnson on, 55; multiplicity of, 237n4; narration and, 166; plurality of, 105; refusal to "explain" films, 187, 199; as subjective, 35. *See also* subjectivity

mechanization of man, 33, 44, 203; in *Barry Lyndon*, 208; in *A Clockwork Orange*, 44, 108–9, 153–56; in *Full Metal Jacket*, 109, 229–31; rote and repetitive behavior, 110; technology and, 109–10, 111, 129–30; in *2001*, 33, 109–11, 129–30, 134–35; war and, 109, 208

The Memoirs of Barry Lyndon Esq., of the Kingdom of Ireland (Thackeray), 14, 20, 45

Meredith, Scott, 43

Merkin Muffley (character in *Dr. Strangelove*), 82–83, 98n8

Metz, Christian, 21

Metz, Toby, 192

MGM, 36–37, 43

Miers, Paul, 115

Milich (character in *Eyes Wide Shut*), 105, 273, 284, 291, 292

Miller, Mark Crispin: cited, 18–19, 214n38

mirrors or doubling: in *Eyes Wide Shut*, 267, 269, 288, 293; Freud on *doppelgänger*, 257, 272; in *The Shining*, 203, 205, 208

mise-en-scène, 3, 8

misogyny, 24, 110, 212, 219, 237n4, 292

Mitterand, François, 67

montages, 8, 33, 165

mood: elegiac mode, 20; strategy and, 83–86

Moonwatcher (character in *2001*), 124–25

Moore, Robin, 223

morality, 107; art and, 285; in *Barry Lyndon*, 180; Chardin and, 172; in *A Clockwork Orange*, 156, 158; in *Eyes Wide Shut*, 264; in *Traumnovelle*, 260

Morning Walk (Gainsborough), 169–70

motherhood: in *Barry Lyndon*, 176, 178, *179;* Marine Corps and patriarchal, 231

MPAA, 39, 40–41, 253, 271–72

Mr. Deltoid (character in *A Clockwork Orange*), 152

Mullin, Molly, 27n51

multiple viewpoints, 35–36

Mulvey, Laura, 21

music, 57; in *A Clockwork Orange*, 149, 150, 151, 155, 285; in *Dr. Strangelove*, 22; in *Eyes Wide Shut*, 117, 209, 253, 262, 263, 285; in *Full Metal Jacket*, 105, 232, 235–36; in *The Shining*, 185, 208–9, 211–12; in *2001*, 106, 110, 114, 122, 129, 192–93, 209; in Vietnam war films, 240n49

Music for Strings, Percussion, and Celesta (Bartók), 209

mythmaking: American superiority as illusory, 221–22; deification of Roman emperors, 62–63; film and, 137–39, 137–40, 142–43, 190; frontier myth and American military, 223; Kubrick as "genius," 17; propaganda and, 137–40, 142–43; war and American mythos, 218, 240–41n56; war films and construction of American masculinity, 218–37

Nabokov, Vladimir, 272; reluctance to sell rights to *Lolita,* 38; as screenwriter, 14, 39–40
Napoleon (1969), 43–44, 77; strategic thinking in, 78–79, 80, 84–86
Napoleon Bonaparte: French revolution and, 93–94; Kubrick's interest in, 4, 187; planned project, 43–44; quoted, *v,* 4
Napoleon Symphony: A Novel in Four Movements (Burgess), 44
narration: in *Barry Lyndon,* 45, 166, 171–72, 182; in *A Clockwork Orange,* 152, 154; in *Day of the Fight,* 32; in *Fear and Desire,* 34; in *Flying Padre,* 33; in *Full Metal Jacket,* 115; in *The Seafarers,* 33
narrative structure: ambiguity and, 137–38; in *Eyes Wide Shut,* 104, 251; flashbacks, 35–36; Kubrick's innovations in, 103; lack of resolution, 105; multiple viewpoints and, 35–36; nonlinear construction, 36, 50–51n11; open narrative, 7, 9–10, 187; of *The Shining,* 60; in *2001,* 187; *2001* as innovative, 53n28, 103, 114
Native Americans, 202, 203, 226–27, 281
Nazism, 186, 192, 194, 197, 199, 203, 207, 209, 211, 285
necrophilia, 272, 273–74
Neider, Charles, 37–38
Nelson, Thomas Allen, 7
Nero, 62–63, 65–66
Nicholson, Jack, 248; cast in *The Shining,* 57; as Napoleon, 44

Nick Nightingale (character in *Eyes Wide Shut*), 113, 253, 267, 274, 293–94
Nietzsche, Friedrich, 5, 19, 64, 197
Night and Fog (Resnaisn), 199
Nixon, Richard M., 138, 139
nonlinear construction, 36, 50–51n11
Nora Brady (character in *Barry Lyndon*), 170–71
Noyce, Phillip, 238n15
nuclear weapons, 40, 92, 129, 141; nuclear deterrent strategy, 78, 82–83

omniscience, 24
O'Neal, Ryan, 45, 282; pictured in stills from *Barry Lyndon, 171, 172, 173, 176–80, 183*
One-Eyed Jacks (1961), 37–38, 51n12
One Flew Over the Cuckoo's Nest (1975), 156–57
"open narrative," 7, 187; ambiguity and, 9–10
operative criticism, 102
Ophul, Max, 24
Orff, Carl, 192–93
otherness: domination of the other, 190, 198; in *Eyes Wide Shut,* 117, 265; frontier mentality and environment as other, 226; in *Full Metal Jacket,* 118, 218–19, 226–28; gender and, 218–19, 234; identity and, 18, 114, 127; self as enemy, 227–28, 233; social exclusion and, 23, 189, 207, 265; subjection and, 119; Willoquet-Maricondi on, 118
Otto, Rudolf, 212
Overlook Hotel, 23, 191, 198–99, 216n77
Ovid, 284–85

pacing, 103, 253
paintings: in *Barry Lyndon,* 19–20, 165–83; in *A Clockwork Orange,* 192; in *Eyes Wide Shut,* 192, 284; in *The Shining,* 201, 203. *See also specific artists and works*

Paths of Glory (1957), 13–14, 50n4, 191, 206, 249; Colonel Dax in, 17, 88–89, 91, 283; conclusion of, 33; General Broulard in, 80, 87–89, 249; General Paul Mireau in, 80, 87–88, 249; German singing girl in, 89, 95, 193; hierarchy in, 77–78, 87–89; as political critique, 140; Rousseauian themes, 77–78, 91, 94–95; spectatorship in, 136; strategic thinking in, 77, 80

Paths of Glory (Cobb), 36–37

patriarchy: boom in horror films and, 188; crisis of, 198; as destructive, 18, 22; *Full Metal Jacket* as critique of, 218, 220; masculinity differentiated from, 234–35; phallocentrism, 110; in *The Shining*, 202

The Pawnbroker (Hilberg), 196

Payback (character in *Full Metal Jacket*), 226

Peckinpah, Sam, 38, 137

Penderecki, Krzysztof, 185, 211–12

Pennebaker, 38

Perfume (Süskind), 47

Perusek, Glenn: cited, 17; introduction by, 3–25

pessimism, 95, 140–41, 185–86, 189–90

photojournalism, 4–5, 31–33, 191, *210*

pie-throwing scene in *Dr. Strangelove*, 41

Pilgrimage to Cythera (Watteau), 170, *170*

Plato, 71

point-of-view: in *Full Metal Jacket*, 115; instability of, 114; omniscient camera, 287; in *The Shining*, 115

political consciousness and film, 137–39

Political Correctness, 68–69

Polito, Robert, 50n10, 51n13

Pollack, Dale, 145

Pollack, Sydney, 239n32

popular culture, film and, 10

postmodernism, 69, 119

power: abuse of power, 139; in *A Clockwork Orange*, 149–50; domination as corruption of, 161; *Eyes*

Wide Shut as interrogation of, 23, 24–25, 280–97; hierarchy and dynamics of, 17–18, 90–91, 189; imbalances of, 4; Kubrick's fascination with, 187, 197–98; reversal in *Full Metal Jacket*, 227; technology as, 230; truth, 161–62; wealth and, 280–97. *See also* artistic control

Preminger, Otto, 38

propaganda, 64, 137–40, 141, 142–43; Nazism, 192; Vietnam war and, 223

prostitution: in *Barry Lyndon*, 168, 176; in *Eyes Wide Shut*, 288, 289; in *Full Metal Jacket*, 97, 226–27, 239n165; in *Traumnovelle*, 266, 273

Psycho (1960), 198–99

Psychoanalysis and the Cinema (Metz), 21

psychology, 5; aversion therapy and behaviorism in *A Clockwork Orange*, 19, 149, 154–56, 158–60, 161–62; of crime in *A Clockwork Orange*, 154–56; in *Eyes Wide Shut*, 262, 281; Foucauldian insight into, 147; Freudian theory, 5–6, 23, 189, 201, 202–3, 231, 262; Jungian theory, 189, 234; Kakutani on Kubrick's neglect of, 281; Lacanian, 21; and *The Shining*, 23, 46, 55–56, 58–59, 201, 202–3. *See also* Freud, Sigmund

"pumpkinification," 63

puns, visual, 20, 170

Puritanism, 5

Pursell, Michael, 221

The Quiet American, 238

Rafterman (character *Full Metal Jacket*), 92–93, 226

Rambuss, Richard, 237n4

Raphael, Frederic, 261–62; cited, 15, 54n38, 245; collaboration, 16–17, 48–49, 268

ratings. *See* MPAA

rationalism, 5; breakdown of rational systems, 92, 95–96, 107, 186, 250; Deleuze on images of, 250; in *Dr.*

rationalism (*continued*)
  Strangelove, 92, 95–96, 250; free will
    and subjectivity, 18; in *Full Metal
    Jacket*, 92, 95–96, 107; HAL as
    representative of logical thought,
    106–8; humanism and, 103; Nazism
    as functioning rational system, 186;
    seven as symbol in Mann's works,
    204; in *The Shining*, 58–59, 60, 250;
    in *2001*, 106–8, 250; Weber on capi-
    talism as rational system, 95–97
Ray, Robert, 227
Reagan, Ronald, 144; and the Great
  Lurch Backwards, 142
realist school, 3, 8
reception theory, 10–11
Red Alert (George), 14, 40, 102
Redmond Barry. *See* Barry Lyndon
religion: Christmas in *Eyes Wide Shut*,
  285; in *A Clockwork Orange*, 154, 285;
  in *Eyes Wide Shut*, 264–65, 290; and
  masculine culture in American, 235–36
"remasculinization," 22, 218–19
The Remasculinization of America
  (Jeffords), 218–19
repetition. *See* rote and repetition
reputation, Raphael on, 62–73
research for films, 33; *Barry Lyndon*,
  165; *Dr. Strangelove*, 40; for Holo-
  caust project, 186; *Napoleon*, 43–44;
  The Shining, 46, 56, 201; *2001*, 42
Resnais, Alain, 199
Reynolds, Joshua, 165, 169
Richardson, Tony, 22
Rivette, Jacques, 250
Roeg, Nicholas, 53n28
Romero, George, 46
Rosenbaum, Jonathan: cited, 23
Ross, Andrew, 235
rote and repetition, 110–11, 116, 202
Rousseau, Jean-Jacques, 99–100n16;
  Paths of Glory and Rousseauian
  themes, 18, 77–78, 88, 89–90
Rousseauian themes: in *Paths of Glory*,
  18, 77–78, 88, 89–90
Russell, Ken, 44

Sackler, Howard O., 34, 35
Sandor Szavost (character in *Eyes Wide
  Shut*), 263, 284–85
Sands of Iwo Jima (1949), 225
Schary, Dore, 36, 37
Schickel, Richard, 245
Schindler's List (1993), 48, 196, 203, 268
Schnitzler, Arthur, 23–24, 44, 48,
  60–61, 71, 245–46, 269, 270–71;
  Freud and, 23–24, 245, 255–60;
  Kubrick on, 261. *See also Traumnov-
  elle* "Dream Story" (Schnitzler)
Scholat, Warren G., Jr., 32
science fiction, 48, 71; blockbusters,
  144–45; Kubrick's generic innova-
  tions, 102, 137; *2001* and, 42
score. *See* music
Scorsese, Martin, 23, 252
Scott, Ridley, 53n28
screenwriting: experimental format
  developed by Kubrick for, 45;
  Kubrick's innovation and, 42;
  Kubrick's process, 15; LoBrutto on
  Kubrick's weakness in, 15; method
  and process of, 46, 59–60; revision
  of script during filming, 39. *See also*
  writing credits
Scurman, Reiner, 101–2
The Seafarers (1953), 33, 50n4
Segal, Erich, 65
self-promotion, 90
Sellers, Peter, 39, 104, 249
semiotic theory, 10
Seneca, Annaeus, 63–64, 65–66
"The Sentinel" (Clarke), 42, 52–53n24
settings and set design, 57, 126, 141,
  249, 252; architecture as symbolic in
  Barry Lyndon, 173, *175;* domination
  and, 23; in *Eyes Wide Shut*, 23,
  282–83, 284, 285–87; Hué City in
  Full Metal Jacket, 220–22; Overlook
  Hotel in *The Shining*, 23, 191,
  198–99, 216n77; in *2001*, 134–35
seven, symbolic use of, 203–6, 216n77
sex: in *Barry Lyndon*, 175, *177, 179;* censorship of sexual content, 23–24, 39,

271–72; in *A Clockwork Orange*, 130, 131, 148–49, 155–56; comedic elements and, 33; as commodity, 289, 291 (*see also* prostitution); *Eyes Wide Shut* and, 60, 71, 117, 253, 262–63, 264–66, 268–70, 273–76, 296; fear and sexual desire, 50n5; film ratings and sexual content, 39, 253; Foucault on, 155; in *Full Metal Jacket*, 105, 107, 229; homosexuality or homoeroticism, 160, 224, 228, 232, 268–70; identity and sexual difference, 21; machinery equated with, 229–30; necrophilia, 24, 272, 273–74; repressed or absent in *2001*, 128, 129–32; sadism and, 23–24, 162, 265–66; Schnitzler's sexual attitudes, 270–71; sexual infidelity, 23, 264, 266–67, 270–71; sexual violence, 23–24, 130, 155, 228; in *Traumnovelle*, 266; violence linked to, 229–30

sexism, 110; gender ideals challenged in films, 139; misogyny, 24, 110, 212, 219, 237n4

The Shadow Knows (Johnson), 46, 55

Sharrett, Christopher, 228

Shaw, Bob, 48

The Shield of Achilles (Bobbitt), 67–68

The Shining (1980), 126; audience engagement with, 114, 115, 187–88; as autobiographical, 200; conclusion of, 201; as critique of American culture, 281; Danny Torrance in, 58, 111, 115, 118, 202; as representative of Kubrick, 187; Delbert Grady in, 111, 132, 206–7; deviations from King's work, 14, 46, 144, 185, 200–201; directing style in, 187; doubling or mirroring in, 203, 205, 208; early draft by Kubrick, 53n33; elevator scene in, 185, 211–12; family in, 46, 198, 200; Freudian theory and, 23, 201, 202–3; Grady girls in, 200, 208, *209;* the Holocaust and, 20; as horror film, 21, 187–88, 246;

identification with characters in, 115; innovation, 102–3; Jack Torrance in, 16, 111, 115, 136, 200, 202; Johnson as collaborator on, 15–16, 46, 55–61, 189–90, 198; *The Magic Mountain* and, 21, 199–200; misogyny and, 292; music in, 185, 208–9, 211–12; narrative structure of, 60; Overlook Hotel in, 23, 191, 198–99, 216n77; as parallel to or reflection of *Eyes Wide Shut*, 23, 285, 290, 291; psychological elements in, 23, 46, 56, 58–59, 202–3; rote repetition in, 111; "scrapbook" scene deleted, 58; screenplay for, 15–16; sound track of, 203, 211 (*see also* music *under this heading*); spectatorship in, 136; stills from, *204, 205, 209;* subjection of will in, 18, 111–12; supernatural elements in, 58–59, 60, 200–201, 212; typewriter in, 200, 203, *204,* 211; Volkswagens in, 202, 207; Wendy Torrance in, 16, 57–58, 111, 115, 118, 202; yellow in, 201, 203–6

The Shining (King), 7, 14, 46; television adaptation of, 46, 144

The Short-Timers (Hasford), 14–15, 191, 218–19, 231, 236

Shostakovich, Dmitri, 209, 262

Shurlock, Geoffrey, 40–41

Siegel, Lee, 102

Singer, Alexander, 31, 50n8

Singer, Isaac Bashevis, 196

Singin' in the Rain, 149, 150

skepticism, 141

sniper scene in *Full Metal Jacket*, 104, 115, 118, 219, 220, 226, 234, 237n4, 292

Sobotka, Ruth, 192

social exclusion, 23, 189, 207, 265

Some Call It Loving (1973), 253

Soper, Kate, 101

sound tracks, 137, 211, 253–54. *See also* music

Southern, Terry, 14, 41, 52n21; on collaboration, 56

Spartacus (1960), 14, 38–39, 136, 251
spectatorship, 136; audience as privi-
    leged spectator, 21; in *Barry Lyndon,*
    136; in *A Clockwork Orange,* 153–54;
    in *The Shining,* 136; surveillance,
    153–54, 199; voyeurism in *Eyes Wide
    Shut,* 136
Spielberg, Steven, 119; completion of
    A.I., 49, 101; *Schindler's List,* 48,
    196, 203
Stadtmueller, Fred, 33
staging, 50n4
stahlhartes Gehäuse (steel-hardened
    casing), 5, 96
Stalin, Joseph, 64–65
Stanley Kubrick: A Biography
    (LoBrutto), 15
Stanley Kubrick, Director (Walker), 7
Stanley Kubrick Productions, 34
stereotypes, interrogation of, 22
Stone, Oliver, 65
storyboards, 11–12
strategic thought: capitalism as
    rational system and, 96–97; chess
    and, 12, 79–80; in *Dr. Strangelove,*
    77, 78, 82–83; in *Killer's Kiss,* 83; in
    The Killing, 83; in Kubrick's works,
    17–18; mood as influence on, 83–86;
    in *Napoleon,* 78–79; timing and, 83
Strauss, Johann, Jr., 106, 110, 122, 129,
    193
subjectivity: antihumanism and, 102;
    discourse and construction of,
    147; Foucauldian, 147–48, 161; free
    will and subjection, 18, 108–14;
    Freudian psychology and decenter-
    ing of human, 5–6; German Expres-
    sionist films and, 9; male "gaze"
    and female, 21; will and subjection,
    118–19
subversion, 123, 136–37, 140, 143, 212,
    225
suffering, *v,* 127
Sullivan, John, 63
"Super Toys Last All Summer Long"
    (Aldiss), 48

surrealism, 9, 21, 108, 245
surveillance, 153–54, 199
Süskind, Patrick, 47
sympathy, 89–91

Tarantino, Quentin, 36
Taylor, Bart, 297
technology: as "elite" power, 127–29;
    in *Full Metal Jacket,* 109; human
    descent and, 125; medical technol-
    ogy in *A Clockwork Orange,* 154–56;
    2001 and, 106–7, 109, 111, 125; will
    and, 108. *See also* mechanization of
    man
Thackeray, William Makepeace, 14, 20,
    191
Thompson, Jim, 13–14, 36, 50nn9–10,
    51n13; collaboration with, 37
Thucydides, *v,* 4, 100n16
Thus Spoke Zarathustra (Strauss), 106,
    122, 193
timing, strategic thinking and, 83
Touchdown (character in *Full Metal
    Jacket*), 92–93
Traumnovelle "Dream Story"
    (Schnitzler), 44, 48, 60–61, 245–
    46, 259, 261–62, 268–69, 272–73,
    275; synopsis of, 260–61
Truffaut, François, 67
Trumbo, Dalton, 14, 38–39
truth, 103, 108; *vs.* constructed mean-
    ing, 105–6; discourse and, 147; film
    as medium for, 4–5; Foucault and
    subjective nature of, 161–62; illusory
    nature of in *Eyes Wide Shut,* 104–6,
    113–14, 248, 274, 293; Parthenon as
    symbol, 173; subjectivity and, 103.
    See also deception
Two Hours to Doom (George). *See Red
    Alert* (George)
2001: A Space Odyssey: audience engage-
    ment with, 114, 122–23; Clarke's
    novelization of, 52–53n24, 124–25;
    collaborative screenwriting for,
    14; conclusion of, 105, 141; Dave
    Bowman in, 107, 114–15; "Dawn of

Man" sequence in, 18, 124–25, 128; dialogue in, 43, 103, 133–34, 135; as expression of Kubrick's world view, 18–19; fan mail regarding, 122–23; Frank Poole in, 107; gender politics in, 18; HAL in, 18, 106–8, 134, 145; Heywood Floyd in, 18, 124, 127–28, 131–34; human relationships in, 117; innovation, 102; Lucas on, 145; mechanization of man in, 33, 109–11, 129–30, 134–35 (*see also* HAL *under this heading*); Moonwatcher in, 124–25, 128; music in, 106, 110, 122, 129, 192–93, 209; narrative structure of, 53n28, 114, 187; Nietzschean thought and, 19, 197; pacing of, 103; sex as repressed or absent in, 128, 129–32; spectatorship in, 136–37; *Star Wars* as antithesis of, 144–45; subjection of will in, 18, 109–11, 112; technology in (*see also* HAL *under this heading*); transcendence in, 106, 114–15, 136–37; as visual experience, 9–10, 137
typewriter in *The Shining*, 200, 203, *204*, 211

The Ugly American (1958), 223
"The Uncanny" (Freud), 201, 267
Une Certain Tendance dans le Cinema Francais (Truffaut), 67
Utrenja (Penderecki), 211–12

Val Cannon (character in *The Killing*), 80, 83
Vavin Inc., 34
Victor Ziegler (character in *Eyes Wide Shut*), 23, 25, 103, 104, 249, 263, 274, 283, 284, 287, 293
Vietnam war, 22, 107, 138–39, 142; American culture and, 218, 235–37, 240–41n56; films about, 220–21, 235–36, 238n15; frontier mentality and, 223, 227; *Full Metal Jacket* and, 47; Hasford's experiences in, 53–54n37; movies about, 219–20;

propaganda and, 223; reporting on, 226
Vincent Rapallo (character in *Killer's Kiss*), 81–82, 86, 193
violence, 186; in *A Clockwork Orange*, 107, 130, 148–49, 150, 151–52, 155–56; copycat crimes committed by audience, 150; Foucault on, 155, 159; in *Full Metal Jacket*, 237; human nature and, 126; sex linked to, 229–30; sexual, 23–24, 130, 155, 228; as spectator sport, 126
Visconti, Lucchino, 73n1
Volkswagens, 202, 207
von Karajan, Herbert, 211
voyeurism, 21, 136, 287

Walker, Alexander, 7
war: as abstraction, 92; American culture and, 142, 235–36, 240–41n56; as evidence of human corruption, 94–95; film noir linked to, 193; as "going ape," 125–26; Kubrick's interest in, 187; mechanization of man and, 109, 208; as pointless, 92–93; seven linked to, 206; in *2001*, 125–26. *See also* Vietnam war; war films
war films, 77; as political critiques, 140; strategic thought in, 17–18; Vietnam and nature of, 219–20. *See also specific titles*
Wartime Lies (Begley), 48, 196
Watergate, 138, 142
Watson, Ian, 48
Watteau, Antoine, 20, 167
Wayne, John, 219, 226; as mythic war hero, 223–24
Weber, Max, 5–6, 18–19, 95–97
web site, authorized, 54n39
Welles, Orson, 23, 49, 251–52
Wendy Torrance (character in *The Shining*), 16, 57–58, 111, 115, 118, 202
Westerns, 37–38, 137, 138, 226, 239n32
White, Lionel, 13, 35–36
White, Susan, 238n16
Wickre, Bille: cited, 20

will: *A Clockwork Orange* and investigation of, 19, 44, 112, 149, 156–57; domination and loss of free, 161; as illusion, 113; as reactive rather than proactive, 112–13; subjection of, 18, 108–14, 117–88, 156

Williams, Dale, 114

Williams, Tony, 226, 234

Willingham, Calder, 13–14, 51n12; collaboration with, 37, 38, 51n13

Willoquet-Maricondi, Paula: cited, 21–22, 118; on otherness, 118

Wise, Robert, 198

wolves, 201

women: in *Eyes Wide Shut*, 23, 24, 113; in *Fear and Desire*, 34; German singing girl in *Paths of Glory*, 89, 95, 193; Kubrick representation of, 21–22; misogyny, 110, 212, 219, 237n4; motherhood in *Barry Lyndon*, 176, 178, *179;* relative absence of, 22; sexual objectification of, 110, 287–88, 292; sniper in *Full Metal Jacket*, 104, 115, 118, 219, 220, 226, 234, 237n4, 292; strength of characters, 22; in *2001*, 130–31, 132

Writer's Guild Award, 41

writing credits: for *A.I.*, 49; auteur status and, 41; black list and, 38; for *A Clockwork Orange*, 45; for *Dr. Strangelove*, 41; for early films, 34, 35, 36, 37, 50n10; for *Eyes Wide Shut*, 48–49; for *Full Metal Jacket*, 47; for *Lolita*, 39; for *Paths of Glory*, 36, 50n13; for *Spartacus*, 38–39; for *2001*, 43

Zweig, Stefan, 37

Wisconsin Film Studies
PATRICK MCGILLIGAN

Marked Women: Prostitutes and Prostitution in the Cinema
RUSSELL CAMPBELL

Depth of Field: Stanley Kubrick, Film, and the Uses of History
Edited by
GEOFFREY COCKS, JAMES DIEDRICK, and GLENN PERUSEK